Total Quality Management

Deming & Juran

Gift to the world

by

Prof. Mohamed Zairi

SPIRE CITY
PUBLISHING

Total Quality Management
DEMING & JURAN
Gift to the World

First Impression 2005

Copyright © 2005 ISBN 1-904208-03-7

Published by
Spire City Publishing

Northern Office
P.O.Box 84
Clitheroe
Lancs
BB7 2WA
Tel/Fax 01200 428823

Printed by
Information Press

Southfield Road
Eynsham
Oxford
OX29 4JB

Cover by
Upstart

25 Aireville Crescent
Bradford
BD9 4EU

To Prof
Mohamed Zairi

Many thanks for the opportunity
to visit with you and learn of your
challenging project.
You have my best wishes for success.

10 February 2005

Contents

List of figures

List of tables

Acknowledgements

I am first and foremost very grateful to all the organizations I have had the privilege to work with over the years, for sharing their best practices, for engaging in the understanding and application of TQM and for being so receptive to new ideas and untried concepts. I hope their quest for advancing and growing competitiveness continues, supported by quality innovativeness.

My sincere thanks and appreciation go to my research team (past and present) for giving me the impetus to explore important and exciting issues associated with TQM and its implementation, and for helping to create various possibilities and opening new paradigms. The work, undertaken continuously over the past 15 years, is a contribution about which all of us can feel proud.

In particular, my thanks are due to the following individuals whose ideas have formed the basis of some chapters in this book: chapters 2-13, Drs T. Thiagarajan, A. Al Nofal, N. Al Omaim and A.N. Ali; chapter 14, Mr David Ginn; chapter 17, Dr A. Mutiran.

My sincere thanks and appreciation are also due to Statit Software, LLC, for granting me permission to reproduce a section from the handbook, *Introduction to Statistical Process Control Techniques – An Introduction for Healthcare Process Improvement*.

Finally, my thanks go to Jenny Collett for preparing the final manuscript.

Dedication

This book is dedicated to all those who believe in total quality management, who have and are applying its concepts and principles and to those who are actively researching in the quality knowledge field, so making it an established science supported by sound theories.

The book is also dedicated to the memory of Dr Deming, for his teachings, theories and beliefs, particularly on variation, and to Dr Juran, the Father of Quality, for his unique contributions and immense impact on the application and teaching of TQM world-wide. The book he is writing currently, at the "tender" age of 101, is eagerly awaited.

Finally, this book is dedicated to the people I treasure most, my family (mother, brother and sisters), my wife Alweena and my sons Adel, Bilal and Nadir. Thank-you for your love and support over the years.

Introduction

This book was written with the primary intention to recognise the duo of Deming and Juran in bringing TQM to the world and for incessant contribution throughout their lives in educating and mentoring senior executives on the competitive benefits and virtues of quality to society.

Deming's personality was, of course, very different to that of Juran. Deming was irritable, brusque and used to get frustrated at senior management's inability to accept quality as their main responsibility and so lead it from the top. He spent his life beating the drums and, until the few days before he passed away, he was determined as ever to send his unequivocal and uncompromising, direct message to CEOs and senior executives. Some referred to him as "a prophet without honour", others described him as the "philosopher" and some mention him as an "idealist". In any case, Deming has left a great legacy. Myon Tribus, in his tribute to Deming, wrote:

> Dr W. Edwards Deming's contribution to science, statistics and economics were important, but his development of a comprehensive theory of management overshadows all else. This theory has already changed the lives of millions of people. Applied to education, it promises to change future generations. Dr Deming is gone. His legacy lives on.

Deming went through a lot of tragedy during his life. His first wife, Agnes, died in 1930, their adopted daughter, Dorothy Deming Baker, died in 1984. His second wife, Lola, a researcher at the National Bureau of Standards, died in 1986. Survivors in his family include two daughters from his second marriage (Diana Deming and Linda Ratcliff), seven grandchildren and three great grandchildren. Deming suffered ill health and although bound to a wheelchair and a pacemaker, he did not stop preaching the same message to CEOs until five days before his death.

Deming always argued that senior managers are to blame for poor quality in most cases:

> I should estimate that in my experience most troubles and most possibilities for improvement add up to proportions something like this: 94% belong to the system (responsibility of management), 6% special" (1986, *Out of the Crisis,* p. 315).

Deming believed that a good leader is one who has theory, who feels compelled to accomplish real transformation and someone who is practical, with a plan and convincing enough to change others and make them allow the change to happen. The Deming management model (system of profound theory) is his great legacy. It has the following four elements: appreciation for a system (people + process); knowledge about variation; theory of knowledge; and theory of psychology.

Juran, on the other hand, has a different approach. He takes the view that although 80 per cent of the problems of quality lie in the hands of senior managers, they have to be helped and supported to tackle those problems. Deming has been criticised very often for putting forward goals and imperatives for CEOs without providing them with any tools and methodologies. Very often when senior managers asked him the question, how to implement his 14 points, Deming tended to respond: "you are the manager, you figure it out". On the other hand, Juran has spent his life being practical, pragmatic, acting as a philosopher, researcher, writer, teacher and consultant. He proposed sound and practical ideas, developed tools and techniques and supporting resources, to show and convince senior executives how TQM can be implemented and how they can achieve positive benefits from it.

In fact one of the biggest compliments that Juran has received about his work and contribution is from Deming himself. Whenever Deming used to be asked about TQM implementation, he always said: "if you need to know how to implement TQM, ask Juran". Juran's contributions are far too many to list in this brief introduction. He has defined quality from the customer's perspective ("fitness for use"), he is the father of the Pareto principle and he has clearly developed a methodology for ensuring that quality is a management responsibility. He has recommended the following seven steps that any CEO must subscribe to in order to bring about the quality revolution:

1. CEOs must create a steering committee or a quality council and they must chair all the meetings.
2. CEOs must realise that quality management is the management of the business operations. As such, they must have clear quality targets as part of the business plan.
3. They need to encourage education and training for quality throughout the whole organization so that people start to believe that quality is part of the job and not a separate activity.
4. CEOs must move away from just looking at financial indicators and develop measures for quality.
5. Quality improvements have to be measured continuously and progress monitored against the set corporate targets.
6. Efforts for quality improvements, problem solving, creativity and innovation have to be recognised.
7. Reward systems have to be compatible with customer quality excellence standards and not necessarily productivity standards and a "working hard" type of approach. Customer quality excellence standards require frequent changes and new innovation and this must be recognised by senior managers.

Juran's trilogy (quality planning, quality control and quality improvement) is the guiding beacon that thousands of organizations use all over the world to implement TQM and derive benefits from it. Juran argues that the revolution from quality is yet to come and that senior managers need to rise to the challenge by quantifying the return on investment from the advent and use of quality. He has always dismissed the myth that quality is a Japanese invention or a "miracle" by arguing that the recipe for success is a generic one and lies in the following practices and beliefs:

- Quality is a senior management responsibility.
- Quality is not product or service related. It is about people's creativity and innovation and therefore their education and training on quality issues is fundamentally important.
- Quality improvement needs to focus on the process, a concern for every employee since everyone is both a supplier and customer.
- Quality is not an act of faith, it has to be measured, improved and monitored against corporate targets.
- The quality challenge is not products/service productivity related but people productivity related. As such reward and recognition has to reflect flexibility, change, creativity and innovation.

Juran's insistence on the adoption of "big-Q" quality through the emphasis on planning and driving it top-down to encompass all the business activities has been a remarkable contribution. It really helped to define TQM by giving it the "total" perspective, by putting quality in the customer context, moving it away from the use of SQC to handle "little q" and by making it a management responsibility. His legacy still lives on and at the "tender age" of 101, Juran is writing a book exclusively for CEOs since he believes that so far there are no clear messages to help CEOs, who will only listen to other CEOs.

Having spent the last 20 years of my life working in the field of quality management as a practitioner, consultant, researcher and teacher I have seen and experienced the issues that impede the implementation of TQM, such as cultural resistance, senior management lack of commitment, an obsession with trivia rather than customer imperatives, a focus on short-termism and the inability to properly plan for quality and the long-term prosperity of business organizations. Deming's and Juran's messages are as valid today as they were in the early 1950s when they preached the quality message to Japan. We have, of course, moved on in leaps and bounds when it comes to the level of awareness and understanding of the TQM concept, its implementation and its integration with business planning. We do, however, still face several challenges and it looks like Juran was right when he said that the 21st century is the century for the Quality Revolution. Deming, on the other hand, appeared to be pessimistic, and a few days before he died, when asked about whether he sees some hope in Western CEOs being able to fully utilise and capitalise on his philosophy of profound knowledge, has said the following:

I don't think so. They'll have to limp along some other way.

The challenges are different and yet they are all to do with how we will manage organizations in a virtual environment and how we continue to deliver extra value for customers who are more and more difficult to satisfy. Here are some of the quality issues for the 21st century:

- The customer is now in the "front seat", dictating *how* things should be managed and *what* they expect to receive. Customers are no longer passive recipients of products and services. They define their own needs, they determine the features, the processes and the levels of innovativeness they would like to get. They determine their own levels of quality, delivery and how much they are prepared to pay. Some authors refer to the theme of Customer plc. This new paradigm is a *pull paradigm* and unless quality is what drives a business organization, it will be difficult to survive.

- The Internet, e-business, means that the levels of customer expectation have gone considerably higher. By putting the controls in the hands of the customer, suppliers are sending the message that performance predictability is guaranteed. If the customer does not get what has been promised, they will be extremely disappointed. Technology has no emotions, the human intervention has been relegated to the background. The art of bargaining, bartering, empathising with the customer are not as evident as is the case with the conventional organization that is yet to fully automated its processes and which does not trade through the Internet.

- The Internet abolishes control. It puts an organization in a very fragile situation by being totally market oriented and dealing with real time issues, where it is expected to be responsive, agile and innovative. Perhaps this is a tall order for organizations that are not customer centric and which do not embed TQM in all aspects of what they do.

- Variation, as advocated by Shewhart, Deming, Juran and others in the early 1950s, has not gone away completely. It has shifted to a new level. The business environment is now more complex. There are different common and special causes of variation that need to be dealt with. Furthermore, as Juran argues, dealing with chronic waste is no longer an answer. Modern competitiveness has to be based on real quality improvement, which has to be based on innovation, creativity and fresh ideas. In other words, "not rocking the boat" style of management has definitely been superseded. Change is a way of life in the modern organization and using the Juran trilogy will certainly help plan, execute, achieve and sustain superior quality standards.

- Quality objectives are the main objectives of any business organization. Everything else is either a sub-set or what one might refer to as a "consequential outcome". Businesses in the 21st century have got to come to grips with assessing the assets of their organizations differently (intellectual and knowledge capital), evaluating performance in the intangible areas such as quality, service, delivery, innovativeness, professionalism etc., evaluating the value of the brands through market capitalization for instance and establishing return on investment through the impact that quality creates on the competitive front.

All of these challenges do and will of course require proper, rigorous research to be undertaken, to establish empirically the logic, the understanding, the prescriptive solutions and the guidelines that will help business organizations propel themselves well into the 21st century and continue to compete with TQM.

This book tackles the issues that pertain to the aforementioned in four parts:

1. a reflection on the critical factors of TQM and their relevance in the 21st century;
2. a perspective on quality planning and learning and knowledge (the two main philosophies and contributions from Deming and Juran), relevant and critical for a modern business context;
3. a practical, holistic model of TQM implementation which is based on empirically research that has been undertaken for the past 15 years; and
4. a reflection on the future of TQM by tackling the theme of sustainability.

The book also covers the philosophies and legacies of both Deming and Juran quite comprehensively. This insight into their work, contributions and the impact their ideas have created, will help readers, both researchers and practitioners, address current issues and future challenges in the light of what has been described and prescribed in the past.

Professor Mohamed Zairi BSc (Hons), MSc, Postgrad. Dipl., PhD, FCMI, FHKQMA, FRSA, Academician IAQ
Juran Chair in TQM
Head of The European Centre for TQM
Dean of the eTQM College (Dubai)
School of Management, University of Bradford

Chapter 1
Quality – where did it all start?

The quality journey – its beginning and various milestones

The author has always argued that there are no poor countries around the world, only rich ones. Indeed the wealth of any nation has to be looked at from the standpoint of its heritage, its history and the way it preserves itself and moves forward to adapt to events and changes. If quality can be described as the means by which society caters for its needs and serves its requirements, then it follows that one could find something useful, unique and innovative to document.

The first and perhaps only book that has attempted to capture the history of quality is the one edited by Dr Juran (1995). This book depicts the evolution of quality in various forms from Ancient China, Greece, India, Europe, Japan and the USA. The final analysis of this longitudinal investigation is that quality is a timeless concept; however, we can be sure that human endeavour has always taken seriously the challenge of finding solutions to problems and developing innovative solutions that serve the purpose at the time, so enabling mankind to adapt. As Juran argues:

> Quality is a timeless concept, so the origins of the human approach to managing for quality are hidden in the mists of the ancient past. Yet, we can be sure that humans have always faced problems of quality. Primitive food gatherers had to discover which fruits were edible and which were poisonous. Primitive hunters had to learn which types of trees supplied the best wood for making bows or arrows. The resulting know how was then passed from generation to generation.

The cycle of evolution started with primitive societies where the life of the village organized people into craftsmen fulfilling needs of the "consumers", the inhabitants. With the growth of commerce and trade, came the importance of warranties, quality specifications. Through the division of labour into professional craftsmanship, more attention was given to training, apprenticeship and experience. Guilds were then set up as bodies to govern apprenticeship and offer qualifying tests. Inspections developed during the ancient Egyptian period for the construction of stone projects where various measurement instruments were used, such as the square, level and plumb bob for alignment control (Juran, 1995).

The industrial revolution brought with it more advancements in quality control and improvement techniques and the proper use of scientifically-based concepts. The Taylor system of scientific management was created in the late 19th century. This was very successful in raising productivity levels, but not so good for human relations and worker motivation. Quality control and quality assurance became very pervasive as concepts during that era and, during the 20th century, the rise of consumerism led to a style of competition which was more focused on quality. The next period is one which has established quality as a key driver for organizational competitiveness and has introduced various concepts that tackle organizational effectiveness and help build capabilities for sustainable competition.

One civilization which is not covered in Dr Juran's seminal book is the Islamic contribution to quality. The golden age, which started in the mid 8th century and lasted for over 400 years, had very significant influences in all fields. This era included, for instance:

- The development of Arabic numerals, logarithms and algorithms. Al-Khawarzmi (790-840 CE) was a renaissance man, a great mathematician, geographer, astronomer and made significant contributions. He introduced the zero, negative numbers, algebra and the decimal system.
- The first medical book was printed in Europe in 1486 AD; the first real hospital was opened in Baghdad by the Caliph Harun Al-Rashid in 931 AD. Doctors and pharmacists were licensed after passing examinations set by the State. The ambulant clinic was developed using camelback transportation to provide medical services to prisoners, people in remote areas, villages without doctors and hospitals.
- The use of precise weights and measures. Gold coins made ten centuries ago had a weight variance of 1/3000th of a gram.
- The invention of spherical geometry, the clock pendulum, the magnetic compass and the art of navigation and the astrolabe.
- The use of postal services, gold coins, windmills, waterwheels, artillery etc.
- Islamic architecture has always been characterised by ostentation and an expression of power. For instance, in the 14th century gates were built with different cross vaults, semi-circular arches. The innovativeness displayed using vaulting techniques was for the purpose of creating strength, preventing fires, particularly for wooden roofs and ceilings. The use of engineering in Islamic architecture, metalwork and woodwork is very prevalent in most monuments, shrines, mosques and palaces.
- The point covered by Dr Juran on the division of labour and craftsmanship was very much evident during the Islamic civilization. Autocratic Muslim rulers could assemble large numbers of workers and materials and with the help of carefully selected architects, projects were conceived and developed very quickly. Various techniques were used, some of them pre-dating the Islamic era. The extent of specialisation in the building trade very much depended on the needs of the local community.
- The labour division and craftsmanship which dominated during the Islamic era can be seen for instance in woodworking. Sawyers prepared the rough timber to the correct dimensions; carpenters did most of the woodwork tasks required for buildings; makers of wooden door locks

sorted out the safety aspects of the buildings; turners had the task of making wooden screens for windows. Other crafts included makers of chests for clothes, carvers or decorators, incrustors who specialised in precious and expensive materials. Similarly, stonemasons were also divided into different specialities. Quarry men prepared the roughly shaped blocks for inner walls and foundations; preparers created finished ashlar blocks; skilled carvers created decorative work; masons worked on the rough stonework of the inner faces of the walls; masons on the rough rubble cores between the outer and inner faces of the walls. Other important building trades included brickwork, clay walling, metalwork, ironmongery, plastering and tiling.

There is no doubt that various civilizations have given a meaning to quality with relative significance, reflecting the time, the place, the occasion, the need and the pride that generations of people wished to see reflected. Simply, one could argue that quality is heritage, quality is answering all the needs and expectations of society, quality is combating waste, quality is the genius and innovative application of human creative contributions.

Quality evolution – predictions for the 21st century

While it is always difficult to predict the future with any certainty, one can, however, attempt to draw parallels between quality and other professions. For instance, as Dr Juran (1995) argues, the accounting profession has evolved over the years to become a well-organized profession, with distinctive processes and disciplines, with newly and customised invented jargon and having professional bodies that influence what takes place in industry at large. The profession even has an impact at a political level through the enactment of special legislation.

Juran (1995) argues that the evolution of quality as it stands is similar to the accounting profession. Indeed, there is great awareness of the importance of quality at the political level, business leaders, legislators and administrators. There are reports and documents demonstrating what can be achieved through the use of quality and hundreds of well-documented case studies available in the public domain. In the future, we will see more of the following:

- reference reports on how to benefit from quality;
- more use of quality indicators by financial analysts for rating credit worthiness;
- national indicators on quality to be used for economic assessment of industry performance, alongside productivity and financial indicators;
- more rigorous studies to demonstrate the direct impact of quality on business performance and to build predictive models of performance;
- more growth in education, with degrees specialising in quality;
- the introduction of quality in schools;

- the development of theories and standardised terminology through the acceleration of research in the field of quality;
- the growth of professional specialisation in quality. Juran suggests, for instance, that similarly to certified professional accountant (CPA), a corresponding title in the field of quality could be "certified public qualitist";
- it is also possible that in the future, licensing for quality may be introduced to protect the best interest of the public. Similar to some professions such as medical, aircraft maintenance, technicians etc., perhaps people who serve the customer directly will have to be certified and must demonstrate competence in providing the expected services or, in the case of developing products, they may have to be certified as competent to design and maintain products and processes.

Western Electric's Hawthorne Works
As a result of Alexander Graham Bell's invention of the telephone, great expansion of the telecommunications' industry took place. The American Telephone and Telegraph Companies created several subsidiaries to handle different processes and operations and to service different sectors of the market. Western Electric Company was established to handle the production of hardware.

AT&T Bell Labs developed the engineering requirements through R&D activities. The Hawthorne branch converted them into designs, which were then transferred to a technical department, which looked after engineering and technical specifications suitable for production. The whole process was then governed by a "quality code of conduct and a body of industrial laws to be obeyed by all employees", as Juran (1997) called it.

Juran (1997) describes the quality strategies adopted by AT&T at the Horthorne's plants as effective. Products were of high quality but there was a concern with high costs due to the rework involved, mass inspection which involved large numbers of inspectors and their support functions. Juran estimates that at least 30 per cent of the activity at the time was tackling rework, handling scrap and repairing defective products.

There were conflicting objectives at the time: to produce and deliver products of high quality standards and to maintain tight schedules in order to serve expanding markets, as well as maintaining human relations by ensuring piecework earnings. Product quality at the time was policed through sampling inspection techniques and dealing with defects. Juran (2004) argues that despite the fact that inspection has led to a lot of benefits, such as detecting and eliminating defects, maintaining the precision of measurement and helping establish quality standards where they did not exist previously, they have several limitations, including for instance:

- The chronic waste identified did not help management design strategies for reducing it.

- The planning of manufacturing processes did not include capability analysis.
- Production workers had little say in controlling their own quality.
- Inspection gauges were designed for sorting out good from bad rather than giving employees feedback on improving processes and eliminating waste.
- Governing quality through "acceptable levels" creates subjectivity and compromises standards.

Walter Shewhart and SPC

Dr Walter Shewhart (1891-1967) is greatly recognised for his contribution in developing the control chart and the concept of statistical control. He had a background in sciences and engineering from the University of Illinois and received a doctorate in physics from the University of California at Berkeley in 1917. He taught at Illinois and California Universities. Most of his professional career was spent in Western Electric where he served as an engineer. Dr Shewhart lectured in various countries including the UK and India. He was a consultant to the War Department, the United Nations and the Government of India.

The adoption of the control chart came about as a result of the Bell Labs' inspection engineering department. It enabled the department regularly to publish reports on quality at Western Electronic. The charts were used to indicate performance of the company month by month. The charts would highlight variation and its causes. Shewhart developed a strategy which divides data into two types of variations: variation as a result of the system (noise) and variation from local (signal) sources. Shewhart called each type of variation chance causes and assignable causes. Deming labelled them later as common causes and special causes. Juran on the other hand describes them as variation due to chance (noise in the signal) and real variation (actual change in performance).

Shewhart invented the control chart on 16 May 1924 (p chart for percentage defects). He then extended the concept to include control charts for average, standard deviation and other measures.

Deming had a lot of admiration and respect for Shewhart and very often their relationship was described as the master and student. Deming's deep respect for Shewhart's contribution can be found in his forward to Dr Shewhart's classic book on *Economic Control of Quality of Manufactured Product* on the occasion of its reprint to commemorate 50 years (Shewhart, 1931).

To Shewhart, quality control meant every activity and every technique that can contribute to better living, in a material sense, through economy in manufacture. His book emphasises the need for continual search for better knowledge about materials, how they behave in manufacture, and how the product behaves in use. Economic manufacture requires achievement of statistical control in the process and statistical control of measurements. It requires improvement of the process in every other feasible way. The cost of inadequacy of inspection are well known. The ultimate aim of quality control should accordingly be elimination of inspection except for small samples for assurance of continuation of statistical control and for comparison of measurements between vendor and purchaser, manufacturer and customer, etc.

Shewhart's original PDCA cycle is shown in Figure 1.1 at the end of this chapter.

An insight into variation and SPC[1]
What is statistical process control?
Statistical process control is an analytical decision-making tool which allows you to see when a process is working correctly and when it is not. Variation is present in any process; deciding when the variation is natural and when it needs correction is the key to quality control.

Where did this idea originate?
The foundation for statistical process control was laid by Dr Walter Shewart working in the Bell Telephone Laboratories in the 1920s conducting research on methods to improve quality and lower costs. He developed the concept of control with regard to variation, and came up with statistical process control charts which provide a simple way to determine if the process is in control or not.

Dr W. Edwards Deming built on Shewart's work and took the concepts to Japan following WWII. There, Japanese industry adopted the concepts whole-heartedly. The resulting high quality of Japanese products is world renowned. Dr Deming is famous throughout Japan as a "God of quality".

Today, SPC is used in manufacturing facilities around the world. SPC is rapidly becoming required in healthcare and other service industries as well.

What exactly are process control charts?
Control charts (Figure 1.2) show the variation in a measurement during the time period that the process is observed. In contrast, bell-curve type charts, such as histograms or process capability charts, show a summary or snapshot of the results (Figure 1.3).

Process control charts are fairly simple-looking connected-point charts. The points are plotted on an x/y axis with the x-axis usually representing time. The plotted points are usually averages of sub-groups or ranges of variation between sub-groups, and they can also be individual measurements.

Some additional horizontal lines representing the average measurement and control limits are drawn across the chart. Notes about the data points and any limit violations can also be displayed on the chart.

What is the purpose of control charts?

The control charts is an essential tool of continuous quality control. Control charts monitor processes to show how the process is performing and how the process and capabilities are affected by changes to the process. This information is then used to make quality improvements.

Control charts are also used to determine the capability of the process. They can help identify special or assignable causes for factors that impede peak performance.

How do they work?

Control charts show if a process is in control or out of control. They show the variance of the output of a process over time, such as the time it takes for a patient to see a doctor in the immediate care facility. Control charts compare this variance against upper and lower limits to see if it fits within the expected, specific, predictable and normal variation levels.

If so, the process is considered in control and the variance between measurements is considered normal random variation that is inherent in the process. If, however, the variance falls outside the limits, or has a run of non-natural points, the process is considered out of control.

What is the relationship between variation and assignable causes?

Variation is the key to statistical process control charts. The extent of variation in a process indicates whether a process is working as it should.

When the variation between the points is large enough for the process to be out of control, the variation is determined to be due to non-natural or assignable (special) causes.

How are the normal-predictable variance levels determined?

One of the beauties of control charts is that the process itself determines the control limits. The process itself shows what can and cannot be expected. The control limits are automatically calculated from the data produced by the process. These calculations are done painlessly by Statit QC software, no need to calculate them by hand. By definition, control limits cannot be pre-assigned, they are a result of the process or the "voice of the process".

Control limits are not specifications, corporate goals or the "voice of the customer". These two concepts must never be confused. "Get real" might be a nice way of putting the concept of control limits vs. specification lines.

What about the rule violations for determining if a series of points within the control limits is unnatural?

The work done by Shewart and his colleagues gave them a base of empirical knowledge on which to base rules violations. For example, six points in a row steadily increasing or decreasing. These have been codified and are contained in the *AT&T Statistical Quality Control Handbook*. Statware uses these time-tested and industry proven standards to automatically check for rules violations. Full details of these rules are provided in the on-line help at Statit QC.

In control? Out of control? What is the point?

If a process is in control, the outcomes of the process can be accurately predicted. In an out of control process, there is no way of predicting whether the results will meet the target. An out of control process is like driving a bus in which the brakes may or may not work and you have no way of knowing!

If a process is out of control, the next step is to look for the assignable causes for the process output, to look for the out-of-controlness. If this out-of-controlness is considered negative, such as patients waiting hours to see a doctor, the reasons for it are investigated and attempts are made to eliminate it. The process is continuously analysed to see if the changes work to get the process back in control. On the other hand, sometimes the out-of-control outcomes are positive, such as patient wait time in the immediate care facility is abnormally short – immediate service! Then the assignable cause is sought and attempts are made to implement it at all times. If successful, the average wait time is lowered and a new phase of the process is begun. A new set of capabilities and control limits is then calculated for this phase.

What about capabilities?

A control chart shows the capabilities of a process that is in control. The outcomes of the process can be accurately predicted, you know what to expect from the process.

Sometimes an organization's requirements, specifications or goals are beyond what the process is actually capable of producing. In this case, either the process must be changed to bring the specifications within the control limits, or the specifications must be changed to match the capabilities of the process. Other activities are a waste of time, effort and money. For example, buying a lot of signs which say "Patient wait time is our top priority" or putting employees on probation for providing slow service.

Can any type of process data be judged using control charts?

Processes that produce data that exhibits natural or common-cause variation will form a distribution that looks like a bell curve. For these types of processes, control charts should provide useful information.

If the data is not normally distributed, does not form a bell curve, the process is already out of control so it is not predictable. In this case we must look for ways to bring the process into control. For example, the data may be too broad, using measurements from different work shifts that have different process outcomes. Every process, by definition, should display some regularity. Organizing the data collection into rational sub-groups, each of which could be in control, is the first step to using control charts.

What specifically do they look like, what are their key features and how are they created?

There are a handful of control charts which are commonly used. They vary slightly depending on their data, but all have the same general fundamentals (see Figure 1.2).

Control charts have four key features:

1. Data points are either averages of sub-group measurements or individual measurements plotted on the x/y axis and joined by a line. Time is always on the x-axis.
2. The average or centre line is the average or mean of the data points and is drawn across the middle section of the graph, usually as a heavy or solid line.
3. The upper control limit (UCL) is drawn above the centre line and often annotated as UCL. This is often called the "+ 3 sigma" line. This is explained in more detail in section "Fundemantal concepts and key terms" later in this chapter.
4. The lower control limit (LCL) is drawn below the centre line and often annotated as LCL. This is called the "- 3 sigma" line.

The x and y axes should be labelled and a title specified for the chart.

How are control charts constructed?

In the past, creating control charts was a difficult process requiring statisticians and mathematicians to remember the formulas and actually calculate the various data points and control limits.

Today, using QC software and computers, the complicated part of the task is done quickly and accurately. We can concentrate instead on the problems, solutions and increasing levels of quality, rather than poring over formulas. The time saved allows us to get immediate feedback on a process and take corrective actions when necessary.

Steps involved in using statistical process control

Proper statistical process control starts with planning and data collection. Statistical analysis on the wrong or incorrect data is rubbish; the analysis must be appropriate for the data collected. Be sure to plan, then constantly re-evaluate the situation to make sure the plan is correct. The key to any process improvement programme is the PDSA cycle described by Walter Shewart, shown in Figure 1.4.

Plan

Identify the problem and the possible causes. The QC tools described in this chapter can help organizations identify problems and possible causes, and to prioritise corrective actions.

Do
Make changes designed to correct or improve the situation.

Study
Study the effect of these changes on the situation. This is where control charts are used – they show the effects of changes on a process over time. Evaluate the results and then replicate the change or abandon it and try something different.

Act
If the result is successful, standardise the changes and then work on further improvements or the next prioritised problem. If the outcome is not yet successful, look for other ways to change the process or identify different causes for the problem.

Control charting is one of a number of steps involved in statistical process control. The steps include discovery, analysis, prioritisation, clarification, then charting. Before using Statit QC software, appropriate data must be collected for analysis. Then, you need to begin again and do it over and over and over. Remember, quality is a cycle of continuous improvement.

Specific SPC tools and procedures
The preparatory phases of SPC involve several steps using a number of different tools. These tools are described below and most are available in Statit QC. Eight quality tools are available to help organizations to better understand and improve their processes. The essential tools for the discovery process are:
- check sheet;
- cause-and-effect sheet;
- flowchart;
- Pareto chart;
- scatter diagram;
- probability plot;
- histogram;
- control charts; and
- brainstorming.

Identification and data gathering
When you set out to improve quality, the first thing to do is identify the processes that need improvement. This can be done using a number of methods such as surveys, focus groups or simply asking clients about their experiences. For example, perhaps patients at a clinic have been complaining to management about the allegedly increased times they are having to wait in the immediate care ward.

Once the problem areas are identified, a brainstorming session should occur with a variety of people who are involved with the processes. The target problems are decided upon and a list of possible causes is identified.

After a number of possible problems are noted, the next step is to prioritise. The problems that are having the greatest effect are the highest priority items. It has been "discovered" time and again that a great percentage of the trouble in nearly all processes is caused by a small percentage of the total factors involved. Service departments routinely find that 5 per cent of the problems are taking over 80 per cent of their time. Therefore, in order to maximise effectiveness, identify the key opportunities for improvement, those items that will provide the most benefit to your organization.

Pareto charts
The Pareto chart can be used to display categories of problems graphically so they can be properly prioritised. The Pareto chart is named after a 19th century Italian economist who postulated that a small minority (20 per cent) of the people owned a great proportion (80 per cent) of the wealth in the land.

There are often many different aspects of a process or system that can be improved, such as the number of defective products, time allocation or cost savings. Each aspect usually contains many smaller problems, making it difficult to determine how to approach the issue. A Pareto chart or diagram indicates which problem to tackle first by showing the proportion of the total problem that each of the smaller problems comprise. This is based on the Pareto principle: 20 per cent of the sources cause 80 per cent of the problem.

A Statit QC Count Pareto chart is a vertical bar graph displaying rank in descending order of importance for the categories of problems, defects or opportunities. Generally, you gain more by working on the problem identified by the tallest bar than trying to deal with the smaller bars. However, you should ask yourself what item on the chart has the greatest impact on the goals of your business, because sometimes the most frequent problem as shown by the Pareto chart is not always the most important. SPC is a tool to be used by people with experience and common sense as their guide.

Figure 1.5 is a Pareto chart of patient complaints from a customer satisfaction survey.

Analysis of selected problem
Once a major problem has been selected, it needs to be analysed for possible causes. Cause-and-effect diagrams, scatter plots and flowcharts can be used in this part of the process.

Cause-and-effect or fishbone diagram
One analysis tool is the cause-and-effect or fishbone diagram, shown in Figure 1.6. They are also called Ishikawa diagrams because Kaoru Ishikawa developed them in 1943.

The fishbone chart organizes and displays the relationships between different causes for the effect that is being examined. This chart helps organize the brainstorming process. The major categories of causes are put on major branches connecting to the backbone, and various sub-causes are attached to the branches. A tree-like structure results, showing the many facets of the problem.

The method for using this chart is to put the problem to be solved at the head, then fill in the major branches. People, procedures, equipment and materials are commonly identified causes.

This is another tool that can be used in focused brainstorming sessions to determine possible reasons for the target problem. The brainstorming team should be diverse and have experience in the problem area. A lot of good information can be discovered and displayed using this tool.

Flowcharting

After a process has been identified for improvement and given high priority, it should then be broken down into specific steps and put on paper in a flowchart. This procedure alone can uncover some of the reasons a process is not working correctly. Other problems and hidden traps are often uncovered when working through this process.

Flowcharting also breaks the process down into its many sub-processes. Analysing each of these separately minimises the number of factors that contribute to the variation in the process.

After creating the flowchart, you may want to take another look at the fishbone diagram and see if any other factors have been uncovered. If so, you may need to do another Pareto diagram as well. Quality control is a continual process, in which factors and causes are constantly reviewed and changes made as required.

Flowcharts use a set of standard symbols to represent different actions:
- Circle/oval: beginning or end.
- Square: a process, something being done.
- Diamond: yes/no decision.

An example of a flowchart is shown in Figure 1.7.

Scatter plots

The scatter plot is another problem analysis tool. Scatter plots are also called correlation charts. A scatter plot is used to uncover possible cause-and-effect relationships. It is constructed by plotting two variables against one another on a pair of axes. A scatter plot cannot prove that one variable causes another, but it does show how a pair of variables are related and the strength of that relationship. Statistical tests quantify the degree of correlation between the variables.

In the example shown in Figure 1.8, there appears to be a relationship between height and weight. As the student gets taller, generally speaking they get heavier.

Data gathering and initial charting

This is the time to begin gathering data related to the problem. The following tools will help with this task.

Check sheets
Check sheets are simply charts for gathering data. When check sheets are designed clearly and cleanly, they assist in gathering accurate and pertinent data, and allow the data to be easily read and used. The design should make use of input from those who will actually be using the check sheets. This input can help make sure accurate data is collected and invites positive involvement from those who will be recording the data.

Check sheets can be kept electronically, simplifying the eventual input of the data into Statit QC. Statit QC can use data from all major spreadsheets, including Excel and Lotus 123, all major database programs and some other SPC software programs. Since most people have a spreadsheet program on their desktop PC, it might be easiest to design a check sheet in a spreadsheet format.

Check sheets should be easy to understand. The requirements for getting the data into an electronic format from paper should be clear and easy to implement.

Histograms
Now you can put the data from the check sheets into a histogram. A histogram is a snapshot of the variation of a product or the results of a process. It often forms the bell-shaped curve which is characteristic of a normal process.

The histogram helps you analyse what is going on in the process and helps show the capability of a process, whether the data is falling inside the bell-shaped curve and within specifications. See Figure 1.20 for more information.

A histogram displays a frequency distribution of the occurrence of the various measurements. The variable being measured is along the horizontal x-axis, and is grouped into a range of measurements. The frequency of occurrence of each measurement is charted along the vertical y-axis (see Figure 1.3).

Histograms depict the central tendency or mean of the data, and its variation or spread. A histogram also shows the range of measurements, which defines the process capability. A histogram can show characteristics of the process being measured, such as:

- Do the results show a normal distribution, a bell curve? If not, why not?
- Does the range of the data indicate that the process is capable of producing what is required by the customer or the specifications?
- How much improvement is necessary to meet specifications? Is this level of improvement possible in the current process?

Probability plot
In order to use control charts, the data needs to approximate a normal distribution, to generally form the familiar bell-shaped curve. The probability plot is a graph of the cumulative relative frequencies of the data, plotted on a normal probability scale (see Figure 1.9). If the data is normal it forms a line that is fairly straight. The purpose of this plot is to show whether the data approximates a normal distribution. This can be an important assumption in many statistical analyses.

Although a probability plot is useful in analysing data for normality, it is particularly useful for determining how capable a process is when the data is not normally distributed. That is, we are interested in finding the limits within which most of the data fall.

Since the probability plot shows the percentage of the data that falls below a given value, we can sketch the curve that best fits the data. We can then read the value that corresponds to 0.001 (0.1 per cent) of the data. This is generally considered the lower natural limit. The value corresponding to 0.999 (99.9 per cent) is generally considered the upper natural limit.

Note: To be more consistent with the natural limits for a normal distribution, some people choose 0.00135 and 0.99865 for the natural limits.

Control charts: fundamental concepts and key terms

Whether making mother's recipe for spaghetti sauce or admitting patients to the emergency room, the outcome of a process is never exactly the same every time. Fluctuation or variability is an inevitable component of all systems and is expected, arising naturally from the effects of miscellaneous chance events. However, variation outside a stable pattern may be an indication that the process is not acting in a consistent manner. Events which fall beyond expected variability or events forming a pattern that is not random, indicate that the process is out of control.

From a quality control perspective, an out-of-control service or production system is trouble! It is probably not meeting customer specifications or achieving business goals, and there is no way of predicting if it will or can.

There are two general ways of detecting that a process is out of control. The first test for an out-of-control process asks, "Is any point falling above or below the control limits on its control chart?" This particular test is very easy to perform by viewing the control chart. The second form of rule violations is based on patterns of points on the control chart and can be difficult to detect.

Statistical process control charts graphically represent the variability in a process over time. When used to monitor the process, control charts can uncover inconsistencies and unnatural fluctuations. Consequently, SPC charts are used in many industries to improve quality and reduce costs.

Control charts typically display the limits that statistical variability can explain as normal. If your process is performing within these limits, it is said to be in control; if not, it is out of control.

It is important to remember what you can conclude about a system that is in control: control does not necessarily mean that a product or service is meeting your needs, it only means that the process is behaving consistently.

Rules testing

How do you judge when a process is out of control? By plotting a control chart of the output of a process, it is possible to spot special or unnatural causes of variability and indications that the process is drifting. Drifting is defined by the mean or range of the variation changing as the process in running. The most common indication of change is a point falling outside of the control limits, but other tests for process instability are also valuable.

Zones in control charts
Many of the standard rules examine points based on zones. The area between each control limit and the centre line is divided into thirds. The third closest to the centre line is referred to as zone A, the next third is zone B, and the third closest to the control limits is zone C. Note that there are two of each of the zones, one upper and one lower. Zone A is also referred to as the "3-sigma zone", zone B is the "2-sigma zone", and zone C is the "1-sigma zone" (see Figure 1.10). These sigma zone terms are appropriate only when 3-sigma is used for the control limits, as it is in Express QC. Sigma is the Greek letter for s and is used in this context to denote the spread of data.

Standard control limits are located 3-sigma away from the average or centre line of the chart. The centre line is also called the control line. These are called 3-sigma limits or 3-sigma zones. The distance from the centre line to the control limits can be divided into three equal parts of one sigma each.

Statistics tell us that in normal data dispersion, we can expect the following percentages of data to be included within the sigmas:

- 1-sigma – 68.3 per cent;
- 2-sigma – 95.5 per cent; and
- 3-sigma – 99.7 per cent.

We can expect 99.7 per cent of the process outcomes to be within the 3-sigma control limits.

Control limits
Control limits are calculated statistically from the data. They are referred to as the lower control limit (LCL) and the upper control limit (UCL) on a control chart. These are set at 3-sigma by default since this is the most commonly used limit (see Figure 1.2).

Control limits define the zone where the observed data for a stable and consistent process occurs virtually all of the time (99.7 per cent). Any fluctuations within these limits come from common causes inherent to the system, such as choice of equipment, scheduled maintenance or the precision of the operation that results from the design. These normal fluctuations are attributed to statistical variability.

An outcome beyond the control limits results from a special cause. Special causes are events external to the ordinary operation of a production or service. Special causes indicate that there have been one or more fundamental changes to the process and the process is out of control. Special causes need to be investigated and eliminated before a control chart can be used as a quality-monitoring tool.

The automatic control limits for Express QC have been set at 3-sigma limits. Warning limits are set at 2-sigma by default, and they can also be displayed.

Sub-groups

An important factor in preparing for SPC charting is determining if you will measure every product of the process, such as timing every patient's wait time, or if you will use sub-groups. Sub-groups are a sample of data from the total possible data. Sub-groups are used when it is impractical or too expensive to collect data on every single product or service in the process. Decisions to use sub-groups or not needs to be carefully thought out to ensure they accurately represent the data.

Sub-groups need to be homogenous within themselves so that special causes can be recognised, so problem areas stand out from the normal variation in the sub-group. For example, if you are in charge of analysing processes in a number of affiliated hospitals, a separate group should represent each hospital, since each hospital has different processes for doing the same tasks. Each hospital sub-group should probably be broken down even further, for example by work shifts.

Sub-groups in variable control charts. All data in a sub-group has something in common, such as a common time of collection, all data for a particular date, a single shift, or a time of day. Sub-group data can have other factors in common, such as data associated with a physician, or data associated with a particular volume of liquid. In Express QC, this is referred to as a grouped sub-group and there is a categorical variable that holds the grouping category, for example, Physician_ID or Volume.

Sub-groups in attribute control charts. A sub-group is the group of units that were inspected to obtain the number of defects or the number of rejects. The number of defects is displayed using c charts and u charts. The number of rejects, also called defective items, is displayed using p charts and np charts.

Phases

In Express QC, phases can be used in a variable control chart to display how a process behaves in response to a change in a particular characteristic of the system. For example, outside factors can cause disruptions in the normal process, such as a construction project in a hospital that could cause additional in-patient falls.

Phase analysis can be helpful in identifying special causes of variation or trends. It is also useful when studying the impact of changes you make to your process, changes which you hope will be improvements.

An example of a phase chart showing the changes that came about after new guidelines were established for shortening patient wait time is shown in Figure 1.11. You can see how the horizontal lines representing the upper control limit, centre line and lower control limit change with the new guidelines.

Sample size. This is the number of cases making up the sample. The sample is a collection of observations used to analyse a system. In SPC applications, "sample" is a synonym with "sub-group".

Rejects – non-conforming items data. Non-conforming items are rejects. A reject is tallied when an entire unit fails to meet acceptance standards, regardless of the number of defects in the unit. This includes defective products or unacceptable outcomes.

Defects – non-conformities data. Non-conformities are defects. A non-conformity is any characteristic which should not be present but is, or a characteristic which needs to be present but is not. A defective item can have multiple non-conformities, for example, errors on insurance forms, incorrect medication, or service complaints.

Using process control charts
This involves the task of determining what data there is and then selecting the correct chart for that data, before analysing it to see if the process is in control.

Data definitions for proper chart selection
Choosing the correct chart for a given situation is the first step in every analysis. There are actually just a few charts to choose from, and determining the appropriate one requires following some fairly simple rules based on the underlying data. These rules are described in the flowchart given in Figure 1.12.

Control charts are divided into two groups:

1. *Variable data.* Variable charts are based on variable data that can be measured on a continuous scale. For example, weight, volume, temperature or length of stay. These can be measured to as many decimal places as necessary. Individual, average and range charts are used for variable data.

2. *Attribute data.* Attribute charts are based on data that can be grouped and counted as present or not. Attribute charts are also called count charts and attribute data is also known as discrete data. Attribute data is measured only with whole numbers. Examples include:
    ○   acceptable vs. non-acceptable;
    ○   forms completed with errors vs. without errors;
    ○   number of prescriptions with errors vs. without.

    When constructing attribute control charts, a sub-group is the group of units that were inspected to obtain the number of defects or the number of defective items. Defect and reject charts are used for attribute data.

Types of charts available for the data gathered
Variable data charts – individual, average and range charts
Variable data requires the use of variable charts. Variable charts are easy to understand and use. The variable data and different charts to use are shown in Figure 1.12.

Individual charts – I chart. The I chart is also referred to as an individual, item, i, or X chart. The X refers to a variable X. An example of an I chart is given in Figure 1.13. Individual charts plot the process results varying over time. Individual observations are plotted on the I chart, averages are not plotted on this type of chart. Individual charts are used to plot variable data collected chronologically from a process, such as a patient's temperature over time. These charts are especially useful for identifying shifts in the process average. When monitoring a system, it is expected that equal numbers of points will fall above and below the average that is represented by the centre line. Shifts or trends can indicate a change that needs to be investigated.

The individual control chart is reserved for situations in which only one measurement is performed each time the data is collected, where it is impractical or impossible to collect a sample of observations. When there are not enough data points to calculate valid control limits, an individual chart functions as a simple run chart.

Average charts – X-bar chart. Average charts are made by simply taking the averages of a number of sub-groups and plotting the averages on the chart. The average chart is called the X-bar chart because in statistical notation, a bar or line over the variable (X) symbolises the average of X. "X-bar" is a shorthand way of saying "the average of X". An example of an X-bar chart is given in Figure 1.14.

An X-bar chart is a variable control chart that displays the changes in the average output of a process. The chart reflects either changes over time or changes associated with a categorical data variable. The chart shows how consistent and predictable a process is at achieving the mean.

X-bar charts measure variation between sub-groups. They are often paired with either standard deviation (S) or range (R) charts, which measure variation within sub-groups.

A definition of variable data sub-groups is: all data in a sub-group has something in common, such as a common time of collection. For example, all data for a particular date, a single shift, or a time of day. Sub-group data can have other factors in common, such as data associated with a physician, or data associated with a particular volume of liquid. In Express QC, this is referred to as a grouped sub-group and there is a categorical variable that holds the grouping category. For example, Physician_ID or Volume.

Range chart – R chart. The range chart can be combined with I charts and X-bar charts. The chart names combine the corresponding chart initials. Range charts measure the variation in the data. An example is the weather report in the newspaper that gives the high and low temperatures each day. The difference between the high and the low is the range for that day. An example of an R chart is given in Figure 1.15.

Moving range chart – MR chart. This type of chart (Figure 1.16) displays the moving range of successive observations. A moving range chart can be used when it is impossible or impractical to collect more than a single data point for each sub-group.

This chart can be paired with an individual chart, which is then called an individual moving range (IR) chart. An individual chart is used to highlight the changes in a variable from a central value, the mean. The moving range chart displays variability among measurements based on the difference between one data point and the next.

Combination charts

Individual and range charts – IR charts. This pair of variable control charts is often offered together for quality control analysis. The individual chart, the upper chart in Figure 1.17, displays changes in the process output over time in relation to the centre line which represents the mean. The moving range chart, the lower chart in Figure 1.17, analyses the variation between consecutive observations, which is a measure of process variability.

Average and range charts – X-bar and R charts. Variable and range control charts are often displayed together for quality control analysis. The X-bar chart, the upper chart in Figure 1.18, is a graphic representation of the variation among the sub-group averages; the R chart, the lower chart in Figure 1.18, looks at variability within these sub-groups. The variation within sub-groups is represented by the range (R). The range of values for each sub-group is plotted on the *y*-axis of the R chart. The centre line is the average or mean of the range.

X-bar standard deviation charts – X-bar and S charts. This pair of variable control charts is often displayed together for quality control analysis. The X-bar chart, the upper chart in Figure 1.19, displays the variation in the means between the sub-groups. The S chart, the lower chart in Figure 1.19, looks at variability within these sub-groups. In this pair of charts, the variation within sub-groups is represented by the standard deviation. The standard deviation is plotted on the *y*-axis, and is a measure of the spread of values for each sub-group. The centre line is the average or mean of these sub-group standard deviations.

Range vs. standard deviation. In Statit QC you can choose to use a standard deviation chart, the S chart, instead of the moving range chart. The range chart is often used because the standard deviation is a more accurate and therefore a more difficult measurement. Now that computers are automatically calculating the standard deviation, the S chart can be used in all situations. This is called the X-bar S chart. A standard deviation formula is used to calculate the differences in the data. This calculation can be used in cases where the sub-group sample size is large and sampling methods support the modelling of the data as normal distribution.

Process capability chart – cp chart

Process capability analysis is used to adjust the process until virtually all of the product output meets the specifications. Once the process is operating in control, capability analysis attempts to answer the question: Is the output meeting specifications, or is the process capable? If it is not, can the process be adjusted to make it capable?

The process capability chart (see Figure 1.20) contains a normal curve superimposed over a histogram of the data, followed by several statistics. A process is said to be capable if its output falls within the specifications virtually 100 per cent of the time.

Note: specification limits are the boundaries, or tolerances, set by management, engineers or customers which are based on product requirements or service objectives. Specification limits are not established by the process itself, and may not even be possible within the given process.

One goal of statistical process control is to determine if specifications are in fact possible in the current process. If the following statements are true, a process capability chart can be an appropriate tool for measuring the inherent reproducibility of the process and monitoring the degree to which it can meet specifications:

- The process is stable and in control.
- The data are normally distributed.
- Specification limits fall on either side of the centre line.
- You are investigating whether your process is capable of meeting specifications.

Attribute data charts

Figure 1.12 shows which charts to use with the different types of variable data.

Defects data vs. rejects data. Again, attribute data represents particular characteristics of a product or system that can be counted, not product measurements. They are characteristics that are present or not present. This is known as discrete data, and is measured only with whole numbers. Examples include:

- acceptable vs. non-acceptable;
- forms completed with errors vs. without errors; and
- number of prescriptions with errors vs. without.

Attribute data has another distinctive characteristic. In quality control analysis, this countable data falls into one of two categories:

1.   Defects data is the number of non-conformities within an item. There is no limit to the number of possible defects. Defects charts count the number of defects in the inspection unit.
2.   Rejects data is where the entire item is judged to conform to product specifications or not. The count for each item is limited to 1 or 0. Rejects charts count the number of rejects in a sub-group.

One way to determine what type of data you have is to ask, "Can I count both the occurrences and non-occurrences of the defective data?" For example, you can count how many forms have errors and how many do not, however you cannot count how many errors were not made on the form. If you can count both occurrences and non-occurrences, you have rejects data. If the non-occurrences cannot be determined, then you have defects data.

For example: If you are counting the number of errors made on an insurance form, you have an example of the defects per form. There is no limit to the number of defects that can be counted on each form. If you are counting the total number

26

of forms that had one or more errors, then you have a count of the rejected units. This is either one or zero rejects per unit.

Summary of defects vs. rejects data:

- Defects charts: attribute charts for cases in which the possible occurrences are infinite or cannot be counted. They count the number of non-conformities within an item.
- Rejects charts: attribute data charts for the cases in which rejected whole units are counted. These figures can be described as ratios instead of just counts.

Sub-group size – constant or changing? Sub-group size is another important data characteristic to consider in selecting the right type of chart. When constructing attribute control charts, a sub-group is the group of units that were inspected to obtain the number of defects or the number of rejects.

To choose the correct chart, you need to determine if the sub-group size is constant or not. If constant, for example 300 forms are processed every day, then you can look at a straight count of the defective occurrences. If the sub-group size changes, you need to look at the percentage or fraction of defective occurrences. For example: a hospital may have a day in which 500 insurance forms are processed and 50 have errors vs. another day in which only 150 are processed and 20 have errors. If we only look at the count of errors, 50 vs. 20, we would assume the 50-error day was worse. But when considering the total size of the sub-group, 500 vs. 150, we determine that on the first day 10 per cent had errors while the other day 13.3 per cent had errors.

Now that we understand the different types of attribute data, the following will discuss the specific charts for analysing them.

Attribute charts – defects and rejects charts
There are four different types of attribute charts. For each type of attribute data, defects and rejects, there is a chart for sub-groups of constant size and one for sub-groups of varying size. Remember: defects charts count the number of defects within the inspection unit; and rejects charts count the number of rejected units in a sub-group.

Defects charts. The two defects charts are the c chart and the u chart. The c refers to count of defects in a sub-group of constant size. The u is a per unit count within a variable size sub-group. A mnemonic to help you remember that the c chart represents defects data is to think back to your school days and the C grade you got in a class when the number of defects or errors within one test exceeded the threshold. Another way to remember which sub-group type goes with which chart is that c is for "constant" and u is for "un-constant".

c chart – constant sub-group size. A c chart, or count chart, is an attribute control chart that displays how the number of defects, or non-conformities, for a process or system is changing over time. The number of defects is collected for the area of opportunity in each sub-group. The area of opportunity can be either a group of units or just one individual unit on which defect counts are performed. The c chart is an indicator of the consistency and predictability of the level of defects in the process.

When constructing a c chart (see Figure 1.21), it is important that the area of opportunity for a defect be constant from sub-group to sub-group since the chart shows the total number of defects. When the number of items tested within a sub-group changes, then a u chart should be used, since it shows the number of defects per unit rather than total defects.

u chart – varying sub-group size. A u chart (u is for unit) is an attribute control chart that displays how the frequency of defects, or non-conformities, is changing over time for a process or system. The number of defects is collected for the area of opportunity in each sub-group. The area of opportunity can be either a group of items or just one individual item on which defect counts are performed. The u chart is an indicator of the consistency and predictability of the level of defects in the process.

A u chart (Figure 1.22) is appropriate when the area of opportunity for a defect varies from sub-group to sub-group. This can be seen in the shifting UCL and LCL lines that depend on the size of the sub-group. This chart shows the number of defects per unit. When the number of items tested remains the same among all the sub-groups, then a c chart should be used since a c chart analyses total defects rather than the number of defects per unit.

Rejects charts. The two types of rejects charts are the p chart and the np chart. The name of the p chart stands for the percentage of rejects in a sub-group. The name of the np chart stands for the number of rejects within a p-type chart. You can also remember it as "not percentage" or "not proportional". A mnemonic to remember that the p chart and its partner the np chart represents rejects data is to think of p as a "pea" and a canning plant which is rejecting cans of peas if they are not 100 per cent acceptable. As p and np are a team, you should be able to recall this with the same story.

np chart – number of rejects chart for constant sub-group size. An np chart (Figure 1.23) is an attribute control chart that displays changes in the number of defective products, rejects or unacceptable outcomes. It is an indicator of the consistency and predictability of the level of defects in the process. The np chart is only valid as long as your data are collected in sub-groups that are the same size. When you have a variable sub-group size, a p chart should be used.

p chart – percentage chart for varying sub-group size. A p chart (Figure 1.24) is an attribute control chart that displays changes in the proportion of defective products, rejects or unacceptable outcomes. It is an indicator of the consistency and predictability of the level of defects in the process. Since a p chart is used when the sub-group size varies, the chart plots the proportion or fraction of items rejected, rather than the number rejected. This is indicated by the shifting UCL and LCL lines that depend on the size of the sub-group. For each sub-group, the proportion rejected is calculated as the number of rejects divided by the number of items inspected. When you have a constant sub-group size, use an np chart instead.

The birth of quality in Japan

Japan was facing a great challenge after World War II. Having lost the war and faced complete destruction of its capability and infrastructure, it needed total reconstruction and to rebuild its economy right from the beginning. General Douglas MacArthur was appointed as head of the Allied occupying forces to lead the reconstruction of Japan and to ensure that they had no military capabilities again.

General MacArthur enlisted the help of several professionals and specialising agencies to assist with the task of rebuilding Japan. Amongst them was the Civil Communication Section (CCS) which had the task of establishing an information and education centre. Since there were no radios to communicate with the Japanese population at the time, CCS looked at the possibility of establishing a manufacturing base for producing radios. At the time, however, the Japanese engineers and managers were highly unskilled and poorly trained. The radios produced were of low quality and there was a lot of scarp and rework.

The establishment of a National Electrical Testing Laboratory was useful as CCS wanted to embed quality into the culture of Japanese organizations and it was thought the best way was to focus on training supervisors, managers and employees on management techniques. In partnership with JUSE (Japanese Union of Scientists and Engineers), training programmes were designed on statistical quality control (SQC). JUSE asked Mr Sarasohn (Head of CCS at the time) to recommend American experts. Dr Shewart was at the time unavailable and instead, a professor at Columbia University by the name of W. Edwards Deming, who was mentored by Shewart and who had used his techniques, was recommended.

The Japanese were already familiar with Deming's name since he had visited Japan in 1947 as part of an economy survey. In 1950, Deming conducted many seminars for engineers, scholars and managers, focusing mainly on the use of the PDCA cycle, explaining the meaning of variation and its causes and the use of control charts. Deming helped to change the Japanese workers' mindset. The use of SQC became very prevalent. The focus, however, became more on statistics rather than on quality improvement, although Deming's contributions did show significant improvements in the work environment.

JUSE, therefore, decided to approach Dr Joseph Juran in 1954, to address senior management teams and to help with management issues of quality and move away from the obsession with technological issues. Juran talked to hundreds of senior managers and emphasised the importance of management's role and commitment to driving quality improvement. He further indicated the importance of having a quality policy that can be written and communicated at all levels so that there was wider buy-in and commitment to continuous improvement. He further indicated to his Japanese audiences that a quality planning process is an essential task. Using Peter Drucker's ideas on management by objectives (MBO) and Deming and Juran's teachings, the Japanese started to develop strategic quality plans. Using the criteria of the Deming Prize, which was launched in 1951, papers published by the likes of Kaoru Ishikawa in 1957 in the importance of integrating quality in operational management and the role of management in setting goals and cascading them at all levels, several best practice applications started to emerge. Juran paid subsequent visits and in 1960, he emphasised the importance of setting goals and planning for improvement.

One of the key emerging developments and perhaps a concept that has created a revolution in the quality movement is the concept of *Hoshin Kanri*. In 1965, Bridgestone Tire published a best practice report analysing the planning techniques used by Deming Prize winners and they referred to a technique called *Hoshin Kanri*.

Hoshin became a must in most Japanese organization by 1975, and in the early 1980s it started to pervade in the Western world, with its name changing to *Hoshin* planning and then quality policy deployment.

The birth of total quality management in the West
History of total quality management

Total quality management was "coined" in the first instance in the US military. The following is a chronology of historical events which led to the birth of total army quality (TAQ) and which then became universally known as total quality management.

In 1988, the Secretary of Defence issued guidance to the services to implement the principles of total quality management (TQM) to improve performance and efficiency. The army's approach to achieve organizational performance excellence and continuous improvement included several initiatives:

- Army Regulation (AR) 5–1, Army Management Philosophy, dated 12 June 1992, established total army quality (TAQ) as the army's management approach. The TAQ provided the methodology, tools and techniques to perform the systematic analyses of organizations, business and work processes to achieve process improvement.
- In 1992, the Chief of Staff endorsed the army concept plan for TAQ implementation, Leadership for total army quality. The plan was built on the foundation laid by AR 5–1 and addressed army-wide implementation of TAQ.
- In 1993, the President of the United States initiated the National Performance Review (NPR) with the mission to make the entire federal government both less expensive and more efficient and to change the culture of the national bureaucracy away from complacency and entitlement toward initiative and empowerment. The NPR (an interagency taskforce led by the Vice President of the United States) implemented four guiding principles: cutting red tape, empowering employees, putting customers first, and cutting back to basics. These building blocks formed the foundation for the re-invention effort . The NPR was renamed in 1998 to the National Partnership for Reinventing Government.

- In 1995, the army developed and implemented a set of army performance improvement criteria (APIC) as a framework for improving operational performance. The Malcolm Baldrige National Quality Award criteria and the criteria for the President's Quality Award, which are Baldrige criteria tailored to fit the federal government rather than private industry, formed the basis for the APIC. The army's criteria were further "greened" to fit the army's mission while remaining true to the "world-class" standards of the Baldrige criteria. Since 1995, army applicants have been recognised as the top performers among all federal organizations competing for the President's Quality Award. This provides external validation of the TAQ management approach.

In August 1997, the Secretary of Defence reinforced this commitment to quality management by directing defence agencies and military services to:
- support quality management initiatives;
- practice proven quality management methods; and
- encourage the shared use of best practices to achieve an even more effective and efficient organization.

Note

1. This section is reproduced from Introduction to Statistical Process Control Techniques – A Introduction for Healthcare Process Improvement, Statit Software, LLC. Reproduced with special permission, © Statit Software 2005. All rights reserved.

Figure 1.1 The Shewhart cycle for continual improvement in Deming's own handwriting

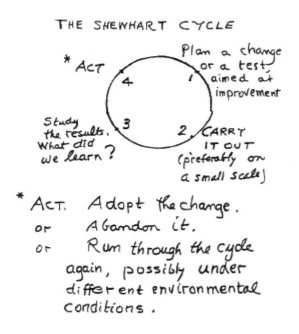

THE SHEWHART CYCLE

* ACT

4

1 Plan a change or a test, aimed at improvement

Study the results. What did we learn?

3

2 CARRY IT OUT (preferably on a small scale)

* ACT. Adopt the change.
or   Abandon it.
or   Run through the cycle again, possibly under different environmental conditions.

Figure 1.2 Control chart

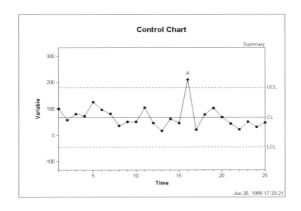

33

Figure 1.3 Histogram

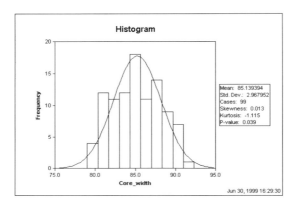

Figure 1.4 The PDSA cycle

Figure 1.5 Pareto chart

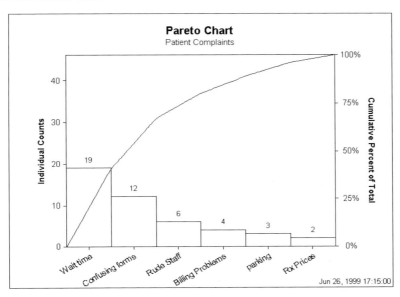

Figure 1.6 Cause and effect/fishbone diagram

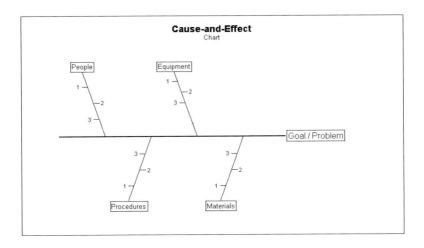

Figure 1.7 Flowchart of product development

PRODUCT DEVELOPMENT

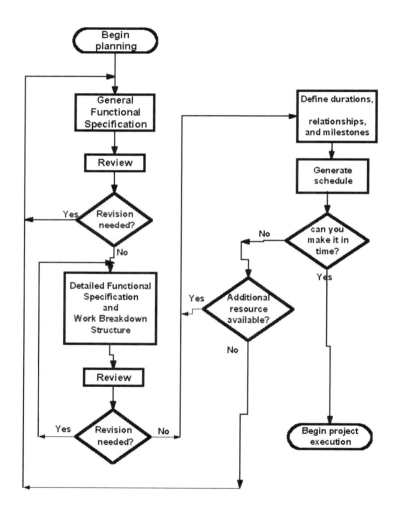

Figure 1.8 Scatter plot

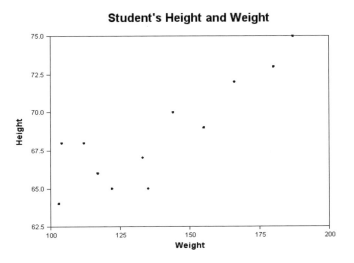

Figure 1.9 Probability plot

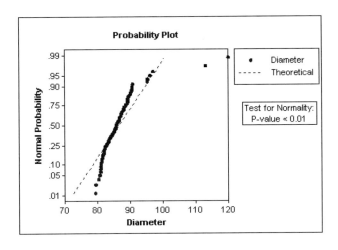

Figure 1.10 Control chart zones

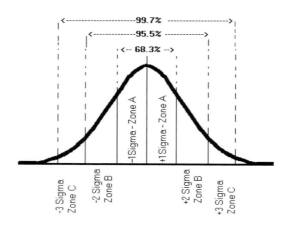

Figure 1.11 X-bar chart with phases

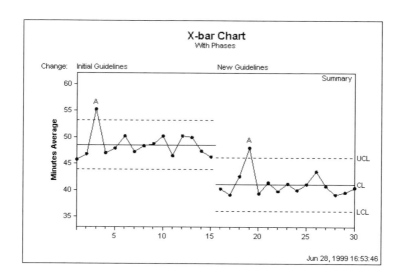

Figure 1.12 Chart selection

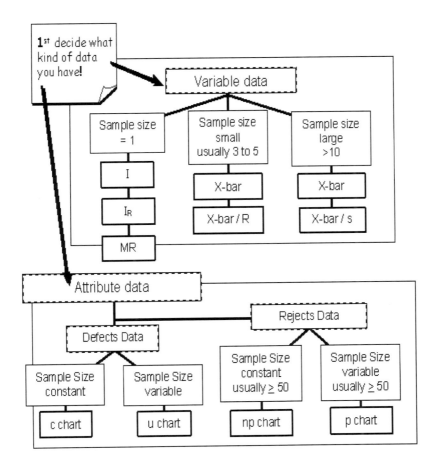

Figure 1.13 Individual chart

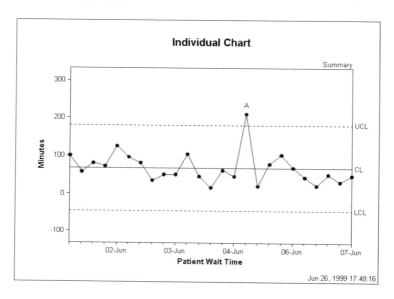

Figure 1.14 Average chart – X-bar chart

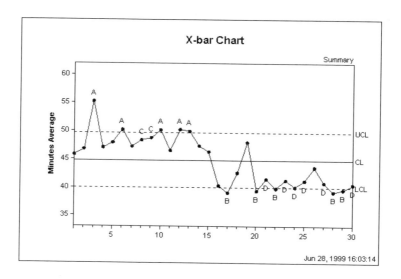

Figure 1.15 R chart

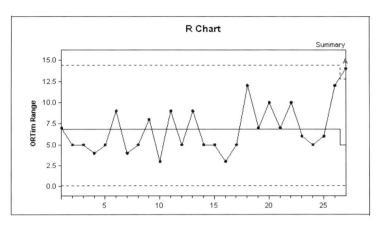

Figure 1.16 Moving range chart

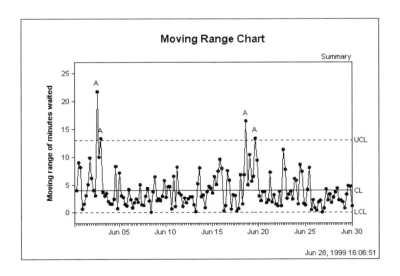

Figure 1.17 Individual/moving range chart

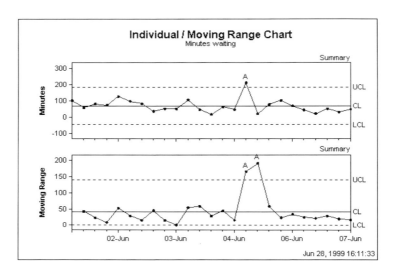

Figure 1.18 X-bar/range chart

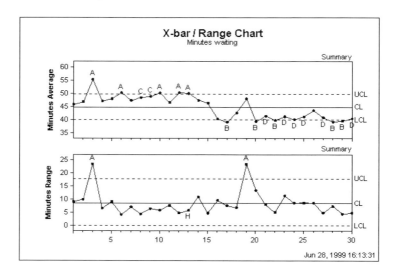

Figure 1.19 X-bar/s chart

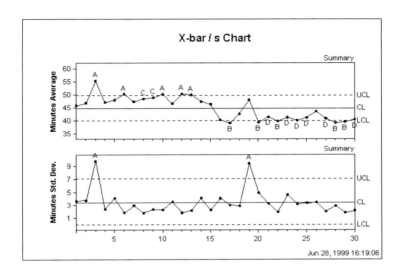

Figure 1.20 Process capability chart

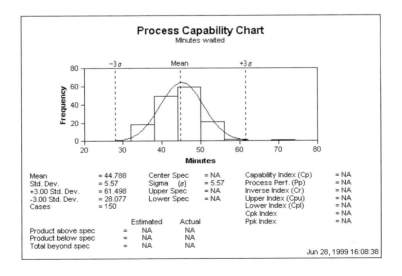

Figure 1.21 c chart

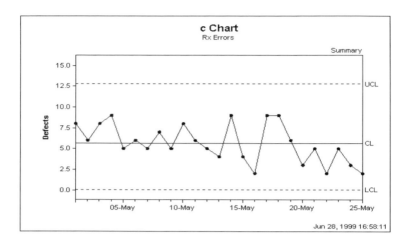

Figure 1.22 u chart

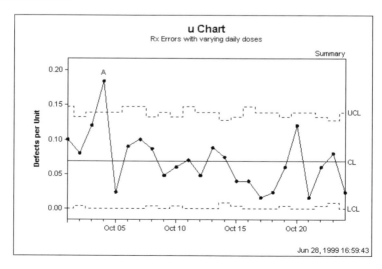

Figure 1.23 np chart

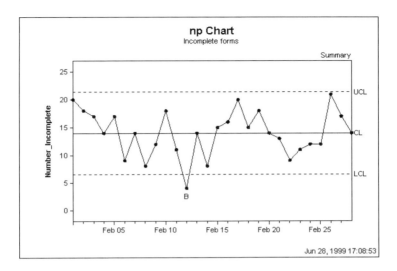

Figure 1.24 p chart

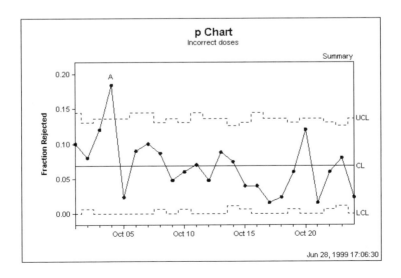

Chapter 2
Quality...what does it mean?

Definition of TQM

The literature on TQM reveals that while there is general agreement on the importance of quality management and on the broad basis in which it should be managed, there is no such consensus on what quality management actually means (Gehani, 1993; Dobyns and Crawford, 1991).

Hill and Wilkinson (1995) argue that TQM is a "notoriously imprecise term". They indicated a number of reasons for this. First, the original quality management "gurus" have been long on prescription but short on analysis and, moreover, have differed among themselves. Second, practitioners tend to use the term to describe a very wide range of practices. Third, the intellectual origins and part of the theoretical basis of TQM derived from the application of statistics to production management are in contrast to most other contributions to management theory, which derive from one of the social sciences and have different applications (Grant *et al.*, 1994).

Hill and Wilkinson (1995) made further important contributions to the debate about the definition of TQM. One is that quality gurus have been disinclined "... to refer to previous management literature or indeed to reference much outside the quality management field". Also, and more importantly, Wilkinson and Willmott (1995) say that the academic establishment, business schools and academics specialising in management have been slow to get to grips with TQM, leaving the leading advocates of quality management "... to enjoy a virtual monopoly over the discussion".

The available literature, however, suggests that there is now reasonable agreement on the basic principles underlying TQM as a generic approach to the management of organizations and on the range of techniques of implementation. In this regard, and in an attempt to identify and define the basic elements of TQM, Hill and Wilkinson (1995) perceive TQM as a way of managing or philosophising management by drawing from work by Crosby (1979), Deming (1986), Feigenbaum (1989), Ishikawa (1985) and Juran (1988). In their opinion, TQM is now seen as a holistic and organization-wide approach based on three fundamental principles:

1. customer orientation;
2. process orientation; and
3. continuous improvement.

These three principles, as argued, are implemented in a specific manner and the mode of implementation is itself a defining feature of TQM. Implementation is by means of appropriate improvement tools, measurement systems and the processes of management and organization. Zairi and Youssef (1995) defined TQM as:

A positive attempt by the organization concerned to improve structural, infrastructure, attitudinal, behavioural and methodological ways of delivering to the end customer, with emphasis on consistency, improvements in quality, competitive enhancements, all with the aim of satisfying or delighting the end customer.

Oakland (1993; 2000) defines TQM as an approach to improving the effectiveness and flexibility of business as a whole through planning, organizing and understanding each activity and involving everyone at each level.

Another way to look at TQM is to analyse the three words: total, quality and management. According to Kanji (1990), quality means satisfying customers' requirements continually. Total quality is to achieve quality at low cost. Total quality management aims to obtain total quality by involving everyone's daily commitment.

This emphasises that TQM is not just a programme or a group of specific techniques, rather it is "a management approach" and a "culture", which implies a shift in an organization's collective thinking and operation (Sashkin and Kiser, 1992). Ross (1999) regarded TQM as an integrated management philosophy and a set of practices that emphasises, among other things:

- continuous improvement;
- meeting customer requirements;
- reducing rework;
- long-range thinking;
- increased employee involvement and teamwork;
- process redesign;
- competitive benchmarking;
- team-based problem solving;
- constant measurement of results; and
- closer relationships with suppliers.

TQM has evolved as an approach to quality that is now characterised in terms of an integrated, systematic, organization-wide strategy for improving product and service quality (Saylor, 1996). Kruger (1999) referred to TQM as a universal business strategy that is not culture-bound. It is equally applicable to manufacturing and service industries, private and public organizations, structures of different sizes, and to companies of any socio-cultural background.

Development of TQM

We can examine the evolution of the development of TQM from a historical perspective. For example, Martinez-Lorente *et al.* (1998) have listed all the important events in the development of TQM from the 1924 to 1987. In the past eight decades, the concept of TQM has undergone many changes (Nwabueze, 2001a, b). For example, in 1950, Juran produced the first edition of the *Quality*

Control Handbook. After ten years, Feigenbaum produced the first edition of *Total Quality Control* in 1961. In the mid-1970s, quality circles began to be widely introduced in the USA. Crosby's *Quality is Free* was produced in 1979. Then Deming's *Out of the Crisis* became the bestseller in 1985. The publication of the Malcolm Baldrige National Quality Award started in 1987. All these give us a clear picture of the development of TQM. Before we start discussing the contribution of the quality gurus, we first examine the definition of the term TQM (Leitner, 1999) and the section at the end of this chapter presents a detailed chronolgy.

The concept of quality has, therefore, evolved gradually. The development in the perception and management of the quality movement can be directly traced back to the roots of the principles of scientific management in the work of Shewart (1931), Crosby (1979), Ishikawa (1985), Deming (1986), Imai (1986), Juran (1988). They, along with others, have provided a steady stream of contributions to the field of quality management. Zairi (1994) outlines the evolution of quality concepts and points out that they have evolved from two extremes: from control driven to culturally driven; and from controlling-in to managing-in quality.

Feigenbaum (1993) identified the following six phases in the evolution of quality:

1. *Operator quality control* was developed before 1900. In this stage, one worker or a very small group of workers was responsible for the manufacture of products. Each worker could easily control the quality of his or her own work.

2. *Foreman quality control* was practised between 1900 and 1918. It came about as a result of mass production, which is characterised by the division of labour, specialisation of skills and standardisation. The classical management approach known as the scientific management method was initiated by Fredrick Taylor and became very popular. Workers performing similar tasks were grouped under the supervision of a foreman who then assumed responsibility for the quality of his group's output.

3. *Inspection quality control* was developed during the World War I. By World War II, the manufacturing system had become more complex and large numbers of workers were reporting to each foreman who could quite easily have lost control of the work. As a result, it was necessary to engage full-time quality inspectors. Quality inspection was adopted to separate non-conforming parts, and so the term "quality" meant inspection. In this era of mass production all finished products were examined for defects to ensure quality.

4. *Statistical quality control* peaked in the period between 1937 and 1960. There became an increased need for quality inspection in the late mass production era because the volume and variety of components increased dramatically. Due to the huge costs involved in quality inspection, Taylor's scientific management approach became inappropriate.

Statistical quality control concentrated on the statistical tools and made the quality inspection department more efficient and contributed most to sampling inspection rather than complete inspection. However, its slow growth was not due to its development of technical and statistical ideas but to other problems, which included process capability, incoming material control, design control and ability of business. Consequently the fifth phase, total quality control, evolved. As organizations began looking for better ways for management to reduce inspection costs, Deming (1986) introduced the idea of statistical quality process control to aid Japanese industries in their post-war reconstruction. The importance of quality control was recognised in the business world. Deming taught the Japanese statistical techniques as a means of ensuring quality in production. He also offered his 14 points as the quality improvement path.

5.   *Total quality control* (TQC) phase started in the 1960s. Organizations that adopted TQC found it possible to examine designs regularly, to analyse while the product was in process and to take action at the manufacturing stage or source of supply. It also provided the structure in which early statistical quality control tools could be joined by additional techniques. For example, metrology, reliability, quality information equipment, and quality motivation were linked with modern quality control and with the overall quality function of business. In the1960s, some researchers (Feigenbaum, 1993; Ishikawa, 1985) extended the idea of quality control and considered its management implications. The strategic focus, which concentrated on customers, broadened the responsibility and scope of quality control. This quality control approach expanded beyond statistics and included ideas of quality systems, quality costs, and quality assurance. It was known as total quality control (Feigenbaum, 1993) and included total quality management. The application of Deming's ideas in Japan proved to be an influential approach within management thinking. Deming's ideas along with those of Crosby (1979), Ishikawa (1985), Juran (1988) and Feigenbaum (1993) were to form the foundation of present day concepts of TQM in the business world. Evans and Lindsay (2001) pointed out that the above researchers' influence removed quality from being seen as a purely technical issue to a management issue and from this concept total quality management was born.

6.   *Total quality management* (TQM) is a term that was initially coined by the Department of Defence in the United States (Evans and Lindsay, 2001). TQM evolved in the 1980s and began to have a major impact on management and engineering approaches to long-term success through customer satisfaction. It is based on the participation of all members of an organization in improving processes, products, services and the culture in which they work. Garvin (1988) outlined the evolution of

TQM as the outcome of four major eras of development. He illustrates the evolutionary process where quality has moved from an initial stage of inspecting, sorting and correcting standards to an era of developing quality manuals and controlling process performance. The third stage was to develop systems for third-party certification, more comprehensive manuals including areas of an organization other than production, and the use of standard techniques such as SPC. The present and fourth era of TQM is primarily strategic in nature with continuous improvement as the driving force.

Mangelsdorf (1999), in tracing the evolution of TQM thought and application, has provided an up-to-date indication of how the various threads of TQM theory have worked together to create the immediate, present day impact of TQM. That present impact Mangelsdorf described as "an integrative management system based on TQM", as opposed to simply "quality management". In his view, companies themselves, through their exposure to and involvement with the various quality theories and concerns over time, have extracted, implemented, adapted and refined whatever was essential for themselves. By the 1990s quality programmes for productivity and innovation had been intensified to respond to new, often harsh, world conditions and contingencies. Quality management provided the basis for "a new approach in business management for the turn-around" (Mangelsdorf, 1999).

In the 1990s, in response to global business factors, management increasingly used TQM theory and experience as a means of integrating quality into the production of goods and services.

The definition and design of processes were reformulated in response to global competition, increased technological complexity, more elaborate sequences of operations and increased division of labour within companies. Quality engineering and control factors were transferred and integrated throughout companies: "Every department manager and every employee is now responsible for his results and deliverables" and "TQM has evolved in combination of [sic] theoretical elements through the present to provide the basis of current integrative management" (Mangelsdorf, 1999).

Further definitions of TQM

Although TQM has become a key management issue and has appeared to be a well-accepted system of management, there is no universally recognised definition of TQM, and almost all writers on the subject have their own definition, by and large devising it to suit their own beliefs, prejudices and business and academic experiences (Kruger, 2001).

TQM provides a generic concept of continuous improvement in quality and other performances. Researchers agree that TQM is a philosophy that stresses a systematic, integrated and consistent perspective involving everyone and everything. Quality award models provide a general framework for quality management (Nwabueze, 2001a, b). The criteria include quality leadership, human resource development, quality strategy, information resources, quality assurance in process and product, people satisfaction, customer satisfaction, social and environmental impact and the performance results.

Hellsten and Klefsjo (2000) define TQM as some form of management philosophy based on a number of core values, such as customer focus, continuous improvement, process orientation, everybody's commitment, fast response, result orientation, and learn from others. Kruger (2001) considers TQM as a universal business strategy which is not culture-bound. It is equally applicable to manufacturing and service industries, private and public organizations, structures of different sizes, and companies of any socio-cultural background.

McAdam *et al.* (1998) divide TQM into two broad overlapping areas: holistic TQ and continuous improvement TQ. The holistic approach defines TQ as an all-embracing philosophy covering concepts such as business process re-engineering, benchmarking and total productive maintenance. For example, Hutchins (1992) defines TQ as "everything that an organization does which in the eyes of others determines its reputation on a comparative basis with the best alternatives". This view of TQ includes both business efficiency and proficiency. The continuous improvement (CI) approach to TQ is defined by Hill (1993) as both a mechanism and a cultural definition of TQ. Continuous improvement is one of the fundamental tenets of the quality movement.

Zairi (1994) attempts to balance the argument by describing TQ as "essentially a whole array of techniques, management principles, technologies and methodologies which are put together for the benefit of the end customer".

Henderson (1992) gives a definition of TQM to include: total means everyone in every function within the company accepts acceptability for the quality of his own output; quality means conformance to agreed customer requirements; and management means that for any major business strategy, it is management-led but with a strong involvement of employees.

Oakland (2000) describes TQM as: "a comprehensive approach to improving competitiveness, effectiveness and flexibility through planning, organizing and understanding each activity and involving everyone at each level. TQM ensures that the management adopts a strategic overview of quality and focuses on prevention rather than inspection. It is useful in all types of organizations".

According to Crosby (1979), "TQM is a management discipline concerned with preventing problems from occurring by creating attitudes and controls that make prevention possible".

Conclusion

There are 15 characteristics of TQM distilled from the above definitions – TQM:
1. is a management philosophy to guide a process of change;
2. ensures quality is recognized as a corporate strategic priority, along with financial and other priorities ;

3. starts at the top;
4. calls for planning;
5. requires organization-wide improvement;
6. calls for everyone to be skilled and knowledgeable;
7. promotes teamwork;
8. is about achieving results by process-based approach;
9. focuses on customer;
10. recognises internal customer-supplier relationship;
11. considers suppliers as part of the organization's processes;
12. seeks disciplined approach in continuous improvement efforts;
13. aims to instill a 'prevention not inspection" ethic;
14. emphasises importance of measurement; and
15. reduces total cost of meeting customer requirements.

Important events in the development of TQM
This chronology is based on Martinez-Lorente *et al.* (1998).

1924-32	Hawthorne studies demonstrated the importance of the social and psychological climate in work.
1924	Shewhart developed statistical process control.
1926	Bell Telephone began to apply statistical control methods.
1940s	US army pushed the use of sampling methods during World War II.
1950s	Many attempts at work improvement undertaken (e.g. job enrichment, work re-design, participative management, quality of work life, worker involvement).
1950	Deming's first visit to Japan.
1951	Creation of Deming Application Prize in Japan.
	First edition of Juran's *Quality Control Handbook* published.
1954	Juran's first visit to Japan.
	Maslow's theories about human needs.
1960	Liberalisation of economy in Japan with pressure to improve quality to compete with foreign companies.
	McGregor's X and Y theories.
1961	First edition of Feigenbaum's *Total Quality Control* published.
1962	The idea of quality circles appeared in the first issue of the *Japanese Journal Quality Control for the Foreman*.
1970s	The pressure of Japanese companies began to be felt in US companies.
1972	QFD was developed at Mitsubishi's Kobe shipyard.
1973	After the 1973 oil crisis the JIT system was adopted by a vast number of Japanese companies. A small number of US and European companies began to apply this system in the 1980s.
1974	Quality circles began to be widely introduced in the USA, the first quality circle programme was launched in Lockheed in 1974 and in the UK Rolls-Royce introduced the concept in 1979.

1979	First edition of Crosby's *Quality is Free* published.
	Xerox Corp. started to apply benchmarking concept to processes.
	Publication of the BS5750 quality management series.
1980	An NBC television documentary about the "Japanese miracle" proposed Deming as a key element in this miracle.
1981	Ouchi's Z theory.
1982	First edition of Deming's *Quality, Productivity and Competitive Position* published.
1983	"Quality on the line", published by Garvin in *Harvard Business Review*, analysed the differences between Japanese and US companies, showing some of the reasons for the better performance of the Japanese.
	A paper about Taguchi's design of experiments was published in *Harvard Business Review*.
1985	Naval Systems Command named its Japanese-style management approach "total quality management".
1986	First edition of Deming's *Out of the Crisis* published. It became a bestseller.
1987	First edition of ISO 9000 quality management system series.
	Publication of the Malcolm Baldrige National Quality Award.

Chapter 3
The quality gurus

Introduction

The conceptual root of TQM can be traced to the work of Walter Shewhart in statistical process control (SPC) at the Bell Laboratories in the USA during the 1920s. Shewhart's concern was to develop a system to measure variables in production. Additionally, he designed the plan-do-check-act cycle, which applied the scientific method to improve the work process (Evans and Lindsay, 2001).

Shewhart's early work on the statistical control of processes and the control chart established a foundation for the quality of management movement. His emphasis on the need for statistical analysis to create adequate understanding of work processes was clearly seminal for grasping the essence and causes of variation, both controlled and uncontrolled (Bank, 1992).

Following Shewhart's innovations, the three major pioneers in the quality movement emerged – all Americans – W. Edwards Deming, Joseph M. Juran and Philip B. Crosby (Evans and Lindsay, 2001). Fundamentally, through Shewhart's work, these later pioneers, or quality gurus as they are referred to, grasped the significance and the basis of variation in production (Tribus, cited in Bank, 1992). Deming himself specified that: "If I had to replace my message to managers to just a few words, I'd say it all had to do with reducing variation" (cited in Bank, 1992).

The contributions of Deming, Juran and Crosby to improving quality have had a profound impact on countless managers and organizations around the world. Other, somewhat more derivative theorists, important to the revolution in quality management, include Armand V. Feigenbaum, Kaoru Ishikawa, Bill Conway, Genichi Taguchi, Shigeo Shingo, and W.G. Ouchi. In the following sections, each of these nine contributors to our present day understanding of TQM is considered individually. In subsequent sections, the individual TQM approaches of major theorists are compared. Models and frameworks of TQM derived from theory are described; and, finally, empirical studies of TQM and associated critical factors are presented.

Deming's philosophy and contribution

The origins of the quest for quality management in the minds of many analysts may not be so certain and clear as those outlined above. Some controversy is apparent (Dow et al., 1999). Powell (1995) for example, credits the Union of Japanese Scientists and Engineers (JUSE) in 1949. Deming appears to defer to Stewhart's 1930s statistical process control work. However, most management gurus who have contributed to the development of TQM, find their origins in Deming (1986). Deming outlined a new theory of management based on 14 points, which "... provide criteria by which anyone in the company may measure the performance of management". The focus is on improving the quality of the products or services by reducing uncertainty and variability in the manufacturing processes (Deming, 1986; Evans and Lindsay, 2001). In addition to stipulating the criteria of effective management performance, Deming's analysis indicates that higher quality, established through systems of monitoring, analysis and control, would instigate higher productivity. These two, working in tandem, establish a methodology aimed at the achievement of long-term competitive strength. The system, known as Deming's chain reaction theory (Deming, 1986, p. 3), is as follows:

Improve quality → productivity up → Cost down → Price down → Markets increased →
→ Stay in business → More jobs and better return on investment

The derivation of Deming's 14 points follows from his analysis of the critical situation of Western (mainly US) management approaches. Factors contributing to this situation were identified as follows:

- Lack of constancy of purpose and focus of short-range planning.
- Emphasis on short-term profits and immediate reviews.
- Annual merit reviews and individual performance evaluations.
- Mobility of top management.
- Managing the company only by visible figures.
- Excessive medical cost for employee healthcare, which increases the final cost of goods and/or services.
- Excessive costs of warranty fuelled by lawyers on contingency fees (Deming, 1994).

Deming's solution consisted of 14 points:

1. Create constancy of purpose in order to improve both products and services.
2. Learn a new philosophy and reject commonly accepted levels of delay and mistakes by understanding that it is possible for something to be done right the first time.
3. Cease the dependence on mass inspection to achieve quality by incorporating quality into the product.
4. End the practice of awarding business based on the price tag alone.
5. Improvements must be continuous and not just a one time effort. Management must look for ways to reduce waste and constantly improve quality.
6. Institute on-the-job training to ensure that employees are trained properly.
7. Institute modern methods of responsive supervision.
8. Drive out fear.
9. Break down barriers between departments.

10. Eliminate slogans, exhortations and numerical targets for the work force – these have never helped anyone to do a better job.
11. Eliminate numerical quotas for both the work force and the management.
12. Remove barriers that rob people of their right to take pride in their work, such as misguided supervisors, faulty equipment and defective materials – people are anxious to do a better job and become distressed when they are unable to do so.
13. Institute a vigorous programme of education and retraining.
14. Take action to accomplish the transformation.

Deming's work, which helped him to formulate his theory, was carried out with the Japanese in the 1950s, as they rebuilt their industry after World War II. The contribution of Deming to Japanese attitudes to business and manufacturing is indisputable. His role as a key player in the country's turnaround labelled him as the "father of the third wave of the industrial revolution" remarked Bank (1992). Deming (1986) defined quality as "satisfying the customer beyond expectations". Satisfying the customer is central to Deming's approach to quality and quality management. In his opinion, improved quality leads to a reduction in rework, fewer delays, and better utilisation of equipment. Improvement in the company's productivity makes it able to market better quality products at a lower price, and this offers employees a good chance of secure employment with a company likely to "stay in business". It is variability, as referred to in this discussion, which matters. Quality and productivity increase as variability decreases, Deming argued. Central to his approach are the nature of variation and what companies need to do about it. Deming identified two types of variation, "special" and "common". Special causes are assignable to individual machines or operators, and common causes are those shared by operations and are the management's responsibility. In this way, root causes can be identified, and an action to remove variability may be taken by the appropriate persons.

Deming's work went on to considerably extend quality management beyond statistical methods, focusing on senior management becoming actively involved in quality management. He estimated that management was accountable for over 90 per cent of potential improvement. Elimination of numerical targets and performance appraisals are key points in reducing variation. Targets are often beyond the reach of the target managers. They distort the system and cause "knock-on" problems in other production areas. Likewise, performance appraisal becomes manifestly unfair if there is a great deal of common cause variation, which effectively hampers an employee's personal contribution. Deming maintained that "workers work *in* the system, not *on* the system which remains a management activity" (cited in Bank, 1992).

Beyond Deming's concern for the deficiencies of ordinary management practice, and the 14 points essential for rectifying it, his paradigm for change includes a seven-point action plan. This action plan begins with management struggling over the 14 points, the obstacles, and finishes with the construction of a system of organization for quality, which he regards as requiring the participation of knowledgeable statisticians (Mann, 1992). The action plan includes the following:

- Management struggles over the 14 points and their obstacles and agrees to the meaning and plan direction.
- Management takes pride and develops courage to move in a new direction.
- Management explains to people in the company why change is necessary.
- Every company actively is divided into stages, identifying the customer of each stage as the next stage. Continual improvement of methods should take place at each stage, and stages should work together towards quality.
- Start as soon and as quickly as possible to construct an organization to guide continual quality improvement.
- Everyone can take part in a team to improve the input and output of any stage.
- Embark on construction of the organization for quality (Mann, 1992).

In the Deming cycle, the activity of quality improvement is designed to be a continuous process. His plan-do-check-act cycle comprises a sequence of steps to improve the end result of the process and then to ensure continued improvements. The plan phase begins with a study of the current situation, during which facts are collected and used in formulating an appropriate set of actions that improve quality. In the do phase the planned actions are implemented. During the check phase results are compared with those specified in the plan phase and techniques and procedures used to identify the extent to which they really solve the identified problems. Finally, the act phase is used to standardise successful methods so that new techniques are continuously applied.

Deming's review of his quality management philosophy comprises four areas:

1. *Application for a system.* This means everyone needs to understand the constituent parts of the system in which they work and the various inter-relationships that occur; a failure in one part of the system affects success in another part.
2. *Knowledge of statistical theory.* This requires that all staff are conversant with the general methods of statistics and are able to apply them effectively.
3. *Theory of knowledge.* This relates to effective planning and implementation of those plans to determine what works and what does not.
4. *Knowledge of psychology.* Quality development requires changes in people's attitudes, values and behaviours. Consequentially, management and workers alike need to understand what drives people and how those

drives can be tapped for the continuous development of quality (James, 1996).

Juran's philosophy and contribution
Juran's philosophy of quality was originally developed during his work with Western Electric in the USA in the 1920s and in the 1940s he worked with Deming. Certain similarities and, equally importantly, differences were established between the two theorists. Juran, like Deming, taught principles of quality management to the Japanese in the 1950s. His work was fundamental to their post-war re-organization. Juran's approach has had considerable influence throughout the world. His overall approach was designated as "managerial breakthrough" (cited in Flood, 1993).

Juran echoed Deming's conclusion that US businesses faced a major crisis in quality due to the increase in poor quality products and services and the loss of sales to foreign competition. Both concluded that the solution to this crisis depended on developing new thinking concerning quality that would include all levels of the management hierarchy. Upper management in particular required training and experience in managing to achieve higher quality (Evans and Lindsay, 2001; Flood, 1993).

Unlike Deming, Juran specified a detailed procedure for quality improvement through his "quality trilogy" (Flood, 1993; Evans and Lindsay, 2001):
1. Quality planning:
   - Identify the customers, both internal and external.
   - Determine customer needs.
   - Develop product features that respond to customer needs.
   - Establish quality goals that can meet the needs of customers.
   - Develop a process that can produce the needed product features.
   - Prove process capability – show that the process can meet the quality goals under operating conditions.
2. Quality control:
   - Choose control subjects – what to control.
   - Choose units of measurement.
   - Establish measurements.
   - Establish standards of performance.
   - Measure actual performance.
   - Interpret the difference (actual vs. standard).
   - Take action on the difference.
3. Quality improvement:
   - Prove the need for improvement.
   - Identify specific projects for improvement.
   - Organize a guide for the projects.
   - Organize a diagnosis for the discovery of causes of problems.
   - Diagnose to find these causes.

- Provide remedies.
- Prove that the remedies are effective under operating conditions.
- Provide for control to hold the gains.

The quality trilogy consists of three basic managerial processes through which the management of an organization can achieve quality (Juran, 1988):

1. *Quality control* emphasises the prevention of quality problems and the correction of defects to create a product that is free from deficiencies.
2. *Quality improvement* is based on looking for opportunities to improve quality before problems arise.
3. *Quality planning* provides the operating forces with the means of producing products that meet consumer needs.

"Fitness for use" is Juran's definition of quality. He uses this in the context of a user-based view, which signifies that quality lies with the actual use of a product or service. Juran applied two different meanings to quality – features and freedom from deficiencies. Effective management of these quality types is achieved by using the quality trilogy (Juran, 1986). This emphasises the connection between quality planning, quality control and quality improvement. Only the customer can determine the quality of the product or service using Juran's definition. James (1996) argues that "… consequently, manufacturers do not like to use it, but prefer a more controlled conformance to specifications". Therefore, fitness for use is a utility value concept, which varies from one customer to another. According to Juran (1974), this concept is based on five quality characteristics:

1. technological (e.g. strength);
2. psychological (e.g. beauty);
3. time-oriented (e.g. reliability);
4. contractual (e.g. guarantees); and
5. ethical (e.g. sales staff courtesy).

Juran emphasised a structured approach to planning for product quality. Within Juran's system, the quality of a manufactured product is defined primarily by technological and time-oriented characteristics, whereas a service product may involve all the characteristics indicated above. Further, he determined that fitness for use could be broken down into four elements:

1. quality of design;
2. quality control;
3. availability; and
4. field service.

Quality of design concentrates on quality of market research, product concept and quality of specification; quality of conformance includes technology, manpower, and management; Availability focuses on reliability, maintainability, and logistical support; Field service quality comprises promptness, competence and integrity (James, 1996).

Quality improvement was always Juran's focus, he determined that the goal was to increase performance to levels never achieved previously. To do this he indicated that companies must achieve a series of breakthroughs in attitude, organization, knowledge, cultural patterns and results. Consequently, he developed six phases of problem solving for quality improvement which include (James, 1996, p. 65):

1. Identify the project:
    o   nominate projects;
    o   evaluate projects;
    o   select a project;
    o   ask: "is it quality improvement"; and
    o   prepare a mission statement.
2. Establish the project:
    o   select a team;
    o   verify the mission; and
    o   analyse symptoms.
3. Diagnose the cause:
    o   confirm/modify mission;
    o   formulate theories;
    o   test theories;
    o   identify root cause(s);
    o   identify alternatives.
4. Remedy the cause:
    o   design remedy;
    o   design controls;
    o   design for culture;
    o   prove effectiveness;
    o   implement; and
    o   design effective controls.
5. Hold the gains:
    o   foolproof the remedy;
    o   audit the controls; and
    o   replicate the results
6. Replicate and nominate:
    o   nominate the new project.

In these phases, 23 activities are carried out. The first three phases and activities involved are described as the journey from "symptom to remedy" and the remaining three phases and the activities are considered as the journey from remedy to further opportunity. According to Juran, the process is cyclic in nature and reflects the continuous spiral of quality development in an organization.

Unlike Deming, Juran did not propose making a major cultural change to the organization, but rather sought to improve quality by working within the system. Juran's programmes were designed to fit into an organization's current business planning with a minimal risk of rejection. He argues that employees at different levels of an organization speak in their own "language", while Deming believes that statistics should be the common language (Flood, 1993; Evans and Lindsay, 2001).

Juran's approach recommends ten steps to quality improvement as follows:

1. Build awareness of the need and opportunity for improvement.
2. Set goals for improvement.
3. Organize to reach the goals (establish a quality council, identify problems, select projects, and appoint teams, designate facilitators).
4. Provide training.
5. Carry out projects to solve problems.
6. Report progress.
7. Give recognition.
8. Communicate results.
9. Measure all processes and improvements.
10. Maintain momentum by making annual improvement part of the regular systems and processes of the company (Juran, 1992).

Crosby's philosophy and contribution

Crosby worked as Corporate Vice President for Quality at International Telephone and Telegraph (ITT) for 14 years after working his way up from line inspector. Crosby's had a straightforward attitude to quality management. He states that top management in an organization should adopt a quality management style, not because it is the right thing to do, but because it is good for the bottom line (Crosby, 1979; 1984). This approach substantiates Juran's insight into management motivation for TQM.

Crosby states that quality is free and that "unquality things" cost money when organizations are not doing the "right things right" (Crosby, 1979; 1984). Crosby argues that quality does not cost money. "What costs money is not doing the job right the first time". He sets out four pillars of quality in terms of making quality certain:

1. management participation and attitude;
2. professional quality management;
3. original programme; and
4. recognition.

In Crosby's approach, the focus is on altering the attitudes and behaviours of the workforce. He attributes quality problems to a lack of standards and attention to detail among employees (Harris, 1995). Crosby's quality slogan is "conformance to the requirements and quality is free". Crosby (1979) developed "five absolutes of quality":

1. Conformance to requirements. Once the requirements have been determined, the production process will exhibit quality if the product or service resulting from that process conforms to those requirements.
2. There is no such thing as a quality problem.
3. There is no such thing as the economics of quality – it is always cheaper to do the job right the first time.
4. The only performance measurement is the cost of quality.
5. The only performance standard is zero defects.

In the opinion of Crosby, the underlying philosophy behind these absolutes is a "conformance mentality". It breaks down if the design of the product or service is incorrect or does not match the actual customer requirements effectively. Crosby argues that since management deals predominantly in the language of money, putting the cost of non-conformance in cash terms makes sense. This concept clearly illustrates the effect of non-conformance and focuses attention on prevention issues. It is Crosby's basic thesis that quality is free.

Crosby (1979) believes that the first step for an organization to move toward a quality management profile is to determine its current level of management maturity. A management maturity grid is developed based on the concept that there are five stages in quality management maturity:

1. Uncertainty exists – when management does not recognise quality as a positive management tool.
2. Awakening exists – when management starts to recognise that quality management can help but will not commit resources to it.
3. Enlightenment begins when management learns about quality management and becomes supportive.
4. Wisdom evolves when management participates personally in quality activities.
5. Certainty is established when quality management is a vital part of organizational management.

Crosby developed a 14-point plan for quality improvement. These points were meant to deal predominantly with implementation issues:

1. Management commitment: determining where management stands on quality, developing a quality policy and management visibly becoming serious about quality.
2. The quality improvement team.
3. Quality measurement for each activity throughout the company.
4. The cost of quality: Crosby suggested that cost of quality is a "catalyst that brings the quality improvement team to full awareness of what is happening".

5. Quality awareness: according to Crosby this means providing the sort of support necessary to raise the level of concern and interest in quality among all staff in order for them to understand, acknowledge, and support the reason for the quality programme.
6. Corrective action: Crosby suggested that there is a need to develop systematic methods to solve problems previously exposed.
7. Zero defects (ZD) planning: Crosby's main points of ZD planning are:
    ○   explain the concept and programme to all supervisors;
    ○   determine what material is required;
    ○   determine the method and process of delivery of the ZD programme; and
    ○   identify the error-cause-removal programme and make plans for its execution.
8. Supervisor training: Crosby suggested this is necessary in order to ensure that supervisors are able to carry out the tasks and responsibilities of the quality improvement programme.
9. ZD day: hold a ZD day to establish the new attitude.
10. Employee goal setting should take place.
11. Error causes removal.
12. Recognition.
13. Quality councils.
14. Do it over again: emphasising that quality is about continuous improvement (Crosby, 1979).

In the opinion of Crosby, the above-mentioned points should be used as a guide to help in the rapid development of a programme. He also identified four absolutes of quality management:
1. Quality is conformance to requirements.
2. The system of quality is prevention.
3. The measurement of quality is the price of non-conformance.
4. The performance standard must be zero defects.

Feigenbaum
Feigenbaum's career in quality started more than 40 years ago as President and Chief Executive Officer of General Systems Co. He is widely regarded as one of the world's best quality control thinkers and practitioners. Feigenbaum (1961) coined the term total quality control, which he defines as:

> An effective system for integrating the quality development, quality maintenance, and quality improvement efforts of the various groups in an organization so as to enable marketing, engineering, production, and service at the most economical levels, which allows for full customer satisfaction.

Feigenbaum's work also emphasised employee involvement, teamwork and long-term commitment to planning for continuous improvement. He made a major contribution by studying quality cost and indicated that quality and cost are a sum not a difference; they are partners not adversaries. Feigenbaum identified ten benchmarks necessary for total quality competitive success:

1. Quality is a company-wide process.
2. Quality is what the customer says it is.
3. Quality and cost are a sum, not a difference.
4. Quality requires both individual and team work.
5. Quality is a way of managing.
6. Quality and innovation are mutually dependent.
7. Quality is an ethic.
8. Quality requires continuous improvement.
9. Quality is the most cost effective, least capital intensive route to productivity.
10. Quality is implemented within a total system connected with customers and suppliers (Stevens, 1994).

Ishikawa

Ishikawa was probably not known for his contributions to quality management through statistical quality control. His development of the Ishikawa diagram (fishbone) and the employment of the seven tools of quality provided the capacity to use problem-solving techniques throughout an organization. In Ishikawa's own words these seven tools were described as "indispensable for quality control" (Bank, 1992), and consist of:

1. pareto analysis;
2. fishbone diagrams;
3. stratification;
4. check sheets;
5. histograms;
6. scatter diagrams; and
7. control charts.

With these tools, Ishikawa argues, managers and staff could tackle and solve the quality problems facing them. According to James (1996), Ishikawa was more people oriented than statistically oriented. He believed that everyone in the company should be involved in quality development, not just the management who drove it, and he remarked that, in many Western organizations, grass-root workers were, and still are, denied the opportunity to make a contribution to quality. From the experience of Japan, he argues that the Japanese insistence on teamwork, and all staff being equal on the basis of contributions to quality, illustrates the major gap existing between Japanese and Western management quality practices.

Ishikawa advocated total quality control (TQC) in Japan prior to World War II. As a professor at the University of Tokyo, he was one of the creators and early champions of quality circles, and founder of the Union of Japanese Scientists and Engineers (JUSE).

Ishikawa's philosophy for quality management is company-wide quality, which involves both vertical and horizontal co-operation. Vertical co-operation occurs between managers, supervisors and the workers, while horizontal co-operation means looking beyond the internal organization, caring about end customers through customer service and the quality that suppliers offer.

According to Ishikawa, TQC embraces five strategic goals:
1. Quality must be sought before profits.
2. The infinite human potential occurs when inspection is no longer necessary.
3. A long-term consumer orientation must be fostered within and outside the organization.
4. Facts and statistical data must be used to communicate throughout the organization, and measurement must be used as motivation.
5. A company-wide TQC/M system should be developed with the focus of all employees on quality implications of every decision and action (Brocka and Brocka, 1992).

Key elements of Ishikawa's quality philosophy are as follows:
- Quality begins and ends with education.
- The first step in quality is to know the requirements of customers.
- The ideal state of quality control occurs when inspection is no longer necessary.
- Remove the root cause, not the symptoms.
- Quality control is the responsibility of all workers and all divisions.
- Do not confuse the means with the objectives.
- Put quality first and set your sights on long-term profits.
- Markets are the entrance and exit of quality.
- Top management must not show anger when facts are presented by subordinates.
- Of problems in a company, 95 per cent can be solved with simple tools for analysis and problem solving.
- Data without dispersion information (i.e. variability) is false data (Evans and Lindsay, 2001).

Conway

Bill Conway is referred to as the "Deming disciple" (Zairi, 1991). In Conway's approach, quality management equates with management of all stages of development, manufacturing, purchasing and distribution. Conway (1991) emphasises consideration of economic viability, improvement in activities to reduce material waste and time wastage.

Problems of failure in quality management often point to management's lack of conviction and commitment. In Conway's system, TQM combines consistency, pervasive application of a statistical approach and tools with a new way of management thinking. His system incorporates six guidelines or quality improvement tools (Zairi, 1992, p. 26):

1. Human relation skills: management responsibility to create a working climate built on trust, mutual respect and common goals.
2. Statistical surveys: use the power of surveys to identify areas for improvement and to be better informed about various development.
3. Simple statistical techniques: use simple charts and diagrams to highlight problems, analyse them and propose various solutions.
4. Statistical process control: minimise variations within various processes using control charts.
5. Imagineering: problem-solving techniques using problem visualisation with the view of identifying ways for waste elimination.
6. Industrial engineering: the use of various techniques to redesign work, methods and plant layout for the purpose of achieving great improvements.

Taguchi

Taguchi was awarded the Deming prize in 1960 in recognition of his techniques involving industrial optimisation. From 1978-1982 Taguchi acted as director of the Japanese Academy of Quality. Taguchi notably developed methods for on-line and off-line quality control. These methods comprise the basis of Taguchi's total quality control assurance approach. For his contribution to Japanese industrial standards, Taguchi received MITI's Purple Ribbon Award from the Emperor of Japan.

Taguchi's employment of statistics primarily focused on their use by designers and engineers "to optimise the settings so that products are robust" (Zairi, 1991). In the early stages of product development, these approaches act as trouble-shooting/problem-solving tools. Control variables, dealt with by SPC, and noise variables, are identified through Taguchi's methods. If left unaccounted these factors may affect product manufacture and performance.

Taguchi defined quality from a social perspective: "The loss imparted by the product to the society from the time the product is shipped" (Zairi, 1991). Loss may include customer complaints, damage to company's reputation, market lead loss, and added warranty expense. Taguchi's argument concerning the loss function is that loss is not initiated until the product is out of specification. More critically, loss is initiated when deviation from target value exists. The QLF concept allows management awareness of deviation at the early stages of product development. Cost estimates are also provided. Taguchi's guidelines for quality improvement are (Zairi, 1991, p. 30):

- Quality losses result from product failure after sale; product "robustness" is more a function of product design than on-line control, however, stringent, the manufacturing processes.
- Robust products deliver a strong "signal" regardless of external "noise" and with a minimum of internal noise.
- Any strengthening of a design, that is, any market increase in the signal-to-noise ratios of component parts, will simultaneously improve the robustness of the product as a whole.
- To set targets of maximum signal-to-noise ratios develop a system of trials that allows you to analyse change in overall system performance.
- To build robust products, set ideal target values for components and then minimise the average of the square of deviations for combined components averaged over the various customer-user conditions.
- Before products go on to manufacturing, tolerances are set.
- Virtually nothing is gained in shipping a product that just barely satisfies the organization standard over a product that just fails. Get on target; do not just try to stay "in specification".
- Work relentlessly to achieve designs that can be produced consistently.
- A concerted effort to reduce product failure in the field will simultaneously reduce the number of defectives in the factory.
- Strive to reduce variances in the components of the product and variances will be reduced in the production system as a whole.

Shingo

Shingo pioneered the area of zero quality control (ZQC). He established that ZQC does not significantly raise production costs in any important way. Shingo has consistently promulgated his concepts that both statistical quality control and typical inspection processes should be totally eliminated. His basic idea is that control must occur at the problem's source, not after the problem emerges. Incorporation of inspection is used in the process where the problem is identified. At that point the problem is eliminated. Statistical quality control (SQC) focuses on effects, not the cause, of process imperfection and abnormalities. SQC concentrates on errors related to operators. Human error is completely eliminated with checklists for each operation. This checklist process is termed *Poka Yoke,* this is similar to automation or *Vikhoda* in which operators stop automatically when operations are complete or mistakes occur. Shingo's guidelines are (Zairi, 1991, p. 31):

- Control upstream, close to the source of problem by, for example, incorporating devices to warn on defects in materials or abnormalities within the process.

- Establish control mechanisms to deal with different problems to enable operators to know which problem to cure and how to cure it with minimal disruption to the operating system.
- Take a step-by-step approach by taking small strides, simplifying control systems and having economic viability in mind. Efficiency, technological sophistication, available skills, work methods have all got to be carefully studied for effective usage of *Poka Yoke*.
- Do not delay improvements by over-analysing: Although many manufacturers' main objective is to achieve closeness between design manufacturability, many *Poka Yoke* can be implemented as soon as the problems have been identified with no cost to the companies concerned. *Poka Yoke* encourages interdepartmental co-operation and is a main vehicle for continuous improvement because it encourages continuous problem-solving activity.

Ouchi

Ouchi's famous contribution to management is Theory Z. Ouchi has examined overall Japanese management philosophy in terms of its effect on business in the USA. He concluded that Japanese success was built on a commitment to quality and a participative management style. US business is burdened with great inefficiencies – acute specialisation is the problem. Ouchi's plan for improvement is simply implementation of his analysis of the Japanese system (Zairi, 1991). The basis of Theory Z is (Zairi, 1991, p. 32):

- Understand the Type Z organization and your role.
- Audit your company's philosophy.
- Define the desired management philosophy and involve the company leader.
- Implement the philosophy by creating both structures and incentives.
- Develop interpersonal skills.
- Test yourself on the system.
- Involve the union.
- Stabilise employment – avoid layoffs and share the misfortune.
- Decide on a system for slow evaluation and promotion.
- Broaden career path development.
- Prepare for implementation at the lowest level.
- Seek out areas of implement participation.
- Permit the development of relationships (for example, promote good communication).

Chapter 4
Deming's life and contribution

"Quality is not something you install like a new carpet or a set of bookshelves", he would say. "You implant it. Quality is something you work at. It is a learning process." (from an obituary on Dr W. Edwards Deming that appeared in the 21 December 1993 edition of the *Washington Post*, "W. Edwards Deming dies; his lecture on quality control fueled Japan's rise", by Claudia Levy, *Washington Post* Staff Writer).

Deming's birth in Sioux City – the start…
W. Edwards Deming's father, William Deming, craved education all his life. In 1891, William Deming showed up at the school in Correctionville, Iowa, scruffy, penniless and after a 20-mile walk from his family's remote farm. In just three years, he managed to obtain a teaching certificate. He then got married and moved to Sioux to study law. W. Edwards Deming was born in 1900 in Sioux City. In 1906, the Deming family moved to a rented house in Cody, Wyoming. The family went through a period of struggle and William's dream of a legal career did not take off so he had to contend with the job of a travelling land salesman, while his family were waiting anxiously, fearing their property would be seized for back taxes.

The harsh realities of life taught the Deming family to survive on the miserly income of the mother who gave piano lessons (50 cents per lesson). The family (one daughter, two sons and their parents) realised their aspirations could only be realised with having good education. In the meantime, everyone was taught to help make ends meet. W. Edwards had a lot of determination in him. Before going to school each morning, he fired a boiler in a boarding house which gave him a weekly earnings of $1.25 so that he could treat his family to Sunday dinner. At the age of 14, he got $10 a month from the local council for shining up poles and lights in the village where he lived.

Edwards Deming was extremely bright. He graduated from high school by skipping some grades and enrolled at the University of Wyoming in 1917 to do a degree in circuits and switches. He graduated in 1921 and then stayed on for an additional year as an instructor. He then moved on to Colorado School of Mines and then The University of Colorado as an Assistant Professor in Physics.

Before joining Yale University to do a PhD in physics, Deming had a brief industrial placement at Cicero, Illinois (working at Western Electric). His brief was to help improve mica transmitters. It was then that he came across the principles of statistical quality control, though he did not actively get involved with it at the time.

Working for the government
Deming returned to Western Electric in the summer and was offered a job there on graduation (at a starting salary of $5,000). However, once he graduated he decided to join government services instead. His first job was with the Fixed Nitrogen Research Laboratory (US Department of Agriculture). He specialised in physics and properties of materials which led him automatically to statistics through the theories of measurement errors and least squares. The fact that he also had to study the kinetic theory of gases made him learn a lot about probability theory.

The influence of Shewhart on Deming
As Hoopes (2003) puts it: "Deming, with his combined love of big ideas and practical work, could only be attracted to Shewhart's vision of an intimate relation between new physics and mass production".

The 40-year friendship between these two geniuses began in 1927. The introduction took place through Kunsmann, who was Deming's boss in Washington and who knew Dr Shewhart quite well. Both of them met at Shewhart's home in New Jersey on a regular basis and exchanged thoughts and ideas continuously. Deming was impressed with Shewhart who then became his mentor. This mild, well-mannered scientist was described by Deming as: "never ruffled, never off his dignity".

Shewhart's argument was that minute variations inside the company, could have drastic effects on customer satisfaction. According to him, production managers and senior executives, should "accept as axiomatic that a controlled quality ... must be a variable quality" (Hoopes, 2003). He argued that unfortunately senior managers wrongly attribute variation to "chance", an excuse that he likened to our ancestors blaming the lack of success on the gods.

He famously coined two types of variation (assignable and special). He argued that extreme variations are most improbable and, therefore, are most likely to be "assignable" to some "special" cause such as flawed raw materials, a malfunctioning machine, or a careless worker. It is, therefore, management's responsibility to find and eliminate such problems. Shewhart's advice is that managers should not waste their time investigating causes of variation that falls within a normal range. He believed that the elimination of all variation is an impossible task (we live in an inexact world according to him).

Shewhart's conclusions had a lot of influence on Deming's theory of management. He could see that the idea of common and special causes of variation could be made applicable to any process, not just to manufacturing. Deming, extending Shewhart's ideas, argued that once a process is in control, continuous improvement means that more special causes of error must be found by not just improvements in the process itself but looking at the whole system. This, he argued, is the function of senior management.

Deming became a fierce critique of senior management and their lack of focus on people. On a positive note, he argued that although things have got better because of the growth in using SPC (statistical process control) charts, workers are only allowed to report on any variation they might observe but not to influence the improvement of the process or system itself.

Deming was also influenced by other experts on SQC, including for instance Colonel Leslie Simon and Harold Dodge, a Bell Labs statistician. Dodge described the philosophy of SQC to Deming as: "Quality has to be 'built in' rather than 'inspected out'".

Deming continued to further his knowledge of statistics by communicating with eminent scholars and experts, including Professor Birge (Berkeley Physics Department) and Karl Pearson (philosopher and statistician, University of London). From 1930 until 1939, Deming taught statistics at the Bureau of Standards and then in the Graduate School of the Agriculture Department. In 1938, Deming continued to build on a tradition of inviting eminent speakers, including Shewhart who conducted four sessions on quality control. The difference between Deming and Shewhart was that the latter was a poor speaker and people found it difficult to understand him.

In 1939 Deming moved to the Bureau of the Census as head mathematician and adviser on sampling. He gave several other courses including statistics courses at Stanford. He was, however, discouraged because most of the people who attended his courses had a background in engineering and technical subjects. He lamented that managers were only attending a half-day appreciation talk and that engineers and technicians, despite the fact that they had gained good competence by attending his courses, would go back to their work environment and gradually lose the knowledge gained because they had very little influence to make decisions and change things.

In 1940, a year before Pearl Harbour was attacked, Deming moved to the War Department to introduce SQC to weapons manufacturers. It was Shewhart who suggested that a committee was formed with Deming as a member. The committee was called the American War Standards on Quality Control with the purpose of providing guidance to weapons manufacturers and military ordnance inspectors. With his determination to convert top management to the usefulness of SQC, Deming continued to give lecturers and courses. In July 1943 at Stanford University, he ran a ten-day course for 30 managers which was a successful and well received programme. He followed this with another crash course at UCLA in Southern California. The outcomes, generally speaking, were however disappointing (Hoopes, 2003, p. 212):

> Senior corporate managers showed no wartime interest in SQC. Production managers embraced Deming's teachings, but top executives forfeited the opportunity to make quality a unifying,

company-wide concern, an oversight that later gave a huge competitive advantage to the Japanese.

Hoopes goes on to say:
> Deming tried but failed to get his message to the top floor. Giving his course in Detroit in December 1943, he added a one-day session for executives. Promising to avoid technical discussion, he hoped that a general explanation of SQC would win over the brass. But Ford, General Motors, and Chrysler did not send a single senior manager.

In 1947 and 1950 Deming was invited to Japan to work as an adviser on sampling techniques under MacArthur's Supreme Command Allied Forces. This time round, he decided to make sure that SQC was sold to upper management levels, convinced that their role is extremely crucial in driving quality improvement.

Deming's own views on the Japanese miracle

Deming corrected an assertion made by many in that Japan started down the road of quality after 1950. He argued that the Japanese very much knew what quality was well before 1950 and that they were working confidently behind the scenes to put their house in order and optimise their products and services. Although as Deming said, this was not so evident at an international trading level.

The upsurge of quality in Japan did, however, take place in the period 1950-1954 and beyond. So what happened? Deming (1986, p. 486) argued:
> ...top management became convinced that quality was vital for export, and that they could accomplish the switch. They learned, in conference, after conference, something about their responsibilities for the achievement of this aim, and that they must take lead in this aim. Management and factory workers put their forces for quality and jobs.

The first invitation for Deming to make a contribution in the teaching of SQC was in 1949, although he had previously visited Japan in 1947 as part of a census team. He accepted the visit in June 1950. JUSE facilitated the introduction of top executives to Deming (21 in 1950, more in 1951, 1952 and subsequent years). In his first address to Japanese managers, executives and engineers, Deming said:
> We are in a new industrial age, created largely by statistical principles and techniques.... Statistics had revolutionised "requirements of international trade" such as quality, price, standardization, and communication (Hoopes, 2003).

Deming taught the Japanese to get away from the old model of designing, making and launching the product by emphasizing the importance of the customer. He stressed the importance of doing consumer research, to study the market and the needs of the customer and to redesign the product according to real needs and requirements. Deming argued that between 1950-1970 JUSE taught statistical methods to 14,700 engineers and thousands of foremen. Courses for managers had a waiting list of seven months. Deming was so confident that the Japanese could rival the USA and the rest of the world because he had seen first hand their undivided attention to continuous improvement and their determination to compete in foreign markets. He predicted that the Japanese dominance in world markets would take place within five years and his prediction was based on looking at Japanese workers apply themselves, the knowledge and commitment of Japanese managers, the confidence employees had in their top management teams in guiding their companies and in making the right decisions and the level of attention and focus given to education by the likes of JUSE.

Deming saw the growth of quality circles and the establishment of this movement by Professor Kaoru Ishikawa, the son of the JUSE president who introduced Deming to top managers in 1950. Ishikawa argued that QCCs complete the process of continuous improvement, and having top management focus on QC and its management allowed the workers bottom-up to look at their own local work environments.

Deming understood Japanese society extremely well, he embraced their culture and endorsed their management practices. He decided to donate the royalties from his printed lectures to JUSE. The latter used the money to fund the Deming Prize, which is still considered one of the most prestigious and special quality awards in the world. The medallion has inscribed on it Deming's own words:

The right quality & uniformity are foundations of commerce, prosperity & peace.

Chapter 5
Juran's life and contribution

...every successful quality revolution has included the participation of upper management. We know of no exceptions (Joseph Juran).

My job of contributing to the welfare of my fellow man is the great unfinished business (Joseph Juran).

Intrinsic is the belief that quality does not happen by accident, it must be planned! (Joseph Juran).

Without a standard there is no logical basis for making a decision or taking action (Joseph Juran).

Juran's birth in Braila

Joseph Moses Juran was born in Braila, Romania on 24 December 1904. His father was born in Gura Humora (Austria) in 1874. His mother was born in Braila, in either 1877 or 1880. His family moved to Gura Humora in 1907. His father Jakob left Romania for the USA as an immigrant in 1909. The entire family joined Juran's father in Minnesota on 20 May 1912. Full of dreams for a better life, the Jurans were not so fortunate when they landed in America. Juran recalls (Juran, 2004):

> We were not greeted by the statue of liberty; our ship did not land at Ellis Island...our new home was a tarpaper shack set in a wooded area. The shack was a rectangle of about 360 square feet. It was partitioned into three areas without doors. In the rear was the kitchen, which included a cast-iron stove that was the sole source of heat for the entire shack. The middle area provided sleeping quarters. On one side the three boys slept crosswise in one bed; the girls slept on the other side. The front area held the curtained bed for the parents.

The USA – a land of opportunity

To make ends meet, various members of the family had to take on labouring jobs. At school, however, Joe Juran was found to be extremely bright. He did very well, being three years ahead of his age group. He was particularly good at maths and physics. In 1918, things got better and the family moved from the shack to a more conventional house (Juran, 2004):

> We welcomed the conveniences of the house. The kitchen stove was heated by gas, and the living room had a "self-heater" stove – it

burned coal briquettes. Suddenly we were rid of woodcutting. Gas also provided the brilliant incandescent lighting from the Welsbach mantles. A welcome luxury was indoor plumbing and its array of services; hot water from the gas-fired boiler; hot baths in the second floor bathtub; and waste disposal from the indoor toilet – two of them.

Joe Juran enrolled at the University of Minnesota in 1920. He was the first member of his family to register at a college, ever. He graduated in 1924 with a BSc in Electrical Engineering and found a job at Western Electric. He worked in the inspection department of Hawthorne Works, which at the time employed over 40,000 people. Juran's brilliance in absorbing detail, his analytical skills and his overall knowledge of the work place was soon noticed and he moved up the ranks.

By the mid-1926 and after two years of trouble shooting, Juran understood how the Hawthorne works was linked to the holding mother company (AT&T). He realised how quality was defined at the strategic level and how it was driven by each of the subsidiary companies. In order to deal with the problem of defects and rework, the control chart was introduced by the inspection engineering department. The charts were used to track quality performance with the control limits so that decisions could be made by supervisors and managers. Dr Walter A. Shewhart was a member of the Bell Laboratories' inspection engineering staff at the time. Juran argues that at the time, the use of control charts was not really effective (Juran, 2004, p. 109):

The control chart was a brilliant invention; today many such charts are in use world-wide. Nevertheless, the inspection branch managers made virtually no use of the control chart. At the time it was one of my responsibilities to "sell" the chart to inspection supervisors. I rarely made a sale, and I was puzzled by their reasons for rejection; they seemed illogical and even irrelevant. Today the reasons for rejection seem clear. The inspection supervisors saw no way in which control charts could help solve their chief problems. Shop foremen's top priorities were to meet schedules and maintain piecework earnings. Quality was no higher than third on their priority list.

Being involved in the Bell Labs' initiative had a significant impact on Juran's career. He was selected to attend various courses on probability theory and then he joined the inspection statistical department to train senior managers. As he says "Such fortuitous events lifted me out of obscurity and placed me on a fast track".

In 1928 he wrote a pamphlet called "Statistical methods applied to manufacturing problems" which looked at the use of sampling and analysing techniques for the control of manufacturing quality. This contribution was used in an AT&T *Quality Control Handbook*. In 1937 Juran moved to the headquarters in New York as an internal consultant to the various subsidiaries and started to develop external interests and networking through professional associations and large consultancy houses.

In 1941, Juran was seconded to the Lend-Lease Administration as an administation assistant. On 20 December 1941 Western Electric President (C.G. Stoll) received a telegram which read (Juran, 2004):

Very anxious to secure services of J.M. Juran … on loan basis for six weeks to make very important analysis of Statistics Division of Lend-Lease Administration and assist in reorganizing it (signed by E.R. Stettinius, Jr – Lend-Lease Administrator).

Juran was in charge of re-organizing the shipment of goods and materials to friendly nations that were supporting the war effort. He simplified processes, re-engineered them and using an able and competent team to assist him, he eliminated bureaucracy, waste and helped build efficient storage and delivery processes.

The canoe journey

By the age of 40, at the end of 1944, Juran decided that he wanted to embark on a new career. As he called it at the time, disembarking from "the ocean liner" (corporate comfort of Western Electric) and jumping into "the canoe" as an independent: "By the end of 1944, my mind was made up – my goal was to be a freelancer in the field of management".

Juran's career took off and the seaworthiness of his canoe was confidently proven. He published *Quality Control Handbook* in 1951. The book was the key to Juran's success and established his reputation world-wide. As he puts it (Juran, 2004):

The Handbook became the "bible" of managing for quality and has increasingly served as the international reference book for professionals and managers in the field. It has retained that position; no serious competitor was visible as the year 2000…Publication of the Handbook was also a milestone on my journey through life. Over the years it attracted many followers, opened many doors, and contributed to my being sought after by institutions in the United States and internationally. It vaulted me into a position of leadership in the field; the decades that followed would solidify and enlarge that status.

The book is now in its 5th edition and has been renamed *Juran's Quality Handbook*. The handbook became the launch-pad for Juran's career. Subsequent books were written and each helped to move managing for quality closer towards a complete science.

In 1964, Juran published *Managerial Breakthrough*, which established the know-how in terms of capitalising on the benefits of quality. Some people refer to it as the start of the six sigma movement. The book was organized in two parts:

1. Breakthrough – creation of beneficial change.
2. Control – prevention of adverse change.

Quality Planning and Analysis (QPA) was written jointly with Professor Frank Gryna and was published in 1970. It was meant to be a textbook for the quality professionals, particularly quality engineers seeking certification. The American Society for Quality (ASQ) used it for its Certified Quality Engineer (CQE) examinations.

Juran on Planning for Quality (JPQ) was published in 1988. It discusses in detail the planning process as the third key component of Juran's famous trilogy. The other two components were covered in *Managerial Breakthrough*.

Juran's training and consulting services grew at a phenomenal rate. Alongside his research and writing interests, Juran thrived on consulting activities and meeting senior executives to disseminate his ideas. As he says in his memoirs (Juran, 2004, p. 275) he was so overwhelmed with demand that he started to use the tactic of raising his fee:

> A measure of my selectivity in accepting invitations was my rising consulting fee structure. By the early 1960s, my usual fee was $300 *per diem*. By the mid-1960s it was $500; by the early 1970s it had reached $1,000 *per diem*. In a sense I was using the fee structure to price myself out of the excess invitations. I felt no shame in accepting those fees. No one but me knew how much time I was devoting to *pro bono* engagements, reading articles, attending conferences, maintaining my database, writing books and training manuals, preparing lecture notes, keeping up with correspondences, and so on.

Interest in Juran and his ideas continued even when he decided to terminate his professional engagements in 1991. He goes on to say:

> I was still receiving numerous overtures to provide consulting services or to hold in-house courses. Increasingly I declined to make the journeys, but the requests persisted. I then resorted to the tactic of pricing myself out of the market – I raised my *per diem* rate to $10,000. Most of my would-be clients balked at that rate, but some did not. I then gave the wheel another turn – I raised the rate to $25,000. That did it. Only one client needed me badly – and bought two days of my time. That income was a far cry from what I earned at my early morning job in 1912, when I sold copies of the *Minneapolis Tribune* for one cent each (p. 336).

Juran Center for Leadership in Quality

Juran has always felt the need to repay his debt to the USA, the country that has welcomed him and his family and given him the opportunity to achieve and be very successful, recognised all over the world. Realising that his needs were more or less fulfilled and that he has no financial worries, Juran started to focus more on spending his time, providing service to society as *pro bono publico*. In 1983, he created the Juran Foundation Inc. (JFI) with the following mission statement: "…to identify the quality-related problems of society and develop remedies for their solution".

Although JFI did not manage to accomplish its various ambitious goals, nevertheless it did provide a lot of useful support by giving grants to schools to buy books and training materials, research grants to scholars, supporting some conferences and a donation to the Malcolm Baldrige National Quality Award for the sum of $100,000.

A book on the history of quality was published with contributions from authors from all over the world. The royalties were to be kept for the benefit of JFI.

A proposal was made by Minnesota University's Carlson School of Management to create the Juran Center for Leadership in Quality and to transfer the JFI papers. The agreement was signed in April 1998 and the vision and work of Dr Juran were set to continue through a centre that had the knowledge and expertise to establish itself as a benchmark in the world for leading management of quality.

Juran's influence on Japan

Juran admits that the invitation to go and lecture in Japan came as a result of the publication of *Quality Control Handbook*. Through the Japanese Union of Scientists and Engineers' (JUSE) first managing director (Ken-ichi Koyanagi), Juran was invited because Juran tackled other issues than just statistics in his book, including economics of quality, specifications, organization for quality, the role of inspection, quality assurance, supplier relationships among others.

Koyanagi thought that there was sufficient knowledge and competence with SQC and there was then an urgent need to look at ways and means for managing quality at all levels. Although the invitation to have Juran visit Japan was issued in December 1952, it was not until 1954 that Juran was ready and could spare the time to go there and give lectures and conduct consultancy projects.

Juran visited several Japanese organizations and conducted several seminars. In Tokyo, the courses he ran for senior managers (two days) had 62 attendees; the courses for middle managers were attended by 160 delegates. In Osaka, he had 106 enrolments from middle managers and 62 enrolments from senior managers.

Juran also conducted several courses at prestigious universities and professional associations including Waseda University, Chamber of Commerce in Osaka amongst others. He was asked by JUSE to present a report at the end of his visit, with useful observations and recommendations. The following are extracts from the report he produced for JUSE (Juran, 2004):

- A strong wave of interest in the statistical tools for quality control.
- Some over-enthusiasm and over-extension of the use of statistical tools, with under-emphasis on other essential tools.
- A search for a broader base for the solution of quality problems through use of additional essential tools. (This is the present stage).

- Japanese industry appears to have compressed these steps into fewer years than have some Western countries. In this way, though starting later, Japanese industry has reduced the extent to which it was lagging behind Western development.
- The present trend toward broadening the approach to managing for quality (by setting quality goals, quality planning, organization changes and economic analysis) is wholly constructive.
- It is conviction that notwithstanding the grave obstacles facing the Japanese economy as a whole, the outlook for improved quality and improved quality reputation for Japanese goods is bright.

Juran's visit created the right impact; so much so that he was asked to visit Japan several times over the coming years. Juran visited Japan on numerous occasions over the years, to conduct seminars and speak at conferences and to offer consultancy advice to a large number of prestigious and well-known corporations.

Japan's recognition of Juran's contribution

There are millions of people who have, over the years, kept asking the question: was Deming better recognised than Juran in Japan? Is this the reason why a prize was created in Deming's name, to signify the importance of his contribution? Why didn't the Japanese create an award with Juran's name?

Juran tackles the question in his memoirs (Juran, 2004). He said that during 1966 while at a seminar, Professor Kondo (from Kyoto University) who had just finished his presentation, gave the cue to Dr Juran's presentation, being the speaker who followed him. Prof. Kondo commented: "we have a Deming Prize; why don't we have a Juran prize?" It appears that the Japanese had discussed the idea of creating a quality prize to be awarded to companies that have managed to win the Deming Prize for a the second time. They had in mind the idea of the Juran Prize as the new quality award.

Since Juran did not explicitly express an interest, the Japanese took it that he has decided that he was not interested and instead named the new award The Japan Prize. Juran writes:

> In retrospect, I realize now that Kondo's query was actually in accordance with the Japanese custom of avoiding bluntness. Nevertheless it confused me, and today I regret the outcome. I would have been delighted to lend my name to something so symbolic of excellence in quality.

Juran was however rewarded for his efforts in supporting the quality movement in Japan. In 1981, he received a high honour – the emperor's award of the Order of the Sacred Treasure, Second Class (the Second Class is the highest award that is given to a non-Japanese). It was presented to him by the then Minister of Science and Technology (Ichiro Nakagawa) with the following citation: "...for the development of Quality Control in Japan and the facilitation of U.S. and Japanese friendship".

Even now, Dr Juran is still so humble about the influence he has had on Japanese management thinking. He argues that it is better to leave the final analysis and judgement to others. He goes on to say (Juran, 2004, p. 300):

> While some of the Japanese comments include biases and embellishments, their actions do not. The following list of those actions provides a useful basis for appraising the Japanese view of my contribution:
>
> - JUSE invited me to make nine visits to Japan and to participate actively in the planned events.
> - While my correspondences was chiefly through JUSE, I had many invitations to visit Japanese companies, including Toyota, Matsushita, and Bridgestone.
> - JUSE translated several of my books into Japanese, along with many of my papers.
> - They published Japanese translations of my lecturers.
> - They incorporated much of my text material into their array of training courses (for professionals, foremen, middle managers, and senior executive).
> - They succeeded in having me decorated with the Order of the Sacred Treasure.
> - They planned to name an important prize after me, but because of mis-communication, it ended up as the "Japan Prize".

Chapter 6
Models of TQM implementation

Models proposed by quality experts and consultants
There are many experts and consultants who have identified success factors for TQM implementation. There is no one-size-fits-all model. However, the various models offered by experts can help firms in the implementation process.

Some of the models that have been adopted by UK companies are those of Kanji *et al.* (1999, 1998) and Oakland (1993, 1989, 2000). The model proposed by Oakland (1993, 2000) at Bradford's European Centre for TQM, which is adopted by the DTI, has as its core theme the identification and management of processes within the organization.

The processes are seen as chains of internal and external customer-supplier relationships that must be managed effectively and efficiently. Surrounding the processes are the "soft" outcomes of TQM – culture, communication and commitment, and "hard" management necessities of TQM – the use of teams (ranging from high-powered quality councils to work-area quality circles), quality tools (for systematic data collection and analysis) and systems (based on recognised international standards).

Kanji (*et al.* 1993) use a four-sided "pyramid" model to show the structure of TQM:
1. Delight the customers: customer satisfaction; internal customers are real.
2. Management-by-fact: all work is a process; measurement.
3. People-based management: teamwork; people make quality.
4. Continuous improvement: continuous improvement cycle; prevention.

It encompasses a set of four general governing principles, represented by the four sides. Each of the principles is translated into practice by using two core concepts. "Leadership" sits at the base of the pyramid, aptly emphasising the critical role of leadership to make TQM happen.

Kanji *et al.*'s (1999,1998) modified pyramid model is based on the proposition that to achieve customer satisfaction level (delight the customer), the organization has to improve continuously all aspects of its operations (continuous improvement); this can be achieved through leadership by making decisions on objective evidence of what actually was happening (management-by-fact), and by involving all employees in quality improvement activities (people-based management), leading ultimately to business excellence. His modified pyramid model, together with the four-stage process of implementing TQM, represents an attractive and practical implementation framework for companies to follow (Yusof and Aspinwall, 2000).

The four stages are identification and preparation, management understanding and commitment, scheme of understanding, and critical analysis. Kanji (1999) points out that there is a need to identify and collect information where improvement will have the most impact. This requires management information from a data collection system with a fact-based approach.

Oakland (1993, 2000) proposes a model for TQM implementation where the customer-supplier chains form the core, which is surrounded by the hard management necessities of a good quality system, tools and teamwork. He proposes seven steps for senior management to begin the task of process alignment to a self-reinforcing cycle of commitment, communication and cultural change. The seven steps are:

1. Gain commitment to charge.
2. Develop shared vision and mission for business or desired charge.
3. Develop critical success factors.
4. Defining the core processes.
5. Gain ownership.
6. Break down the core processes into sub-processes, activities and tasks.
7. Ensure process and people alignment through a policy deployment or goal translation process.

Dale and Plunket (1990) identified 21 points which organizations should consider important in the process of TQM implementation:

1. Top management commitment and support vital for credibility, continuity and longevity of process.
2. Establishment of multi-disciplinary quality-improvement steering committee chaired by chief executive officer is essential.
3. Quality control activity separated from quality improvement process.
4. Set goals for improvement and develop quality objectives and strategies.
5. In development of TQM, use of management tools, techniques and package required at different stages in different organizations.
6. Success of process depends on timing of introduction of particular tool, technique or package.
7. Senior management team must identify and tackle main quality problems.
8. Integration of quality improvement process with other organizational improvement initiatives is vital to success.
9. Efforts to ensure that all potential non-conformances are identified and eliminated at design stage.
10. Dedication to remove basic causes of errors.
11. Teamwork vital to success of TQM. People should be involved. Develop them by providing quality education and training to bring about changes in their behaviour and attitudes.
12. Quality assurance system well documented and also provide direction and feedback.
13. Mistake-proving operations to be investigated and remedied.
14. Customer and supplier relationships to be developed and improved.

15. No ideal way recommended for assuring the quality of organization's product or service. In order to sustain process, results must be cost effective.
16. Establish measures of customer satisfaction and quality indicators for all internal functions/departments and encourage attitude that "the next process/person is the customer".
17. Internal and external customer must be able to complain, and customer complaints must be analysed and feedback ensured into organization.
18. Develop system by which all staff can raise problems faced by them in conducting error-free performance.
19. Statistical methods used to support the analysis.
20. Effective internal audit procedure of quality assurance system developed and in place.
21. With patience and tenacity, always develop future plans for at least ten years.

Meanwhile, Frank Voehl (1995) summarised the major concepts and principles of TQM in the form of the "House of Quality", as shown in Figure 6.1. The roof, or the superstructure of TQM, consists of three sub-systems: the management, social and technical sub-systems of the organization. Four pillars of quality support the superstructure, which are basically the principles in quality management. They are customer satisfaction, continuous improvement, managing with facts, and respect for people. The foundation of TQM, he said, is made up of four managerial levels, which are strategy, process, project and task management. Meanwhile, the cornerstones for the quality house are the strategic, operations, project and personal quality planning. This planning will underline the organization's mission, vision, values, and goals and objectives. Lewis and Smith (1994) suggest that TQM based on the House of Quality framework requires quality planning by experienced individuals working together, that is, a team. Total quality efforts frequently fail because the individuals are unable to carry out their responsibilities.

In his book *Beyond TQM*, Flood (1993) defines quality as, "Quality means meeting customers' (agreed) requirements, formal and informal, at lowest cost, first time, every time". Flood underlines ten principles to summarise the definition of TQM:
1. There must be agreed requirements, for both internal and external customers.
2. Customers' requirements must be met first time, every time.
3. Quality improvement will reduce waste and total cost.
4. There must be a focus on the prevention of problems, rather than an acceptance to cope in a fire-fighting manner.
5. Quality improvement can only result from planned management action.
6. Every job process must add value.
7. Everybody must be involved, from all levels and across all functions.

8.   There must be an emphasis on measurement to help to assess and meet requirements and objectives.
9.   A culture of continuous improvement must be established.
10.   An emphasis should be placed on promoting creativity.

Therefore, from the above discussion, we can conclude that TQM is a management philosophy that requires total involvement and commitment of organizational members at all levels in the process of continuous improvement to ensure quality outputs to satisfy customer needs. Effective and efficient resource management is the key principle to ensure competitive advantage and excellent results.

Kano (1993) showed the structure of TQM using "The House of TQM" concepts. The theory of quality and theory of management form the first pillars of the house. These concepts are promoted by the practice of the plan-do-check-act cycle that ensures customer satisfaction. The concepts from the second pillar (techniques) for collection and analysing data are the basis of actual practices.

Of these techniques, seven quality control tools and statistical methods are typical. At some stage of the TQM initiative, it becomes necessary to effectively and efficiently promote these two pillars within an organization for which the third pillar called the "vehicles" is engaged, which comprises management policy for continuous improvement and training as well as employee involvement.

Evans and Lindsay (2001) suggest that TQM is a philosophy or an approach grounded on three core principles:
1.   customer focus;
2.   teamwork and participation; and
3.   continuous improvement.

These aforementioned three principles are thought to be supported and implemented by:
•   integrated organizational infrastructure;
•   variety of management practices; and
•   wide range of tools and techniques.

Leadership, strategic planning, data/information management, process management and resource management must also form part of the TQM architecture of which the major components are organizational infrastructure, management practices and tools/techniques.

Brocka and Brocka (1992) recommended seven principles to achieve TQM implementation success:
1.   Top leadership commitment and participation.
2.   Develop and sustain culture committed to continuous improvement.
3.   Dedicated focus on satisfying customer needs and expectations.
4.   Involve and help every individual to achieve improvement in his/her work.
5.   Develop constructive working relationships and create teamwork.

6.   Value people as most important resource.
7.   Best available management practices, techniques and tools are employed.

Hunt (1993) supports the view that the essence of quality management is the concept of TQM. The essence of quality management is the ultimate customer satisfaction that can be brought about by the employees, by involving and empowering them improve the quality of services and goods. This level of performance can be reached only when the workforce are able to identify the customers and their needs/expectations, as well as a clear knowledge of how the organization plans to achieve the goal of meeting customer needs/expectations. He also suggests the following quality concepts:
  • top management leadership;
  • strategic planning;
  • customer focus;
  • employee teamwork and empowerment;
  • continuous process improvement;
  • commitment to training and recognition; and
  • measurement and analysis.

According to Stamtis (1997), the following five assumptions are essentially required for TQM implementation:
1.   *Customer focus (both internal and external)*: customer needs must be identified and understood.
2.   *Total involvement (commitment)*: commitment and leadership must be demonstrated by management through providing opportunities for employees to improve quality. Set up multi-disciplinary, cross-functional and self-directed teams for employees to be included and empowered to improve their work environment.
3.   *Measurement*: management must establish appropriate measures of process and results and also establish measures with customers as the focus.
4.   *Systematic support*: managing quality process is the responsibility of management and there the quality infrastructure be tied up to the internal management structure, thereby linking the quality to existing management systems.
5.   *Continuous improvement*: all work must be viewed as a process. Management's responsibility is to anticipate or expect changes in the needs, wants and expectations of customers, employees and society.

Figure 6.2 shows that management through leadership is the basis for TQM. It is asserted by Stamtis (1997) that once the leadership has been defined, thereafter policy, resources and general management together will guide the TQM process, which transforms the input into results in satisfying society, customers and the organization.

Zeitz *et al.* (1997) proposed TQM dimensions based on existing theoretical and empirical studies. These dimensions include:

- management support;
- suggestions;
- use of data;
- supplies;
- supervision;
- continuous improvement;
- customer orientation;
- social relationships; and
- communication innovation.

They believe that these dimensions are key prerequisites for successfully implementing TQM. The five key elements of TQM suggested by Grahn (1995) are:

1. people quality;
2. entrepreneurial and innovative quality;
3. information quality;
4. planning and decision quality; and
5. process and execution quality.

This model aims to address all five drivers in a balanced way such that it considers the organization's underlying systematic structure and how each of the elements influences the other. Figure 6.3 illustrates the five drivers of TQM and their relationships.

Model in a service context

The definition of service in the *Guidelines for Services* published by the International Standards Organization (ISO, 1990) is:

Supplier's activities at the interface with a customer, and the results of all supplier's activities to meet customer needs.

The definition stresses that the interactions between employees, who are the service provider, and customers are critical to determine customer satisfaction. This definition is general to both product-manufacturing and service-oriented organizations, where service quality is associated with tangible and intangible products. Service-oriented organizations are those involved in basically service business operations, including financial services, health care, tourism and hospitality, insurance, postal service and teaching and education services. However, the concept of service has change radically over the years, and assumed significant importance. Sinha and Ghoshal (1999) argued that, in a marketing perspective, the dividing line between manufacturing and service is vanishing. Similarly, this study has no aim to differentiate between the two sectors, although research constructs are mainly based on a theoretical framework in the service context.

Furthermore, in the service sector, where production, delivery and consumption can occur simultaneously, the concept of quality refers to the matching between what customers expect and what they experience. Customers assess service quality by comparing what they want or expect to what they actually get or perceive they are getting (Berry *et al.*, 1988). This is perceived quality and any mismatch between expected service and perceived service is a "quality gap". As perceived quality, being a user-based category, is always a judgement by the customer, quality in this context is whatever the customer says it is. Narrowing the quality gap is one of the prime goals of service quality management.

Meanwhile, Groth and Dye (1999) suggest that service quality is when customers buy a service because they require the service and the related quality of service offers the best perceived value-to-resource choice available. ERD (expectations-realisation-divergence) identifies the difference between *ex ante* expectations of the service quality and the perceived *ex post* realisation of the service/service quality. ERD is positive (negative) if the customer feels realisation exceeded (fell short of) expectations.

Comparatively, Beckford (1998) argues that most manufacturing organizations which implement TQM are involved with formal reports, documents and record keeping on operational systems and procedures. However, service-oriented organizations, or those operating through a distributed delivery network, also require a standardised approach for management purposes and for customer satisfaction. Therefore, flexibility and creativity needed for the quality systems developed in a manufacturing context, are also important to quality service operations.

From a different perspective, Boaden and Dale (1994) argues that TQM for service demands more understanding, interest and commitment of top management as an absolute precondition for success. This is because TQM depends on the creation of a quality culture in a service organization, which puts emphasis on everyone being involved in continuous improvement. He refers to Edvardsson's (1991) service chain model, that management should understand internal customers' expectations in order for them to take responsibility for making quality improvements and being committed to the initiatives to fulfil the end customers' expectations.

Parasuraman *et al.* (1988) analyse service on a consumer perspective based on the four following characteristics:

1. *Intangibility.* In contrast to goods, service is intangible, cannot be touched, smelled, tasted or seen. Consumers who pay for services typically have nothing tangible to take home. Thus, tangible products associated with services like degree certificates, plastic credit cards,

insurance cover notes, and service agreements, may represent the service, but are not the service itself.

2. *Heterogeneity*. Services always vary because human beings usually perform them. Therefore, in a quality perspective, service is difficult to standardise. Each lecturer may deliver a same course module with specific outlines differently.

3. *Inseparability of production and consumption*. A service is usually consumed or experienced while being delivered, with the customer often involved in the process. Student-lecturer interactions cannot be avoided in the teaching process. For this reason, mistakes or excellence in service may happen at any point of the process of service delivery. It is important to note that customer evaluation happens along the process.

4. *Perishability*. Most service cannot be stored and packaged for each customer on each service transaction. Referring to the first three characteristics, each customer will experience a different level of service quality provided by the same company or even by the same employee.

Zeithaml *et al.* (1990) have identified four overall gaps within a service organization that, individually or in various combinations, cause the important fifth gap in customer evaluation. It is the gap between customers' service desire or expectation and their perceptions of the service that is actually delivered (Figure 6.4). The four gaps will determine customers' perception of the service rendered:

1. Management's perceptions of customer service expectations are different from actual customer desires. Management failures to understand customers' desires for the service expected could be a fundamental mistake that may lead to further wrong decisions. A chain reaction of mistakes that are likely to follow are setting up wrong human resource training, wrong approach to performance measurement, and also wrong promotion activities.

2. Management's specifications for service are different from its perceptions of customer expectations. Management may have understood the customer expectations of the service, but fail to translate the understanding into equivalent specifications for service performance.

3. The difference between service specifications determined and the level of service actually delivered. Even if the management does understand customer service expectations (minimum at gap 1) and does set appropriate specifications for the service standards (minimum at gap 2), the service delivery may still fall short of customers' expectations. This is the most relevant aspect (of people management) to be explored in this study. The "service performance gap" is the quality level at which there are discrepancies between the service delivered by employees as compared to the standard specified by the management. The main reasons that may cause this gap are:

- Lack of employees' ability and capability. A screening process in human resources' selection and recruitment is critical to identify the capable workers that fit the job. It is important to note that even if the worker is trying to do his/her best (in the case of hard working workers), if he/she does not have the capability, the quality mission may still fail.
- Lack of motivation and willingness to perform quality service. Motivated workers will put in all efforts to ensure excellent results and quality service performance. Berry *et al.* (1989) describe willingness to perform in terms of "discretionary effort", that is, the difference between maximum amount of effort and commitment a worker could put into the given job or responsibility, and the minimum amount of effort required in avoiding being fired or penalised. Specified operational factors that affect employee motivation and willingness to perform quality service are role conflict, role ambiguity and too few or overloaded job functions.
- Inadequate role support and attention by the management. Organizations implementing quality need to invest in appropriate technology and support systems to facilitate role performance. At the same time, workers with lack of skills and capabilities need relevant and adequate training to improve service performance. In other words, insufficient attention to support facilities, skills and knowledge development from the management will affect the workers' ability and willingness to perform to the expected quality service standards.

4. The differences between delivered service and external communication about the service. Many service organizations fall prey to the promotional temptations of promising more service than they can consistently deliver. Over-promising in promotion is especially pernicious, because it raises customers' expectation, and consequently affects perceptions of the service. Customers with high expectations for a certain level of service will be more disappointed or dissatisfied than those with moderate expectations.

5. This is the potential gap between the customers' desired or expected service and the perceived service that they received. Customers' service quality judgements are a function of the expectations in the customers before they pay for the service and make their perception of the service they experienced. Therefore, the degree of gaps 1 and 4 constitutes the level of quality service performance. Consequently, closing or minimising gap 1 to 4 will close or minimise gap 5.

The challenge to quality service organizations is to meet or exceed precise customers' expectations for the four dimensions (reliable, responsive, reassuring and empathetic) of service performance. The extent to which customers' expectations and the delivery of service performance are similar or different will influence the degree of customers' satisfaction.

Gronroos (1990) made an empirical study to test his service quality theory and the internal marketing concept as a strategic management instrument. Basically, his service quality theory says:

...the perceived quality of a given service will be the outcome of an evaluation process where consumers compare their expectations with service they perceive they have got, i.e. they put the perceived service against the expected service (Gronroos, 1990, p. 38).

The "perceived service quality" model shown in Figure 6.5 explains that superior perceived quality of service is obtained when the experienced quality meets the expectations of the customer.

The discussion on TQM in a services context suggests that customer expectations are the main factor to consider in quality planning. Furthermore, the management has to inculcate the quality culture to ensure quality service delivery. As the nature of the operations is intangible, heterogeneous, inseparable and perishable, service performance is not quantifiable, and is mainly bound to customer perception. The gap between perceived quality and expected level of service is the key determinant of performance evaluation, from the customer perspective. Therefore, employee competency, motivation and the right attitudes are very important to ensure quality of service. Adequate facilities and support would create a favourable working environment to produce excellent service performance.

Models based on quality awards

As cited by Evans and Lindsay, 2001, various quality awards instituted by several countries help promote awareness of quality and productivity, facilitate exchange of information among organizations, as well as encourage organizations to adopt strategies to improve quality, productivity and competitiveness. Organizations that have successfully implemented quality business strategies are recognized and are projected as role models for other business organizations in the country. Vokurka et al. (2000) emphasised that many organizations, in their drive for TQM, have turned to quality award programmes because they help to perform self-assessment, offer excellence models, tools and techniques for implementing strategies in addition to recognition offered by these quality awards.

However, Vokurka et al. (2000) clearly advised the organizations that the use of excellence models need not be considered a perfect solution to all problems and ills; instead, these models provide only a basis or foundation for self-assessment to encourage and assist TQM implementation.

In 1987, the Malcolm Baldrige National Quality Award (MBNQA) was established. Senior managers in the West started looking at quality award criteria as guiding frameworks to plot the approach for effective TQM implementation. Over one million copies of the MBNQA criteria are requested and used by organizations world-wide as a roadmap, a planning tool and diagnostic framework in assisting TQM implementation efforts (Pannireselvam and Ferguson, 2001).

Malcolm Baldrige National Quality Award (MBNQA)

On 20 August, 1987, the Malcolm Baldrige Quality Improvement Act was, by then President Reagan, named after Malcolm Baldrige, who served as Secretary of Commerce from 1981 until his death in an accident in 1987.

The American Society for Quality Control (ASQC) put forward the idea of a National Quality Award as a focal point of a quality revolution in the private sector, which led to the introduction of the Malcolm Baldrige Quality Improvement Act and subsequently the Malcolm Baldrige National Quality Award. The aim of the award was to:

- promote quality awareness and its impact on competitiveness;
- share information on successful quality strategies and the benefits derived from implementing these strategies; and
- propose a set of criteria that can be used by business, industrial, government and other enterprises in evaluating their own quality improvement efforts.

The Baldrige Award framework has four basic elements: driver system, measures of progress, results and goal. Two key assumptions underpin the model. First, top management leadership is the primary driver of the business (Terziovski *et al.*, 2000).

Baldrige recognises the crucial role of the top management in creating the goals, values and systems that guide the pursuit of continuous performance improvement and external orientation. This is an award for US companies only. The purpose of the Baldrige Award is to promote awareness of quality as an integral part of competitive strategy, to highlight to US companies the key elements of a superior quality programme, and to share information on successful outcomes from implementing effective quality strategies (Ghobadian and Woo, 1996).

Second, the basic goal of the quality process is the delivery of ever-improving quality and value to customers. The model implicitly assumes that maximising customer satisfaction is one of the most important corporate objectives, and that enhanced customer satisfaction translates itself into improved market share and profitability.

The system comprises a set of well-defined and designed processes capable of meeting the customer's quality and performance requirements. The Baldrige model divides the system into four elements: management of process quality, human resources development and management, strategic quality planning, and information and analysis (Woon, 2000). The four basic elements of the Baldrige award are divided into seven examination categories. The Baldrige model is strongly prescriptive in terms of underlying philosophies and values (Zairi, 1998). It is an audit framework which enables organizations to perform internal self-assessment and identify the areas that need improvements and the values they need to enact in order to attain a culture and operating system capable of attaining continuous improvement and customer satisfaction.

The human resource development and management area looks at how people are developed and involved to realise their full potential using company's quality objectives, and also examines how companies are determined to maintain a climate where there is continuous employee development, full participation and involvement towards realising future company goals (Finn and Porter, 1994).

As asserted by Pannireselvam and Ferguson (2001), the Malcolm Baldrige National Quality Award (MBNQA), since its inception in 1987, has evolved in its role from being a measurement of organizational quality into a guideline for companies striving for performance excellence. Evans and Lindsay (2001) point out that the Baldrige Award criteria are built from a set of core values and concepts derived from real experiences that can be applied to organizations of any type and size.

The Baldrige Award criteria (2003) are built on the following set of interrelated core values and concepts (NIST, 2003):

- Visionary leadership.
- Customer-driven excellence.
- Organizational and personal learning.
- Valuing employees and partners.
- Agility.
- Focus on the future.
- Managing for innovation.
- Management-by-fact.
- Social responsibility.
- Focus on results and creating value.
- Systems perspective.

These core values and concepts (NIST, 2003) are embodied in seven categories as follows:

1. Leadership.
2. Strategic planning.
3. Customer and market focus.
4. Measurement, analysis and knowledge management.
5. Human resources focus.
6. Process management.
7. Business results.

Figure 6.6 provides the framework connecting and integrating the categories. From top to bottom, the framework has the following basic elements.

Organization profile: (top of Figure 6.6) sets the context for the way the organization operates. Environment, key working relationships and strategic challenges serve as an overarching guide for the organizational performance management system.

System operations: composed of the six Baldrige categories in the centre of the figure that define operations and the results which can be achieved. Leadership, strategic planning and customer and market focus represents the leadership triad. These categories are placed together to emphasise the importance of a leadership focus on strategy and customers. Senior leaders set organizational direction and seek future opportunities for the organization. Human resource focus, process management and business results represent the results triad. The organization's employees and its key processes accomplish the work of the organization that yields business results. All actions point toward business results – a composite of customer, product and service, financial, and internal operational performance results, including human resource and social responsibility results. The horizontal arrow in the centre of the framework links the leadership triad to the results triad, a linkage critical to organizational success. Furthermore, the arrow indicates the central relationship between leadership and business results. The two-headed arrow indicates the importance of feedback in an effective performance management system.

System foundation: measurement, analysis and knowledge management are critical to the effective management of an organization and to a fact-based system for improving performance and competitiveness. Measurement, analysis and knowledge serve as a foundation for the performance management system.

European Quality Award (EQA)

The European Quality Award (EQA) is the most prestigious award for organizational excellence and is the top level of the EFQM levels of excellence. The EQA is administered by the European Foundation for Quality Management (EFQM) which was formed by 14 leading European companies.

EFQM, in partnership with the European Commission and the European Organization for Quality (EOQ), launched the EQA in 1991 to recognise companies showing a high level of commitment to quality. In 1996, the award was extended to include a separate category for organizations in the public sector, and in 1997 the award was further extended to include operational units such as factories, assembly plants, sales and marketing functions and research units. Also launched in 1997 were the two categories for small and medium-sized enterprises (SMEs), which were for companies of fewer than 250 persons.

The primary purpose of the award is also to support, encourage and recognise the development of effective TQM by European companies. The EQA, essentially, was introduced also to promote quality excellence in Western Europe and particularly to encourage the need for self-examination/assessment on a regular basis by companies, so that areas of weakness are constantly identified and improved upon (Zairi, 1998).

The award was designed also to increase the awareness throughout the European Community, and businesses in particular, of the growing importance of quality to their competitiveness in the increasingly global market and to their standard of living (Evans and Lindsay, 2001).

The objective of the EFQM is to enhance the position of European industry and commerce by strengthening the strategic role of quality in corporations. This is because quality is perceived to be an important contributor to superior competitiveness (Taylor, 1997). Thus the EFQM's two declared missions are: to accelerate the acceptance of "quality improvement" as a strategy for attaining global competitive advantage; and to stimulate and assist the development of "quality improvement" activities on a wide front.

The EQA is based on the EFQM excellence model, which is also used as the basis for many other national and regional quality awards. The rigorous criteria of the EQA sends out a rallying call "European businesses need to pay even more attention than ever to the principle of systematic and continuous improvement". The hurdles are getting higher and overall standards are increasing. The EQA assessment model is divided to two parts: enablers and results. The enablers are policies and processes that drive the business and facilitate the transformation of inputs to outputs and outcomes. The results are the measures of the level of output and outcome attained by the organization. The model consists nine elements: five enablers and four measures of results (Iaquinto, 1999).

The model is prescriptive in terms of the philosophy and values which it expounds, but it does not stipulate any particular tools, methods, procedures and practices. It is based on an apparently sound and logical assumption that the end results are the by-product of managerial competence, policies and processes.

The model recognises that management plays the key role in the development of the structures and infrastructures necessary to meet its output and outcome goals (Zairi, 1998).

The significance of developing human resources, process capability and planning is emphasised (Zink and Schmidt, 1998). On the result side, the EQA model emphasises correctly the fact that financial results are not the sole measure of performance. The EQA model assumes that there is a causal relationship between outputs (financial results) and outcomes (customer satisfaction and acceptance by society) as well as employee satisfaction. Measures are related to training, education, communication, effectiveness of vision, values and policy, recognition and rewards schemes, involvement, and appraisal, and quantitative measures such as staff turnover and absenteeism (Van der Wiele et al., 2000).

The year 2003 marked the twelfth running of the European Quality Award, which is open to every high-performing organization in Europe and focuses on recognising excellence and providing detailed independent feedback to all applicants to help them on their continuing journey to excellence. Entries for the European Quality Award (2003) are judged against the EFQM excellence model, which is shown in Figure 6.7.

The nine boxes in the EFQM excellence model correspond to the criteria:

- Leadership.
- Policies and strategy.
- People.
- Partnerships and resources.
- Processes.
- Customer results.
- People results.
- Society results.
- Key performance results.

These are used to assess an organization's progress towards excellence, and are grouped as enablers and results. The enabler criteria are concerned with how results are being achieved. The results criteria are concerned with what the organization has achieved and is achieving. The arrows emphasise the dynamic nature of the model. They show innovation and learning which help to improve enablers, which in turn lead to improved results.

These nine criteria and their 32 sub-criteria together offer organizations the benefit of a structured approach to identify organizational strength and areas for improvement. The EQA is open to all European organizations annually in the following categories:
- large organizations and business units;
- operational units of companies;
- public sector organizations;
- small and medium-sized enterprises (SMEs) in two categories:
  ◦ independent SMEs; and
  ◦ subsidiaries of larger organizations.

There are four levels of recognition in each category available to applicants for the EQA, shown below in descending order:
- Award winners: the EQA, is presented to the organization judged to be the best in each of the award categories.
- Prize winners: prizes are presented annually to organizations that excel in some of the fundamental concepts of excellence. In 2003, there were special prizes in each category in the following areas:
  ◦ Leadership and constancy of purpose.
  ◦ Customer focus.
  ◦ Corporate social responsibility.
  ◦ People development and involvement.
  ◦ Results orientation.
- Finalists: finalists are organizations that demonstrate a high degree of excellence in the management of quality as their fundamental process for continuous improvement.
- Recognised for excellence: indicates that the organization is well-managed and aspires to achieve role model status. EFQM excellence

model is a non-prescriptive framework that recognises there are many approaches to achieving sustainable organizational excellence. Within this non-prescriptive approach, there are some basic concepts which underpin the EFQM excellence model. Behaviours, activities or initiatives based on these concepts are often referred to as quality management.

Deming Prize

In July 1950, the Union of Japanese Scientists and Engineers (JUSE) invited W. E. Deming, one of the foremost experts of quality control in the USA, to present a series of lectures. He lectured day after day on his "eight-day course on quality control", followed by his "one-day course on quality control for top management". Through these seminars, Deming taught the basics of statistical quality control plainly and thoroughly to executives, managers, engineers and researchers of the Japanese industries. His teachings made a deep impression on the participants' mind and provided great impetus to quality control in Japan, which was in its infancy. In appreciation, JUSE created a prize to commemorate Dr. Deming's contribution and friendship, and to promote the continued development of quality control in Japan. The Deming Prize was established in 1950 and is wholly administered by the JUSE, and annual awards are still given each year. The Deming Prize, especially the Deming Application Prize that is given to companies, has exerted an immeasurable influence directly or indirectly on the development of quality control and management in Japan. The Deming Prize has gone through several stages of evolution, and in 1984 it became international, thereby allowing overseas companies to apply for and receive the Deming Prize upon successfully passing the examination. In 1997, another change was made to enable overseas companies to apply for the Quality Control Award for Operations Business Units. However, the Deming Prize for Individuals is open only to Japanese candidates (Evans and Lindsay, 2001).

There are two categories of the annual Deming Prize: the Deming Application Prize and the Deming Prize for Individuals.

The Deming Application Prize is awarded to companies or divisions that have achieved distinctive performance improvements through the application of TQM in a designated year. The Deming Application Prize is given to an applicant company that effectively practises TQM suitable to its management principles, type of industry and business scope. More specifically, the following criteria are used for the examination to determine whether or not the applicant company should be awarded the prize:

- Reflecting its management principles, type of industry, business scope and business environment, the applicant has established challenging and customer-oriented business objectives and strategies under its clear management leadership.

- TQM has been implemented properly to achieve business objectives and strategies.
- The outstanding results have been obtained for business objectives and strategies as stated above.

The Deming Prize for Individuals, is given to individuals who have made outstanding contributions in the dissemination of TQM. This is awarded in recognition of outstanding contribution in the area of research and education (Evans and Lindsay, 2001).

The Deming Application Prize is awarded to all companies that meet the prescribed standard. Evans and Lindsay (2001) assert that only a small number of awards are given every each year, which they believe to be an indication of the difficulty of achieving the performance required. The objectives are to guarantee that the company has completely set up the process in such a way that it will continue to improve even after the prize is awarded.

The examination process of the Deming Prize encourages each organization's self-development. The Deming Prize examination does not require applicants to conform to a model provided by the Deming Prize Committee. Rather, the applicants are expected to understand their current situation, establish their own themes and objectives, and improve and transform themselves company-wide. Not only the results achieved and the processes used, but also the effectiveness expected in the future, are subjects of examination. To the best of their abilities, the examiners evaluate whether or not the themes established by the applicants were commensurate to their situation; whether or not their activities were suitable to their circumstance; and whether or not their activities are likely to achieve their higher objectives in the future. Every factor such as the applicants' attitude toward executing TQM, their implementation status, and the resulting effects is taken into overall consideration. In other words, the Deming Prize committee does not specify what issues the applicants must address, rather the applicants themselves are responsible for identifying and addressing such issues, thus this process allows quality methodologies to be further developed.

Items included in the October 2000 Deming Application Prize Examination are:

- Top management leadership, vision, strategies:
  1.1 Top management leadership.
  1.2 Organizational vision and strategies.
- TQM frameworks:
  2.1 Organizational structure and its operations.
  2.2 Daily management.
  2.3 Policy management.
  2.4 Relationship to ISO 9000 and ISO 14000.
  2.5 Relationship to other management improvement programmes.
  2.6 TQM promotions and operation.
- Quality assurance system:

3.1 Quality assurance system.
3.2 New products and new technology development.
3.3 Process control.
3.4 Test, quality evaluation and quality audits.
3.5 Activities covering whole life cycle.
3.6 Purchasing, sub-contracting and distribution management.
- Management system for business elements:
4.1 Cross-functional management and its operations.
4.2 Quality/delivery management.
4.3 Cost management.
4.4 Environmental management.
4.5 Safety, hygiene, work environment management.
- Human resources development:
5.1 Positioning of people in management.
5.2 Education and training.
5.3 Respect for people's dignity.
- Effective utilisation of information:
6.1 Positioning of "information" in management.
6.2 Information systems.
6.3 Support for analysis and decision making.
6.4 Standardisation and configuration management.
- TQM concepts and values:
7.1 Quality.
7.2 Maintenance and improvement.
- Scientific methods:
8.1 Understanding and utilisation of methods.
8.2 Understanding and utilisation of problem-solving method.
8.3 Respect for humanity.
- Organizational powers (core technology, speed, vitality):
9.1 Core technology.
9.2 Speed.
9.3 Vitality.
- Contribution to realisation of corporate objectives:
10.1 Customer relations.
10.2 Employee relations.
10.3 Social relations.
10.4 Supplier relations.
10.5 Shareholder relations.
10.6 Realization of corporate mission.
10.7 Continuously securing profits.

The Canadian Quality Award

The Canadian Ministry of Industry introduced the Canada Awards for Business Excellence in 1984, but revised the programme in 1989, to reflect the MBNQA concept (Vokurka *et al.*, 2000). Canada's National Quality Institute (NQI) recognises Canada's foremost achievers of excellence through this prestigious award. The NQI is a non-profit organization designed to stimulate and support quality-driven innovation within all Canadian enterprises and institutions, including business, government, education and healthcare. The quality criteria for the Canadian Awards for Excellence (Figure 6.8) are similar in structure to those of the Baldrige Award with a few key differences (Evans and Lindasy, 2001). The major categories and items within each category for 1995 are:

- Leadership (170 points): strategic direction, leadership involvement and outcomes.
- Customer focus (200 points): voice of the customer, management of customer relationships, measurement and outcomes.
- Planning for improvement (130 points): development and content of improvement plan, assessment and outcomes.
- People focus (200 points): human resource planning, participatory environment, continuous learning environment, employee satisfaction, and outcomes.
- Process optimisation (200 points): process definition, process control process and outcomes.
- Suppliers, partners and outcomes.

Dubai Government Excellence Programme

The government of Dubai, an Emirate of the United Arab Emirates (UAE), has been concerned to develop the performance of the government sector. Goals include remaining up-to-date in all fields; applying modern administration concepts to increase public satisfaction; developing resources; eliminating unnecessary official procedures; documenting organizations; and encouraging innovation and development of potential. Dubai is also concerned to improve the official governmental working environment throughout all departments. Goals include adoption of policies and strategies conducive to comprehensive development and support of free trade (Dubai Government Excellence Programme).

Specific objectives and principles of the Dubai Government Excellence Programme are summarised as follows:

- The programme emphasises leadership by the government in demonstrating co-operation with positive competition.
- Efficiency, quality and rationalisation of expenditure are sought.
- Awareness of quality is promoted as the private sector is consolidated and enhanced.

- Evaluation of performance is standardised, and government employees are motivated (Dubai Government Excellence Programme).

Six programme groups are defined as follows:
1. *Department*: comprising all government departments.
2. *Administration*: departments and sections at the level of administration.
3. *Work-team*: groups doing special projects.
4. *Administration experiment*: projects implemented by departments to improve performance and services.
5. *Technical project/distinctively creative group*: concerned with technical application and systems.
6. *Vocational/occupational excellence groups*: provide moral and material incentives.

Participation is intended to encourage efficiency, commitment, giving, co-operation, initiative, loyalty, devotion and innovation.

The overall concept of the programme is directed toward modernisation; incentive reward is the basis; the Arabic language is the official language; participation is mandatory for department, administration, administrative excellence and vocational/occupational excellence groups (Dubai Government Excellence Programme).

Singapore Quality Award (SQA)

The government of Singapore established the Singapore Quality Award (SQA) in 1994. The purpose was to encourage organizations to strive for business performance at world-class standards. The Prime Minister of Singapore is the Patron of the Award. The Singapore Productivity and Standards Board (PSB) administers the award. Private sector organizations provide financial support and expertise. These organizations include Arthur Anderson Business Consulting, DHL, the Sony Group of Companies in Singapore and Micron Semiconductor Asia. The governing council creates policies and guidelines for programmes and awards. Sponsor organizations provide the membership of the council. A management committee supports the council and reviews award criteria, develops training and certifies applicants and assessors (Department of Statistics, 1990).

The SQA follows the model of the Malcolm Baldrige, the European, and the Australian Award. Strengthening of management systems is encouraged. Benefits to organizations include provision of a framework for comparison against world-class standards. Winners use the SQA symbol for publicity. All applicants receive feedback for improvement (SQA, 1999).

The award framework has seven core values:
1. leadership and quality culture;
2. use of information and analysis;
3. strategic planning;

4.   human resources development and management;
5.   management of process quality;
6.   quality and operational results; and
7.   customer focus and satisfaction (SQA, 1999).

The framework of the award (Figure 6.9) is established by three basic elements, which connect and integrate the above criteria. These elements include:
- *Driver*: senior executive directions and guideline excellence.
- *System*: well-defined process for performance requirements.
- *Results*: continuous improvement of customer value and organizational performance.

Australian Quality Award
The Australian Quality Award provides a model certified by the Australian Quality Council, an organization recognised by the Commonwealth Government of Australia as the highest organization for quality management (Figure 6.10). The council was formed in 1993 with the merger of Enterprise Australia, the Total Quality Management Institute, the Australian Quality Awards Foundation and the Quality Society of Australia (Canchick, 2001).

The goal of the award programme is to develop and deploy a comprehensive and contemporary body of quality principles and best practices. The award measures quality performance through seven categories of criteria: leadership; policy and planning; information and analysis; people; customer focus; quality of process, product and service; and organizational performance. According to the model, people, information and analysis, and strategy, policy and planning categories have the greatest effect on the quality of processes. The quality of the processes, in turn, affects organizational performance. Customer focus and leadership are key elements, interacting with all the other parts of the model (Vokurka *et al.*, 2000).

Figure 6.1 House of Quality

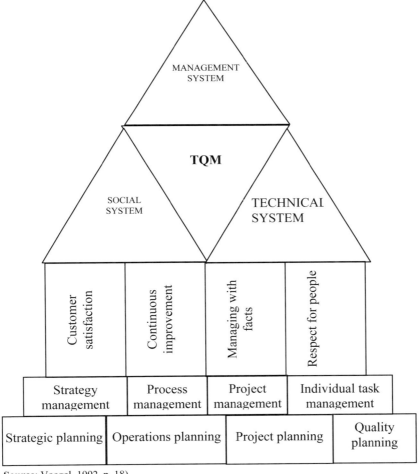

Source: Voegel, 1992, p. 18)

Figure 6.2 Assumptions required to implement TQM

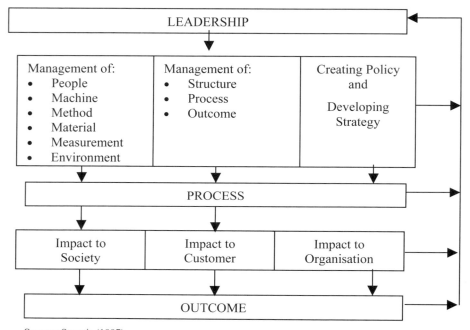

Source: Stamtis (1997)

Figure 6.3 Five drivers of TQM

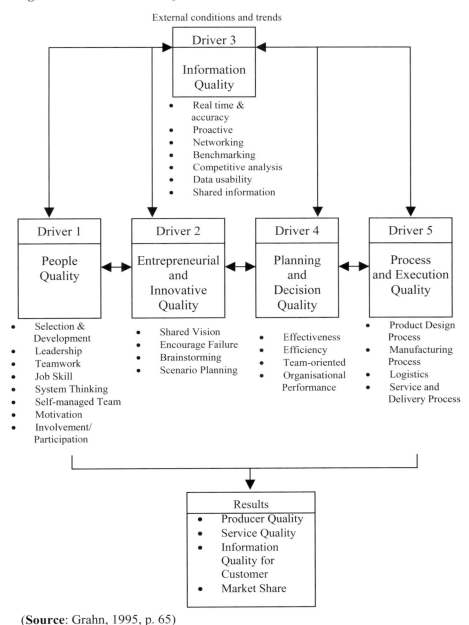

External conditions and trends

Driver 3

Information
Quality

- Real time &
  accuracy
- Proactive
- Networking
- Benchmarking
- Competitive analysis
- Data usability
- Shared information

Driver 1	**Driver 2**	**Driver 4**	**Driver 5**
People Quality	Entrepreneurial and Innovative Quality	Planning and Decision Quality	Process and Execution Quality

- Selection & Development
- Leadership
- Teamwork
- Job Skill
- System Thinking
- Self-managed Team
- Motivation
- Involvement/ Participation

- Shared Vision
- Encourage Failure
- Brainstorming
- Scenario Planning

- Effectiveness
- Efficiency
- Team-oriented
- Organisational Performance

- Product Design Process
- Manufacturing Process
- Logistics
- Service and Delivery Process

Results
- Producer Quality
- Service Quality
- Information Quality for Customer
- Market Share

(**Source**: Grahn, 1995, p. 65)

Figure 6.4 Service quality model

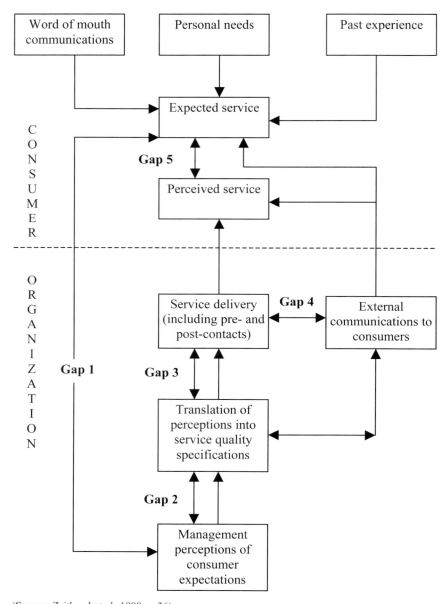

(**Source**: Zeithaml *et al.*, 1988, p. 36)

Figure 6.5 The perceived service quality

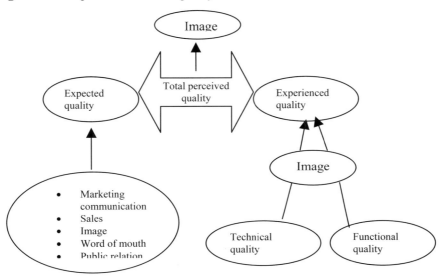

Figure 6.6 Dynamic relationship between Baldrige Award evaluation criteria

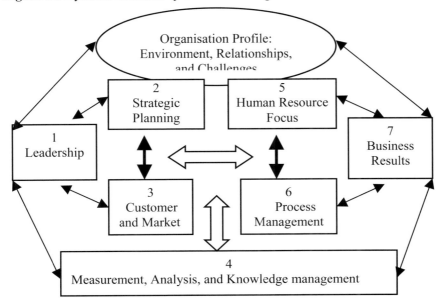

Figure 6.7 EFQM excellence model (2003)

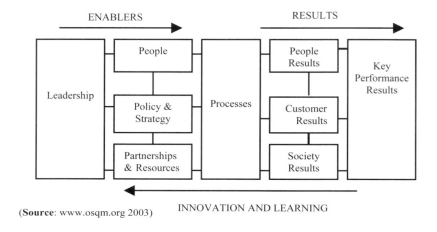

(**Source**: www.osqm.org 2003)

Figure 6.8 Canadian Award for Excellence

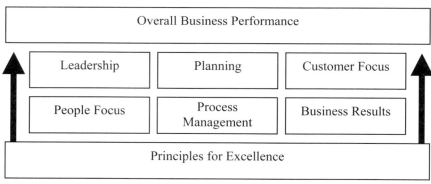

(**Source**: Vokurka *et al.*, 2000)

Figure 6.9 Singapore Quality Award framework

(**Source**: Singapore Quality Award, 1999)

Figure 6.10 Australian Quality Award criteria framework

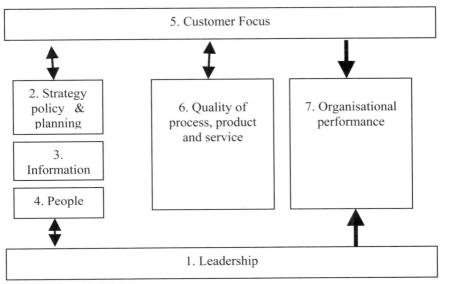

(**Source**: Canchick, 2001)

Chapter 7
The critical factors of TQM implementation

Studies of critical factors of quality management
Identification of critical factors of quality management derives from empirical research. These investigations of quality have contributed to further understanding of the basic principles of TQM. Understanding the components of quality and establishing a "paradigm" of success has characterized TQM research and analysis. In addition to the research described in this section, an outline of the methodologies used in empirical research is described.

The Saraph et al. study
The pioneer study to address the determination of the critical factors of TQM was conducted by Saraph, Benson and Schroeder (1989). They extracted 120 organizational prescriptions for effective TQM. Using a judgemental process, they categorised these prescriptions into eight critical factors:
1.   The role of management leadership and quality policy.
2.   The role of the quality department.
3.   Training.
4.   Product/service design.
5.   Supplier quality management.
6.   Process management.
7.   Quality data and reporting.
8.   Employee relations.

An operational instrument of critical factors was established to measure them.

The Ramirez and Loney study
Ramirez and Loney (1993) conducted an empirical study to investigate which factors mentioned in the literature were critical factors for TQM success. This study covered US companies from the manufacturing and service sectors recognised for their quality achievements in the Malcom Baldrige National Quality Award (MBNQA).

The survey was based on a list of 22 items that were considered in the literature as critical to TQM. The study aimed to identify the factors needed for a successful quality process.

A questionnaire survey of 63 persons (26 quality consultants and 37 managers of quality award winning organizations including MBQNA winners) took place in order to rate each of the 22 factors on a three-point scale. Respondents were required to give a level of importance to each quality factor relying on their experience of the implementation of a quality management process in their firms.

Using the three-point scale, each respondent was asked to indicate if the factor was:

- neutral regarding the factor;
- important but not essential to total quality management process; and
- critical and absolutely essential to the successful implementation of TQM.

Ramirez and Loney assigned scoring weights of 1, 2 and 3 for neutral, important and critical, respectively. Applying this scoring approach, each factor was given a numerical value for its criticality. The results of this study showed that ten factors out of 22 were found to be critical, seven factors important and five factors neutral. The critical factors were classified as tier 1 factors, the important factors were classified as tier 2, and the neutral factors were classified as tier 3. Tier 1 factors were:

- management commitment;
- customer satisfaction;
- clear vision statement;
- culture change;
- education;
- participation management;
- strategic planning;
- goal clarity;
- error prevention; and
- top management steering committee.

Tier 2 factors include:

- problem solving;
- measurement;
- problem identification;
- goal setting;
- recognition programme;
- quality control circles; and
- vendor partnership.

Tier 3 factors include:

- project improvement process;
- publicised successes;
- statistical process control;
- cost of quality; and
- zero defect attitudes.

Tier 1 factors are associated with management support and related activities. Tier 2 factors are associated with shop floor activities while tier 3 factors represent important techniques and tools such as statistical process control, cost of quality and attitude towards achieving zero defects.

The study of Ramirez and Loney contributes significantly to the body of knowledge of quality management. The study suggests a hierarchy of factors that can be used to plan for the implementation of TQM.

The Black and Porter study

Black and Porter (1996) noted that, up to the time of their writing, the literature was "patchy" in its understanding and that extant empirical studies (Saraph *et al.*, 1989) notably were derived from this deficient coverage. They surmised that a set of criteria based on the perception of actual industrial practitioners might be more valid. One way to obtain such a framework would be to make a *post hoc* synthesis of Saraph *et al.*'s items from the collected perceptions of respondents. Alternatively, improved measurement methods could be employed to determine the relative importance of inter-relationships between different items.

To develop an empirical framework from TQM practitioners' perceptions and experience, the Baldrige Award model framework was modified through additional literature review to account for the model's perceived variables. Seven variables were added:

1. use of specific improvement tools;
2. customer-supplier chain concept and department purpose analysis;
3. use of specific organization structures to support quality improvement;
4. management of suppliers;
5. determination of quality costs;
6. encouragement of company quality culture; and
7. active management leadership (Black and Porter 1996).

The European Foundation for Quality Management (EFQM) was queried as to its ratings of the final 39 items according to the item's "magnitude of importance" in relation to "assessment and improvement of quality systems and documentation" (Black and Porter 1996).

Factor analysis of the 204 valid questionnaires returned extracted ten critical factors. In comparison with the Saraph *et al.* model, the study covered a wider domain. New areas were covered in customer satisfaction orientation, teamwork structures and communication of improvement information. The factors derived do not match the Baldrige model categories, but do correspond to established literature. Black and Porter's critical factors are:

- corporate critical culture;
- strategic quality management;
- quality improvement;
- people and culture management;
- operational quality planning;
- supplier partnership;
- teamwork structures;

- customer satisfaction orientation; and
- communication improvement information.

The Zeitz et al. study

Zeitz *et al.* (1997) attempted to clarify the necessary distinction between TQM practices as a management programme and TQM as related to organizational culture. The view, set out in 1997, was that TQM practices seen as "formal, programmatic and behavioural" must be differentiated from "attitudes, firmly held beliefs and situational (and often not formally sanctioned) interactions". To maintain this distinction, knowledge and judgement are required to account for cultural factors, which, legitimately, are involved in the support for the implementation of TQM. Some cultural dimensions must exist as prior conditions to TQM implementation; others "facilitate acceptance and adoption" (Hunt's study, cited in Zeitz *et al.*, 1979). At the other end of the spectrum, cultural change, in many interpretations, is the logical outcome for "TQM programmatic efforts" (Schmidt and Finnegan's study, cited in Zeitz *et al.*, 1997). Ten supportive cultural dimensions were identified:

1. communication;
2. resolution;
3. empowerment;
4. innovation;
5. challenge;
6. commitment;
7. rewards;
8. expectation;
9. cohesion; and
10. trust.

Non-cultural TQM dimensions were also identified:
- quality philosophy;
- quality planning;
- management leadership;
- quality supervision;
- continuous improvement;
- quality procedures;
- equipment adequacy;
- quality training;
- employee suggestions; and
- customer orientation.

A factor analysis of results from 886 respondents indicated that seven TQM and five culture dimensions accounted for most of the scale variance. The seven TQM items were:

1. management support;
2. suggestions;
3. use of data;
4. suppliers;
5. supervision;
6. continuous improvement; and
7. customer orientation.

The five culture dimensions were:
1. job challenge;
2. communication;
3. trust;
4. innovation; and
5. social cohesion.

All 12 dimensions were viewed as consistent with TQM literature. The chief benefit of the instrument to organizations was seen as assessing the cultural readiness of the organization for the implementation of TQM. The specific barriers to TQM included "lack of proper fit between people and structure, in which we include inconsistency between the culture and the demands of a formal TQM programme". The study supports the findings that, when fully implemented, TQM benefits quality, productivity and employee development "but TQM is often not well implemented" (Zeitz *et al.*, 1997).

The Krasachol and Tannock study
Studying TQM implementation in Thailand with an initial focus on limitation of adoption by Thai-owned companies, Krasachol, and Tannock (1998) noted support in the literature for culture change in organizations as a requirement to effect TQM adoption. TQM change models should be culturally feasible. Four paradigms cognizant of culture factors were studied extensively, including a meta-paradigm "which informs and enables movement between" the other ones (Whittle's study, cited in Krasachol and Tannock, 1998). The four paradigms are set out as follows.

Visionary total quality (VTQ): a strongly top-down management-led approach. Culture change is promoted to be the strategic quality vision and ideology of top management, which is communicated clearly and widely to all levels of employee. People are seen as programmable pawns. Providing management development and training for quality is one of the key issues in this model. The strategic quality programme is usually led and driven by the most senior executives.

Learning total quality (LTQ): emphasises a bottom-up style of organizational culture change. People are seen as willing participants. Employee empowerment and involvement are the key factors in TQM implementation. The natural work team is one of the important features emphasised in the LTQ organization. The approach to TQM implementation is not explicitly strategic. Human resources or personnel specialists tend to drive the process.

Planning total quality (PTQ): is concerned with rational and systemic approaches to TQM implementation. An explicit programme is introduced to provide systematic direction in TQM implementation. Project teamwork is one of the key activities in this model. Members of the project teams are trained to apply problem-solving tools and techniques in order to improve quality performance effectively. The PTQ approach tends to be introduced and developed by engineers or technologists, and the activity is mainly focused on manufacturing or production.

Transformational total quality (TTQ): is the meta-paradigm that allows an overview of the type and status of the organizational approach to TQM. Companies may reach a "saturated" stage of diminishing returns using any of the paradigms above, when TQM progress starts to falter. From the viewpoint of the TTQ paradigm, TQM implementation is a cyclical process by which a company can choose the most suitable of the other models and move between them as necessary to rejuvenate the process and improve organizational performance. TTQ views people as purposive agents, and activities are typically speculative, involving reframing, empowerment and paradigm shifts.

It should be emphasised that practical TQM implementations are unlikely to be based entirely on one paradigm. It might be expected, however, that they would show a tendency towards one or more of the implementation paradigms.

Even with acknowledgement of differences between implementation paradigms, Krasachol and Tannock (1998) maintained that results of their study (three case studies of Thai organizations) identified five common features for the implementation:

1. *Top management commitment.* It is acknowledged that TQM implementation cannot be successful without top management commitment and support. In all these three companies, it was obvious that quality activities were fully supported and led by top management.

2. *Effective communication within the organization.* Good and effective communication between management and staff is considered vital for TQM implementation. Although the three companies used different approaches and media to communicate with employees, all of them had effective ways of disseminating TQM information.

3. *Problem-solving tools and techniques.* These tools and techniques are known to be effective methods to help employees improve their work and to assist motivation and involvement. TQM companies have to facilitate and empower their employees so that they can apply these tools effectively. All three companies used these methods extensively.

4. *Group activity.* "Working as a team" is at the heart of TQM. All the studied companies emphasised the importance of group activity in their TQM programmes.

5. *Employee training and development.* Human resource development is considered to be a key success factor in TQM implementation. Effective training programmes were a feature of all three companies studied.

Kraschol and Tannock (1998) suggested that social factors of a given particular culture, the Thai culture in this case, are facilitative of TQM implementation and adoption: "The Thai national culture has many of the social qualities which should support effective implementation of a variety of approaches to TQM". In addition to such socio-cultural forces or contexts (presumed, one must suppose, in the researchers' thinking, to shape organizational culture) economic factors and conditions, national, regional and global were viewed in the study as conducive to successful TQM implementation.

The Bradford study

Another empirical study of TQM implementation conducted in the Malaysian industrial context identified factors for effective TQM implementation (Thiagaragan *et al.*, 2001). The survey is based on a list of 22 items that are considered in the literature as critical to TQM. The study aims at finding an answer to the following question: what factors do we really need to have a successful quality process? A total of 63 persons (26 quality consultants and 37 managers of quality award-winning organizations including MBQNA winners) were asked through a self-report questionnaire survey to rate each of the 22 factors on a three-point scale. Respondents were required to identify the level of importance of each quality factor, relying on their experience of quality management process implementation in their firms. Using the three-point scale, each respondent was asked to indicate if the factor was:

- neutral regarding importance, 1 point;
- important but not essential to successful implementation of TQM process, 2 points; or
- critical and absolutely essential to successful implementation of TQM, 3 points.

The authors assigned weights of 1, 2 and 3 for neutral, important and critical, respectively, to classify the criticality of the factors according to their scores. The results of this study show that ten factors out of 22 are critical, seven factors important, and five factors neutral, as in the study by Ramirez and Loney (1993).

The study by Thiagaragan *et al.* (2001) aimed at constructing a generic framework of TQM implementation in Malaysia based on the following critical categories:

- Institute leadership.
- Maximise internal stakeholders' involvement.
- Manage by customer-driven processes.
- Adopt continuous improvement.

Thiagaragan *et al.* (2001) used a descriptive approach in the context of their study which involves best organizations agreeing to a set of quality factors critical to a successful TQM implementation. The emphasis is on what best organizations do or did in practice. To achieve this purpose, a slight adaptation was carried out on the approach devised by Ramirez and Loney (1993). Respondents were asked to rate each of the quality factors as to their level of importance to a successful implementation process in their organization using the following criteria: critical, important and minor.

The Motwani et al. *study*

Motwani *et al.* (1994) examined quality practices in India using an empirical approach. First, a further synthesis of the literature of quality concepts and identification of quality factors was carried out to create an organizational evaluation framework. Second, a field survey examined the level of conformance to identified practices in Indian manufacturing. Results were seen as potentially assisting management to:

- increase the understanding of quality management practice;
- determine the current quality position of an organization;
- assign organizational responsibilities; and
- monitor quality and improvement programmes.

It was hoped that quality management research would yield the following benefits:

- test the reliability and validity of the Saraph model within the international context;
- identify the critical factors used by researchers to structure their models and theories;
- develop a database for cross-cultural comparison; and
- use the identified critical factors to provide quality management guidelines for manufacturing in India (Motwani *et al.*, 1994).

Hypotheses derived from the following nine critical factors distilled from quality management literature were tested:

1. top management;
2. quality policies;
3. the role of the quality department;
4. training;
5. product design;
6. vendor quality management;
7. process design;
8. quality data; and
9. feedback and employee relations.

Quality managers and general managers were surveyed using Saraph *et al.*'s (1989) instrument. Results of the study indicated that top management assisted in quality policy development but not in implementation. Quality issues were not reviewed regularly at top management meetings. Quality policies were found to be directed toward customer satisfaction, they were well documented with specific documentation for each department. All personnel were aware of their responsibilities. Policies also addressed goals of compliance with government regulations, market share growth and the organization's profit and reputation (Motwani *et al.*, 1994).

The role of the quality department involved formulating and refining quality improvements in conjunction with all other departments. All business facets were covered and summary reports of processing and inspection drawn up. Training emphasis for quality was present and supported generally by survey respondents. Some complaints were registered that sophisticated training was wasted on "illiterate workers" (Motwani *et al.*, 1994).

Systematic product design was not supported as a quality improvement factor. Research and development departments and activities were limited. "Lack of sufficient interaction between the research and development department and the quality assurance and manufacturing departments" was described (Motwani *et al.*, 1994).

Vendor quality management was determined as a key factor for improvement and success. Availability of alternative vendors, however, was generally deemed preferable. Price, with minimum acceptable quality, was the predominant preference for more than 90 per cent of respondents. Nevertheless, a feedback system for raw material quality was determined, as was technical assistance to vendors and visitations to vendors by plant personnel. Comprehensive process design was confirmed along with product quality. Organizational help was provided by the Indian Statistical Institute. Statistical techniques were used extensively to:

- determine acceptance/rejection for both manufactured and purchased products;
- ascertain quality standard rationality; and
- point out and correct process discrepancies (Motwani *et al.*, 1994).

The availability and use of quality data were confirmed as critical components of the quality programmes in Indian organizations. Quality cost reporting systems were reported as efficient. Data was available throughout the organizations and regularly updated. Data was displayed in control charts at workstations. Management of quality was revealed as being highly dependent on data access. Feedback and employee involvement was not supported as being critical factors to the attainment of quality. Quality circles, although introduced, had become non-functioning in many cases. Quality performance appreciation at all levels was lacking. Quality performance was not necessarily the basis for employee promotions. Rewards did not prove sufficient to motivate superior quality performance. Rewards, however, tended to be random and were not found to be consistent policy components (Motwani *et al.*, 1994).

For the study of quality management in Indian organizations, researchers determined three major implications. The research method (derived from Saraph *et al.*, 1989) employed was determined as useful for analysing an organization's quality management in terms of principles established in the literature. The approach, as in the Indian study, can help to establish alternate models or variations in quality management implementation. Contrasts between empirical findings concerning organizations and identified criteria provide a basis for more intensive organizational study and possible improvement. Finally, after improvements are put in place, the approach is again applicable to evaluate new positions, levels of improvement and cost effectiveness. The general conclusion of the study was that all the critical factors of the Saraph *et al.* model were not necessary for quality management success: "....quality levels were obtained even in the absence of top management support, proper product design, and continual feedback about quality processes" (Motwani *et al.*, 1994). It is also suggested that in terms of practical application universal acceptance, or at least wide knowledge of critical quality factors consistent with Saraph *et al.* (1989) and Garvin (1983) must encourage "management regardless of their position [to] expect an organization to implement these critical quality factors to a great extent" (Motwani *et al.*, 1994).

The Badri et al. *study*
Badri *et al.* (1995) examined Saraph *et al.*'s organization quality requirements in a more "broadly based" environment than Saraph's investigation. Results from 84 randomly selected firms in the UAE indicated that the constructs developed by Saraph did indeed measure the traits intended. Problems for quality implementation in the UAE were newness of exposure to, and use of the concept of quality; low levels of expertise and skill development, preference for alternative suppliers' dependence on "cheap" expatriate labour from Third World countries and postponement of automation. Follow-up interviews revealed only two of the 424 participating firms had tried quality circles, and then only as experiments carried out by an international agency. Programmes were soon abandoned due to their high cost and insufficient results. Large firms successfully used open communication and employee participation as means of employee involvement.

Quality factors given high practice ratings by both manufacturing and service industries were:

- acceptance of quality responsibility;
- visibility and effectiveness of the quality department;
- top management commitment to quality training for all;
- building employee quality awareness;
- interdepartmental co-ordination of product/service development;
- consideration of implementation predictability issues;
- regulate in-process and final inspection/review; and
- effective supervisor problem solving.

Saraph *et al.*'s (1989) findings, synthesis and approach were further confirmed through examination of UAE management with the following important proviso:

> To develop a true profile of quality management in UAE firms, workers and managers at the different levels of the organization should also be surveyed. In addition, customer satisfaction should be taken into account to understand and evaluate the practice ratings better through "adequacy" ratings as seen by customers (Badri *et al.*, 1995).

The Capon et al. *study*

Capon *et al.* (1994) examined five key measures of TQM success using the Baldrige framework. Twelve TQM projects at Colt International, UK, were carried out. A "company-wide picture" or measurement was sought reflecting the "holistic nature of TQM" which requires "customer, shareholder and competitor reactions". The five TQM success measures were:

1. customer perceptions of service;
2. encouragement of continuous improvement;
3. process consistency, both administrative and mechanical;
4. cost effectiveness of the quality programme; and
5. ease of understanding and updating (Capon *et al.*, 1994).

The Baldrige criteria were summarised for the study as:

- management involvement;
- strategic quality planning;
- employee involvement;
- training;
- process capability; and
- customer perceptions.

The study concluded that 10-15 per cent improvement per month is likely with TQM programme measurements. Participant opinions expressed during the study indicated five key TQM success factors:

1. team leaders with enthusiasm and determination;
2. management setting TQM as a priority;
3. measuring success;
4. involving customers in meetings; and
5. early success in achieving improvements.

Monitoring, measuring and displaying improvement results increases the TQM success rate, following Baldrige Award recommendations (Capon *et al.*, 1994).

The Garvin study

Garvin (1983) conducted a study on nine US and seven Japanese window air conditioner manufacturers of their quality management practices and the associated impact on performance, and published the first empirical investigation of quality management factors. Using self-report questionnaires and on-site observations, Garvin examined the management practices such as quality programmes, policies and management attitudes, quality information systems, product design, production and employee policies, and supplier management. Assembly line reject rate and rate after delivery service calls were also examined as surrogate measures. Garvin's conclusions are:

- Quality is management's top priority and quality-related issues are part of agenda for regular meetings.
- Quality department reports direct to top management. In some companies, vice president is responsible for quality.
- Quality is customer-driven. Definition of quality derives from customers' perspectives. Production, marketing and design do not define quality.
- Defect-free output and performance appraisal of employee are aligned.
- Consistent improvement witnessed as result of comprehensive goal deployment at all levels.
- Data reported to management are timely, detailed and accurate. Effective monitoring and improvement of quality due to support of superior quality information systems.
- Product design supported by reliability of engineering techniques, thorough review and testing of new designs prior to production, and involvement of all affected departments in the review process.
- Reduction of variation achieved by training new employees in all job aspects, problem identification and remedial techniques.
- All production processes controlled by quality techniques and control charts.
- Production that operates smoothly and defect-free ensured by effective communication.
- Commitment to quality in product and service, value for money, and manufacturing capability define selection of supplies through close monitoring and quality audits.

Critical factors of TQM in SMEs

A study by Yusof and Aspinwall (2000) identified ten critical factors for successful TQM implementation in SMEs, based on extensive review of the literature. These factors include management leadership, continuous improvement system, education and training, supplier quality management, systems and processes, measurement and feedback, human resources management, improvement tools and techniques, resources and work environment, and culture. The study revealed the lack of practice in the areas of continuous improvement systems, supplier quality assurance, and improvement tools and techniques.

Another study about SMEs was conducted by Quazi and Padibjo (1998) in Singapore. They targeted SMEs which were attempting to move towards TQM through the ISO 9000 certification route to assess the training and consultancy needs of these organizations. A questionnaire built around the Malcolm Baldrige/Singapore Award model was developed to cover seven critical factors identified from the literature review. These factors included leadership, information and analysis, strategic planning, human resources utilisation, management of process quality, quality results and customer satisfaction.

Gorman (2001) intends to explore the factors that determine the sustainability of growth in small- and medium-sized enterprises (SMEs), and investigates the dynamic between these two conflicting explanations. Two in-depth longitudinal case studies are presented of SMEs in the wholesale sector. For SME managers, this research suggests that the first key managerial choice is "where to compete", but that this is followed by other key choices concerning "how to compete", and it is in the contribution of these that sustained growth is found. Moreover, there may be circumstances when innovative decisions are made regarding these questions that sustained growth is found. Moreover, there may be circumstances when an innovative decision about "where to compete" endows the creative first mover with the opportunity to both drive growth and to be the prime beneficiary of market growth.

Critical factors of TQM in service industries

In another empirical study, Prabhu and Robson (2000) used data from 750 manufacturing and service sector companies in the North East of England to investigate the impact of leadership and senior management commitment on business excellence. They found the results indicate that for all the internal measures selected a significant level of association exists between the level of practice or performance and the world-class status of the responding company. In each case, significant results can be explained by a greater than expected number of potential winners/world-class organizations scoring highly and, conversely, a greater than expected number of room for improvement and could do better scoring poorly.

Zhang et al. (2000) developed 11 constructs for TQM implementation based on a comprehensive review of the literature. The study used data from 212 Chinese manufacturing companies in nine industrial sectors for testing and validating the instrument. The purpose of this study was to develop an instrument for measuring TQM implementation for Chinese manufacturing companies. The constructs of TQM implementation include leadership, supplier quality management, vision and plan statement, evaluation, process control and improvement, product design, quality system improvement, employee participation, recognition and rewards, education and training, and customer focus.

Quazi and Padibjo (1998), using the eight critical factors employed by Saraph *et al*. (1989), examined 33 manufacturing and service firms in Singapore, which also was considered useful for international comparative study of quality factors. Because of the economic transformation of the country since independence, Singapore companies felt the need to emphasise and upgrade quality to compete on an equal global footing (Quazi and Padibjo, 1998).

The results of the study initially focused on the widely accepted perception that TQM had evolved to act as more of a competitive framework for management and not so much as a statistical and quality control function. A higher level of TQM deployment was observed in Singapore than in the UAE (Badri *et al*., 1995). The construct validity for the eight critical factors differed from both Badri *et al*. (1995) and Saraph *et al*. (1989). While Badri *et al*. (1995) found all eight factors to be uni-factorial, Saraph *et al*. (1989) found seven to be uni-factorial, but Quazi and Padibjo (1998) found only three uni-factorial factors and five multi-factorial factors. Quazi and Padibjo confirmed Saraph *et al*.'s approach to be appropriate for self-assessment.

Critical factors of TQM in education and professional services

Lidetka *et al*. (1999) adopted a different approach. They examined the development and assessment of a customised executive education experience designed for the managers of a large financial services organization. It was designed to incorporate many of the desirable outcomes of "action learning" such as organizational impact and sustainability, while being more parsimonious in the involvement of senior executives and in a single-period design, in the time intensity of participant involvement. A total of 542 managers who participated in the programme, over a four-year period, were surveyed concerning the effectiveness of the programme. The research is intended to examine whether participants believed that the value of their learning diminished over time, the effects of demographic characteristics, and the extent to which the sharing of the learning and support of organizational colleagues affected participants' perception of the programme's effectiveness. They found less degradation over time than anticipated and more powerful influence by subordinates in sustaining learning.

In another empirical case study, Rao *et al*. (1999) develop a measurement instrument for international quality management practices. They identified 13 constructs of quality practices through detailed analysis of the literature. These constructs were empirically tested using data collected from the USA, India, China, Mexico and Taiwan. The instrument is validated with a holdout sample set. The constructs include top management support, quality citizenship, quality information availability, quality information usage, benchmarking, employee training, employee involvement, product/process design, supplier quality, internal quality results, and customer orientation.

Wemmenhove and de Groot (2001) describe the process of identifying principles for the re-design of courses and programmes towards the aim within the

University of Dar-es-Salaam, Tanzania, from staff's and students' own visions of the issues involved. They interviewed 16 university staff members in prominent positions concerning environment and environmental education. They held group discussions and informal talks with five young environmental professionals who were graduates or former students. They also distributed 371 questionnaires containing 14 open-ended questions. They found that the principles are environment for development; in interaction with Tanzanian society; and in a student-activating style. This contrasts with the usual conceptualisation of environment and development as normatively separate issues, with the trend to globalise the environmental issue, and with a top-down teaching style that still dominates most universities.

In recent years, more empirical studies have been conducted. Simon and Kumar (2001) summarise the findings of a study which canvassed clients' views of strategic capabilities which lead to management consulting success. The survey was undertaken among 171 executives in the top 500 companies in Australia.

The major elements that were investigated were the reasons for hiring the consultants and the strategic capabilities related to successful performance indicators as identified by clients. The findings show that the main reasons consultants are hired are insufficient in-house resources and quick resolution of issues. The top five strategic capabilities which clients identified as important to success, in order, were ability to listen to and comprehend the client, quality of service, client-consultant communication, integrity and honesty, and technical knowledge. Therefore, the contemporary management consultant needs to be multi-skilled and technically competent, and should have excellent people skills. Consultants also need to note that their view on what constitutes successful performance is not quite the same as that of their clients.

The culture change paradigm

Krasachol and Tannock (1998) noted support in the TQM literature for culture change in organizations as a requirement to effect TQM adoption. The TQM change model should be culturally feasible. Four culture-based paradigms were studied extensively, including a meta-paradigm which informs and enables movement between the other ones (Whittle's study, cited in Krasachol and Tannock, 1998). The four paradigms are as follows.

1. Visionary total quality (VTQ) is a strongly top-down management-led approach. Culture change is promoted to be the strategic quality vision and ideology of top management, which is communicated clearly and widely to all levels of employees. People are seen as programmable pawns. One of the key issues in this model is providing management development and training for quality. Usually, the most senior executive leads and drives the strategic quality drive.

2. Learning total quality (LTQ) emphasises a bottom-up style of organizational culture change. People are seen as willing participants. Key factors in TQM implementation are employee empowerment and involvement. The natural work team is one of the important features emphasised in the LTQ organization. The human resources or personnel specialists tend to drive the process, and therefore the approach to TQM implementation is not explicitly strategic.

3. *Planning total quality (PTQ)* is concerned with rational and systemic approaches to TQM implementation. A systematic direction in TQM implementation is provided by the introduction of an explicit programme. One of the key activities of this model is the project teamwork. Project team members are trained to apply the problem-solving tools and techniques in order to improve quality performance effectively. The PTQ approach is mainly focused on manufacturing or production activities.

4. *Transformational total quality (TTQ)* is the meta-paradigm that allows an overview of the type and status of the organizational approach to TQM. At some point of the TQM journey, when the TQM progress starts to falter, the companies may reach a saturated stage of diminishing returns using any one of the three paradigms above. TTQ views the TQM implementation as a cyclical process by which a company can choose the most appropriate and suitable of the other models, and move between them as necessary to rejuvenate the process and improve the organizational performance. TTQ views the people as purposive agents, and activities are typically speculative, which involves reframing, empowerment, and paradigm shift.

From the practical point of view, it is highly unlikely that the TQM implementation is based entirely on one paradigm, but the tendency would be to employ one or more of the implementation paradigms. Despite acknowledging the differences between implementation paradigms, Krasachol and Tannock (1998) maintained that the results of their case studies on three organizations identified five common features for the implementation:

1. *Top management commitment.* It is acknowledged that TQM implementation cannot be successful without top management commitment and support. In all these three companies, it was obvious that quality activities were fully supported and led by top management.

2. *Effective communication within the organization.* Good and effective communication between management and staff is considered vital for TQM implementation. Although the three companies used different approaches and media to communicate with employees, all of them had effective ways of disseminating TQM information.

3. *Problem-solving tools and techniques.* These tools and techniques are known to be effective methods to help employees improve their work and to assist motivation and involvement. TQM companies have to facilitate and empower their employees so that they can apply these tools effectively. All three companies used these methods extensively.

4. *Group activity.* Working as a team is at the heart of TQM. All the studied companies emphasised the importance of group activity in their TQM programme.

5. *Employee training and development.* Human resource development is considered to be a key success factor in TQM implementation. Effective training programmes were a feature of all three companies studied.

Based on the study conducted in the Thailand context, Kraschol and Tannock (1998) also suggested that social factors of a given particular culture, the Thai culture in this case, are facilitative of TQM implementation and adoption. The Thai national culture has many of the social qualities which should support effective implementation of various approaches to TQM. In addition to the socio-cultural qualities, the researchers also view the economic factors and conditions, national, regional and global, as conducive to successful implementation of TQM.

Chapter 8
Leadership and senior management commitment

The aim of leadership should be to improve the performance of people and machines, to improve quality, to increase output, and simultaneously to bring pride of workmanship to people. Put in a negative way, the aim of leadership is not merely to find and record failures, but to remove the causes of failure: to help people do a better job with less effort ... The leader has also the responsibility to improve the system – i.e. to make it possible, on a continuing basis, for everybody to do a better job with greater satisfaction (Deming, 1986).

Introduction
The next few chapters are based on a comprehensive review of the literature discussing critical factors of TQM in key areas often stressed in implementation case studies, and supported by quality gurus and various writers. Such factors have consistently been considered to be conducive to the success of TQM implementation. At the end of this chapter, 98 examples of BEST PRactice applications are listed. These range from small to very large organizations and cover different sectors of marketing.

It is often argued that total quality management (TQM) should be tailored to an organization's needs (Robin and Dennis, 1995). This view has also been supported by the work of a number of quality practitioners who argue that TQM needs to take account of the different technology histories and backgrounds of organizations. Other differences include different markets that are served with different products and the workforce which may comprise people from different cultures (Atkinson, 1990). Basic characteristics of the organization, its culture and climate (Kanji and Yui, 1997), affect the implementation of TQM (Van Der Akker, 1989). The drive to improve quality, therefore, has to be managed differently. This chapter presents the most important factors of TQM implementation often stressed by researchers, supported by the writings of quality gurus (Crosby, 1979, 1984; Deming, 1986; Feigenbaum, 1983; Garvin, 1987,1988; Groocock, 1986; Juran, 1979, 1988; Oakland, 1989), and based on case studies for each factor presented.

The notion of leadership
"Everything starts with a committed and passionate leader of the business organization. A leader who is really committed to making fundamental changes. Without that very little else is possible" (Steven Stanton in Watts, 1995).

The critical role of top management and their leadership in quality management is emphasised over and over again in the literature covering implementation case studies and the writings of quality gurus. Top management commitment to the quality process and their leadership in fostering an environment where quality is a way of life set the foundation for the implementation of TQM in an organization.

Deming (1986) calls for managers to institute leadership to usher the transformation process. Feignbaum (1961) views senior executives' commitment as the means for promoting organizational commitment (Kano, 1993; Oakland, 1993). Kano (1993) talks about senior executives' commitment as a (more) important factor of TQM, and their doubt as the greatest enemy. Crosby (1979) places management commitment on top of the essentials of TQM implementation. Juran (1993) attributes the quality excellence of the Japanese companies to senior managers' commitment to quality.

In explaining why most of the quality initiatives failed in the West in the 1970s and 1980s, Juran (1993) focuses on senior managers' lack of personal involvement in managing quality; leaving such responsibility to middle managers and confining it to the quality department. The quote by Theodor Krantz, the President of Velcro USA put this reality into perspective:

A year earlier we had made a toothless attempt to modernise Velcro's quality programme. The effort had been delegated to the quality assurance manager, and it ended stillborn (Krantz, 1989).

Responsibilities of leaders

Quality is too important to be delegated; it must be the responsibility of top management (Crosby, 1879; Deming, 1986). Bertram (1991) echoes the gurus' caution by stressing that TQM is not just another management policy decision to be implemented by others. He states that a lack of requisite management commitment is the main reason for 80 per cent of TQM failures (Atkinson, 1993). Easton (1993) also pinpoints deficient leadership as the reason why TQM programmes of some of the US companies achieve only moderate results.

Given the importance of leadership, it is not surprising to find that, in all quality awards, leadership issues are not only placed at the top of the list of criteria but are emphasised in the other criteria necessary to make a quality implementation successful (NIST, 1994; EFQM, 1992).

The importance of top management commitment and involvement is also highlighted in the findings of several studies in the USA and Europe. In a study carried out using Malcom Baldrige National Quality Award (MBNQA) winners as respondents, Ramirez and Loney (1993) reported that management commitment was rated as the most critical step in quality improvement process activity. In fact, management-related activities such as the need for a clear vision statement and focusing the business processes on customer satisfaction were listed among the top ten critical steps for a successful quality improvement process. The overall conclusion of the study was that success or failure of a quality process hinges in a significant way on what happens regarding management commitment and other related top management activities. Similar conclusions were obtained by Zairi and Youssef (1995) when Ramirez and Loney's (1993) study was repeated in the UK and six other countries in the Middle and Far East.

Based on a study, Porter and Parker (1993) showed that the presence of certain management behaviours as the single most critical success factor. Johnston and Daniel (1991) described that senior management on both sides of the Atlantic visited during a study tour assumed active responsibility for the success of the TQM process in their companies. A similar conclusion was reported by Bertsch and Williams (1994) from a study of 20 large international companies based in the US, Europe and the Far East.

Based on his experience as an MBNQA examiner, Easton (1993), in capturing the state of leadership of top management in the Baldrige applicants, states that senior management are committed to quality. Senior managers are actively involved in promoting the importance of quality and customer satisfaction and they devote a substantial part of their time to quality-related issues. Their involvement includes activities such as meeting with employees, meeting customers, giving formal and informal recognition, receiving training and training others. Senior management also develop and communicate key company quality values which place emphasis on the importance of the customer, process orientation, continuous improvement, teamwork, management-by-fact, mutual respect and dignity, and value of individual employees and their contributions. They ensure that the entire workforce understands its role in satisfying the customer. To support and promote the quality process of the organization, senior management develop and put in place elements of quality management structure. These include a senior management TQM council or division and departmental councils.

How can leaders lead quality?

Discussions of implementation case studies in the literature are also unanimous and reinforcing this reality. The examples range from large to small companies, service to manufacturing, multi-nationals to family businesses, and government to non-profit agencies (Powers, 1994; George, 1990; Olian and Rynes, 1991; Wiggenhorn, 1990). At ICL Product Distribution UK, the chief executive and senior executives spearheaded the company-wide quality drive, while at Ciba-Geigy Italy, the total quality initiative was led by the group chief executive, with the active support and involvement of senior executives (Binney, 1992).

First and foremost in the quality evolution process, senior management must start by understanding what TQM really means (Smith, 1994). They must be convinced of its benefits to the organization, and acknowledge the fundamental change it will bring in the running of the organization. It is critical that they build the requisite commitment before getting the rest of the staff involved. There must be consensus among themselves regarding what the organization needs to achieve its quality goal.

At the Aluminium Company of America (Alcoa), it was the chief executive officer who initiated the quality initiative. The directors and senior managers then laboured over six months to identify the challenges and opportunities, and then to design and begin the total quality process there. During this period, the top management team, including the CEO, spent many hours in quality education and training, and visiting and benchmarking companies that had acquired reputations as leaders in quality management. All these helped form a consensus among top management about why they were interested in quality and what needed to be done to achieve the goals (Kolesar, 1993).

At Ciba-Geigy Italy, the management team spent two years "owning" and shaping the quality initiative themselves before consultants were involved (Binney, 1992). At Rockware Glass Ltd, UK, a series of workshops for senior executives was held at the outset resulting in a unanimous recognition of the importance of quality management for the organization's survival (Durrant, 1990). The first stage of implementing TQM at Ilford Ltd was the acceptance by top management that they had to fundamentally change the way they operated. "Acceptance of this was difficult but vital to achieving real change" (Hunt and Hillman, 1990).

The importance of employee involvement

One of the precepts of TQM is employees' greater involvement and commitment to the process and its goal. It is through the actions and behaviour of the management that employees identify with the goals of the company and extend their commitment towards its success (Feigenbaum, 1961; Kano, 1993; Oakland, 1993; Olian and Rynes, 1991). Ramirez and Loney's (1993) study also highlighted the fact that it is not sufficient for management to be committed, but they must also be obvious (Crosby, 1979; Townsend and Gebhardt, 1992). Bertsch and Williams' (1994) study also found that senior executives see being visible in their commitment to quality sends strong signals about what is expected and desired from the staff. It is through their demonstrated actions and behaviour that management can harness the involvement of employees, and thence their commitment to the quality goals of the company will be assured (Barker, 1991).

Johnston and Daniel (1991), in relating Fuji Xerox experiences, stress that if top management command employees to improve but are not themselves constantly seeking ways to improve systems, continuous improvement initiatives will fail. In describing the experiences of TQM implementation at Johnston Matthey plc, UK, George (1990) emphasises that senior management demonstrating involvement in the quality process is just as critical as commitment. There were initial hiccups in the implementation process when staff felt that senior executives were not committed (George, 1990).

The CEO of Alcoa stressed the need for his directors and senior managers to be visible in terms of their commitment in the eyes of the staff involved (Kolesar, 1993). The findings of a survey carried out among employees at two Hewlett-Packard factories in the UK showed that the degree of buy-in amongst the respondents was favourable amongst those who saw their management staff using the TQM techniques themselves to improve processes (Browning and Shaw, 1990).

Some of the ways CEOs and senior executives of best companies make this commitment evident is by leading quality initiatives and investing the requisite time and effort. A study found that most CEOs of the 62 major US-based companies spend at least 10 per cent of their time in quality improvement efforts (Olian and Rynes, 1991). At Southern Pacific Lines, leadership meant role modelling. This involved leaders being out on the "track and yards" with the employees to demonstrate and speak about the quality-driven approach to doing business (Carman, 1993). The CEO of Motorola spent a significant amount of time explaining the corporate vision to enable every employee to translate it into personal work goals (Wiggenhorn, 1990). The president and his senior executives at Short Brothers were the first to be trained in the theory, practice and tools of quality improvement (Oakland and Porter, 1994). The managing director of Rockware Glass Ltd UK meets every employee in a series of TQM-related sessions at various locations and times convenient to the works (Durrant, 1990). A high-powered steering committee to manage the TQM process at Paul Revere Insurance Group is a visible sign of top-level commitment to the process (Bank, 1992). The vice-president at Philips Electronics personally leads a company-wide task force on quality improvement of software development, while at Ericsson Sweden, a top executive took ownership of analysing and improving the order-make-market system (Bertsch and Williams, 1994).

Steps for effective leadership
According to Juran (1993), there are seven steps that a responsible CEO must take to achieve quality in any organization:
1. Set up and serve on the company's quality council.
2. Establish corporate quality goals and make them a part of the business plan.
3. Make provision for training the entire company hierarchy in managing for quality.
4. Establish the means to measure quality results against quality goals.
5. Review results against goals on a regular basis.
6. Give recognition for superior quality performance.
7. Revise the reward system to respond to the changes demanded by world class quality.

Oakland (1993) lists the five requirements for effective leadership:
1. Clear beliefs and objectives in the form of a mission statement.

2. Clear and effective strategies and supporting plans.
3. The critical success factors and critical process.
4. The appropriate management structure.
5. Employee participation through empowerment and EPDCA (evaluate-plan-do-check-amend) helix.

"Getting quality results is not a short-term, instant-pudding way to improve competitiveness; implementing total quality management requires hands-on, continuous leadership" (Feigenbaum, 1989). Leadership and top management play a critical role in quality management, an aspect that has been emphasised in most of the literature on TQM. In this respect, leadership involves envisioning the future, co-ordinating the development of a coherent mission for the organization, overseeing the development, controlling the process, and providing motivation towards organizational culture and climate (Wilsy, 1995; Master, 1992; Lorentzen, 1992; Nanus, 1992). George and Weimerskirch (1998) argue that without clear and consistent leadership, a company can never be a quality leader.

While some principles and practices of TQM may differ among firms and industries, there is an almost unanimous agreement as to the importance of leadership by top management in implementing TQM. According to Makower (1993), such leadership is a prerequisite to all strategy and action planning. In the quality process, top management must understand what TQM really means. Senior management must be convinced of its benefits to the organization, and acknowledge the fundamental change it will bring in the running of the organization.

Strategic stewardship
Given the importance of leadership, it is not surprising to find that in all quality awards, leadership issues are not only placed at the top of the list of criteria but also are emphasised in the other criteria as necessary to make implementation successful (Thiagaragan and Zairi, 1997). Zairi (1999) suggests that if organizations are to compete effectively in this millennium, they will have to equip and renew themselves by challenging the status quo and re-examining their corporate leadership process. Curt (1991) identifies seven major characteristics of excellent leadership:
1. Visible, committed, knowledgeable and dedicated to promoting quality and knowing relevant details and how well the company is doing.
2. A missionary zeal in which leaders are trying to effect as much change as possible.
3. Aggressive targets, going beyond incremental improvements, and looking for large gains.
4. Strong drivers with attention to cycle time and zero defects.
5. Communication of values that effect cultural change related to quality.
6. Flat organizational structures that allow more authority at lower levels.

7.   Senior management maintains strong customer contacts.

Robin and Dennis (1995) point out that TQM aims to encourage a participative style of management throughout the organization and that an organization with this style of management is likely to be more enthusiastic towards TQM and will have less need to change its systems and communication structure. Jacqueline and Shapiro (1999) in their study on employee participation conclude that a participative supervisory style is positively related to employee participation and that the extent of employee participation is positively related to the assessment of the benefits of TQM. Furthermore, participation in an improvement structure represents a major vehicle by which employees can contribute to continuous improvement (Lawler, 1994; Soin, 1992).

On the other hand, it is argued that organizations with an authoritative style of management, wherein employees/managers who are promoted, are aggressive, career minded and not team workers, are likely to find it more difficult to cope with the pressures of TQM implementation.

The Malcolm Baldrige Award Criteria (1995-1999) considers leadership in terms of four major factors, namely:

1.   the active involvement of top management;
2.   communication across different organizational levels;
3.   leadership in quality activities for all levels of management; and
4.   inter-functional co-operation.

By the same token, Glenn (1992) points out that leaders must do the following four critical factors:

1.   create a vision;
2.   show commitment;
3.   build trust; and
4.   rid themselves of all sense of failure.

George (1998) argues that since management is responsible for directing the activities of the people within the organization, the control of the management process itself is necessary to implement an overall quality programme. In this respect, management must provide the appropriate leadership in demonstrating its commitment. Similarly, Juran (1993) attributes the failure of most of the quality initiatives in the West in the 1970s and 1980s to the lack of personal involvement of senior managers in managing quality, thereby leaving the responsibility to middle managers and confining it to the quality department.

Organizations involved in best practice applications

Post Office Counters Ltd
Catton and Company (UK) Ltd
Shell Chemicals UK
Velcro USA
ICL Product Distribution UK
Ciba-Ceigy Italy
Aluminium Company of America (Alcon)
Rockware Glass Ltd UK
Ilford Ltd
Fuji Xerox
Johnston Maltkey plc UK
Hewlett-Packard UK
Southern Pacific Lines
Motorola
Shorts Brothers
Paul Revere Insurance Group
Philips Electronics
British Construction Machinery Manu.
Ericsson Sweden
Matsushita Japan
Federal Express
Club Med
LeaRonal (UK)
Mitel Telecom UK Ltd
Tioxide Group Ltd
Thomas Interior System
Milliken Industrial
Globe Metallurgical
Eastman Chemical Company
Wainwright Industries
Norand Corporation
Charrette Corporation
STC Cables Products Ltd
Nissan UK
Rank Xerox
AT&T
Istel UK
Mitel
Telecom Ltd UK
Wallace Co
Grundos of Denmark
GTE Directories

Charrette Corporation
AMP of Canada Ltd
British Steel
GPT Ltd
BP Chemicals UK
Exxon Chemicals Ltd UK
IBM UK Ltd
Hartford Insurance Group
Florida Power & Light
Pascal Corporation Japan
BMA Pie
STC Cables Products UK
General Electric
National Westminster Bank
Rover Cars
Procter and Gamble
NEC Japan
Komatsu
Unilever Personal Products
Thomas Cork SML
Suntory Brewery Japan
Elida Gibbs Ltd in Belgium
Philips Signetics
Bekaeit in Belgium
Toyota
Jaguar Cars
Carnaud Metalbox plc
Esso Research Centre UK
Saturn Corporation
Unipart
Global Contribution Circle
Yutaka Gigen
Royal Mail
3M
Heinz
Oklahoma City Works
Prudential Assurance Co
Thomas Interior Sys. (USA)
Electrolux
ITT Hancock Industries
Caterpillar Tractor Company
Solectron Corporation

Honda

Corning

General Electric

Baxter Healthcare Group

Mercury Marine

Hilti (GB) Ltd

British Airways

L.L. Bean Inc

Ford

Digital Equipment

Nestle

DuPont

Panasonic

Co-operative Bank plc

Chapter 9
Internal stakeholder management

Creating participation requires creation of an atmosphere of mutual trust….[participation] also requires a stimulus, since the forces of sub-optimization are usually in charge (J.M. Juran).

When companies address the problem of recognition, they usually do a superb job. They enlist the collective ingenuity of those who have special skills in communication as well as the line managers (J.M. Juran).

Employee involvement

While top management involvement and leadership are essential for TQM success, they are not sufficient on their own (Haksever, 1996). TQM succeeds only with employees' involvement in the TQM process and their commitment to its goals (Kano, 1993; Crosby, 1979; Bank, 1992; Reeves and Bednar, 1993). In 1979, when the founder president of Matsushita Japan spoke of how Japanese products swept aside Western products in the world market, he attributed it to the involvement of every one in the company in the quest for quality (Bank, 1992). This fact was also captured in a study which found that organizations with a high level of employee involvement stand a greater chance of success (*Quality Progress*, 1994).

Crosby (1989) talks about the need for every individual in the organization to understand his or her role in making quality happen. In fact, the need to maximise the involvement of all employees is one of the basic principles of change implementation in an organization. It involves the employee having a common understanding of quality and the importance of their involvement to maintain the quality momentum.

According to the chief executive of Federal Express, the foundation for the success of the quality improvement process at this company is the involvement of every employee in that process (Townsend and Gebhardt, 1992). He calls it the "human side of quality". LeaRonal (UK) believes that "for a quality improvement programme to be successful, the commitment to total quality must encompass a whole workforce who must be encouraged to participate actively in the search for continuous improvement (Smith and Tee, 1990). The success of the quality improvement process at Mitel Telecom Ltd UK is attributed to the total involvement of the workforce (Boyer, 1991). In implementing the quality process, Shorts Brothers views greater involvement of its workforce as important evidence that the company is progressing in the right direction (Oakland and Porter, 1994).

The critical importance of employees' involvement in the quality process of an organization is based on the belief that the best process innovation ideas come from the people actually doing the job (Haksever, 1996). The quality reputation of Japanese companies is mainly credited to their great success in this area.

A total quality management environment demands that people participate in continuous improvement activities in an unhindered manner, that pushing decision making to the lowest practical level is the way. In TQM terminology, this is called empowerment. Deming (1986) and Juran (1991) also stress the importance of giving employees the authority and autonomy to do their job or empowerment when they talk about "pride of workmanship", "self-improvement", "self-control" and "self-inspection" respectively. At Tioxide Group Limited, empowerment to enable its employees to participate in continuous improvement activities was seen as a key element in the development of its total quality strategy (Oakland and Porter, 1994).

Zink (1995) emphasises that employee empowerment is an important area of assessment of major quality awards around the world. Empowered employees are given many labels: self-managing teams, self-directing teams, autonomous groups. Zink (1995) even includes participation in employee suggestion schemes.

Promoting employee involvement by operating suggestion schmes are common in the majority of the 158 US companies in the Fortune 1,000 surveyed (Conference Board in Olian and Rynes, 1991). While such schemes are also common in non-TQ organizations, enthusiasm is often stifled due to poor follow-up from management. TQ organizations, however, generally design schemes that are responsive and user friendly. Employees who wish to make a suggestion at Thomas Interior System simply fill out a half-page pre-printed form and drop it in a designated suggestion box (Johnston and Daniel, 1991). Response to the suggestion is ensured within 72 hours. At Thomas, ideas are submitted at an average monthly rate of 40, with an implementation at 80 per cent.

At Milliken, which received 262,000 ideas in 1989, suggestions are acknowledged within 24 hours and acted on within 72 hours, while at Globe Metallurgical, ideas discussed at the weekly quality circle meeting are implemented the same day where possible (Nadkarni, 1995). However, at Eastman Chemical Company, the suggestion system was eliminated because it was found to impede teamwork (Bemowski, 1992).

Greater employee involvement in quality efforts can only come about when the employees know that the organization cares for them (Townsend and Gebhardt, 1992). Baldrige winners treat their employees as partners rather than hired hands (Nadkarni, 1995). The chief executive of Wainwright Industries, the 1994 winner of the Baldrige Award, sums up this point well when he said:

> An internal customer (employee) will treat the external customer the
> way he or she is treated by the company (Bemowski, 1995a).

This message is echoed by Townsend and Gebhardt (1992):

> Without the co-operation of the latter group (employees), the loyalty
> of the former (external customers) is always in jeopardy.

The value of employee participation and involvement

In the context of TQM, it is widely acknowledged that participation in an improvement structure represents a major vehicle for employees to contribute to continuous improvement (Vermeulen and Crous, 2000; Lawler, 1994; Soin, 1992). An organization will only be successful when those at the bottom co-operate. It is difficult to achieve the higher goals that globalisation demands unless employees from all levels perceive continuous improvement as a benefit and become committed to the goals (Tan, 1997). Employee involvement provides a powerful means of achieving the highest order needs of self-realisation and fulfilment (Evans and Lindsay, 2001).

Flynn *et al.* (1995) noted that employee involvement is the most significant variable in understanding the percentage of parts passing final inspection without requiring rework. Employees who have been trained, empowered and recognised for their achievements see their jobs and their companies from a different perspective. They "own" the company, in the sense that they feel personally responsible for its performance (George and Weimerskirch, 1998). Crosby (1989) argues that every individual in the organization must understand his or her role in making quality happen. The need to maximise the involvement of all employees is one of the basic principles of change implementation in an organization (Thiagarajan and Zairi, 1997).

Marchington *et al.* (1992) uses employee participation as an umbrella term covering all forms of employee influence. In this respect, employee involvement describes managerially inspired initiatives aimed at winning employee commitment and working toward industrial democracy. Such practices support the rights of employees to participate in management decisions.

Employee involvement should begin with a personal commitment to quality. If employees accept and commit to a quality philosophy, they are more apt to learn quality tools and techniques and use them in their daily work (Evans and Lindsay, 2001). A number of key practices are employed by quality leaders to foster employee involvement. These include the following:

- all employees are involved at all levels and in all functions;
- the effective use of suggestion systems to promote involvement and motivate employees;
- the support of teamwork throughout the organization; and
- monitoring the extent and effectiveness of employee involvement (Evans and Lindsay, 2001).

The strength of employee involvement for expediting quality and fashioning organization success is noticeable perhaps particularly in service organizations. Employee involvement and organization commitment to the well-being of each employee appears to be two handles on the same water jug. They reinforce each other and work toward maximising employee contribution and organization benefit. Letting one or the other slip wastes the effort. Federal Express and its unique success is an outstanding example of a caring organizational attitude and practice integration with employee involvement. Both reinforce employee job satisfaction, which in turn reinforces customer satisfaction. The correlation is direct and positive (Evans and Lindsay, 2001).

The company credo of Federal Express is simply "people, service, profits" (Evans and Lindsay, 2001). Frontline employees are positioned for promotion to management positions. At the same time, all organization decisions are evaluated in terms of how employees are affected. That is, the organization puts "people" first, as the best path to customer service and the key to profitability and overall success, which for Federal Express with its "no lay-off" philosophy, and its "guaranteed fair treatment procedure" has been astounding. The recognition programme for individual and team contributions to the company is a primary focus. Employee involvement for high quality service at Federal Express entails reward systems that recognise satisfaction, results and customer-focused behaviours, appropriate skills and abilities for performing the job, and supervisors who act more as coaches and mentors than as administrators. Training is particularly important, as service employees need to be skilled in handling every customer interaction, from greeting customers to asking the right question. (Evans and Lindsay, 2001).

Empowerment
During the last few years the term "empowerment" has been intensively used in the literature of management (see for example, Collinson and Edwards, 1998; Cunningham and Hyman, 1996; Wilkinson, 1998). However, an adequate definition of empowerment, beyond the most rudimentary, is difficult to find. Conger and Kanungo (1988) define empowerment as:

a process of enhancing feelings of self-efficacy among organizational members through the identification of conditions that foster powerlessness and through their removal by both formal organizational practices and informal techniques of providing efficacy information.

According to Wilkinson (1998), "empowerment" is generally used to refer to a form of employee involvement initiative, widespread since the 1980s, and focused on task-based involvement and attitudinal change. It provides a solution to the age-old problem of "taylorised" and bureaucratic workplaces where creativity is stifled and workers become alienated, demonstrating their discontent through individual or collective means. Furthermore, employee empowerment can unleash the potential of individuals, or groups of low status for taking over task-centred elements of managerial responsibilities.

While it is well-established in the literature that empowerment is an essential component of successful transformation programmes, the findings of Prybutok and Kappelman (1995) suggest a mechanism for demonstrating the organization's commitment to empowerment early in the implementation of an organizational transformation. According to their study, such a demonstration reduces employees' resistance to the process of change by meeting their need to feel some sense of control during a time of change and by increasing their consciousness of management's commitment to the principles of empowerment during the transformation.

Collinson and Edwards (1998) argue that when practising empowerment more precision is desirable. It is more fruitful to see empowerment as a "constrained process", and as essentially referring to "the use of employees, abilities within goals defined by management". Widman (1994), in addition to recognising the importance of empowerment, claims that fully empowering people is what the people side of quality is all about. From a study of a major re-engineering effort at the Principal Financial Group (Rohm, 1993) it was found that it was essential to define empowerment as a component of the re-engineering effort.

Lashley (1997) groups empowerment into the following four categories:
1. Empowerment through participation (e.g. autonomous work groups, job enrichment).
2. Empowerment through involvement (e.g. quality circles, team briefings).
3. Empowerment through commitment (e.g. employee share ownership, profit-sharing).
4. Empowerment through de-layering, such as job re-design and job enrichment.

A strong argument for the importance of empowerment in making successful organizational transformations is provided from case studies by Gilbert (1992), whereby it was demonstrated that TQM efforts failed because the commitment to TQM was not coupled with involvement and training came too late, and obstacles were placed in the path of the information gatherers; the management was poor and the training was inadequate.

Empowerment requires substantial training. In their study Prybutok and Kappelman (1995), found that training alone provided little benefit and explained almost nothing about success, but training combined with empowerment provided a great deal more benefit and explanatory power. They conclude that providing employees with an empowering experience in conjunction with their training significantly improved the outcome of that training. Edosomwan (1992) suggests the following critical elements of empowerment lead to an increase in organizational performance:
- involve employees in developing the organization's strategies;
- provide the skills required to solve problems and make decisions; and
- define empowerment based on the mission of the organization.

Ross (1999) indicates that greater employee autonomy and discretion, implied by team working, are invariably accompanied by an intensification of work and increased self-monitoring. According to Simmons *et al.* (1995), true empowerment provides a critical clue that contributes to organizational growth, to achieve the organization's goal, and to create a new managerial behaviour. By the same token, Gilbert (1993) argues that the essence of TQM's operation in an organization is focusing on customer and process improvement through sound empowerment, since empowerment establishes the initiative to activate people toward accepting and fulfilling the organization's goal.

Recent studies identified employee empowerment as a critical factors of TQM implementation (Martinez-Lorente *et al.*, 1998, Lui *et al.*, 2000; Claver *et al.*, 2001; Davidson *et al.*, 2001; Dale *et al.*, 2001). Eastman Chemical Company implemented successful employee empowerment through, isolating employee factors or characteristics that make empowerment difficult, unlikely or impossible. The characteristics are that employees "don't care, don't have authority, don't have appropriate skills"(*The X Factor Executive Report*, 1999). Eastman addressed the issues by outlining processes for giving employees the skills and authority needed to assume increased responsibility. Employees were surveyed to this end. They discussed disturbing aspects of the employee appraisal system that were a major obstacle to their dedicated and sincere involvement. Revision of the appraisal system was made.

Dana Commercial Credit Corporation (DCC), winner of the 1996 Baldrige Award (as was Eastman), pursued employee involvement through development of empowerment processes:

- involving employees in setting their own goals and judging their own performance;
- encouraging them to assume ownership of the actions; and
- encouraging employees to identify with DCC and to become stock shareholders (*The X Factor Executive Report*, 1999).

Texas Instruments Europe builds empowerment into its organizational approach, organization by processes. Creativity is stimulated and quality teams are developed. Hewlett-Packard combines empowerment and teamwork with freedom for employees to set their own objectives. Empowerment is viewed as supporting employees and encouraging them in problem solving, issue identification voluntary, process improvement, and elimination of the need for process re-engineering (*The X Factor Executive Report*, 1999).

AT&T's Consumer Markets Division (CMD) established empowerment as "a way to encourage individual initiative and self-directed responsibility without compromising the integrity of its communication network" (George and Weimerskirch, 1998). Six approaches were combined and integrated to achieve this purpose. Notable among the six was "Common Bond", a values statement developed by AT&T in 1992 through internal focus groups and external experts. The statement committed the company to special "values to guide our decisions and behaviour". Values were as follows:

- respect for individuals;

- dedication to helping customers;
- highest standards of integration;
- innovation; and
- teamwork.

Internalisation of the values followed from further focus groups discussing what the values meant to them and how they could guide their decisions and behaviours. Publication or distribution of all results allowed embedding of the values within the organization. The spirit of Common Bond became the common language of organizational discourse. Exploratory questions were encouraged according to guidelines:

- Why am I doing this?
- Have I notified everybody directly affected by this work?
- Can I prevent or control service interruption?
- Is this the right time for the work?
- Have I been trained or am I qualified for this work? (George and Weimerskirch, 1998).

Employees were empowered with freedom and responsibility to use their maximum ability for the organization's benefit. Frontline people are increasingly empowered and the organization's structure has been increasingly flattened. Information flows to an increasingly larger group of employees who progressively assume responsibility for fundamental decisions. Empowerment creates a demand for communication change. Organizations' vision and policy communication flow through the empowered groups (George and Weimerskirch, 1998).

Middle management role

The act of maximising employee involvement in the quality process requires middle managers within the organization to make major adjustments. They must give up some authority as power and control are pushed to lower levels in the organization. In addition, managing according to the philosophy of TQM requires new attitudes and skills from middle managers (Wilkinson *et al.*, 1994). The transition towards TQM can be an uncertain and troubling process for middle managers (Townsend and Gebhardt, 1992; Manz and Sims, 1993).

Only when middle managers are convinced that the transition process that may cost them in status, power and recognition leads to a better world, can the implementation of TQM be smooth (Johnston and Daniel, 1991). If they do not see it, they may react with suspicion, uncertainty and resistance (Durrant, 1990; Wilkinson et al., 1994; Manz and Sims, 1993; Wacker, 1993). Crosby (1989) says

It is hard to get people interested in improvement of any kind if they perceive it is a threat to their authority or life style.

Unless there is a middle management buy-in, they soon become barriers rather than champions of the new system. According to Manz and Sims (1993):

> On the road to a total quality culture, the biggest obstacle to success is the middle management brick wall.

This fact was also reflected in a survey of 161 organizations. It was established that one of the elements that differentiated the successful TQ organizations from the less than successful ones was middle management support. A survey concluded that without middle managers' committed support for the quality process, the process will be derailed.

Another survey reported in *Quality Progress* (1993), which examined 536 organizations using TQM, returned similar findings. The study, which aimed to identify specific practices that have contributed to or detracted from TQM success, revealed that middle management are the main roadblocks to successful TQM. The study recommends that senior management should work hard to understand and involve middle managers in TQM efforts, such as involvement in designing and promoting TQM, creating different but meaningful roles for them in supporting widespread quality improvement initiatives, and providing training and development not only in TQM concepts and practices, but also in new leadership skills.

In this sense, getting middle managers' buy-in and being involved in a positive manner is viewed as key to the success of TQM (Ishikawa, 1985; Glover, 1993; McDermott, 1993; Crosby, 1989; Olian and Rynes, 1991). Ishikawa (1985) says that middle management can contribute greatly to quality improvement but conventional organizational arrangements do not encourage their contributions. He calls for senior management to provide greater attention to encourage new roles for middle managers.

At Norand Corporation, management discovered that without middle management's committed support, the total quality process could fail. Middle management training and acceptance were made a priority. Training was created for middle managers to show them how to manage empowered employees and to become facilitators of quality improvement initiates and coaches of employee development (Wacker, 1993).

At Charrette Corporation, it was recognised at the outset that the new role of middle managers, especially in the transition stage, would be critical to achieving a successful implementation (Manz and Sims, 1993). At Nissan UK, the supervisors have a wide range of responsibilities where people management skills feature prominently. For example, supervisors are involved in staff selection, developing and training their staff and motivating and maintaining morale. They are also the channel for all communications to manufacturing staff.

Training and education

Introducing new systems such as TQM when people do not have the fundamental skills to work in the new system is a prescription for disaster (Dumas, 1989). There should be no doubt that for TQM to succeed, the entire workforce must acquire new knowledge, skills and abilities. Training and education based on total quality must be planned and provided if this is to be realised. Oakland (1993) stresses that training strategy must be planned and provided if this is to be realised. Oakland (1993) stresses that training strategy should be addressed early alongside other strategies within the quality policy. He goes on to say that training is the single most important factor in improving quality once the necessary commitment has been assured.

The importance of training and education is also echoed by other quality gurus. Ishikawa (1985) says "Quality begins and ends with training" (also Imai, in Clemmer (1990)). Crosby (1989), Juran (1974) and Feigenbaum (1961) also emphasised the need for organization-wide education and quality awareness programmes.

Top management of best organizations, recognising the link between education and successful TQM, also focus their implementation process around it. The point is well summed up by Durrant (1990) in discussing TQM initiative at Rockware Glass Ltd UK:

> There would be more training for all in one year than the previous ten years.

At Shorts Brothers, training is a number one priority (*Quality Progress*, 1994). Some 400 training sessions were conducted, catering to the president, the management committee and the shopfloor workers.

Rank Xerox has had a comprehensive training programme for all its employees since the beginning of its TQ initiatives. It considers training to be an essential element in developing the TQ process throughout the company (Cullen and Hollingum, 1987). AT&T Istel UK and Mitel Telecom Ltd UK have also ensured that all employees are provided with formal and rigorous education at the outset of the TQM process (Hutt, 1990; Boyer, 1991). Both organizations believe that education provides a firm foundation for a common language and for understanding the organization's quality aspirations.

Best companies do not just confine education and training to its shopfloor employees and managers. Top executives are actively involved in the learning process themselves. Wallace Company's five top leaders each underwent more than 200 hours of intensive training in the methods and philosophy of continuous improvement. The managing director of Grundos spends an average of 30 days a year sitting in seminars with all levels of managers (Binney, 1992).

According to Garvin (1993), organizations failing to grasp the basic truth that TQM requires a commitment to learning is the reason why failed programmes far outnumber successes and success rates remain distressingly low. This statement may come as a surprise as many organizations embarking on total quality initiatives allocate a considerable amount of resources in providing the employees' training in new skills and knowledge. Garvin (1993) is not just referring to the mechanism of providing skills and knowledge but is including the accompanying – and perhaps more critical – process of applying what was learnt in the workplace. Potential for involvement will not exist just by creating systems and processes for the provision of training. Skills and knowledge acquired must be applied and integrated into the fabric of daily operations. He says that some of the less than successful initiatives, although effective at creating or acquiring new knowledge, may have been less successful in applying the knowledge to the workplace.

It is critical for training and education programmes to be linked explicitly to implementation if they are to have maximum effectiveness. Management should not assume that the new knowledge from such programmes will be applied when trainees return to their workplaces. Management should have in place a system to ensure employees follow through what they have learnt when they return to their jobs after training. For example, the management at GTE have put in place a system whereby employees know that they will be evaluated on the implementation of the new knowledge acquired during training. Organizations such as Honda, Corning and General Electric are other examples where new knowledge has been effectively translated into new ways of behaving. These companies actively manage the training process to ensure that it occurs by design rather than by chance.

Best organizations also direct training towards supporting other quality initiatives within the organization. For example, Baxter Healthcare Corporation believes that the objectives of its Baxter Quality Award can only be realised if applicants receive training relating to the award – the process, criteria and the scoring system – and the examiners are familiar with the objectives of the award and how to conduct assessments (Sanford, 1992). At Mercury Marine, the absence of relevant training resulted in setbacks to its quality circle initiative (Ingle, 1982). Problem-solving teams, set up as part of the quality process at Hilti (Great Britain) Ltd, encountered problems during the early stages when project teams were set up without the requisite skills (Findlay *et al.*, 1990).

Proper timing and spacing of training programmes to ensure what is learnt is applied right away and not lost is also crucial. Maximising the impact of training by the correct timing of training programmes was highlighted in a recent study of 536 TQM organizations in the USA (DDI, 1994). Hence, conducting organization-wide training in TQM before the need or desire for TQM is created could have a negative impact in the TQM implementation process. Employees unable to apply their knowledge forget the details by the time they encounter a real need, and thence lose enthusiasm in the quality initiative.

As training and education prepare employees for greater involvement in the organization's quality process, providing them with the right type of training is crucial. Generally, leading organizations ensure their education and training programmes include both the basics of quality and TQM and the set of skills for continuous quality improvement.

The literature gives a good indication of the type of new skills best organizations provide for their workforce to nurture a quality ethic (Johnston and Daniel, 1991; Sanford, 1992; Oakland and Beardmore, 1995; Cashbourne, 1991; Bank, 1992; Carman, 1993; Westbrook and Barwise, 1995). A study in the USA reported that training in continuous improvement skills, interpersonal skills and leadership skills are common amongst 536 TQM organizations. Another study of 20 companies that were high scorers in 1988/89 MBNQA assessment rounds found that initial training typically encompasses TQM awareness and leadership, followed by sessions in problem-solving and continuous skills (Olian and Rynes, 1991).

It is also evident from the studies that organizations are emphasising both interactive and technical skills. According to a survey, good communication skills is one of the two employee characteristics most valued by quality-driven organizations (*Quality Progress*, 1995). British Airways' training for its crew is a 50-50 split between the technical and the behavioural. The latter type of training includes treating customers as individuals and taking ownership of their problems. At Charrette Corporation, training for supervisors and managers to develop the necessary facilitator skills and behaviours are essential to overcome the initial uncertainty and suspicion amongst middle managers (Manz and Sims, 1993). Only with a considerable amount of suitable training and education can this be achieved.

Organizations such as Fuji Xerox commence training for all employees immediately upon hiring. They believe that putting everyone through the same TQM training provides the employees across the organization with a common language of quality and a shared way of thinking. TQM concepts are generally understood and used, making communication much easier (Johnston and Daniel, 1991).

TQM is a leadership issue at all levels. Middle managers become leaders of empowered employees, facilitators of the new management system, and coaches of new methods. Only with a considerable degree of training and education can this changed role be assumed (Townsend and Gebhardt, 1992). Organizations are investing a significant amount of resources in preparing their managers to be different types of leaders. Based on a survey among UK managers (Wilkinson *et al.*, 1994), concluded that the effective training of managers may be an important factor in the success of TQM implementation.

At Nissan UK, where supervisors are empowered to recruit their own staff and people management skills feature prominently in their functions, the company puts a great deal of emphasis on training and developing supervisors as leaders. In addition to standard training elements, professional programmes conducted cover personal effectiveness, and impart knowledge required by a supervisor in one function which is different from that needed by his or her peer in another function (Vallely, 1993).

AMP of Canada Ltd has implemented a training programme whereby managers participate in learning a different way of managing. This on-going programme, which takes 300 hours during the first year, deals with the soft side of managing and draws extensively on the disciplines of psychology, sociology and philosophy. Milliken managers take a seven-week leadership orientation programme, which is topped up by at least another 40 hours in a year (Johnston and Daniel, 1991).

It is important that education and training materials used should be readily associated with the company, its "culture" and implementation strategy:

A week of training in a vacuum .....doesn't make TQM happen (DDI, 1994).

Kano (1993) stresses the importance of adapting training programmes to the company's workplace. At British Steel, top management spent considerable time defining the challenges to be faced by the organization and clarifying their vision and values before embarking on training. In designing their training courses, they matched the methodologies and content to the specific culture and values of their organization (Johnston and Daniel, 1991). At Rank Xerox a task force was set up to develop a training curriculum to support the implementation plan.

On the same note, Oakland (1993) cautioned that training for quality is too important to be totally left to the so-called external quality professionals (Smith and Tee, 1990). Bought-in training courses may not be compatible with the philosophies and culture of the company. In fact, some TQM organizations perceive the generic nature of off-the-rack education and training materials as a barrier to steady progress in the quality drive (Cashbourne, 1991). GPT Ltd is one such organization. It produced its own education package comprising a work book, manual and videos.

In many TQ organizations that conduct internal training, cascading of training is common (Bendell et al., 1993), this basically involves a number of managers and supervisors who, after undergoing training and education themselves, are selected to be trained as course instructors for internal training. These trainers then develop their own training package best suited to their team's needs. In some organizations, the process starts at the top (Bertsch and Williams, no date). The CEO who is trained first, trains managers who report to him or her, and who in turn teach their immediate staff and so forth.

By accepting responsibility for, and conducting training courses themselves, managers are seen as visible supporters and get buy-in from their "students". Training will have more impact as a result as employees, seeing that management is committed, will also be more willing to get involved. In the process, managers also develop self-discipline and expertise in promoting TQM within the organization (Kanji and Asher, 1993).

GPT Ltd UK call such training "family group training" (Cashbourne, 1991). The majority of its training workshops were designed and run by line managers. The cascading approach was used at Ilford Ltd to great effect (Hunt and Hillman, 1990). A top management committee delivered the training, starting with themselves and followed by the next level. This level then trained their reporting managers. At Southern Pacific Lines, internal staff deliver most of the formal quality training for the company's 23,000 employees (Carman, 1993). Rank Xerox Limited, whose first line managers also worked with their staff during training, sees the line management ownership of the training process as critical to effective continuing implementation (Wright, 1988).

In some TQ organizations, however, training is led by employees who are recognised by the management as having particular inter-personal skills. This is done without reducing or compromising the role of the work group leader in any way. At LeaRonal UK, training achieved a high degree of success using dedicated in-house trainers (Smith, 1994).

Before they develop tailor-made training packages, some organizations start by using training materials put together by external consultants, gradually reducing their involvement. BP Chemicals UK started by using the Crosby programme (Stark, 1990). While they retained Crosby's key principles and philosophy, the training materials were now their own. After getting training help externally in the initial years, Paul Revere Insurance Group has now taken responsibility for its own training (Bank, 1992). At Shorts Brothers, the training was initially consultant-led (Oakland and Porter, 1994). In the later stages, the employees took ownership of all courses. The three organizations view the ownership of the training process as an important factor in their quality initiatives.

In almost all the 20 best companies surveyed in the USA, Europe and the Far East, Bertsch and Williams (no date) found that quality trainings are frequently conducted by line managers with consultants used sparingly and with specific short-term assignments. The use of cascade systems is common.

In TQ organizations, most employees receive a substantial amount of annual training. Employees of Baldrige applicants receive 40 to 80 hours of training per year (Easton, 1993). At Grundos, an average of 4 per cent of employees' working time is devoted to training (Binney, 1992). In terms of training expenditures, top US organizations, Baldrige applicants included, commit 2-5 per cent of total corporate payroll.

In the USA, several top companies, in recognising the importance of training and education, have come together to form a co-operative venture to identify training's best practices and generate comparative data to set a standard for their individual efforts. The American Society for Training and Development's Benchmarking Forum is represented by 37 companies, and includes many Baldrige winners. One of their motives is a desire to learn how to adopt or adapt training practices that clearly provide a competitive advantage (Kimmerling, 1993).

Rao *et al.* (1996) state that training typically covers problem-solving techniques, problem analysis, statistical processes, quality measurement, organizational diagnosis, group processes and decision making. Zhang *et al.* (2000) assert that all management personnel, supervisors and employees should accept education and training. This would typically include quality awareness education and quality management methods.

According to a survey conducted by the Conference Board (Ross, 1999), top management commonly addresses the following topics in quality training:

- quality awareness;
- quality measurement (performance measures, quality-cost benchmarking, data analysis);
- process management and defect prevention;
- team building and quality circle training;
- focus on customers and markets; and
- statistics and statistical methods.

Benefits from training and education

Investment in training is at a high level for companies integrating or linking business results and people management. Since 1989, Trident Precision Manufacturing Inc. has invested an average of 4.4 per cent of the company payroll on education and training. This level of training investment is "three times above the average for all US industries" (*The X Factor Executive Report*, 1999). Currently 80 per cent of Trident employees received training in at least two job functions to encourage diversification of employee abilities (Bemowski's study, cited in *The X Factor Executive Report*, 1999). For Trident, the benefits from training include:
- an increase in sales volume from £4.4 million in 1988 to £14.3 million in 1995;
- never losing a customer during 18 years of business; and
- a dramatic decline in employee turnover (*The X Factor Executive Report*, 1999).

Deming notes that in Japanese organizations of the 1950s, "entry-level managers spend 4 to 12 years on the factory floor and in other activities to learn the aspects of production" (Evans and Lindsay, 2001). From Deming's training perspective, all organization members needed training in problem solving and mastery of appropriate statistical tasks. Honda of America requires that all employees, no matter their job classification, start out on the production floor. People improvement comes through comprehensive, continuous, effective training.

Not only does training result in improvements in quality and productivity, but it adds to worker morale, and demonstrates to workers that the company is dedicated to helping them and investing in their future. In addition, training reduces barriers between workers and supervisors, giving both more incentive to improve further. (Evans and Lindsay, 2001).

Rewards and recognition

Drawing a conclusion based on best practices of quality leaders in the USA, Europe and Japan, Johnston and Daniel (1991) cited rewards and recognition as one of the enablers which maximises employees' potential and involvement and, in doing so, becomes one of the main contributors to the company's journey to quality. A study which focused on 86 major corporations found that best practice units within these organizations used rewards as incentives to advance their TQM process (*Quality Progress*, 1994). According to Easton (1993), the practice of providing an employee recognition scheme for quality is widespread amongst Baldrige applicants.

Crosby (1989) considers recognition as one of the most important steps of the quality improvement process. Many other authors also talk about recognition and rewards as being part and parcel of a well-defined quality process (Haksever, 1996; Townsend and Gebhardt, 1992; Stark, 1990; Johnston and Daniel, 1991; Titman and Callum, 1991; Eastman, 1993; Cullen and Hollingum, 1987; Binney, 1992). In best organizations, rewards and recognition are linked to sustaining the appropriate behaviour (Bertsch and Williams, no date; Williams *et al.*, 1993).

Titman and Callum (1991), in discussing the experience of Exxon Chemicals Ltd UK, see reward and recognition as an essential element of the TQ process and a prerequisite to achieving and maintaining a corporate culture which embraces the TQ process. Rank Xerox Ltd identified recognition as one of the major areas of change to be leveraged within its quality initiative strategy (Smith, 1994). At IBM UK Ltd's Havant site, it is generally recognised that the company's recognition programme has played a major part in the overall success of the site's quality initiative (Kyte, 1991). The emphasis on recognition of its employees' contributions and achievements is a special feature of the TQ initiative at Hartford Insurance Group (Cullen and Hollingum, 1987). When the enthusiasm of its employees of the TQ work faded after two years, top management at Ciba-Geigy Italy rekindled their enthusiasm by rethinking the reward system to include quality objectives (Binney, 1992).

At Exxon Chemical Ltd UK both reward and recognition systems are in place. The reward mechanism comprises an across-the-board salary increment and individual merit awards. Those whose behaviour is in line with company business needs are made known to management and encouraged. Individuals who succeed in establishing the desired behaviour and results are provided with higher benefits.

As the individual reward mechanism gives little external recognition, the company provides a channel for more public recognition through the rewards of teams. The annual presentation of the President's Awards are for outstanding and exemplary achievement in certain well-defined areas, including TQ. There are no direct financial rewards. However, winners are accorded world-wide publicity through company news bulletins.

Rewards do not have to be monetary (Haksever, 1996). Employees are motivated by different things and organizations need to ascertain in each case what these are. Paul Revere Insurance Group designed its recognition awards for successful ideas from quality teams along the lines of Olympic medals, i.e. bronze, silver and gold lapel pin medals. Employees attach value to, and proudly wear, them (Bank, 1992). Employees at Florida Power & Light Company wanted as recognition the full implementation of their improvement suggestions (Johnston and Daniel, 1991).

It is also important that employees perceive that the achievement of the goals tied to rewards and recognition is within their power. A system in which employees cannot have direct impact on the achievement of the goals will cause frustration and a lack of identification with the goals (Johnston and Daniel, 1991). On a similar note, Titman and Callum (1991) stress the importance of clear communication as a tool to support the reward mechanism, i.e. employees need to know what is expected of them, what it is that they are trying to achieve and why they are trying to achieve it. Rewards and recognition schemes must continually evolve to meet the organization's changing needs.

Offering rewards that employees fail to attach value to is unlikely to have a positive effect on them, and is an inefficient use of resources. Therefore, the implication is that motivation schemes should be designed in such a way that, at the changing career stages, the focus should especially be on jobs that are designed to augment internally-mediated rewards (Twomey and Twomey, 1998). These would be consistent with feelings of accomplishment in terms of increasing profitability, market share and reducing costs for the company, as well as recognition and respect from peers and superiors (Kastetter, 1999).

Teamwork

One step by 100 persons is better than 100 steps by one person (Koichi Tsukamoto, President, Wascoal Corporation, Japan cited in Clemmer, 1990).

Teamwork is a critical element of TQM (Kanji and Asher, 1993; Crosby, 1989; Creech, 1994; Clemmer, 1993; Aune, 1991; Bank, 1992; Manz and Sims, 1993). Teamwork promotes a bottom-up thrust for quality improvement (Heath, 1989) and delivers synergistic enhancement of quality efforts (Bank, 1992).

Successful organizations are run with teams – for solving problems, for improving quality, for introducing new processes and products (Hoevemeyer, 1993). Compared to employees who work individually, effective teams tend to have higher morale and productivity, and take pride in the job and the company. A 1991 Conference Board study (Olian and Rynes, 1991) found the formation of teams working together for continuous improvement to be the single most commonly-employed TQM implementation tactic amongst 158 companies. In Japan, teams are a fundamental component of the management system (Garvin, 1983). Perlman and Zacharias (1991) say that in many organizations, one of the greatest barriers to TQM is the territorialism that has evolved over many years.

At Southern Pacific Lines, there is a strong emphasis on teamwork. It was in fact made clear at the outset that the quality process would survive only if the employees could form themselves into teams. There are now over 890 teams, of which 25 percent are cross-functional (Carman, 1993).

The importance of active participation by every employee and a team approach was recognised as vital at an early stage of implementation at Tioxide

Group Ltd (Oakland and Porter, 1994). At IBM UK Ltd's Havant site, the success of its quality "programme" is due to each and every one of its employees working as a team (Kyte, 1991). Teamwork is one of the guiding principles of total quality at BMA Pie in the USA (Powers, 1994). At STC Cables Products UK, the team approach is seen to create an environment where employee involvement is maximised, morale improved and job satisfaction increased (Davies and Wilson, 1990). At Rank Xerox, people from all levels come together to share ideas and best practices in an effort to innovate and continuously improve business processes.

Teamworking and the breaking down of functional barriers were given great emphasis in Ilford Ltd's quality initiatives (Hunt and Hillman, 1990). This helped to underpin a total company approach rather than allow initiatives to become too functionalised. At the heart of Eastman Chemical Company's quality is the interlocking team structure (Bemowski, 1994). This structure starts with a team composed of Eastman's president and the vice presidents who report to him. Each vice president then forms a team with his or her reports. This continues all the way down the organization until, essentially, all 17,750 employees are involved in teams. With this structure, teamwork is improved and information flows both up and down the organization.

Employees who involve themselves in quality group activities are also more convinced of the benefits of the quality process. The findings for a survey carried out among employees at two Hewlett-Packard factories in the UK showed that the degree of buy-in among the survey respondents was favourable with those who were part of a quality team (Barker, 1991).

In pursuit of teamwork, some organizations set up formal team systems. Such systems can play a major role in promoting employee involvement – one of the cornerstones of TQM. Florida Power & Light Company which maintains a team process improvement system saw a significant involvement of its employees in the quality process as a result (Johnston and Daniel, 1991).

There are typically two types of formal team systems. One of these is the natural, or functional, team which usually focuses on the regular daily work processes, and involves a voluntary problem-solving group made up of workers in the same work area. The quality circle is an example of a voluntary work area team. Organizations attempting to foster a teamwork ethic may find this type of team allows discrete pilot development (Lawler and Mohrman, 1985). Given its existence across a wide range of industries, including the public sector since the 1970s, the opportunity for learning from the experiences of others are also plentiful.

Although functional teams help towards the improvement of teamwork within local work areas, working within functional boundaries keeps individuals and groups isolated and reinforces pre-conceptions (Hirschhorn and Gilmore, 1992; Kordupleski, 1993). This may create resistance to integration within organizations and thus hamper the creation of a total quality culture.

Best organization such as Xerox Canada and General Electric are blurring functional boundaries to integrate all players across the organization to work together as a team towards greater accomplishments in the organization's quality journey (Hirschhorn and Gilmore, 1992). Organizations are linking together traditional functions by forming a second type of team system – cross-functional teams. Price and Chen (1993) believe that a properly managed cross-functional team system can assist in scaling down organizational boundaries to satisfy the customer (Oakland, 1993). According to National Westminster Bank plc UK cross-functional teams are important in the design of quality delivery service (Goodstadt, 1990).

Getting employees together in groups does not guarantee a successful outcome (Cashbourne, 1991). Members need to work effectively as a team. Organizations keen to promote integration through teams create an enabling system which promotes teamwork and eliminates barriers to successful performance. Florida Power & Light Company employees are trained on how to work in teams, and have officially been given the responsibility and authority to form natural teams as they see fit (Johnston and Daniel, 1991).

Team activity represents the principal source of process improvement. The significance of teams rests on the fact that they provide opportunities to individuals to solve problems that they may not be able to solve on their own (Evans and Lindsay 2001). Furthermore, teams perform a variety of problem-solving activities, such as determining customer needs, developing a flowchart to study a process, process analysis and documentation, process stabilisation, brainstorming to discover improvement opportunities, selecting projects, recommending corrective actions, and tracking the effectiveness of the solutions. In this connection, Zhang *et al.* (2000) advise resorting to measures such as cross-functional teams, within functional teams, quality control circles, voluntary teams and suggestion activities, for encouraging employee participation. Teamwork is defined as the engine that drives many improvement efforts and the following key elements for successful teambuilding are suggested:

- facilitate team development and activity;
- guide teams in employing a systematic approach to improvement;
- create cross-functional teams for cross-functional purposes;
- work at everyone becoming part of an improvement team;
- support and reinforce team behaviour and performance; and
- ensure the process improvement teams are linked vertically and horizontally into the organization.

Teams should be the basic unit of performance for most organizations because they represent a combination of multiple skills, experiences and judgements. This point has been consolidated by Hoevemeyer (1993), who states that successful organizations are run with teams for solving problems, improving quality, and for introducing new processes and products. Compared to employees who work individually, effective teams tend to have higher morale and productivity and take pride in the job and the company (Thiagaragan and Zairi, 1997). Shapiro (1995) argues that teamwork could be viewed and interpreted as the collaborative activity of individuals and co-operative interactions within the group. In this respect, Heath (1989) points out that commitment, support, trust and satisfaction are key elements for establishing a sound environment for teambuilding. Creating teams allows organizations to apply diverse skills and experiences toward their processes and problem solving. According to Longenecker and Scazzero (1994), the process of team goal setting, feedback and problem solving can be a useful tool assisting an individual manager in his/her efforts at quality improvement. Tan (1997) identifies five reasons why teams are successful, namely:

1. *Flexibility*: as teams are easier to assemble, deploy, refocus and disband.
2. *Commitment*: teams with commitment to clear objectives produce excellent results.
3. *Synergistic response to challenge*: complementary skills and experiences enable teams to respond synergistically to challenges changing events and demands.
4. *Enhance work*: teams help members to overcome barriers and establish confidence; this reinforces the intention of each team to achieve its goal and develop satisfaction.
5. *Focus*: teams help members to develop a shared sense of direction.

Scholtes (1995) suggests other key elements for team building, namely: teams must support customers, systems and improvements; and they must not only support the system, but they must also be a system.

In a field experiment on quality improvement through team goal setting, feedback and problem solving, Longenecker and Scazzero (1994) conclude that when a manager of a production cell sets up quality problem-solving teams to respond to defect rate problems, he receives not only quicker response times but better decision making and more rapid implementation of solutions. In this respect, effective teams can be a potent force to ease the pressure traditional managers experience to fix quality problems themselves or with the assistance of engineers alone.

According to Evans and Lindsay (2001), the central role of teams and the needs for such team skills as co-operation, inter-temporal communications, cross-training, and group decision making, represent a fundamental shift in how the work of organizations is performed in the USA and most countries in the Western world. An ASQC/Gallup telephone survey of 1,293 randomly selected full-time employees in 1993 reported the prevalence and impact of teamwork (Rayan, 1993). Eight out of ten employees reported that some type of team activity is taking place at work and two out of three employees participated in team activities.

The concept of teamwork in quality has been developed and refined through quality circles in Japan and evolved into powerful self-managed teams today. Quality circles, which are defined as small groups of employees from the same work area, were instituted in Japan in the early 1960s and then taken to the USA in the early 1970s (Evans and Lindsay, 2001). In Japan, the rapid push for quality became a national priority and the results were dramatic. Such efforts of quality improvement as well as the cultural bias toward group activity resulted in the formation of the quality control circle, attributed to Dr Kaoru Ishikawa. A fundamental difference in quality circles is whether they include specific problem-solving training.

The Western approach to quality circles moved towards improvement of employee satisfaction and communications (Luzon, 1988). According to Evans and Lindsay (2001), the quality of work-life programmes developed in the early 1960s was related to circle concepts but tended to emphasise behavioural interventions, re-organization of groups or tasks, or efforts to build or enhance morale. Ross (1999) argues that a useful way of conceptualising the role of teamworking in quality strategies is to consider how it relates to "employee empowerment".

At ADAC laboratories, most workers participate in highly empowered function and/or process teams, and all manufacturing employees are members of self-directed teams. Throughout the course of a year, every ADAC employee is on at least one team (George and Weimerskirch 1998).

The University of Michigan Medical Admission Department was receiving many complaints. The Director of Admission set up a team consisting of housekeepers, nurses, admission clerks and members of the transport department. Using TQM tools, the team made several recommendations, which when implemented, led to the mean number of complaints per month falling from 37.3 to 1.5 in one year (Rao et al., 1996).

The role of employee unions
There is a lot of debate on the role of employee unions within the concept of employee involvement. For the unions, past experiences of management "productivity" initiatives to turn around the organizations had often resulted in job losses and redundancies. Productivity and efficiency are thus not positive words for them to support new initiatives in whatever form.

Some hold the view that if an organization is substantially unionised, management must take the initiative to encourage union involvement. It is recognised that because most unions exert influence at the grassroots level –where quality must become an uncontentious way of life – some form of workable partnership is needed for TQM to succeed. Glover (1993) also stressed the importance of keeping the union informed and involved in what the organization is doing with the TQM transformation process.

At the outset of the implementation of the quality process, the management at Shorts Brothers was very aware that one of the potential barriers to progress was trade union resistance. However, by involving the trade union at the early stages and in discussing the objectives of the initiatives, resistance was avoided (Oakland and Porter, 1994).

Southern Pacific Lines also involved the unions in its quality initiative from the very beginning with much success. Union officers were briefed on the poor economic and performance status of the company and asked to discuss the plan with the local people and participate in the TQ process. In fact, the union leaders knew about the strategy before middle and lower managers (Carman, 1993). At Rover Cars, its total quality improvement initiative yielded significant gains in performance with the support and co-operation of the unions (Rose and Woolley, 1992).

While the above organizations would agree wholeheartedly on the importance of union involvement in the TQM initiative, Ciba-Geigy Italy is one organization that felt unions should be kept at arm's length in the corporate TQM projects (Binney, 1992). It believed that this would enable the management to establish a stronger direct line of control and communication to the shopfloor, which is vital to effective TQ process. Its TQM initiative was started without union involvement. In fact, when the union asked to be included, the company refused.

The structure of collective bargaining occupies a central position in the debate on the effectiveness of any industrial relations system (Clarke, 1998). It is posited that the structure of collective bargaining exerts an important influence on the local autonomy of both management and employees, and the pattern of strikes and pay outcomes. For some managers, depending on their ideology and style of management, multi-employer bargaining has a further advantage in that it can "neutralise" or, at the very least, minimise workplace trade unionism. However much workers and trade unions might seek to improve the terms of the labour contract and to strengthen their legal rights, the legal codification of the employment relation in contractual form has almost universally been seen as providing a minimum guarantee of the rights and interests of labour (Bratton, 2001).

This understanding has defined the framework within which trade unionism has become institutionalised within developed capitalism, and the basis of the separation of the trade union from the political functions of the movement (Sawchuk, 2001). Trade unions negotiate with employers within the framework of the law, while organizing politically to lobby for legislative improvements (Small and Yasin, 2000). The separation and complementarity of these two functions rests on the effective rule of law. There is no point in the trade union either negotiating a contract or lobbying for changes in legislation if the law is systematically disregarded (Tith, 1998). In the absence of the rule of law, the inevitable conflict between employer and employee can only be resolved by the threat or the use of force. The establishment of the rule of law is, therefore, an essential condition for the development of effective trade unionism (Floyd *et al.*, 1999).

Trade unions as a part of the democratic movement, sought to develop "civilised" forms of trade unionism, formally eschewing politics and negotiating directly with employers on behalf of their members (Sawchuk, 2001). The trade unions lacked the institutional and financial resources of the former official unions, but sought to build up membership by supporting rank-and-file action against employers, particularly through the provision of legal advice and representation of small groups of workers in the courts. This was an extremely time consuming and costly process, requiring frequent appeals (Small and Yasin, 2000).

Although the formal mechanisms of collective bargaining, labour contracts and tripartite collaboration have been installed, and the independence of the judiciary has notionally been guaranteed, it has proved very difficult for trade unions to adapt to the new role (Tith, 1998). The former official trade unions have been in no hurry to adapt, and while the labour legislation, constitutional provisions and international conventions are systematically violated with impunity by employers and by the government, then the essential framework for the development of trade unionism is absent (Gruenberg, 1998).

Chapter 10
Policy and strategy

Deployment provides for communication both up and down the hierarchy. It also provides the lower levels with the opportunity to participate in the planning process (J.M. Juran).

The quality policy imperative
It is clearly evident that successfully implementing TQM in any organization requires the alignment of every member's efforts with the aim of the organization (Olian and Rynes, 1991). Deming (1986) through his first point, "strive for consistency of purpose", stresses the need to link quality efforts within an organization to a larger sense of corporate purpose. Crosby (1979) explains that the quality policy must be given the same emphasis as the financial policy and is the responsibility of top executives. Mitel Telecom Ltd UK views the publishing of its quality policy as the first evidence of its commitment to quality improvement (Boyer,, 1991). Carman (1993) in relating the experience of Southern Pacific Lines in implementing continuous quality improvement emphasised that a strong and clear leadership statement of mission and strategy is essential. This statement must make clear that quality is the strategy.

Although most organizations have sophisticated planning processes, many strategies fail to deliver because "what is planned and what is implemented are not the same" (Zairi, 1995). This contention is supported by Easton (1993):

> The (strategic quality) plans generally stop at setting goals and objectives and developing budget. They do not realistically address implementation issues or deployment of the plan throughout the organization. Even in companies with a fairly well-developed planning process, failure to realistically consider implementation issues is common and is a key reason the planning process is ineffective.

Articulating goals and communicating the vision
This is not surprising as policy deployment and implementation are generally acknowledged as difficult processes (Groocock, 1986). A study of strategic development and implementation found that 73 per cent of managers believed that implementation was more difficult than development (Zairi, 1994). Zairi (1995) views the problem as being due to strategies often undergoing frequent changes and causing misalignment and disruption in performance. Failure to address this fundamental link was attributed to ICL Product Distribution (Binney, 1992) and GPT Ltd UK (Cashbourne, 1991) who had little success with their quality initiatives in the early years.

However, best organizations such as Procter and Gamble, NEC Japan, Komatsu, Unilever Personal Products, Hewlett-Packard, Rank Xerox and Florida Power & Light attained much success in developing, communicating and reviewing strategic plans at levels within their organizations by using a structured strategic planning process. This is sometimes termed quality policy deployment (Bemowski, 1992; Johnston and Daniel, 1991; Smith, 1994; Zairi, 1994) and is defined by Rank Xerox as:

> A key process which Rank Xerox can articulate and communicate the vision, mission, goals and vital few programmes to all employees. It provides answers to the two questions. What do we need to do? And How are we going to do it? (Zairi, 1994).

At NEC Japan, the quality policy deployment process (called *hoshin kanri*) starts with the chief executive first setting the long-term policy in line with the aims and philosophy of the corporation (Smith, 1994). This is done after full discussion with his senior managers and when consensus is achieved. Out of this, a few strategic factors (*kanri*) that will give the corporation an edge in the marketplace are created. The long-term plan is then divided down into medium and short-term objectives. This is handed down the line and debated with the three levels involved, thus overlapping discussions. This will go up and down and across the lines until the plan has a shape and everyone understands and agrees to it. The strategic aims generally stay intact – the debate is mostly about how to achieve them and the acceptance of responsibilities.

At Rank Xerox, the process is also deployed in a top down fashion, with active participation at all levels (Zairi, 1994). In order to gain organization-wide commitment, a "catchball" technique is used. The technique is similar to NEC Japan's whereby through negotiation at all levels, across levels and across departments using hard data and facts "thrown" at each other, goals are accepted and everyone is committed to delivering them. At Thomas Cork SML, the board directors and senior management had a joint meeting to reach consensus on the two sets of company's policy and objectives drawn by each group (Oakland and Porter, 1994).

Developing action plans

The next step of policy deployment is taking the defined corporate focus and converting it into action with targets within every department and at every level of the organization. Smith (1994) sees this step as "a key way of locking the quality process into the management process; making linkages from a five or ten year vision into daily actions". Johnston and Daniel (1991) explain how corporate objectives are translated into meaningful ones and cascaded down the levels at Suntory Brewery in Japan:

> The policy deployment process forces the organization to develop plans for action ... after the plant manager announces his policy,

section managers set targets. Supervisors then set targets for each group and individual operators defines their role, targets and plans of action.

At Rank Xerox, with the company's objective defined, each director identifies a list of actions to meet his objective. These are then cascaded down the organization, with each level agreeing their own list of actions. At the end of the cascade, all its 28,000 employees have personal objectives (Smith, 1994).

An important element of QPD is the regular monitoring of progress and performance checks to ensure that goals are still achievable (Johnston and Daniel, 1991). At NEC Japan, the *kanri* element ensures that progress to goals is monitored (Smith, 1994). Annual presidential audits are conducted to check if the plan is on schedule, and regular checks on progress at all levels are made before the president's audit. Changes are made whenever necessary. At the Soap Sector of Procter and Gamble, management reviews are conducted for the purposes of ensuring the quality of results, assessing strengths and weaknesses and ensuring that there is goal congruence and total alignment within the company (Zairi, 1994).

Johnston and Daniel (1991) reported that Deming Award winning organizations also continuously standardise or modify processes based on the results of the review. The actual results, and the processes used to achieve them, become input for the planning phase the following year.

Making policy deployment a driver for continuous improvement
While the subject on strategic quality planning in organizations is not widely discussed in the literature, unlike many other topics of TQM, what is reported generally tends to give a good degree of indication of how best organizations achieve success, namely, they ensure that it:
- is a corporate-wide process;
- focuses on the vital few;
- builds contributions from all levels into the planning;
- approaches deployment through consensus;
- is accessible to everyone and open to challenge;
- ensures everyone understands and is committed to it; and
- keeps it a live document by regular review and adjustment.

An increasing number of organizations, as part of a strategic planning approach to continuous improvement, are starting to use policy deployment, suggested by Lee and Dale (1998). In Western organizations, the interest in policy deployment has primarily been generated by the use of self-assessment against a recognised model for business excellence, such as the European Foundation for Quality Management model and Malcolm Baldrige National Quality Award (Watson, 1998). The bodies of knowledge of strategy formulation and TQM have been dominated by contributions from different disciplines: business policy and industrial engineering/production management, respectively. As a result, the management literature has treated strategy formulation and TQM as distinct, separate organizational processes (Gouvea *et al.*, 2001). In the pursuit of strategic quality management, managers require a system to develop policy, communicate, allocate resources, focus and align actions, and control corporate drift. Although there are many ways in which to plan (i.e. formal strategic planning, issue-based planning, and strategic assumption analysis and dialectic inquiry), they are all fraught with difficulties and often charged with bureaucracy, short-termism, and failure to adapt to changes. Policy deployment helps create cohesiveness within a business that is understood throughout the company; it provides a structure with which to identify clear organizational goals. In recent years, policy deployment has been a topic in which organizations have shown an increasing interest, but it is still not a well-known technique in many companies (Civi, 2000).

Policy deployment and strategic planning are fundamental to TQM. They are the ways to align all efforts in the company towards its major goals (Rees, 1998). Policy deployment connects TQM to the strategic planning process and is fundamental to the success of TQM. Strategic planning is considered by many organizations as a necessary business tool, but after considerable effort and much budgetary commitment, the strategic plan is filed and never used. There are five reasons why strategic plans fail:

1. Daily management not distinct from breakthrough objectives.
2. Vague mission/value and weak organization linkage.
3. Vague vision/strategic intent and weak organizational linkage.
4. Lack of data analysis during plan creation.
5. Lack of periodic review and process improvement (Lee and Dale, 1998).

Policy deployment offers a planning process which can respond to and resolve these issues, and ensure that the policy and the plan remain alive and vibrant. For instance, management by policy deployment is characterised by the purposes of the organization, the principles that guide actions, a vision of where the firm is going, the objectives that move the firm toward its vision, the priorities assigned to the objectives, and an action plan in which everyone participates (Civi, 2000). Policy deployment and strategic planning help to reshape the corporate objective-setting process to conform to customers' needs (Southern, 2001). They are processes of developing plans, targets, controls and areas for improvement based on the previous level's policy and an assessment of the previous year's performance. The concept of policy deployment as providing a bridge between the corporate "plan" and the "do" steps in continuous improvement is re-emphasised as the process embraces the concept of empowerment as a balance between alignment of activities to the goals and the freedom people have to take action. The ultimate purpose of this process is to empower people to make meaningful improvement.

Policy deployment works on two levels to manage continuous improvement and achieve business results: strategic objectives and daily control of the business (Drew, 1998). There is a four-step policy deployment process:

1. Prepare the organization to create policies that will change the way it does business.
2. Create the plan, using input from key customers and managers from the organization's key activities.
3. Deploy the policies through a schedule of regular updates and follow-up, and by committing resources to ensure accomplishment of the goals and objectives.
4. Revisit the first three steps during the annual review to ensure continuous improvement of the process.

These simple steps belie the complexity of the real process, and fail to emphasise that the daily control of activities is the foundation of policy deployment, pinpointing performance strengths and weaknesses (Pitt, 1999).

The principles of policy deployment can be summarised as focus on processes, not results; founded on daily control; goals based on customer needs; thorough analysis of previous stage; top-down, bottom-up planning; catchball between layers of organization; objectives aligned throughout the organization to achieve common goals; all members of the organization are responsible for the process leading to the results; focus on a small number of breakthrough items; widespread understanding of TQM; means deployed with targets; regular review mechanism, focus on corrective action; and dynamic, flexible, never-ending improvement (Lee and Dale, 1998). In terms of benefits, policy deployment helps create cohesiveness within an organization and provides a consensus on the company objectives at all levels, brings into focus a vision of the future of the organization, integrates and orchestrates the efforts of all within an organization into actions that move the entire organization towards its objectives; creates and establishes process to execute breakthrough year after year; creates commitment to both the direction and implementation paths chosen; increases interdepartmental co-operation; draws on and reinforces the cycle in monthly progress reviews; creates a planning and implementation system that is responsive, flexible, yet disciplined; gives leadership a mechanism to understand the key problem areas in a company, and facilitate prioritisation; creates quicker and more accurate feedback loops, and by means of the catchball process, it provides optimum communication both between levels and departments concerned (Anderson *et al.*, 2001).

Chapter 11
Resource management

[on the important of the supplier to the customer] An over-riding criterion is the supplier's burning desire to work with the customer on a long-term relationship backed up by a demonstratable store of specialized knowledge, with management that is trying to adopt the new philosophy (W.E. Deming).

The importance of resource management

The significance of resource management undoubtedly deserves more attention. Cornford (2001) argues that resource management can be analysed in two sections. First, regarding communication management and supplier management, he suggests that local resources are important in the day-to-day work of people in higher education. Second, he also stresses the role of local information resources, arguing that there are six roles: "grey" information specific to the discipline or field of study or research, departmental or central contacts lists, locally-produced materials information about locally-based research projects, information about events (seminars, workshops and lectures), and room and equipment booking information. Regarding organizing local information, paper information could be transferred to a database connected to a Web server so that information is available at the desktop. In the case of locally-produced materials, these can be easily stored in electronic form. In other cases, it may not be appropriate or cost effective to transfer information to an electronic format. Therefore, local information remains important to the day-to-day activities of most people working and studying in higher education. Capturing, organizing and sharing it, whether locally or more widely, and integrating it with material from further afield add a further dimension to the notion of the hybrid library.

The importance of knowledge management

McAdam and Reid (2000) suggest that knowledge management is an emergent and eclectic body of knowledge, which covers the systematic management of knowledge of all kinds, within all levels and types of organizations. The relative newness of the area of a management philosophy has resulted in most research and practical application studies being based in large private sector organizations. There is relatively little information on knowledge in the private sector, and even less on private-public sector knowledge management comparisons. They compare the perceptions of both private and public sector organizations in regard to knowledge management to improve overall understanding and to develop sector-specific learning (Fernandez et al., 2001). They mention three points: first, the key dimensions of knowledge management are identified using a developed knowledge management model. Second, a survey of public and private sector organizations is used to investigate perceptions of the knowledge management dimensions. Third, there are a series of qualitative social constructionist workshops, involving both private and public sector organizations, which were run to gain a deeper insight into sectoral comparisons. It is found that knowledge management was more developed as a management philosophy in the public sector. This development has been caused by continual pressure for increased efficiency, reduced resources, and improved quality within the public sector (Szwejczewski *et al.*, 2001).

Communicating for quality
The need for continuous quality improvement must be conveyed effectively and regularly if TQM is to take root and be sustained (Smith, 1994; Oakland, 1993). Kanji and Asher (1993) are most forthright about the need for effective communication for the development of awareness of, and commitment to, quality in an organization's environment:

> Communication is part of the cement that holds together the bricks of the total quality process supporting the principle of people-based management.

Best organizations also recognise that communication could make the difference between success and failure. They see effective communication as a means to maintain enthusiasm for quality initiatives within the organization. At IBM UK Ltd Havant, communication, along with management direction, was identified as most important if the quality process was to succeed (Kyte, 1991). At ICL Product Distribution UK, various modes of communication were used in an effort to motivate staff and increase understanding of the role that everyone could play in improving quality (Binney, 1992). At Ciba-Geigy Italy, a comprehensive communication campaign was launched to support the TQ initiative. A special feature of the TQ initiatives at Hartford Insurance Group is the emphasis on communications up and down the hierarchy and between departments (Cullen and Hollingum, 1987).

Effective communication is vital in aligning the workforce towards corporate expectations. Leaders of Grundos of Denmark believe that effective communication brings out the best in people:

> The key is to keep people as informed as possible. People want to do things right. It's up to management to give them the chance to do so (Binney, 1992).

Unclear and inconsistent communication results in employees, front-line and middle managers focusing on priorities which have little or no relevance to the organizational focus (Williams *et al.*, 1993). Smith (1994), in citing the experience of Elida Gibbs in Belgium, also warns that poor communication can lead to loss in momentum in the quality drive.

Typically, best organizations tend to use a wide range of techniques to communicate. At Ciba-Geigy Italy, management briefings are held regularly in an effort to develop commitment to quality, supported by posters, brochures and notice boards all emphasising the need for quality improvement. The company even used its suggestion scheme to improve communication and inter-departmental understanding by requiring that suggestions had to be outside the person's own area of work. IBM UK Ltd in Havant even set up a communication department to keep everyone informed of quality activities (Kyte, 1991). In ICL Product Distribution UK, posters and slogans were used in the effort to motivate staff and increase understanding of the role that everyone could play in improving quality. Measurement charts dealing with customer service levels, process improvement and personal and departmental performance were widely maintained and displayed (Binney, 1992).

Many TQ organizations have realised that over and above the usual array of newsletters, memos and bulletins, personal communication needs to be emphasised (Bertsch and Williams, no date). Smith (1994) says that there is no real substitute for direct contact.

A survey of 158 US companies in Fortune 1000 concluded that not only do they emphasis top down communication, but also increase bottom-up and lateral communications (Olian and Rynes, 1991). The need to develop channels to receive feedback from workers is also stressed by many writers. Employees need ways to present ideas, vent their feelings and voice their opinions.

Open, two-way communication also helps foster good relationship between management and employees, which is vital if quality is to be an integral part of "business as usual". British Airways has a programme whereby, in a public form, the CEO answers questions that have been previously submitted by the staff (Binney, 1992). Bertsch and Williams (no date) also reported that top managers in 20 best companies in the USA, Europe and the Far East make a point of personally interacting with staff at various levels. Regular luncheon meetings where CEOs discussed quality matters with a cross-section of the staff are common in Philips Signetics and Bekaert in Belgium. The CEO of Philips Electronics conducts question and answer sessions about the company's TQM process with all his employees in 18 European countries via TV-satellite connection. Crosby (1989) also talks about TQ organizations having communication systems that utilise in-house TV circuits, and satellite transmission to ensure that the communication linkage is maintained.

Nissan UK, on the other hand, does not rely on corporate videos, in-house news bulletins or notice boards for communication with its staff. Its supervisors are the channel for all communication to manufacturing staff. At the start of every shift, each has a five minute meeting with his team (Ashton, 1992).

Lateral communication or communication across the organization is vital if the customer is to be continuously satisfied. Digital has a world-wide system called "Notes" which literally allows any one of 100,000 Digital employees to talk to anyone else and obtain information on any subject (Smith, 1994).

166

The literature also highlights the fact that clear and effective communication is also vital to support other quality initiatives such as performance-related reward mechanism and training (Titman and Callum, 1991). In the former case, for example, the appraiser needs to communicate to the employee what is expected of him or her, and why it is important. Having in place a feedback mechanism from training course attendees is useful to monitor carefully and improve the quality of subsequent events.

Communication is vital in the empowerment process. If employees are to share the decision making in the company, they must know and understand company objectives and values, and have access to the information relevant to their area of responsibility. British Steel communicates to its employees the results of all customer surveys, highlighting both positive and negative comments. It has monthly newsletters, and even mails relevant information to employees' houses (Johnston and Daniel, 1991). British Airways has a programme whereby, in a public forum, the CEO answers questions that have been previously submitted by the staff (Johnston and Daniel, 1991).

Communication between managers and workers is critical to TQM implementation. TQM can be sabotaged when bureaucratic barriers combine with management misunderstanding of what TQM needs if it is to function. If communication fails, TQM fails, and this is more likely to happen when management, individuals or factions are not bought into the process (Ross, 1999).

Communication of TQM from top management to organization members and the communication of commitments are "inextricably linked in the quality process" (Ross, 1999). Management may have difficulty in communicating this in an understandable way, or the filtering process down through the ranks of management may create distortion so that the plan and vision lose clarity and momentum. Information critical to TQM requires encoding according to organization-wide agreement and commitment so that quality is precisely defined and implementation measures are agreed on (Ross, 1999).

Spechler (1993) identified four virtues for consideration in developing communication for quality. The plan should:

- convey to all that quality is a team effort;
- establish recognition for quality achievement;
- provide information to all about both long-term and short-term quality goals and initiatives; and
- create shared understanding and language for quality.

Kanji and Asher (1993) emphasise that effective communication is needed for the development and awareness of quality, and for commitment to it as part of the organization's environment.

Open, two-way communication also helps foster good relationships between management and employees. A director of FedEx emphasises "open, two-way communication is absolutely essential to achieving our quality goals". He and his senior executives hold regular meetings at a local hotel and they are open to any employee. So popular was this that they outgrew the space and now use a television network as the vehicle for continuing two-way communication. The director broadcasts live on the network every six months to discuss the state of the company and to field questions from employees throughout the FedEx network (cited in George and Weimerskirch, 1998).

Many organizations use a variety of communication techniques. Redland Roof Tiles UK produces a monthly newsletter, which is used to introduce or reinforce concepts of TQM and continuous improvement. The tone is friendly and informal with cartoons and anecdotes (Whitford and Bird, 1996).

The Digital Switching and Customer Service Division of North Telecom Canada Ltd has received awards and international recognition for its quality systems and procedures. Continually communicating the importance of quality to its 5,000 employees is considered vital by divisional management and three internal communications specialists generate daily newsletters, monthly newspapers and videos (Ross, 1999).

The manufacturing division of ICL UK uses face-to-face communication as a key feature of its communication strategy. The managing director talks to the whole workforce in small groups of 50 people at least once per year. This involves seven meetings per day starting with the first shift and going through to 10:30 p.m. Staff express their views and listen to the managing director. A formal cascade process is used for announcements of organizational changes, company news, quality results, customer feedback and quality training. Managers and supervisors gather their staff together and make announcements assisted by prepared questions/answers. Managers take responsibility for finding answers to questions which staff raise and cannot be resolved immediately. On-line satellite broadcasts are used where appropriate and staff not able to see the broadcast are given a video the next day (Zairi, 1999b).

At D2D, the managing director holds annual "kick-off events". At these, he talks to every employee in small groups about the previous year's performance and strategy in a relaxed atmosphere (Zairi, 1999b). At IBM Rochester, posters are important in getting the quality message across to all employees (Zairi, 1999b). Lateral communication across the organization is vital if the customer is to be continuously satisfied. Digital has a world-wide system called "Notes", which literally allows any one of 100,000 employees to talk to anyone else and obtain information on any subject (Smith, 1994).

Managing suppliers

No total quality process is complete if it does not address the issues related to the process of managing suppliers (Elshennaway et al., 1991). This notion stems from the quality management philosophy of "prevention rather than detection". TQ organizations aim for "design and purchase" quality, rather than "inspecting" quality to produce services and products that meet customer requirements.

Quality gurus such as Crosby (1989), Deming (1986), Ishikawa (1985) and Peters (1989) preach about the need for suppliers to be viewed as an integral part of the organization's operation. Crosby (1989) says that the relationship between supplier and buyer is one of the most important parts of the quality improvement process. He estimates that 50 per cent of an organization's quality non-conformances are due to defective in-coming materials (Smock, 1982).

TQ organizations tend to manage and control their supply chain better (Hirschhorn and Gilmore, 1992) by pursuing approaches such as supplier base reduction, limited sourcing arrangement and closer integration and strategic alliance with suppliers (DeRose, 1987). According to the Japanese Ministry of International Trade and Industry, the Japanese manufacturing industry owes its competitive advantage and strength to its supplier relationship structure (Dyer and Ouchi, 1993). Japanese automakers have elaborate supplier relationship programmes. Toyota and Nissan have large supplier assistance management consulting groups with specialised expertise that work full-time – free of charge – with suppliers. They help suppliers to improve their production techniques and achieve total quality in products and service. Both Toyota and Nissan have at least one consultant for every four to six suppliers (Dyer and Ouchi, 1993). At Jaguar Cars, where appropriate, representatives of its suppliers are brought in as team members of task forces set up to deal with specific quality problems (Cullen and Hollingum, 1987).

According to Easton (1993), many Baldrige applicants have set up extensive quality programmes with their suppliers. These include supplier quality systems audits, supplier rating and qualification systems, training, joint design teams, joint quality improvement teams, and supplier (and supplier employee) recognition schemes. In his way, they ensure that the quality movement spreads gradually throughout their entire supplier chain (Crosby, 1989). They offer partnership and extend as much assistance as possible to suppliers to help them manage quality effectively. Florida Power & Light Company provides a two-week training course for its suppliers on how to implement a total quality management initiative in their own company, while Wallace Company has provided over 100 of its suppliers with training on TQM (Johnston and Daniel, 1991).

Deming (1986) strongly advocates supplier base reduction. His fourth principle states:

End the practice of awarding business on price tag alone. Instead, minimise total cost by working with a single supplier.

According to Dyer and Ouchi (1993), reducing the total number of direct suppliers can increase quality while lowering costs. Suppliers developing competency in the customers' requirements, less or no inspection due to confidence in supply quality and quicker and better responsiveness from the suppliers are some of the reasons for this (Kite, 1990). Shorts Brothers are continually attempting to reduce the supply base and to build long-term lasting relationships with a number of preferred suppliers (Oakland and Porter, 1994). It encourages suppliers to embrace total quality by extending support through training services and an invitation to participate in joint improvement teams.

As a vital preventive measure against non-conformance of incoming materials, TQ organizations also undertake supplier evaluation (Newman, 1988). As a key criterion, they select suppliers based on their capability and commitment to product and service quality. Evaluation may be performed by analysing the supplier's history or audits such as on-site assessments or interview. One of the key factors in ICL Product Distribution UK's success in getting its supplies right is its supplier evaluation programme (Binney, 1992). Rover and Ford in the UK also have similar programmes (Gilroy, 1994).

Businesses which do not take customer and supplier relationships into account are less likely to be successful. Liu *et al.* (2000) and Masella and Rangone, (2000) both highlight the critical role played by the supplier in contributing to the overall performance of the purchaser. What types of supplier knowledge, when and how to cultivate the supply base, are questions asked by Fan *et al.* (2000) and Tracy and Tan (2001). They suggest that facilitating the supplier knowledge use in design does matter, and there is a very positive relationship between supplier selection, involvement, customer satisfaction and firm performance.

Liker *et al.* (1998) have a detailed research on supplier involvement in design: a comparative survey of automotive suppliers in the USA, UK and Japan. They highlight several points which deserve attention. They are cross-national differences in supplier involvement, component characteristics and supplier involvement, supplier technical capabilities and supplier involvement, buyer-supplier relationships and supplier involvement, data exchange and supplier involvement, and impacts of supplier involvement in design.

Chapter 12
Systems and process management

Anything less than direction of best efforts of everyone toward achievement of the aim or aims of the whole organization is a directed verdict toward failure to achieve best overall results (W.E. Deming).

Under the Taylor System the experience and creativity of the work force were major underemployed assets of the companies. More recently it has become evident that workforce participation can add significantly to companies' quality performance (J.M. Juran).

Accredited quality management system

En route to a TQ culture, registration with a quality management system such as ISO 9000 is seen by many organizations as a starting point and an important element of the implementation process (Oakland and Porter, 1994; Porter and Parker, 1993; Hirschhorn and Gilmore, 1992). At Carnaud Metalbox plc, the ISO 9000 registration process provided the foundation on which a quality culture was built and helped the company to move on in developing the total quality process (Oakland and Porter, 1994). At Tioxide Group Ltd, the registration programme pushed quality to a much higher profile in the company as everyone was actively involved in the process. The company also saw themselves in a better position to meet the specific requirements of customers and improve their strategic relationships (Oakland and Porter, 1994).

In discussing the implementation of the quality management process at Esso Research Centre, UK, Price and Gaskill (1990) assert that the use of the discipline of a recognised industry accreditation for a quality management system such as the ISO 9000 helps in the integration of the quality process into the site culture. The systematic approach as stipulated under the various elements such as calibration and maintenance of laboratory equipment, staff training and sample management assist in minimising errors and increase the incidents of "right first time".

Companies such as Nissan Motor UK, Federal Express and Club Med view operating standards as an important requirement in the quality stakes. However, they do not see the need to have a recognised industry accreditation (Binney, 1992).

The ISO 9000 system

A quality system has several parts, such as the organizational structure, responsibilities, procedures and processes. For effective TQM implementation, full documentation of this quality system is required to ensure that the customer's requirements are clear, that the supplier has the capability to fulfil them, and all the resources are available at an optimum cost (Oakland, 1993). Many TQM gurus advocate designing the documentation system to conform to the requirements of an internationally acknowledged standard, often ISO 9000. This requires expressing the quality system and specific procedures in a quality manual.

ISO 9000 standards were introduced in 1987 and have become accepted world-wide. Many organizations, regardless of their size and products, accept the ISO 9000 series of standards and adapt it to their own advantage (Tsim *et al.*, 2001; Ross 1999; Mcteer and Dale; 1996). However, the standard cannot be applied directly; it needs to be customised for individual organizations (Schroder and McEachern, 2001).

Evans and Lindsay (2001) point out that these standards are recognised by about 100 countries and the meeting of these standards have become a requirement for international competitiveness. In some foreign markets, purchases are not made from non-certified suppliers. Sun (2000) in this regard mentions that ISO 9000 has become the admission ticket to European markets. Many US companies have claimed that the first barrier to entry into European markets is ISO 9000. According to the International Standards Organization (2000), the total ISO 9000 certification world-wide to the end of 1999 is 343,643.

Evans and Lindsay (2001) identify the ISO 9000 as a:

… series of global quality system standards that guide a company's performance of specified requirement in the areas of design/development, production, installation, and service. They are based on the premise that certain generic characteristics of management practices can be standardised, and that a well-designed, well-implemented, and carefully managed quality system provides confidence that the outputs will meet customer expectations and requirements.

ISO 9000 standards help to ensure that organizations follow specific well-documented procedures in the making of their products or services. Motwani *et al.* (1994) emphasise that ISO is aimed at production systems and in this way it assures that the production process meets the standards or criteria.

The benefits to companies throughout the world that were certified under ISO 9000 can be divided into internal and external benefits. Internal benefits related to the internal functioning of organizations. These include increase in productivity, improvement in efficiency and reduction in costs. Other benefits include better management control, clearly defined task structures and responsibilities, improved co-ordination structures, along with support in decision making. External benefits include concern for the organization in relation to its environment such as maintaining competitive advantage, increasing sales and market share, opening up the possibility for entering new markets and ensuring increased customer satisfaction (Singels *et al.*, 2001; Brown and Van der Wiele, 1995). According to the study of 160 Australian companies (Brown and Van der Wiele, 1995), the benefits obtained by ISO 9000 certification include: increasing the company's quality awareness, improvement of the relationship within the organization, increased customer satisfaction and improvement in customer relations. On the other hand, according to another study carried out in the UK (Lloyd's Register Quality Assurance, 1994), the benefits of certification can be summarised as an important marketing tool that helps market retention, increases the possibility of obtaining new contracts, decreases the number of customer audits, and assists in entering international markets. Tannock and Krasachol (2000) note that the ISO 9000 series have become important in developing countries.

The new version of the ISO 9000 standards was released on 15 December 2000. All organization certified to ISO 9001/2/3:1994 are required to transfer to ISO 9001:2000 (Tsim et al., 2001). Unlike its former editions, ISO 9000:2000 emphasises more the strategic issues of quality management, leading on from a sound mission statement (customer focus), a clear quality strategy formulation (process model) and an effective quality implementation (continuous improvement through Deming's PDCA cycle) (Samuel, 1999).

Many organizations consider ISO 9000 certification as the first step in the implementation of TQM (Oakland and Porter, 1994). A documented quality system as part of a TQM strategy can contribute to TQM by managing the organization's processes in a consistent manner (Zhang et al., 2000).

Organizing for quality

The success of the quality improvement process depends on effective and systematic implementation (Crosby, 1989). Given the corporate-wide nature of TQM, a suitable infrastructure to support quality initiatives is required (Johnston and Daniel, 1991). Oakland and Porter (1994), in fact, highlighted that one of the responsibilities of senior management at the outset of introducing TQM is the need to set up a defined quality organization structure in order to create a framework which will enable quality improvement to develop and flourish (Bendell et al., 1993; Easton, 1993; Davies and Wilson, 1990). In fact, they see the structure as a key element in ensuring the success of TQM.

Some authors such as Oakland and Porter (1994) propose a three-tier quality structure, made up of a quality council, process quality committees (or site steering committees) and quality improvement teams to devise and implement TQM within an organization. The quality council, comprising a top management team and headed by the CEO, reviews the strategic direction on TQM, decides resources, monitors, facilitates and handles impediments to progress Bendell et al., 1993; 1994). Glover (1993) views a quality council as usually beneficial in planning and designing the TQM system. He goes on to say that it is important that the council is high-powered if this is to be realised.

The process quality committees support the council by overseeing and managing quality at process or site levels, depending on the size of the organization. Oakland and Porter (1994) recommend that every senior manager should be a member of at least one committee, and believes that this provides the top-down support for full employee participation, through either a quality improvement team or quality circle programme. The committees control the quality improvement teams and assist by selecting projects, appointing team members and monitoring progress. The team members, themselves cross-functional, are brought together to tackle and solve specific problems on a project basis.

A case example of a three-tier structure is a quality structure introduced at a major British construction machinery manufacturer (Goulden and Rawlins, 1995). The structure is made up of a plant quality council, steering groups and cross-functional/multi-level project teams. Overall strategy and management of the quality programme is provided by the council. The steering groups sponsored and supported individual teams ensuring the required resources were made available. Members of the teams came from areas closely associated with the project.

The quality structure at Shorts Brothers is another example (Oakland and Porter, 1994). To direct a quality management implementation process, a total quality organizational structure was formed at the outset of the implementation process. This consisted of a quality council chaired by the CEO, two divisional councils chaired by their respective vice presidents, and 18 functional quality teams chaired by senior managers. A total quality secretariat was also established to co-ordinate the quality initiatives and to take a leading role in assisting the quality council to develop a total quality strategy.

The quality structure at STC Cables Products UK is aimed at total employee involvement in the quality improvement process (Davies and Wilson, 1990). The company designed a five-element quality structure to harness their full potential at every level of the organization:

1. Quality improvement team:
   ◦ comprises general manager, senior managers and a facilitator;
   ◦ ensures visibility of management commitment;
   ◦ determines quality policy;
   ◦ establishes direction; and
   ◦ provides support.
2. Quality improvement groups (QIGs):
   ◦ operates at all levels on a departmental basis;
   ◦ supervisors as leaders; and
   ◦ address quality issues within work area.
3. Corrective action teams (CATs):
   ◦ brought together to address specific problems allocated;
   ◦ disbanded when permanent solution found;
   ◦ leader is appointed; and
   ◦ leader selects members.
4. Quality improvement process manager:
   ◦ senior manager;
   ◦ facilitates day-to-day operations of QIGs and CATs; and

◦　　co-ordinates quality activities.
5.　　Individuals: the employee is expected to strive for excellence and be totally involved in the quality process.

It is evident from the literature that support structures for quality management vary widely (Black, 1993a). Smith (1994) suggests that the differences reflect the cultures of the organizations. The structures are also seen to be live, evolving as the TQM matures. This may suggest that there is more concern with promoting ownership of the quality process than there is with the structure required.

Promoting ownership of the quality process through structures becomes even more beneficial within organizations with geographically dispersed operating units. At Southern Pacific Lines, several regional steering committees directly reporting to the central quality council were set up (Carman, 1993).

Support structures for quality management are typically changed or dismantled when goals and objectives for setting up have been achieved. For example, BP Chemicals, UK modified and changed its quality structures as its quality system evolved and moved from the planning and education phase to the implementation phase (Stark, 1990). At Thomas Cork SML, the high-powered quality council set up at the outset to oversee the introduction of total quality was disbanded and its functions taken over by the management committee, once the quality initiatives got off the ground (Oakland and Porter, 1994).

Townsend and Gebhardt (1992) recommend the need to have a full-time post to facilitate and manage the day-to-day running of the quality process, especially if the organization is large (Smith, 1994). An individual such as this can provide a vital support function to the corporate quality council. At STC Cables Products UK, the facilitator (quality improvement process manager) has a major role in the on-going success of the QIP. He is responsible for establishing the quality teams and putting together the training programmes at the initial launch. According to Davies and Wilson (1990), the individual selected must be an efficient organizer, a motivator, enthusiastic and sufficiently senior. At Tioxide group Ltd, a group quality manager reporting directly to the executive director responsible for quality was appointed to facilitate the implementation process (Oakland and Porter, 1994).

The vital role of the facilitator is also highlighted by a study at two Hewlett-Packard factories in the UK (Barker, 1991). The finding showed that the degree of buy-in among the survey respondents was better in the factory which had a full-time TQM facilitator who actively coached and supported quality teams and activities.

Quality improvement is through process improvement
The challenge of organizing for quality is to enable quality improvement to develop and flourish. The success of the quality improvement process depends on effective and systematic implementation. Given the corporate-wide nature of TQM, a suitable infrastructure to support quality initiatives is required. Barcala *et*

al. (2000) argue that there is a need to provide the entities and institutions that train retailers with a series of recommendations to improve the quality of the courses they organize, especially concerning the aspects where those actually receiving training detect the greatest shortcomings. Oakland (2000) also highlights that authority must be given to those charged with following TQM through with actions that they consider necessary to achieve the goals. The commitment will be continually questioned, and will be weakened and destroyed by failure to delegate authoritatively.

Then they map the key business processes against the functional organization. The repair process would be mapped to billing, maintenance repair, distribution, manufacturing, product design and product management. The quality council does this. Then a major stakeholder of the process who is committed to its improvement is assigned as process owner. This person puts together a cross-functional team consisting of middle managers from each of the functional organizations. The committee monitors the activities of the formal improvement teams set up to investigate company-wide areas for improvement.

Concerning quality management, Heng (2001) suggests that the focus on quality sets the context for shaping and organizing the work of capturing its core knowledge. The ISO 9000 standard provides convenient categories for knowledge mapping, and presents a common language for consultant-client interaction during the mapping process. An ISO 9000 quality management system would shape the context of its work, as well as the work behaviours of its human resource. It also provides a ready framework for ordering and structuring its knowledge. There needs to be a full-time post to facilitate and manage the day-to-day running of the quality process, especially if the organization is large. An individual such as this can provide a vital support function to the corporate quality council.

Elbadri (2001) considers the success of the quality improvement process to be dependent on effective and systematic implementation. Moran (1998) proposes a quality structure of three tiers. The purpose of this TQM structure is to achieve employee participation. A disciplined and systematic approach to continuous improvement may be established in a TQM or business excellence steering committee or council. A full-time post is needed to manage the quality process. Many organizations have realised the importance of the contribution a senior, qualified director of quality can make to the prevention strategy. In large organizations, it may be necessary to make several specific appointments or to assign details to certain managers. In smaller organizations, a part-time quality manager could be appointed if the cost of employing a full-time quality manager is not justified.

The following actions may be deemed to be necessary. Support structures for quality management are typically changed or dismantled when goals and objectives for setting up have been achieved. For example, BP Chemicals, UK, modified and changed its quality structure as its quality system evolved, and moved from the planning and educational phase to the implementation phase. Rao *et al*. (1996)

show that AT&T-USA started by identifying the key business processes that are critical for achieving customer satisfaction.

The committee/council should meet at least monthly to review strategy, implementation progress and improvement. A case example of a three-tier structure is a quality structure introduced at a major British construction machinery manufacturer (Thiagarajan and Zairi, 1997). The structure is made up of a plant quality council, steering groups and cross-functional/multi-level project teams. Overall, the council provides strategy and management of the quality programme. The steering group sponsored and supported individual teams, ensuring the required resources were made available. Members of the teams came from areas closely associated with the project.

The success of the quality improvement process depends on effective and systematic implementation. Given the corporate-wide nature of TQM, a suitable infrastructure to support quality initiatives is required. Castka *et al.* (2001) in fact highlight that one of the responsibilities of senior management at the outset of introducing TQM is the need to set up a defined quality organizational structure in order to create a framework, which will enable quality improvement to develop and flourish (Paton, 2001). In fact, they see the structure as a key element in ensuring the success of TQM. The integration of marketing, design, purchasing, operations and quality assurance is necessary for success in TQM. This is suggested by the fact that lack of integration of new design control, incoming material control, product control and improvement are the main causes of the high cost of non-quality operation.

Appelbaum *et al.* (2000) view a quality council as usually beneficial in planning and designing the TQM system. They go on to say that it is important that the council is high-powered if this is to be realised. Some authors, such as Deissinger (2001), propose a three-tier quality structure, made up of a quality council, process quality committee (or site steering committees), and quality improvement teams to devise and implement TQM within an organization. The quality council, comprising a top management team and headed by the CEO, reviews the strategic direction on TQM, decides resources, monitors, facilitates, and handles impediments to progress. The process quality team (PQT) and any site TQM steering committees should also meet monthly, shortly before the senior steering committee/council meetings. Every senior manager should be a member of at least one PQT. This may suggest that there is more concern with promoting ownership of the quality process than there is with the structure required. Promoting ownership of the quality process through structure becomes even more beneficial within organizations with geographically dispersed operating units. This system provides the top-down support for employee participation in process management and development, through either a quality improvement team or a quality circle programme. It also ensures that the commitment to TQM at the top is communicated effectively through the organization (Gunasekaran *et al.*, 2001).

Managing by processes

Although most, if not all, organization activities are considered as processes which cross traditional functional boundaries (Kanji, 1995), many organizations maintain and operate along vertical functional structures, stifling the people within the organization and thus preventing them from understanding how their work affects the overall process of providing customer satisfaction. The functional approach therefore allows barriers to customer satisfaction to evolve (Oakland and Beardmore, 1995), it allows critical control points between departments to be vulnerable to organizational "noise" (Edson and Shannahan, 1991) such as "turf protection" and poor communication.

If employee involvement is key to the attainment of customer satisfaction, managing by process is key to engaging an organization's employees to take responsibility for what they are doing in relation to satisfying the customers (Oakland and Beardmore, 1995; Juran, 1993). In many best organizations such as Rank Xerox (Coleman, 1991), IBM (Snowden, 1991), ICL and Shell Chemicals UK (Sinclair, 1994), there is a growing recognition of the need to move away from the traditional functionally-based approach to managing through a set of clearly-defined, customer-driven processes.

McAdam (1996), in relating the experiences of Shorts Brothers, says that the process-based approach or managing by process improves customer focus and avoids the limitations of managing by vertical functions.

If the aim of implementing TQM in an organization is to achieve customer satisfaction, then a first step is managing the internal customer-supplier relationship to support the management of processes. Within each organization there exists an intricate structure of both internal customer (one individual/process/department supplying another). Any weak link or break at any point in the internal customer-supplier chain may find its way to the interface between the organization and the external customer (Oakland, 1993). Deming (1986) and Kanji (1995) also talk about understanding the notion of internal customer-supplier as absolutely critical to a quality transformation. In this sense, the concept of an internal and external customer-supplier relationship forms the core of total quality (Oakland, 1993; Kanji and Asher, 1993).

Best organizations ensure that everyone within the organization understands that they are dependent on each other, know where their work goes, and continuously ensures that the necessary quality at each interface meets overall customer expectations (Crosby, 1989; Bendell *et al.*, 1993). To orient the perspective of its employees to the "next internal customer", the management at Catton and Company (UK) Ltd requested everyone to ask: Who are my immediate customers? What are their requirements? Do I have the necessary capabilities to meet their requirements? Who are my immediate suppliers? What are my true requirements? Do I communicate my requirements? (NIST, 1994). At the outset of the TQ programme at Thomas Cork SML, an exercise called "Needs and expectations" was carried out which involved everyone asking similar questions (Oakland and Porter, 1994). At Shorts Brothers, everyone understood the concept of the internal customer-supplier and that satisfying the internal customer must be realised in order for the company to succeed in its quality quest.

Sinclair (1994) found that the identifying and mapping of processes is one of the activities pursued by TQM organizations to support the management of processes (McAdam, 1996; Hardaker and Ward, 1987).

The role of benchmarking

Benchmarking is an integral part of a total quality process (Beadle and Searstone, 1995; Bendell et al., 1993; Mitchell, 1995; Bank, 1992; Kleiner, 1994). But what is benchmarking? Rank Xerox, which developed benchmarking as part of its quality process, provides the most practical definition:

A continuous, systematic process of evaluating companies recognised as industry leaders, to determine business and work processes that represent best practices, establish rational performance goals (Zairi, 1994).

The primary objective of benchmarking is performance improvement. Identifying opportunities for performance improvement by comparing one organization's performance with that of another is a reflex of TQM (Bank, 1992). Zairi (1994) draws the link between TQM and benchmarking:

TQM is the wheel of improvement ...doing an internal, value-adding activity for the end customer. Benchmarking .... is the external activity for identifying opportunities and ensuring that the wheel of improvement is turning in the right direction and is making the necessary effort towards the end destination, i.e. achieving high standards of competitiveness.

Many best organizations are using benchmarking as a tool for obtaining the information to be used in the continuous improvement process, and to gain competitive edge (McNair and Leibfried, 1992; Booth, 1995). They are attracted to it because it stimulates and challenges the improvement process (Smith, 1994).

At Post Office Counters Limited (POCL), benchmarking is a quality improvement tool (Mitchell, 1995). The company used benchmarking inputs to set realistic targets to benefit the customer. At Southern Pacific Lines benchmarking is viewed as essential for an increased rate of improvement (Carman, 1993). Saturn Corporation built and successfully launched a brand – Saturn – in a saturated market using the benchmarking approach (Bemowski, 1995b). Motorola benchmarks itself against 125 companies, while Wainwright Industries has benchmarked 16 past MBNQA winners (Nadkarni, 1995).

Unipart, a UK car components manufacturer, has an information-sharing scheme – Global Contribution Circle – with Yutaka Gigen, a counterpart in Japan (Bowen, 1993). Bank (1992) reported that organizations such as Royal Mail, 3M, Heinz, British Airways and Federal Express also employ benchmarking as a vital component of their total quality initiatives.

All Baldrige winners used various types of benchmarking to learn best practices (Nadkarni, 1995). There are essentially four types of benchmarking (Zairi, 1994):

1. Competitive benchmarking: comparisons with primary competitors.
2. Functional benchmarking: comparisons with similar functions or processes within the same broad industry leaders as partners.
3. Generic benchmarking: comparison with similar functions or processes regardless of type of industry.
4. Internal benchmarking.

The fourth type, internal benchmarking involves comparison within the set-up of one's own corporation, for example, between sister organizations or branch offices. It is generally ignored in many definitions and played down as unimportant by some writers (Vaziri, 1992). However, Rank Xerox used internal benchmarking with much success, transmitting best practice experiences between its 20 different operating companies across Europe (Smith, 1994).

Typically, the process of benchmarking involves the acquisition both of outputs (the actual benchmark) and information on how those outputs are achieved. Zairi (1994) labels this as process-driven benchmarking. Focusing on just outputs – cost-driven benchmarking – while often resulting in cost reduction, may commit people to unrealistic targets to the detriment of the quality process.

Pulat (1994), in describing AT & T Oklahoma City Works benchmarking experience, offers benchmarking as a continuous process using the plan-do-check-act (PDCA) cycle. The plan phase defines processes to be benchmarked. The do phase involves collecting data on own processes and those of others that are similar. The check phase requires performing gap analysis (numbers and practices). The act phase involves implementing projects to close negative gaps and maintain positive ones.

Haksever (1996), in reference to results of the International Quality Study by Ernst & Young and American Quality Foundation, cautions against the application of benchmarking before a comprehensive quality process is in place. However, Southern Pacific Lines disputed the findings and conducted benchmarking early in their implementation process to set targets for improvement (Carman, 1993):

The target for any particular performance indicator has no credibility unless it is based on what the competition is doing.

Rank Xerox, the concept creator, claims to have worked and benchmarked with competitors. Milliken benchmarked Xerox's approach to benchmarking.

Benchmarking is a qualifying criterion for organizations aiming for the European Quality Award, and the US Malcolm Baldrige National Quality Award (MBNQA). In the MBNQA, applicants are required to demonstrate competitive analysis and benchmarking activities for 510 of the total 1,000 points.

Benchmarking involves a goal-setting process (Robertson *et al.*, 2001). To achieve these goals, benchmarking encourages the organization to empower employees and to effectively assign and integrate the responsibilities, work processes and reward systems (Jarrar and Zairi, 2000). When the employees are totally committed to benchmarking, the organization will benefit from the successful implementation of the best practices. To better prepare for benchmarking projects, one may adopt the process which is a structural approach to problem solving and general management (Cassell *et al.*, 2001). The process consists of four phases: focus, plan, do and review. The functions of benchmarking include using benchmarking to transform to agile pro-activity; to monitor agility programmes, projects or strategies; for planning purposes; for implementation purposes; for continuous improvement processes; and for acquisition of data on agility metrics (Longbottom, 2000).

Benchmarking as a driver for competitive advantage
However, benchmarking is not without its problems (Ball *et al.*, 2000). Davies and Kochhar (1999) mention five points: limited use of benchmarking with no detailed benchmarking studies; lack of use of benchmarking metrics; lack of implementation of best practices; no formal benchmarking strategy, checklist or definition; no feedback of results into business plan targets (Godfrey and Godfrey, 1999). The reasons for lack of benchmarking are pre-occupation with metrics, being mistaken for competitive analysis; lack of implementation of findings; lack of planning; lack of structure in the benchmarking project; failure to involve all levels and areas of organization; no perception of the need to benchmark; belief that a company is unique; and studies too large and superficial (Buyukizkan and Maire, 1998).

Fernandez *et al.* (2001) propose the term "evolutionary benchmarking" to describe a framework that helps to encourage researchers to find answers to both sets of questions. It is a framework that captures and represents the relevant information for analysis, planning and comparison tasks involved in benchmarking organizations (Fernandez *et al.*, 2001; Razmi *et al.*, 2000). There are five processes of benchmarking: self-analysis, pre-benchmarking, benchmarking, post-benchmarking, and observation and adjustment (Razmi *et al.*, 2000). However, there are also misconceptions about benchmarking. For example, if benchmarking motivates visits to other organizations simply to see what they are doing, without any clear learning objective, the "industrial tourist" gains little from the exercise (Ball *et al.*, 2000). How significant is benchmarking? Longbottom (2000) finds that benchmarking can reduce costs, reduce staffing levels, reduce time taken, reduce waste/re-work, improve profitability, and improve customer benefits (Brah *et al.*, 2000). Post-modern benchmarking argues that we should place greater emphasis on benchmarking as a serious research methodology, taking a place alongside quantitative and qualitative research methodologies. This view of benchmarking presumes that the process needs to be subjected to the same rigour as in any serious research project (Fernandez *et al.*, 2001).

The future of benchmarking is discussed in Jarrar and Zairi's article (2000). They argue that a major issue that will affect benchmarking in the future is the advances in IT. It is expected that the Internet and other electronic means will result in best practice transfer (Fong *et al.*, 1998). Already many organizations have their own intranets, and e-mail is becoming a standard means of communication. This spread of IT is accelerated by the fast-paced profileration of knowledge management application and specialized tools (Sarkis, 2001).

Self-assessment

Self-assessment is an effective technique to measure the culture of quality within an organization (Zairi, 1994). In this sense, management can use self-assessment as the means to assess whether their implementation efforts are deployed in the right way. Such was the case at Prudential Life Administration, part of Prudential Assurance Company Limited (Porter and Tanner, 1995).

The ability to assess an organization's progress against an accepted set of criteria would be most valuable (Oakland, 1993; Porter and Tanner, 1995). The Malcom Baldrige National Quality Award (MBNQA) and the European Quality Award (EQA) assessment models are available to organizations for self-assessment (Conti, 1991). For example, it has been suggested that thousands of TQM organizations use the MBNQA criteria annually (Sunday and Liberty, 1992). In this sense, these provide a more widely-accepted technique to measure progress towards TQM than those suggested by authors such as Saraph *et al.* (1989), Black (1993a) and Cupello (1994).

At 3M a self-assessment using the MBNQA criteria is performed annually at all business units (Bertsch and Williams, 1994). Prudential Life Administration used the MBNQA criteria during the first year, before moving on to use the EQA's (Porter and Tanner, 1995). Tioxide Group Limited used the EQA criteria (Oakland and Porter, 1994). Many organizations adapt these well-known criteria to suit their needs and objectives.

In recent years, researchers have attempted to develop a scientifically-based diagnostic framework for TQM (Saraph *et al.*, 1995; Black, 1993a). There are three commonly-used methodologies for self-assessment, namely, discussion group methods, survey methods and award type processes using written reports (Finn and Porter, 1994). The award type self-assessment is deemed to be the most objective. Prudential Life Administration used a hybrid approach of discussion and award type (Porter and Tanner, 1995).

In common with other quality initiatives, providing the necessary training is vital to make self-assessment work. A study of self-assessment practices in 117 leading European organizations found training to be one of the initiatives used to support self-assessment (Van der Wiele *et al.*, 1996). Tioxide Group Ltd has over the years produced a team of professional auditors (Oakland and Porter, 1994). Nearly 400 employees have been trained to undertake quality audits through the group.

How does self-assessment work in practice?

Self-assessment within the TQM framework systematically follows the processes that drive the organization toward continuous improvement and customer satisfaction. Self-assessment is made by systematic design and through application of a structured model, such as Hillman's (1994), which has two objectives: first, to maintain high levels of achievement in success areas; and, second, to identify additional improvement areas and opportunities for positive action. In the Davis model (1993) self-assessment takes three directions: first, establishing the current level of performance and highlighting improvement priorities; second, monitoring achievements and progress in organization improvement; and, third, providing a future planning and development focus. Other models follow various checklists of TQM standards, such as those found in the Deming Award, the Baldrige Award and the European Quality Award. Organizations may elect to develop their own integration of various model elements or elaborate these with individualised elements.

In terms of developing integrated models or overall evaluation systems, the focus of continuous improvement must be maintained. Assessment, therefore, cannot be constructed as negative, hostile, disruptive or combative. It is collaborative. It acts also as a preventative to disturbance or misdirection in the quality process. Even so, the perspective of co-ordinating continuous evaluation with continuous improvement inherently reveals some conflict, since the assessment must be focused on identification of non-conformity and review of corrective action. Hence, assessment manifests a control orientation in conjunction with extension of quality system elements. Therefore, self-assessment extends beyond mere control toward a definite improvement orientation (Conti, 1999).

Executive management involvement and leadership in self-assessment is regarded as being essential due to their instrumental and encompassing role in continuous organizational improvement. The choice of model for implementation depends on top management knowledge and preference (Fountain, 1998). The self-assessment model termed "target assessment" incorporates the following elements and rationale:

1. *People*: not adequately covered by other models, people are the most valuable resource a company has.
2. *Leadership*: this is in common with all other models, as without leadership there would be no direction.
3. *Empowerment*: people need to become responsible, clear understanding of requirements is essential.
4. *Process control*: the backbone must be firm; the basics must be in place.
5. *Change management*: the only certain thing that will happen in life is change; companies are notoriously bad at change management (this may be "time to market", re-organization or process re-engineering).
6. *Supplier development*: by working together with suppliers, huge gains can be made in cost, quality, delivery and lead times.

7. *Business performance*: such as MBNQA and EQA, the inevitable focus of the business is survival.
8. *Customer perception*: the most important person is the customer and what he/she thinks; perception may be different from the company "facts".
9. *Communication*: vertical/horizontal communication is vital for workforce commitment; the cascade must come from the top, but the whisperings at the bottom must be visible to the top.

Strengths and opportunities are the focus of target assessment. Advantages are "increased focus on people, change management, empowerment, communication, and suppliers" (Fountain, 1998). These "softer" areas of traditional elements, neglected by the organization leadership's agenda because of difficulty in their measurement are, in the target model, highlighted and assured of focused debate and analysis. Senior management itself has experienced empowerment through targetted self-assessment, with sharpened focus for improvement potential.

Cost of quality

Cost and quality have long been the centre of attention for both manufacturing and logistics managers as cost centres for most firms. Cost considerations drive a host of strategic decisions, including global manufacturing rationalisation, outsourcing and downsizing, as firms seek ever-lower labour and materials costs (Andersen and Moen, 1999). The need for a new approach to quality cost measurement arises due to difficulties in monitoring and documenting the effects of quality improvement activities in some companies. Top management were not willing to give their long-time support, since they were unable to see the effect in their financial reports. It was also difficult to reveal the effect of the improvements on customer satisfaction (Moen, 1998).

Quality cost measurement has its origin in the early 1950s, and Feigenbaum's classification of quality costs in the familiar categories of prevention, appraisal and failure has been almost universally accepted (Lee and Cunningham, 2001). New costs elements have been added. There are several shortcomings in the traditional approach to quality cost measurement. For example, traditional quality cost systems are mainly internally company focused and reactive by nature. In many organizations, quality management fulfils a need which is not measured or even quantitatively estimated (Millar, 1999). Five common questions regarding this include: How does the manager of such an organization determine quality goals? By what means does the manager of such an organization evaluate the quality management's achievements? Are quality resources efficiently allocated? (Gunasekaran, 1999). What serves as a reference for determining quality assessment worker compensation? How is the return on the quality investment economically justified? (Andersen and Rasmussen, 1999).

A new proactive customer and process-focused poor quality cost (PQC) model has been developed to overcome some of the problems. The term poor quality cost has been used to stress that the prevention and appraisal costs have been left out, since they are difficult to measure and have limited application in the strategic decision process (Sandberg and Strimberg, 1999). There are two main categories of direct and indirect costs. Both internal and external costs are made up of direct failure costs which are the direct financial consequence of every failure that is discovered before shipment, and all direct costs associated with claims, warranty administration, etc., as a result of problems discovered after shipment (Angel and Chandra, 2001). Consequence costs, which are additional costs like administration, disturbances in current and related processes, additional planning, etc., are assigned to direct failure costs through a simplified activity-based costing approach. Indirect poor quality costs (PQCs) consist of customer-incurred costs, intangible costs and environmental costs. Therefore, this new customer and process-focused PQC approach has been developed to give a more accurate picture of the cost of poor quality, and to enable management to make long-term strategic decisions concerning how to best satisfy their customers (Superville and Gupta, 2001).

In other words, PQC provides a very useful tool to change the way management and employees think about errors (Harrington, 1999). PQC helps by getting management attention, changing the way the employee thinks about errors, providing a better return on the problem-solving effect, a means to measure the true impact of corrective action and changes made to improve the process, a simple and understandable method of measuring what effect poor quality has on the organization, and an effective way to measure the impact of the quality-improvement process (Fawcett et al., 2000). Of course, PQC by itself cannot resolve quality problems or optimise the quality system. It is only a tool that helps management understand the magnitude of the quality problem, pinpoints opportunities for improvement, and measures the progress being made by the improvement activities (Moen, 1998). An effective improvement process that will reduce the errors that are being made in both the white- and blue-collar areas must accompany the PQC system.

Managers also need to be aware that an effective cost of quality initiative must be an integral part of any overall quality programme (Andersen and Moen, 1999). Costs of quality initiatives translate quality problems into financial terms that are more easily understood by management. Any cost of quality initiative must identify the activities that produce the quality costs, measure all the costs so that they are reportable and understood by management, and identify those costs for improvement action that provides the greatest benefit to the company (Lee and Cunningham, 2001; Millar, 1999). While the importance of understanding quality cost behaviour cannot be overstated, the overriding issue for the successful implementation of an effective quality programme is management commitment. Management should emphasise a holistic approach that includes a cost of quality programme along with the use of prevention techniques such as process control charts, quality planning and problem-solving teams (Bester, 1999). Of course, several aspects of this research merit further investigation. Costs of quality models are still to be studied and developed for different types of industries. The effect of a firm's maturity level on the relative distribution of quality costs within an industry needs to be explored. Finally, the effect of a firm's strategic direction as a "cost leader" or "product differentiator" on the development of its cost of quality model requires further examination (Andersen and Rasmussen, 1999; Gunasekaran, 1999).

Thomas Interior Systems (USA), which modelled its 14-step quality process on that of Milliken & Co, winner of the 1989 Baldrige Award, considers the cost of quality as an important stage in its quality process (Johnson, 1993). To ensure its people are comfortable with the improvement process, the company introduced the cost of quality in the first year to everyone. It is believed that putting this exercise at the beginning helped employees to believe in the quality process. Hilti (Great Britain) Ltd also conducted a cost of quality analysis as an integral part of the TQM process to show the staff in the early stages the tangible benefits of introducing total quality (Findlay *et al.*, 1990).

At Shorts Brothers, management were quick to realise at the outset of the TQM implementation that the total quality process would only survive if it could provide tangible benefits to the company. It involved the workforce in the cost of quality projects relevant to the business objectives (Oakland and Porter, 1994). The success in savings convinced the staff of the benefits of total quality. LeaRonal (UK) believes that tracking of the cost of quality is an additional spur in its TQM process.

The PAF model

The prevention-appraisal-failure (PAF) model, developed by Feigenbaum is the most widely-applied scheme for categorising quality costs (Poter and Rayner, 1995; Plunkett and Dale, 1987). It is also adopted as the quality cost standard for the American Society for Quality Control (Black, 1993a). Feigenbaum (1983) breaks down the quality costs into three categories:

1. Cost of prevention: the costs of any action taken to investigate, prevent or reduce the risk of non-conformity or defects.
2. Cost of appraisal: the cost of evaluating the achievement of quality requirements.
3. Failure costs: the costs of non-conformity, both internal and external.

Both Rank Xerox (Mercer and Judkins, 1990) and LeaRonal (UK) (Smith and Tee, 1990) added two additional elements to the model:

1. Cost of exceeding requirements: the costs incurred to provide information or services which are unnecessary or unimportant or for which no agreed requirement has been established.
2. Cost of lost opportunities: the lost profits resulting from purchases of competitor products and services or from cancellation or products or

from cancellation of products or services due to not meeting customer requirements.

Quality control techniques
Juran (1974) states that quality techniques are important tools, not only for low-defect production but also for quality improvement. Shewhart defines quality control as the use of statistical procedures to provide guides to produce good parts and to disclose the cause of variations (Modaress and Aussari, 1989). Other quality gurus such as Deming and Taguchi strongly support a comprehensive quality control system to aid the management of quality. Deming says the key to achieving high quality conformance and to overcoming process-related problems is the use of statistical quality control (SQC) techniques (Modaress and Aussari, 1989). The techniques deal with the collection, analysis and interpretation of data related to the causes of variations in quality characteristics.

According to Juran, there are over 50 SQC techniques (Quiros, 1994). However, the fundamental ones, originally assembled by Kaoru Ishikawa as the seven QC tools, are process flow charting, check sheets or tally charts, histograms, Pareto analysis, cause and effect diagrams, scatter diagrams and control charts.

SQC for defect prevention is one of the cornerstones of the quality strategy at Electrolux (Cullen and Hollingum, 1987). The use of SQC techniques was also seen as one of the key elements in the development of Tioxide Group Ltd's total quality strategy, while at Carnaud/Metalbox plc, the SQC initiative was seen as an important vehicle for wide participation in teamwork and gave the total quality process a new boost (Oakland and Porter, 1994). ITT Hancock Industries considers SQC an important tool in controlling key process parameters and monitoring quality improvements (Cullen and Hollingum, 1987). Each level of its workforce is trained in the techniques of SQC.

Measuring customer wants and satisfaction
Quality should be customer driven (Takeuchi and Quelch, 1983). In the Baldrige Award criteria, a key concept is that quality should be "based on the customer" (NIST, 1994). Nearly a third of the award score is related to the customer. Amongst best companies, there is a passionate and generally held commitment to service customers to the best of their abilities (Peters, 1989; Easton, 1993). A major conclusion of Peters and Waterman (1982) was that best organizations align their corporate strategies to their customers' requirements. Satisfying customers' requirements better than the competition is widely recognised today as a key to success in the marketplace (Peters, 1989).

Central to the success of Baldrige winners was their constant focus on satisfying customers and measuring their satisfaction (Nadkarni, 1995). Measuring customer satisfaction is a cornerstone of TQM (Zairi, 1994). Best organizations use a variety of techniques such as customer surveys, focus groups and advisory panels, service visit teams, and close-up interviews to measure customer satisfaction (Clemmer, 1990; Berry, 1991; Taylor, 1995).

Customer survey is the method most commonly used to track customer satisfaction (Bergendahl and Wachmeister, 1993; Oakland and Beardmore, 1995). At Hilti (Great Britain) Ltd, surveys were carried out to assess customers' perception of Hilti quality (Findlay *et al.*, 1990). Caterpillar Tractor Company conducts two customer satisfaction surveys following each purchase, one after 300 hours of product use and the second after 500 hours of use (Takeuchi and Quelch, 1983). Baldrige winner Solectron Corporation calls on each of its 120 customers to enquire about satisfaction with their products and service, while another winner, Wainwright Industries collects weekly and monthly feedback information from customers to determine quality trends and customer satisfaction (Nadkarni, 1995).

While customer satisfaction surveys potentially offer the most efficient and objective means of assessing satisfaction, Deming (1986) calls for frequent direct interaction with customers to determine the level of satisfaction on a continual basis. L.L. Bean Inc., a mail order company, maintains direct contacts with its customers to track customer and non-customer perceptions of the quality of its own and its competitors' products and services (Takeuchi and Quelch, 1983). At Shorts Brothers, customers' representatives are regularly consulted on the level of customer satisfaction (Oakland and Porter, 1994). Xerox holds a visitor quality day for customers every six week (Nadkarni, 1995).

Without understand customers, there can be no true customer satisfaction (Kordupleski *et al.*, 1993; Crosby, 1989). Peters (1989) even equates survival to customer responsiveness. Best organizations listen to their customers in order to serve their requirements effectively (Nadkarni, 1995). National Westminster Bank plc, UK, considers understanding and staying close to its customers' requirements and expectations as the cornerstone of its quality service programme (Goodstadt, 1990). Through surveys, Nat West can identify critical service elements as required by the customers. The CEO of GTE Directories, the 1994 Baldrige winner, attributes their success to the "religion" of listening and responding to the customer (Bemowski, 1992).

In his study, Garvin (1983) found that the Japanese quality leaders had a clear understanding of consumers' wants by collecting expensive customer data. Like measuring customer satisfaction, a variety of methods are used to collect information on customer requirements (Clemmer, 1990; Berry, 1991). At Shorts Brothers, customer representatives are invited to contribute to multi-disciplinary design teams (Oakland and Porter, 1994).

Determining customers' needs is the start; translating these needs in the organization and satisfying them is a major challenge. In recent years, many best organizations have adopted the technique of quality function deployment (QFD) to "bring the voice of the customer into everything they do" (Zairi, 1994). It is a system for translating consumer requirements into appropriate organizational requirements at each stage, from research and product development to engineering and manufacturing to marketing. Best organizations such as Ford, Rank Xerox,

Hewlett-Packard and Digital Equipment have started adopting QFD as a method of designing and optimising the process of developing new products based on the wants of the customers (Zairi, 1994).

The process of QFD involves systematic conversion of non-measurable customer requirements – "what" – into technical specifications/design requirements – "how" (Zairi, 1994). At the centre of the QFD process is the "house of quality". The house of quality is the essential tool used to chart customer requirements and the translation of those requirements into tangible goods and services. The resulting matrix depicts customer requirements, technical specifications/design requirements, target values and competitive ratings on products/services.

Some best organizations, recognising the need to look beyond customers' immediate needs, are also investigating the requirements of customers' customers (Vandermerwe, 1993). IBM, DuPont, AT&T and Panasonic have stopped creating products with just the buyer in mind and have started considering the end user as well.

A strategic focus on customer satisfaction should lead to customer loyalty, achieved and measured through identifying loyalty intention and effective loyalty. Loyalty is the intention to continue purchasing joined with a positive recommendation of the company, its products and services. It also can be measured by recording the empirically verifiable business actually carried out by customers as well as the numbers of customers retained, won and lost (*The X Factor Executive Report*, 1999).

3M Company has emphasised "customer loyalty (as opposed to satisfaction)" (*The X Factor Executive Report*, 1999). The company concentrates on identifying customers who are totally satisfied with 3M and would definitely recommend the company and definitely repurchase. In this way, the company's target for production, business and customer satisfaction can be stated as: "50 per cent of customers should be ... loyalists" (Van de Vliet, 1997, cited in *The X Factor Executive Report*, 1999).

To survive in highly competitive markets, organizations need to provide goods and services that yield highly satisfied and loyal customers. When customers are satisfied, they are more likely to return to those who helped them, while dissatisfied customers are more likely to go elsewhere (Robledo, 2001). Without a unifying vision of customer needs, even the most talented and motivated teams earn only the small satisfaction of narrow competence, and the customer is lost. It is the clear customer-oriented vision of where they are heading that is one of the main factors that distinguish great companies from the rest.

Chapter 13
Issues in TQM implementation

Every organization is also a human society. Large organizations harbour many such societies. Every human society evolves a pattern of beliefs, habits, practices, etc., based on its accumulated experience. This is known as the cultural pattern. This pattern provides the society with certain elements of stability: a system of law and order, explanation of mysteries, rituals, taboos, status symbols, and so on. These elements are viewed by the society as possessing important values.

Any proposed change becomes a threat to these important values and hence will be resisted until the nature of the threat is understood. The resistance is not limited to the organized societies. It extends to the individual members who may feel that their personal values are threatened (J.M. Juran).

Introduction

TQM has sought to enhance operating efficiency through continuous improvement of organizational systems. Quality achievement has become an important measure of organizational success in both manufacturing and services. Throughout previous chapters, an attempt was made to survey the literature on the most important factors in the process of TQM implementation. An extensive review of literature on quality management was performed for the purpose of clarifying critical factors that are essential for TQM implementation. Through the extensive literature review, many critical success elements of TQM implementation are identified based on reviews of various models, quality awards and conceptual frameworks of academics and practitioners along with empirical studies. From the literature review several quality factors for effective quality management implementation were identified. A comprehensive list of the major critical quality factors and literature support is as follows:

- *Leadership*. Feigenbaum, 1989; Deming; 1986; Crosby; 1979; Juran, 1993; Powell, 1995; Saraph *et al.*, 1989; Black and Porter, 1996; Ahire *et al.*, 1996; Motwani *et al.*, 1994; Deming Prize; Baldrige Award; European Quality Award; Australian Quality Award; Canadian Quality Award; Kanji, 1990; Oakland, 2000; Zairi, 1999; George and Weimerskirch, 1998; Ross, 1999; Krasachali and Tannock, 1999; Evans and Linsday, 2001; Ramirez and Loney, 1993; Hoffman and Mehra, 1997; Zeitz *et al.*, 1997; Grahn, 1995; Stamtis, 1997; Garvin, 1983; Anderson and Sohal, 1999; Mohanty and Lakhe, 1998; Laszlo, 1999.

- *Employee involvement.* Deming, 1986; Juran, 1993; Ross, 1999; Ramirez and Loney, 1993; Evans and Linsday, 2001; Crosby, 1979; Zairi, 1999; Flynn *et al.*, 1995; Tan, 1997; European Quality Award; Canadian Quality award; Zhang *et al.*, 2000; George and Weimerskirch, 1998; Ahire *et al.*, 1996.
- *Training and education.* Saraph *et al.*, 1989; Kanji, 1990; Deming, 1986; Juran, 1974; Black and Porter, 1996; Powell, 1995; Motwani *et al.*, 1994; Thiagaragan and Zairi, 1997; Flynn *et al.*, 1994; Oakland, 2000; Zhang *et al.*, 2000; Mann and Kehoe, 1995; Ishikawa, 1985; Crosby, 1989; Porter and Parker, 1993; Feignbaum, 1961; Rao *et al.*, 1996; Mathews, 2001; Evans and Linsday, 2001.
- *Middle management role.* Wilkinson *et al.*, 1994; Thiagaragan and Zairi, 1997; Ross, 1999; Mann and Kehoe, 1995; Evans and Linsday, 2001;Crosby, 1989; Ishikawa, 1985; Deming, 1986; Samuel, 1992.
- *Reward and recognition.* Zhang *et al.*, 2000; Johnston and Daniel, 1991; London and Higgot, 1997; Crosby, 1989; Evans and Lindsey, 2001; Roa *et al.*, 1996; Zhang *et al.*, 2000; George and Weimerskirch, 1998; Thiagaragan and Zairi, 1997; Sweetman, 1996.
- *Teamwork.* Deming, 1986; Zhang *et al.*, 2000; Evans and Linsday, 2001; Thiagaragan and Zairi, 1997; Shapiro, 1995; Tan, 1997; Scholtes, 1995; Longenecker *et al.*, 1994; Rao *et al.*, 1996; Crosby, 1979; Juran, 1993; Ross, 1999; Oakland, 2000; Kanji, 1990; Luzon, 1988; Juran, 1993.
- *Policy and strategic planning.* Deming, 1986; MBNQA; EFQM; Juran, 1993; Crosby, 1979; Feigenbaum, 1989; Garvin, 1984; Saraph, *et al.*, 1989; Black and Porter, 1996; Australian Quality Award; Canadian Quality Award; Powell, 1995; Zairi, 1999; Motwani *et al.*, 1994; Ross, 1999; Oakland, 2000; Sinclair and Zairi, 2001, Sureshandar *et al.*, 2001; Evans and Lindsay, 2001.
- *Communication for quality.* Ross, 1999; Spechler, 1993; Kanji *et al.*, 1993; George and Weimerskirch,1998; Zairi, 1999; MBNQA; EFQM; Smith, 1994; Whitford and Bird, 1996; Garvin, 1988; Juran, 1988; Ishikawa; 1976; Thiagaragan and Zairi, 1997; Powell, 1995; Badri *et al.*, 1995.
- *Supplier management.* Zhang *et al.*, 2000; Crosby, 1989, Deming, 1986; Ishikawa, 1985; MBNQA; Canadian Quality Award; Garvin, 1988; Juran, 1988; Saraph *et al.*, 1989; Powell, 1995; Badri *et al.*, 1995; Richardson, 1997.
- *Process management.* Flynn *et al.*, 1994; Juran, 1988; Powell, 1995; Deming, 1986; Motwani *et al.*, 1994; Oakland, 2000; Ross, 1999; Mcteer and Dale, 1996; Evans and Linsday, 2001; Saraph *et al.*, 1989; Mann and Kehoe, 1995; Ramirez and Loney, 1993; Ahire *et al.*, 1996; Black and Porter, 1996; MBNQA; EFQM; Australian Quality Award; Canadian Quality Award; Tan, 1997.

- *Organizing for quality*. Oakland and Porter, 1995; Spechler, 1993; Ross, 1999; Thiagaragan and Zairi, 1997; Kanji and Yui, 1997; Black and Porter, 1996.
- *Quality measurement and benchmarking*. Deming; and Crosby, 1979; Evans and Linsday, 2001; Ahire *et al.*, 1996; Black and Porter, 1996; Flynn *et al.*, 1994; Powell, 1995; Saraph *et al.*, 1989; Motwani, 1994; Ross, 1999; Zairi, 1994; Booth, 1995; Macdonald 1998; Jackson, 1999; Pitt, 1999; Campanella, 1999; Crosby, 1979; Roden and Dale, 200; Tsai, 1998; Juran, 1978; Taguchi and Clausing, 1983; Ahire *et al.*, 1996; Sincair and Zairi, 2000.
- *Customer focus*. Deming, 1986; Juran, 1988; Crosby, 1979; Powell, 1995; Black and Porter, 1996; EFQM; MBNQA; Flynn *et al.*, 1994; Oakland and Porter, 1994; Zairi and Youssef, 1995; Evans and Linsday, 2001; Richardson, 1997; Ross, 1999; Saraph *et al.*, 1989; Zeitz *et al.*, 1997; Kanji, 1990; Spring *et al.*,1998; Chan *et al.*, 2001; Govers, 2001.

TQM and cultural issues
Many assumptions are made about the cultural influences on TQM implementation. Juran (1993), for example, says that there is no need to redesign a country's culture to instil the disciplines of quality improvements. He stresses that what is needed to make TQM work is the adherence to its principles, practices and techniques. Kano (1993), on the other hand, says that one needs to take cultural background into account when implementing TQM. However, he stresses that culture is not a barrier to the implementation of TQM.

A Bradford-based benchmarking study of 22 critical factors of TQM across several countries of widely differing cultures found that not all the critical factors are relevant in a generic sense (Zairi, 1994). Fundamental factors such as top management commitment, the need for a clear mission statement, and focus on the customer were, however, emphasised as absolutely essential to the success of TQM across borders.

How is culture defined?
Culture is defined as the collective programming of the mind which distinguishes one group from another and the sum total of beliefs, knowledge, attitudes of mind and customs to which people are exposed during their social conditioning (Hofstede, 1984). This definition recognises the fact that when people grow up in different environments, their cultures will be different. These differences were identified as relation to authority, conception of self, relationship between the individual and society, the individual's concept of masculinity and femininity, and ways of dealing with conflicts, including control of aggression and the expression of feelings. National cultures differ in the way the members view the world, how they deal with uncertainty, the degree to which individuals are integrated into groups, how information is processed, and conception of time, how individuals

establish relationships with others, the modality of human activity, and what is a human being's relationship to the environment (Mak, 2000).

It is apparent that different countries implement quality systems in different ways. There is a material variation in all aspects of quality management, from the reasons stimulating the quality management programme, through to the problems faced (Ngowi, 2000). National culture provides an explanation for many of the variations observed, in particular the dimensions of uncertainty avoidance and power distance, and diffuse/specific and affective/neutral. It is not possible with results obtained to be categorical about which approach to quality management is best objectively. It seems that the quality management approaches mirror the culture in which they develop (Douglas and Judge, 2001). Cultures that are consistent with the imperatives of TQM develop styles that will support the underpinning values of quality management. Others, that are at variance, may adopt the tools and approaches, but not the philosophy that TQM requires. Uncertainty avoidance appears to lead to a greater adoption of quality tools and techniques associated with quality management, and so the overall outcome in terms of competitiveness and customer focus may well be similar to countries where other cultural values prevail (Mathews *et al.*, 2001).

The inquiry deals with the relationship between national culture and the company corporate culture, the consequence of manager style change for TQM implementation, and how culture change can be measured adequately. The results are achieved by the use of external and internal measurement devices. Limitations consequent on the number of participants and dual role of the researcher indicate the potential value of further investigations into the topic using these devices. The main conclusion is that the maintenance of TQM systems without continued senior management commitment may not suffice to secure change and prevent a reversion to earlier cultural patterns (Mak, 2000).

Quality culture

Entrepreneurs who start companies, or managers who take over the helm, often create or bring an organizational "cultural scheme" whose philosophy mirrors their own. The organization's success or failure then depends on the relevance of these beliefs to the current opportunities and limitations confronting the organization (Bass and Avolio, 1993; Dellana and Hauser, 1999). The organization's philosophy or culture is then the basic repository of corporate vision and value, and requires that the policies, procedures and processes of the organization be based on this philosophy (Batten, 1994; Dellana and Hauser, 1999).

The boundary between TQM as a management programme and TQM as an organizational culture is not well defined. Many of the TQM classifications reviewed contain individual dimensions or elements that could be interpreted as belonging to organizational culture or climate. Indeed, one might argue that the essence of TQM is culture change and that TQM practices are merely tools for cultural transformation (Flood, 1993; Zeitz *et al.*, 1997). The answer to this puzzle depends on what is meant by organizational culture. In our view, culture consists of the beliefs, values and underlying assumptions supporting behavioural patterns and artefacts (cf. Ott, 1989; Schein, 1992; Zeitz *et al.*, 1997). Defining characteristics typically say what a thing is, but also they say what a thing is not. We assume that culture is distinct from TQM programmes and practices, even though the two often overlap in practice. TQM practices are formal, programmatic and behavioural, whereas culture refers to attitudes, firmly held beliefs and situational (and often not formally sanctioned) interactions. One clear operational distinction between the two is that cultural dimensions can be readily recognised without a TQM programme present (Montes *et al.*, 2003).

Few researchers have developed distinct, general dimensions of organizational culture. Reichers and Schneider (1990) and Zeitz *et al.* (1997) argue that this aversion to such general dimensions stems from the anthropological roots of culture studies, which prefer idiographic (emic) methodologies to nomothetic (etic), a point on which Denison (1996) and Zeitz *et al.* (1997) elaborate. Those in the idiographic tradition use detailed observation and analysis to capture the unique logic or *gestalt* of each organization's culture. They view nomothetic methods, employing ordinal dimensions universally applicable to all cultures, as likely to overlook or even distort important cultural features. The author agrees with Reichers and Schneider (1990), Denison (1996) and Zeitz *et al.* (1997) that culture can be studied using such nomothetic procedures. Indeed, several authors suggest measurable dimensions of culture based on theory. O'Reilly *et al.* (1991), Zeitz *et al.* (1997) have developed a survey measure of culture, and reveal seven dimensions derived from factor analysis: innovation, stability, respect for people, outcome orientation, attention to detail, team orientation, and aggressiveness. In addition, organizational climate bears a strong conceptual resemblance to culture (Denison, 1996; Reichers and Schneider, 1990; Zeitz *et al.*, 1997) and has often been measured quantitatively.

Perhaps the most central prerequisite of successful TQM programmes is good communication between top management and employees, mentioned explicitly by most of the authors reviewed. A second important dimension is employee involvement or empowerment. A third cultural dimension, also closely identified with successful TQM implementation, is trust, especially between management and employees. Indeed, Deming (1986) and Zeitz *et al.* (1997) include trust or "driving out fear" as a core feature of TQM.

The difference between climate and performance

Kangis *et al.* (2000) explore the linkage between organizational climate and corporate performance. The results show that there is a consistent association between climate and performance. Independently of sector, companies performing above average show higher values on climate dimensions than those performing below average. Interest in organizational climate and its link with corporate performance is gaining momentum. The aim of this paper is to contribute to this discourse by examining the extent to which above and below average-performing companies also exhibit different climate measurements. A survey was conducted on a sample of electronic component manufacturers, as a sunrise industry in a growth phase, and hosiery and knitwear manufacturers, as a sunset industry, in decline. In turn, sub-samples of companies that performed above or below average for each of these sectors were selected.

Lee and Howard (1994) attempt to illustrate how an internal climate survey can be used as a measurement tool to assess the level of quality in the service sector. Internal climate should ideally be determined by examining a cross-section of an organization. In an empirical study of two public mental health and mental retardation agencies, middle managers were initially believed to be more resistant to the introduction of a quality improvement process than line workers. Two hypotheses regarding internal climate among different levels of employees were tested. Results from this study provided insight for top managers of both public agencies to facilitate their TQM processes.

Continuous improvement

In recent years, the concept of continuous improvement (CI) has been emphasised by an increasing number of companies. CI consists of activities which contribute to organizational goals through the continuous improvement of work processes, work places and work interactions. Small group activities and the participation of all employees are often considered an integral part of CI. Most definitions of CI include the use of specific methods/tools and established procedures for using them (Berling, 2000).

Groups or project teams normally carry out the improvement work (Cole, 1989; Berling, 2000). Most attention has been centred on problem solving and identifying potential improvements – idea generation techniques. These possible improvements are not always obvious when one has been in the same job for any length of time. In Japanese management practices, especially the Toyota Production System (e.g. Ohno, 1988), systematic methods are available to help employees to see the situation from different angles.

The main reasons for engaging in improvements include both improving operational performance indicators, such as productivity, quality, cost and delivery, and organizational capabilities, such as employee commitment, skill and co-operation (Berling, 2000). Commitment to continuous improvement could lead to excellence (Scheuing, 1999), when continuous quality improvement is applied organization-wide, throughout all activities and functions, and manifested in a fundamental and shared belief in total customer satisfaction (Huq and Martin, 2000).

All organizations have individual and unique, dominant cultures, as well as various, powerful sub-cultures that are fundamental to all actions, operations and relationships in the organization. Huq and Martin (2000), following Schein (1992), classify organizational culture on three levels: artefacts, values and beliefs, and underlying assumptions. It is the latter level that serves as the fundamental definition of culture in this study. It is the underlying assumption that employees will have about accepting the CI initiatives that will result in successful or unsuccessful implementation (Huq and Martin, 2000).

Commitment to continual improvement is the central axiom of CI. Sustained improvements can only come through the commitment and participation of everyone involved. For example, in a hospital's new business environment, staying competitive means offering better care faster with less cost, through more collaboration, more communication, and more commitment. This axiom tells us that every process and every output can be improved without limit (Huq and Martin, 2000). They also claim that the workforce cultural values of CI emphasise democracy and teamwork, ongoing improvement and attention to quality, and customer satisfaction. Implementing a culture change within the industry will introduce new forms of teamworking and bring forward best practice models. Teamworking allows organizations to collaborate and share experiential learning, yet still remain competitive. This collaboration results in significant gains in terms of TQM (Sommerville *et al.*, 1999). Hofstede (1984) argues that culture is the collective programming of the mind, which distinguishes one human sub-group from another. The implementation of a TQM philosophy within the organization requires a cultural change. In any event, a change in culture and philosophy necessitates changes in peoples' behaviour. Changes in individuals are aligned to and affected by organizational change. If organizations are cultures, then cultural change also means organizational change (Bate, 1994; Sommerville *et al.*, 1999). TQM's real purpose is to change an organization's attitudes and skills so that the culture of the organization becomes one of preventing failures, and the norm is operating right first time (Oakland, 1989; Richbell and Ratisiatou, 1999). The drive is towards developing a quality culture, motivating staff and improving processes, thus making quality a continuous "race without a finish" (Fowler *et al.*, 1992; Richbell and Ratisiatou, 1999).

Transforming the vision of a total quality organization to reality requires a complete change in the prevailing attitudes and culture within the company. This change must cascade from the top management to the shopfloor, and must be permanent, consistent and visible. However, the bias towards continuing past modes of behaviour is strong in any organization, but is especially pronounced in large organizations which perceive themselves to be successful. This is often the case in multi-nationals that may have enjoyed considerable success in the market place. Problems may arise in attempting to involve the organization in a change, such as applying TQM that may be hard to discern because of the staff's ingrained ideas about the nature of the business and their reluctance to adapt to the new principles. Another potentially greater problem is that management have to recognise that employees need continuous development to expand their skills and, hence, the organization's scientific base and knowledge base (Richbell and Ratisiatou, 1999).

The real management challenge is how to sustain continuous improvement to stay alive in the organization. Managers finally understand that each staff meeting and/or event is an opportunity to teach, learn about and reinforce the importance of embracing CI. Managers should use those opportunities to celebrate successes, to learn from experience and to build team spirit (Scott, 2001).

Innovation culture

Innovation is also integral to the concept of continuous improvement, and to the proposition that visionary leadership enables the simultaneous creation of a co-operative and learning organization (Deming, 1986). According to Deming, organizational learning generates and encompasses two types of knowledge – the process task knowledge akin to the "science of the process", complete with the understanding of technology, and human task requirement as explicated with precise operational definitions that guide activity and the measurement of quality.

Zhuang *et al.* (1999) argue that striving to survive in the ever-changing world, the ability to innovate has become increasingly crucial. They examined the general understanding of issues concerning innovation among managers and their ability to translate this understanding into practice. They found out that while most organizations have realised the importance of innovation and are prepared to mobilise their managers to be involved in innovative projects, many of the organizations have not yet been able to create an innovation culture and devise suitable policies to encourage innovation positively within the wider context of their organizations. They also discovered that there are low levels of understanding of the most commonly known innovation techniques, and most people dismiss the value of creativity training programmes conducted in their organizations, raising serious concerns over the effectiveness of these programmes.

Macedo-Soares and Lucas (1996) note that quality management practices of leading firms have increasingly been considered benchmarks for other countries in the quest for successful competitive technologies. They identify socio-cultural factors as a root cause for the difficulties of employing these practices effectively in Brazil. They recommend that the development of innovative capabilities and cultural synergies are significant in the scope of the increasing associations with foreign firms and to overcome at least some of the difficulties at issue.

McAdam and Welch (2000) suggest that with increasing market pressure and fragmentation, small and medium-sized enterprises (SMEs) need to move beyond the change philosophy of continuous improvement (CI) and develop a culture of innovation. To find out if SEMs could go beyond CI to achieve effective business innovation as a change management philosophy, a literature survey and a research survey on 15 SMEs were conducted to provide additional relevant information. The main findings include: the SMEs exhibited a range of CI and innovation characteristics – some had adopted a culture of CI, while others had not; the SMEs which had adopted a CI culture found that it could provide a solid foundation on which to build a culture of effective business innovation; and these SMEs were found to have embraced all the different components of innovation more readily than those SMEs which did not have a CI culture.

BPR (business process re-engineering), as a tool for innovation, may lead to high performance processes. However, if the processes are not permanently adapted, process performance will decrease in relation to that of competitors. In order to counter such a performance decline, innovations are needed. Since new ideas are the result of human creativity, it is essential that each process actor becomes active in learning (through personal experience, workshops, literature, etc.) and information sharing. Furthermore, selected members of a business process could be charged with the task of scanning and evaluating emerging technologies. In other words, high process performance means satisfying the four key stakeholders, investors, employees, customers and society, and improving the process continuously in order to guarantee long-term success (Keung, 2000).

Chapter 14
Driving quality through the voice of the customer

Everybody has a customer. And if he doesn't know who it is and what constitutes the needs of the customer … then he does not understand his job (W.E. Deming).

The needs of customers, especially internal customers, go beyond products and processes. They include needs for self-respect, respect of others, continuity of habit patterns, and still other elements of what is broadly called the cultural pattern. A great deal of failure to determine what customer needs are is traceable to failure to understand the nature and even the existence of this cultural pattern (J.M. Juran).

Deploying the voice of the customer through QFD

Karabatsos (1988) quotes Larry Sullivan (chairman of the American Suppliers Institute) as stating in 1986 that QFD is the "mechanism to deploy customer desires vertically and horizontally throughout the company". At a fundamental quality process level QFD can also be seen as a positive quality improvement approach as opposed to a (traditional) negative quality improvement approach to deliver customer satisfaction (Ford Motor Co., 1983), see Figure 14.1.

For a more detailed baseline definition, Sullivan (1986) proposes six key terms associated with QFD:

1. *Quality function deployment*: an overall concept that translates customer requirements into appropriate technical requirements for each stage of product development and production.
2. *Voice of the customer*: the customers' requirements as expressed in their own terms.
3. *Counterpart characteristics*: the voice of the customer expressed in technical language.
4. *Product quality deployment*: the activity required to translate the voice of the customer into technical requirements.
5. *Deployment of the quality function*: the activity required to assure that customer required quality is achieved.
6. *Quality tables*: the series of matrices used to translate the voice of the customer into final product characteristics.

The six key terms of QFD described by Sullivan (1986) can be further simplified as follows:

1. a "concept" for translating customer wants into the product;
2. a requirement to understand "what" the customer "wants";
3. the requirement to identify "how" technically to deliver what the customer wants;
4. the requirement for a team to carry out the "translation" of whats into hows;
5. the requirement for a "team" required to "deliver" the hows into the product; and
6. the requirement for charts that facilitate the translation of whats and hows into the product.

In even simpler terms, this can be distilled down to just one concept of QFD with four key requirements of; customer whats (or wants), technical hows, team(s) and matrices. This can be taken a step further by proposing that the first requirement of customer whats needs the second requirement of technical hows to translate itself into the product, this second requirement in turn needs the third requirement of teams to translate itself into the product, and finally this third requirement needs matrices to translate its decisions into the product. This systematic trace from customer subjectiveness, to technical objectiveness, to team decision making with the aid of matrices into product characteristics is a fundamental basis for QFD.

The quality tool of QFD

QFD is often referred to as a tool in the broad terms (Reynolds, 1992), and in more specific terms; a competitive tool (Kathawala and Motwani, 1994), a communication tool (Fowler, 1991), a marketing tool (Potter, 1994), a design tool (Slinger, 1992), a planning tool (Sullivan, 1988; McElroy, 1989), and a quality tool (Ealey, 1987). This last reference of, quality tool, perhaps best summarises all the tool references, and needs a definition in itself to understand better the basic roots of QFD. Straker (1995) describes quality tools as:

structured activities that contribute towards increasing or maintaining business quality.

By structured activities, Straker (1995) means repeatable and using a defined set of rules; by contribute, he means add value; by increasing or maintaining, he means for use in all areas of quality improvement; and for business quality, he means that the company benefits from the quality tool use. In simple terms Straker (1995) suggests that quality tools are both serious and valuable ways of doing business. Straker (1995) also proposes that tools can be used at either the organizational level (structuring the way people work together), or at an individual level (helping people and groups solve problems and tasks in their everyday business). Straker finally suggests three areas where tools can be used:
1. collecting various levels of numeric and non-numeric information;

2.   structuring the information in order to understand aspects of process and problems; and
3.   using the information to identify and select information and plan for specific actions.

The definition of quality tools and the three areas of use as described above by Straker (1995) help to outline the fundamental basis of any quality tool including QFD as defined already by Sullivan (1988), Barlow (1995) and Clausing (1994). However, according to Straker (1995) who lists some 33 individual tools in a relationship diagram with their information uses, it is apparent that not all tools are suitable for all three areas of use, or are of equal use. Asaka and Ozeki (1988) list some 15 individual quality tool types, while Nickols (1996) lists just three suites of tool types. It is clear then that the interpretation of what constitutes a tool, a tool type or a suite of tools is largely dependent on the perspectives of the various authors and the application of the tool(s) in question. Nickols (1996) considers the question of tools in terms of their problem-solving capability, and proposes his three tool types:

1.   Repair tools: for technical trouble shooting.
2.   Improvement tools: such as *Kaizen*, continuous improvement, TQM and re-engineering.
3.   Engineering tools: for design or solution engineering from scratch.

The matrix diagram of QFD
Asaka and Ozeki (1988) describe matrix diagrams as a method to "show the relationships between results and causes, or between objectives and methods, when each of these consists of two or more elements or factors". Asaka and Ozeki (1988) continue by stating that "various symbols are used to indicate the presence and degree of strength of a relationship between two sets of essential items". They propose some four key benefits of using matrix diagrams with symbols:

1.   The use of symbols makes it visually clear whether or not a problem is localised (symbols appear isolated) or more broad ranging (symbols in rows or columns).
2.   It possible to show the problem as a whole, and view all the various relationships between the various at once.
3.   By testing and evaluating each relationship and intersection of the essential factors, it becomes easier to discuss the problem at finer levels of detail.
4.   A matrix makes it possible to look at specific combinations, determine essential factors and develop an effective strategy for solving the problem.

Asaka and Ozeki (1988) refer to four different types of matrix:
1.   *L-type*: a two dimensional pairing of rows and columns.

2. *T-type*: a three dimensional matrix comprising of two L-type matrices.
3. *Y-type*: a combination of three L-type matrices.
4. *X-type*: a combination of four L-type matrices.

Some basic mechanics of the QFD process
The house of quality mechanics within QFD
To begin explaining the mechanics, Kim and Ooi (1991) argue that "QFD is a set of planning and scheduling routines that has proven effective in producing high quality as well as low cost products". Burton (1995), on the other hand, proposes that the QFD chart, often referred to as a "house of quality" due to its so called construction of "rooms" and a "roof", is essentially a chart comprising nothing more complicated than a series of lists and relationship matrices Clausing (1994) agrees with the term rooms, but adds they can also be referred to as cells and adds that the QFD matrix diagram comprises eight such rooms (or cells) which in turn contains 20 steps in completing the basic QFD matrix. The American Suppliers Institute (ASI) (1992) also refer to ten analytical steps for studying the completed house of quality at the product planning level.

The eight rooms Clausing (1994) describes are effectively the same basic rooms Ford Motor Company use in their house of quality charts at a planning level, but Ford (1994a) go further by adding a ninth quality plan room (excluding the relationship matrix) which is a key strategic aspect of the QFD process within the company. For an example of the nine rooms and relationships matrix format used in a Ford CFE-QFD Phase 1 HOQ see Figure 14.2.

Figure 14.3 (Ford Motor Co., 1994b) shows the subtle difference that a Ford Quick-QFD Phase 1 matrix exhibits, also with nine rooms and a relationships matrix, plus a further four rooms and two relationships matrices to include safety and regulatory requirements as well as the Ford worldwide customer requirements and systems design specifications.

Burton (1995) adds to his description of the house of quality chart, comprising lists and relationships matrices, by stating that they are aligned along two axes, where the x-axis is called the customer axis, and the y-axis is called the technical axis. This twin-axis description is supported by Asaka and Ozeki (1988), who suggest QFD is generally charted using a two dimensional diagram , with customer quality requirements on the vertical axis and the quality requirements needed to satisfy the customer requirements on the horizontal axis. Akao (1988), on the other hand, refers to these symbols within the quality charts used for QFD as indicators of correlation between the customers' "demanded qualities" and the technical "quality elements". Akao (1988) also refers to the traditionally used symbols depicting strong, medium and weak as the double circle, circle and triangle respectively.

For an example of a typical phase 1 house of quality chart see Figure 14.4 (Hochman and O'Connell, 1993), which charts the customer requirements and key measurables for a portable phone.

The cascading phase to phase mechanics of QFD

Sullivan (1988) defines four levels of QFD matrices that reflect different stages of application in the product development cycle. The first of these is the planning matrix that culminates with selected control characteristics (based on customer importance, selling points and competitive evaluations). The second is the component deployment matrix which culminates in defining the finished component characteristics (based the planning matrix targets). The third stage is the process plan chart, which culminates in the production process monitoring plan required by the operators. Finally, the fourth stage, is the control plan which culminates in defining quality controls that would typically include control points, control methods, sampling size frequency and checking methods. In each case Sullivan (1988) outlines that the previous charts key outputs feed into the next chart as key inputs, and represent the transition from the development phase to the execution of the production phase within the product development cycle. The four-phase QFD process can be seen in a cyclical way in Figure 14.5 and as a process clock as used by Ford Motor Company in Figure 14.6. The cascading phase to phase QFD can be seen in Figure 14.7, a typical four-phase QFD process and Figure 14.8, the Ford five-phase QFD process using a "rear view mirror".

Phase 1. Prioritisation mechanics of QFD and its implications within Ford

A key benefit of QFD is its identification of customer requirement priorities to assist the product development engineers to decide where to focus resources. Four areas are crucial components to the phase 1 house of quality (HOQ). The first is benchmarking, and the second is the customer desirability index (CDI) the CDI has also typically been referred to as the customer importance rating (CIR). The third prioritisation process is ultimately an end product of the first two and relates to the technical importance rating of the technical systems expectations (TSEs) which represent the company measurables. These measurables typically take the form of a test or metric that can be assigned a target with technical data to support an actionable follow up by the system/component engineer who is the next internal customer of this data. The fourth, and often least used, form of prioritisation within the QFD house of quality is the roof correlation matrix. The term "roof" is due the triangular nature of this technical relationship matrix on top of the main wants and hows of the relationship matrix. As a result of the roof is rarely completed.

The mechanics of the benchmarking process within prioritisation

Benchmarking within the phase 1 HOQ comes in two forms, the first is the customer competitive assessment (or evaluation) (CCA or CCE). As the title suggests this is the qualitative benchmarking that the customer participates in within the horizontal customer axis. Customers evaluate the products by comparing the relative perceived performance according to the key customer requirements (using customer language). This exercise involves the company product (or service) among its key competitive products (or services). The second benchmarking activity is the quantitative engineering competitive assessment (or evaluation) (ECA or ECE). This technical benchmarking exercise will compare the same products (or services) through conducting tests that are global and measurable and which have been correlated objectively or subjectively to best represent the technical function of the subjective customer wants. These tests have been typically referred to as substitute quality characteristics, design requirements, technical system expectations or hows. These are the technical company measures and make up the key element of the technical axis. The benefit of conducting both benchmarking exercises within the same HOQ matrix is that it is then possible to compare subjective customer ratings to objective engineering ratings. The first benefit is to show the company where improvements are required the most, and where there is already high satisfaction relative to competition. The second key benefit is that it is possible to compare discrepancies between customer perception and technical reality. Where discrepancy occurs it is either due to the wrong technical measure being in place, there are more "hidden" customer wants that require further research or quite simply a complexity of brand image.

Competitive benchmarking to set goals is a powerful tool and is supported by Vaziri (1992) who adds that it assists companies to anticipate customer needs. This ability to anticipate customer wants is a critical measure of success within any QFD exercise, and in the absence of any other form of gazing into the future, it provides the engineer with a key tool in setting so called stretch targets. Vaziri (1992) adds that it is important to obtain this benchmarking data in a timely fashion to be effective. Vaziri (1992) also argues that QFD derived customer requirements are a precursor to benchmarking, but not a prerequisite, although he does reinforce the argument that the combination of QFD and benchmarking culminates in feeding information to quality improvement teams.

The mechanics of the quality strategy plan within prioritisation
The quality strategy or plan is the area or room within the QFD HOQ where consideration of the customer importance rating (CIR), or customer delight index (CDI) for the key customer wants, is effectively weighted using a combination of techniques. First, it is important to emphasise the subtle difference between CIR and CDI. In simple terms the CDI is a customer-assigned rating of desirability for each customer want relative to every other want. From this process a Pareto list of customer wants is developed, where typically only the top 25 per cent of wants are taken and put into the QFD house of quality matrix. Effectively this is a form of prioritisation before the QFD HOQ is constructed in an effort to keep the total matrix size containable.

The mechanics of technical importance ratings within prioritisation
The basic QFD HOQ maths for determining the final technical axis TIR's is universal. Each TIR is the sum of the final weighted CIR multiplied by each respective relationship value (typically 9, 3 or 1) across the horizontal axis, and then the summed down the vertical axis. Typically the CIR's are also normalised between 1 to 5, although the strategic CDI (which is the weighted CDI as a result

of the quality strategy maths and algorithms to produce a future effect) may vary and even include decimal points.

The mechanics of the roof correlation matrix within prioritisation
This last stage of the mechanics of QFD is perhaps the least utilised part . The full function of the roof correlation is to assign weak and strong positive and negative relationship symbols between the technical measurable aspects of the QFD HOQ. As a result it has become the practice just to assign strong negatives that highlight the critical conflicts between optimised technical measurable relationships.

External and internal customer to supplier "voice-quality-satisfaction" chains
Ansari and Modarress (1994) state that it is the role of the QFD team to determine strategies that consider all opportunities presented by both internal groups and external suppliers. The scenario by Ansari and Modarress (1994) suggests that QFD teams make ideal co-ordinators of the external-internal customer-supplier chain, because the four-phase QFD process spans the product development cycle. This scenario is supported by Gopalakrishnan *et al.* (1992) who propose that while the QFD tool defines customer-supplier relationships it also improves internal processes.

To look generically how the customer-supplier chain links to key goals of product quality, product timeliness and customer satisfaction, Chaston (1993) proposes the three overlapping areas of "mutual overlap in a customer/producer/supplier satisfaction circle" (see Figure 14.9). Chaston argues that this requires more than these three areas just working together; they must build a degree of mutual trust through a common set of goals to assure mutual satisfaction. Chaston (1993) concludes this scenario of developing inter-organizational partnerships to deal with future management is becoming increasingly common in high technology industries, such as computing, precision engineering, communications and health care.

If the foundation of the QFD house of quality is based on the premise that products are designed to reflect customers' desires, then the outcome of the QFD process delivers a product that provides a sustained or increased level of customer satisfaction. Increased customer satisfaction as a key outcome of QFD, as supported by many authors including Hochman and O'Connell (1993), assumes the successful deployment of QFD-driven targets. It is this successful delivery process of customer requirements through the customer-supplier chain that is critical (For Motor Co., 1994a). Although the assumption that QFD is deployed effectively, it has already been recognised in the East versus West scenario that QFD needs to be linked into a TQM process such as company-wide quality control.

The role of QFD within total quality management (TQM) processes
Masao Kogure and Yoji Akao (both from Tamagawa University in Japan) are quoted by Karabatsos (1988) as stating that in Japan QFD is incorporated into the company-wide quality control (CWQC) activities, and as a result, QFD is carried

out systematically and continually as routine activities. Only on such a basis, Kogure and Akao (Karabatsos, 1988) conclude, these tools can prove effective.

For a simple definition of TQM, Clausing (1994) states that TQM is a promoter of common set of goals (see Figure 14.10). This is also supported by Shores (1992) and Townsend and Gebhardt (1986). Townsend and Gebhardt (1986) also refer to teamwork as a critical total quality enabler and state that the key motivation of every employee and the first step in everyone attaining quality, is to give every employee well-defined customers. In support of this Shores (1992) also emphasizes teamwork and the plan-do-study-act process. Clausing (1994) also confirms the that TQM and TQC (total quality control) literature supports the use of the plan-do-study-act cycle, which will be reinforced by the following arguments, including Zultner (1993). Clausing (1994) also describes the use of *Hoshin Kanri* as a key philosophy that is important to the TQM culture. Kano (1993) suggests many US companies have had trouble translating *Hoshin Kanri*. The Japanese Society for Quality Control committee for the English translation of TQC terminology (which Kano once chaired) translated *Hoshin Kanri* as "management by policy". This process in the English speaking world has also been given terms such as policy deployment (Greenall, 1995; Barlow, 1995), policy management (Sullivan, 1988) and policy formulation (Bardenstein and Gibson, 1992), all of which are described with the integral use of QFD. As a final statement within this introduction to the role of QFD within TQM, Lorenzen *et al.* (1993) describe TQM as the application of quantitative methods and human resources to control all processes to achieve continuous improvement and total customer satisfaction. To achieve this it is proposed that a combination of tools such as QFD, DoE, Taguchi concepts (to provide robust design and processes), SPC and process capability (or process management) are the key quality tools that can be applied systematically across the product development cycle to deliver this goal. The arguments above for the integration of the disciplines such as QFD, SPC and policy deployment to support a TQM framework are also supported by Zultner (1993) (see Figure 14.11).

Zultner (1993) also recommends use of the plan-do-study-act approach within a *Kaizen* team process, which is also supported and argued by Shores (1992) when discussing *Hoshin Kanri* or policy deployment, later in this section.

Zairi (1993) and Sullivan (1988) have already been referred to in their discussions on the Japanese style total quality management (TQM) process called company-wide quality control (CWQC), which was initiated back in 1968 (about the same time as the early QFD concepts in 1966). This CWQC approach is, however, based on a culture of prevention, while TQM, like QFD, is based on a culture which goes beyond just prevention to proactively develop positive qualities. Zairi (1993) reflects that the ultimate use of QFD as an integral part of the TQM is the use of QFD "horizontally" within a company structure as multi-disciplinary teams that identify and prioritise the technological and business know-how. This horizontal integration of QFD within a company following a TQM path is also supported by Zultner (1993) who illustrates this with a diagram on a TQM structure that also includes SPC and policy deployment (see Figure 14.11).

Zairi (1993) adds that the link between TQM and QFD is the way in which QFD is implemented. That is to say, within a TQM culture, a company may utilise QFD as just an isolated planning tool for the design team, or it may allow its full potential to be realised as a driver for changing the culture of work through multi-disciplinary teams. Zairi and Youssef (1995) reinforce these argument by stating that QFD is a main pillar for TQM and product development. One of the key benefits of QFD to support TQM is that it emphasizes a proactive approach to quality problems, rather then being reactive to quality problems by waiting for customer complaints. The argument for QFD being a proactive support to TQM is also corroborated by Bird (no date). In developing these arguments Zairi and Youssef (1995) review the relationship between QFD and other continuous improvement processes within TQM such as SPC, benchmarking and concurrent engineering. In doing so they suggest that, whether QFD is seen as a process, method, system or a philosophy, it ensures that customer requirements are integrated into products as early as the design stage. In closing, Zairi and Youssef (1995) state the TQM literature indicates that building the quality into the product starts with asking what the customer needs. QFD is a useful tool in answering this question. As a result of this Zairi and Youssef suggest that the practice of QFD is a pre-requisite of TQM.

Case studies
Black & Decker Power Tools UK
Black & Decker Power Tools (B&D) employs 1,500 people and manufacturers consumer goods, specialising in indoor and outdoor power tools. The information in this case study was provided by Mr Neil Atkinson (quality development manager) based at Spennymoor (County Durham).

QFD at B&D is defined as "a quality planning technique which ensures that true customer needs are faithfully translated into the finishing products". QFD was appreciated for its potential of helping to improve design quality of new products, which ultimately has a direct impact on customer satisfaction. Through a strong desire to conduct "right first time product launches", the decision was made to introduce QFD. It was also considered that a new culture of improving the quality of new product development process with a focus on the need of customers needed to be introduced, rather than just focusing on internal company needs.

The company introduced QFD by first sending people on courses to learn about it. QFD implementation was the responsibility of senior managers, who were advised by the quality department on various aspects. The company has made a lot of progress in utilising QFD for new product development (60 per cent of the time is spent in this area), and 40 per cent of the time is spent trying to learn more about the technique and optimising its benefits.

Benefits achieved

In relation to economic benefits such as reductions in cycle time, costs, waste and warranty claims, it is felt that it is too early to evaluate the benefits since the application of QFD is somewhat still at the early stages. However, most benefits achieved are in the intangible aspects. Among the major benefits achieved are the following:

- better innovativeness and more ideas for new products;
- better team work spirit, more effective contributions;
- fuller and better information databases on customer requirements;
- strong relationships with customers and suppliers;
- better competitive knowledge and better confidence about competitive performance;
- a general concern for satisfying all customers' requirements and not just the easy ones;
- QFD has helped prioritise design requirements and as such did expose areas of weakness and poor knowledge;
- QFD helps achieve group ownership rather than individuals' contributions; and
- drives front loading of projects to avoid late design changes.

Major problems encountered

At Black & Decker, it was found that QFD is a complex technique to use and as such did encounter resistence by a number of employees. It soon became appreciated that QFD impacts on existing culture and seeks to modify peoples' attitudes and behaviours. Conflicting objectives among team members tended to occur because people tended to work in a state of independence (individual) rather than inter-dependence (team). There was also realisation that QFD benefits cannot be achieved speedily and that because of its complexity and wider impact, QFD takes time to bring about real changes.

In addition, the following major problems were encountered at B&D:

- The extra "up front" research and development that QFD drives demands extra resources which are not usually planned for in the early stages of projects.
- Learning the QFD process takes a long time.

TQM at Black & Decker was started ten years ago. The company is certainly very strong in teamwork and uses various problem-solving techniques such as SPC, data analysis, Taguchi methods, cost of quality, among others. The company is also launching a new corporate package to re-vitalise what has already been established. At the present time, however, it is felt that QFD is not quite integrated into the TQM programme.

QFD implementation
There was no formal process of introducing QFD, which took about eight weeks. The technique has been used for over a year now. The team members selected tended to represent various major functions, they were all trained on the basic workings of QFD for up to three days. QFD was used on the development of a power tool for global markets and currently on another three projects.

At the moment, because QFD has not been integrated into the TQM programme, no attempts have been made at measuring performance or quantifying various benefits. Progress in its utilisation is, however, checked at various review meetings.

Words of advice for potential users based on B&D experience
- Ensure only the important requirements are focused on. Do this by designing market research to give clear priorities concerning customer requirements.
- The most critical factors for successful implementation include:
  ◦ senior management backing;
  ◦ careful planning and training; and
  ◦ choice of appropriate project.
- The most tangible benefits that companies should expect to achieve include:
  ◦ smoother product launch;
  ◦ higher customer satisfaction (i.e. increased sales); and
  ◦ after several projects – shorter development time.
- Major pitfalls to avoid include the following:
  ◦ Do not try to become overnight experts in market research (a message to engineers).
  ◦ If senior management do not buy in then forget it.
  ◦ Pilot projects will demand a lot of learning time, so do not pick a tight timescale project.

Quality function deployment at Lever-Faberge
The company
Lever-Faberge is a wholly owned subsidiary of Unilever plc and is the largest health and beauty products manufacturer in the UK, with 10 per cent of the market. There are 13 Lever-Faberge companies throughout Europe, each operating as an independent company with its local market, with many others throughout the world.

Lever-Faberge employs approximately 1,400 people, of which 700 are directly employed in manufacturing or production activities. The head office is in London; the factory is based in Leeds; 24 per cent of the factory output is for export and is distributed across the world by an independent Unilever subsidiary, Unilever Export.

The customers

The customers are mainly the retail and wholesale trade, which in turn sell to consumers, the ultimate end users of Lever-Faberge's products. An increasing proportion of sales go to major multiples such as Boots, Superdrug, Tesco, Asda, Safeway and Sainsbury. The customer base is as follows:

- Retail and wholesale: 35 per cent.
- Chemists and drugists: 31 per cent.
- Grocery: 34 per cent.

The products

Lever-Faberge sells over 30 branded products with significant shares in the following market segments:

- deodorants/body sprays;
- cleansers;
- conditioners;
- facial creams/lotions;
- hair colourants;
- hair setting aids;
- hairsprays;
- hand and all purpose creams;
- home perms;
- men's toiletries;
- shampoos;
- toothbrushes; and
- toothpastes.

The major brands are represented in the following table in terms of percentage sales. Lever-Faberge major brands (percentage sales):

- Hair preparation: 33 per cent.
- Dental preparations: 12 per cent.
- Men's fragrances: 10 per cent.
- Anti-perspirants and deodorants: 35 per cent.
- Skin creams: 10 per cent.

In 1991 Lever-Faberge launched new brands to strengthen its portfolio. Kyomi deo-perspirant was launched at the beginning of the year, a mouthwash and a new toothpaste variant (Mentadent sensitive) were added to the existing Mentadent range, a new shower gel (Impulse) was also launched and Creamsilk was re-launched to include a two-in-one shampoo.

Purpose/mission

Our purpose is to create and sell personal products which help people care for their health and looks, and so enhance their sense of well-being.

The goal is to delight all our customers with every product and service we offer.

Lever-Faberge relies heavily on total quality management for running its business operations. TQ is defined as follows:

Continuous improvement towards satisfying our customers' requirement at the lowest cost, through harnessing everyone's commitment.

Managers at Lever-Faberge were very much aware of the potential QFD could bring to their efforts in reducing new product development cycle time and in managing effectively the process with the achievement of total customer satisfaction. It was not, however, until April 1991 that some serious efforts were made to consider its introduction within the company.

A senior development manager attended a seminar on QFD and its benefits, organized by the American Supplier Institute (ASI). Having appreciated the true potential of QFD and its usefulness to Lever-Faberge in its quest to speed up the innovation process, he recommended that other people get exposed to the technique.

As a result, an internal seminar was organized, to raise the level of awareness of QFD among marketing managers, brand managers and development personnel. Two teams of a multi-functional nature were formed to try and apply the technique on two brands: Dimension and New Packaging Format.

How it was implemented
The company decided to pilot the technique in two phases:

1. produce a chart for Dimension; and
2. produce a chart for New Packaging Format.

The company realised that the critical need is to understand real customer wants. As a result, a QFD computer package was introduced in the development department in July 1991 and in September 1991 staff from market research were introduced to the QFD concept. The response was very enthusiastic and two market researchers joined the teams to help in the capturing of true customer requirements.

In November 1991 Lever-Faberge decided to widen the QFD training and pilot its principles on two new projects including the following brands: New Hair Product and Roll-on. During the training of the two pilot project teams, various problems were encountered with the use of the technique.
The problems encountered were:

- Difficulties in group dynamics: in creating group cohesion, team spirit and having a spirit of inter-dependence.
- Challenges to culture: various aspects of the existing culture appeared to be incompatible with the workings of QFD and some team members

objected to any significant change in their working patterns. Typically, the following comments were raised:

- "This will mean changing our whole way of working."
- "My boss won't let me devote time to QFD."
- "To get real consumer wants we need different consumer understanding methods."
- "We can't apply QFD to the soft areas."

Recognition of potential benefits

The various people who have been exposed to the principles of QFD did however appreciate the various benefits which could be gained from using the QFD technique.

The building of multi-functional teamwork

It is recognised that this is perhaps one of the biggest advantages of QFD, by changing working methods, maximising people's creative contributions and making the organization goal well-communicated and everyone's concern. It is also an opportunity for making people realise that the innovation process is not just a marketing or development responsibility but, in order to deliver effectively to the end customer, a wide variety of functions have to be involved.

Structuring the technical design process

QFD is an ideal opportunity for introducing a disciplined approach to converting customer emotional needs into physical outputs. As such it relies very much on facts and data and less on people's perceptions and preferences. The power of QFD is also recognised in the ability of the company concerned to map the innovation process each time, for each project, consistently. As such it offers the possibility of tracing back the history of each individual new product development.

Competitor benchmarking

QFD is also an ideal opportunity for moving from an internally focused culture of "doing more of the same", "doing better than we did last time" to an externally focused culture based on measuring individual practices/methods of delivering to the end customer, against those of key competitors, best of breed, and ensuring that the best practices are constantly being incorporated for the achievement of superior performance.

Computerised product design history

It is recognised at Lever-Faberge that QFD offers the opportunity of creating a powerful database on individual projects by compiling various data and pieces of information on project development implementation and measurement. The computerised package will enable teams to identify problematic areas and conduct improvement efforts by eliminating duplication, cutting down on waste and speeding up the innovation process. Repeat stages in the design process can be identified and can provide the ideal opportunity for slashing down NPD cycle time.

The next steps

Lever-Faberge did not find the use of QFD technique to be a straightforward process. There is, however, realisation that QFD is not just a tool which can be used in the context of "business as usual". It challenges the working methods, the culture and where the point of focus ought to be.

There is, therefore, wide commitment to persevere with the introduction of QFD as an established methodology in managing the new product development process. The experience at Lever-Faberge did show that having a facilitator, preferably a consultant/trainer, is extremely beneficial in diffusing crises, releasing tension and conflict between the groups, in offering guidance and prompting teams to think in the right way and focus on the right issues.

The following, therefore, is a list of action points resulting from the earlier experimental stages:

- Teams have completed phase 1 charts. The charts will be further refined as other projects will be generating further "consumer wants" and extended to tackle specified technical design issues.
- Lever-Faberge decided to provide additional training for all the teams involved in managing projects.
- Lever-Faberge is exploring the possibility of involving more closely Unilever Research Laboratory at Port Sunlight particularly in helping establish "consumer needs".
- More efforts will be devoted to finding new ways of generating consumer wants and also to establish the "soft" attribute issues.
- There will be more encouragement of market research being fully involved in helping to generate real consumer wants.
- The creative contributions of team members should be exploited more fully.
- More senior managers must be exposed to the benefits of QFD and seek their support in introducing it more widely in the management of innovation and quality programmes.
- More commitment must be generated from other heads of departments in helping to spread widely the use of QFD, giving time to individual employees to learn, pilot, participate and contribute in using QFD for managing projects.

QFD at Rover Group

Rover Group first learned of QFD through the general increase and availability of papers and information on the QFD technique. The chief engineer in charge of chassis was particularly interested. In order to find out more about it, companies in North America were contacted to see what they were doing. A senior management workshop was held and a pilot project agreed.

Its main benefit was first seen as a way of capturing design and decision information. The turnover and movement of people meant that a short form design record would be of great benefit.

The first problem encountered was how to get "the voice of the customer". To reduce market research costs, the principle of "surrogate customers" was used, i.e. people from the Rover Group with specific characteristics would use the products as customers. Another problem was focusing on too large a topic, e.g. on the whole car, so the focus was changed to a specific component, e.g. "break pedal feel". This pilot project involved a multi-disciplinary QFD team who had one week of intensive training and involved a steep learning curve. A number of lessons were learned.

To start with, the team used competitors' vehicles as well as their own. They found that people were so busy getting used to the car itself and finding the controls that they could not concentrate properly on the brake pedal. Another problem they encountered was in using a questionnaire with too much technical jargon which could not be understood by the "customers". This taught them what they should not do, so they used identical cars but modified the brakes on each one and asked simple questions such as "how confident do you feel with the brakes?" They asked the customers to test the brakes under different driving conditions, e.g. town and country driving etc. They split the customers according to age, sex, weight, height, etc. They also had a one hour "speak-easy" session after the tests as a check on the QFD. They used a Taguchi approach in conjunction with the QFD technique to great effect.

In terms of the benefits of using QFD, they saw this as a customer satisfaction issue rather than a cost saving issue. One of the other benefits was the involvement of suppliers. Quite often suppliers would receive a specification without really understanding the reasons for some of the requirements. It is a big bonus for them to see what the customer wants and helps them to re-appraise their own manufacturing process as they have an understanding of the important parameters. Another benefit is the impact on warranty costs.

QFD helps at the concept design phase, for example, to see how different parts fit together and why the target brake size is what it is. This helps with decisions for different cars in the range.

QFD is best applied in a teamworking culture and is supportive of this culture. It would be difficult to introduce it in a non-teamworking culture.

Rover currently has about a dozen QFD teams running and is taking a "gardening" approach of awareness and positive encouragement with available training if a team wants to use the technique.

The type of projects QFD is being used on is "Power trains", service from dealers (process), market image, windscreen wipers, in-car entertainment.

The company has developed its own one-day training course. This is supported by coaching when the teams needs more help. The course uses a video. The team generates the requirements and identifies relative importance from the discussion on the video, i.e. the house of quality. This illustrates to them the

214

difficulty of getting customer requirements. Once a team is trained, about 80 per cent of the benefit is obtained in actually getting to a point where they can draw a chart, i.e. getting engineers to listen to the voice of the customer, discover "hidden" requirements and take ownership for decisions affecting the customers.

Computerisation would take some drudgery out of the process as it is sometimes seen as a form filling exercise.

The company explained the positioning of QFD in terms of people, technology and systems, encompassed by the strategy of the organization, as shown in Figure 14.12.

Summary
Rover has been using QFD systematically for about two years. It is relatively restricted to components but also some service areas. It works well in a teamwork culture and the key benefit is getting the engineers to listen to the voice of the customer. The use of "surrogate" customer panels has worked well. The use of "organic" growth through positive encouragement, rather than being enforced, has worked well. The key barrier is time. You have to invest time to get the benefits.

QFD at Crosfield Electronics Ltd
Background
The contacts at Crosfield Electronics for this case study were Angus Hill, director of quality, and Malcolm Shaw, department manager, who led the first QFD project in Crosfield.

Crosfield is an international company, with a turnover of £230 million, employing 2,100 people mostly in the UK. It produces electronic imaging equipment, colour scanners, page planners and creative design systems for the printing industry. The company is based in Hemel Hempstead (the site visited) with further facilities at Peterborough and Milton Keynes and a wholly owned subsidiary (producing specialised optical equipment) at Basildon. The company has sales offices in Europe Canada and Australia and uses distributors elsewhere.

Level of understanding and awareness
Crosfield defines QFD simply as a "tool to assist product definition".

There was very little understanding of the tool initially. Crosfield had used short cycle manufacturing prior to introducing QFD.

Reasons for the introduction of QFD
QFD was introduced as part of an overall TQ strategy which in itself was a response to a perceived need to improve substantially the way in which Crosfield developed new products. Prior to introduction the company suffered the classic problems, namely products that were late to market with a high level of engineering changes just before and after launch. Coopers & Lybrand Deloitte assisted in identifying the need and developing the TQ strategy.

Extent of utilisation of QFD

QFD has been used exclusively in Crosfield's product development process and the company has found it more suitable to enhancement of an existing product than development of a new concept. New products requiring technology breakthroughs and benefit from a parallel technology study. Furthermore, Crosfield's experience is that the QFD tool is most effective at the product definition stage.

Benefits

Because of the development times of the company's product, the major product developed using QFD has not yet been lunched. However benefits seen to date are:

- a very real understanding of customer requirements;
- the ability to translate somewhat vague customer requirements into measurable product characteristics;
- company performance competitively benchmarked;
- improved team working following from the establishment of a multi-disciplinary QFD project team; and
- a well-defined and understood product development process which has been established in parallel with the QFD exercise.

Crosfield is also confident of meeting the launch date for the new project and expects a reduction in engineering changes.

Problems

A number of "roadblocks" were faced along the way as the company mounted the QFD learning curve. None of these proved insuperable. Problems mentioned were:

- Initially the project team met part-time (at first in its "tea breaks!"). Full-time would have been better, reducing the project time from nine months (actual) to, probably, three months.
- A complex project (a colour scanner, value approx £100,000, with 10,000 components) was chosen deliberately to test the technique. This resulted in too much detail (although the QFD was only level 1) with about 120 customer requirements and 140 product characteristics. Help was needed to sort and classify the data.
- From time to time senior management became impatient with perceived slow progress and had to be reminded to stick with it!

Link between QFD and TQM

Crosfield commenced its TQ journey in January 1990. It is not a "TQ company" yet but believes its customers recognise it is trying. QFD is one (albeit important) part of Crosfield's extensive TQ programme. The company has a quality council and, beneath that, a "forward engineering steering team" which is responsible for the QFD project and the product life-cycle process.

Two areas of the company are accredited to BS5750 with manufacturing about 90 per cent there.

Other tools and techniques

Crosfield uses the following tools: statistical process control (pilot), data analysis (extensively), failure modes effect analysis, time charting and analysis, cost of quality, force-field analysis, value engineering and analysis, benchmarking.

All employees are trained in the seven tools. Crosfield also uses Pugh techniques to evaluate design concepts and Boothroyd and Dewhurst techniques to evaluate manufacturing efficiency.

Implementation

QFD was introduced in 1990 with assistance from Coopers & Lybrand Deloitte. The internal sponsor was the deputy managing director, technical operations. The company has piloted the technique on one major project which has not yet reached fruition. The choice of this project was a deliberate test of a methodology which was a radical departure from the previous approach. Key differences were the structured approach, level of detail required and the need for multi-disciplinary teamworking. The company deliberately chose a talented sceptic as team leader – on the basis that his conversion to the approach would bring substantial benefits.

Each team member was given three days training which was regarded as just sufficient. Currently no training is being given as the QFD technique is not being used.

External costs related to QFD implementation are estimated to be £75,000 (although this includes some costs associated with the overall TQ programme). Some 2-2.5 man years were required for the initial QFD project.

Recommendations/conclusions

Crosfield has derived substantial benefit from its initial QFD project particularly in the areas of understanding customer requirements, competitive benchmarking, teamworking and developing an improved product development process.

These benefits are confidently expected to flow through, in time, to shorter times to market and fewer engineering changes. In the words of the managing director:

Doing things the right way takes a helluva long time but it's worth waiting for.

For companies considering using QFD Crosfield recommends:

- start with a small, self-contained project;
- resource it full-time with a maximum of six to seven people;
- use QFD in the product definition phase for enhancing an existing product;
- plan and review as a team but do the work off-line;
- keep the customer requirement on the chart to about 30-50; and
- ensure the support and championship of senior management.

Raychem (UK) Ltd, Swindon
The company
Raychem is a "materials-science" company, with a $1.25 billion annual turnover. The corporation develops and manufacturers a wide range of specialist polymeric products and materials such as heat shrinkable tubing, moulded parts, wire and cable products, interconnection devices, gels, adhesives and self-limiting heaters. Raychem also produces sub-assemblies from these products such as electrical harnesses which are build into, for example, aircraft and automobiles. The products are exploited in commercial and defence electronics, industrial products and telecommunications.

Raychem employs over 10,000 people and has manufacturing, marketing and administrative operations in more than 40 countries. Raychem's headquarters are in Menlo Park California, R&D takes place in California and Swindon in the UK.

Raychem has a strong quality culture and has operated a TQM programme for five years. The company knows about and practices many TQM techniques in addition to QFD.

QFD in Raychem
Raychem's awareness of QFD came about partly as a result of the intellectual curiosity of its development staff and partly as a result of purchaser pressure (especially from the automotive industry). The company has been using QFD techniques for approximately two years.

Raychem employed consultants to introduce staff to QFD techniques. Standard training courses and associated case studies were used. Training was given without regard to when the attendees were to apply what they had learned and, as a result, the training was less effective than if it had been given just prior to undertaking a QFD project.

Current practice
Raychem has built up a body of experience of applying QFD and can identify significant benefits, some of which are regarded as too valuable to disseminate.

Raychem's quality procedures relating to product development now mandate QFD as a means of deriving customer requirements' specifications. Some issues from Raychem's experience are (not in any order of priority):

- QFD is a powerful technique for working with customers to draw out and prioritise customers' needs. Raychem characterises this fact by calling QFD "the voice of the customer".
- Raychem points to one QFD project conducted jointly with a leading aerospace manufacturer that has resulted in significant new business.
- The customer became convinced in the course of a joint QFD project with Raychem that they and Raychem had derived a joint understanding of requirements.
- QFD should, therefore, be seen as a mechanism for building lasting relationships with customers, that is for "customer bonding".

- The process of drawing out, specifying and prioritising customer needs relies heavily on listening skills and interviewing techniques. It is most essential that QFD project teams are trained in these mechanisms.
- QFD is a complex technique with a very valuable pay off. However its complexity is such that it is not easy to learn or to apply. As a consequence:
  - Staff need to be trained in QFD theory in a context relevant to products they produce.
  - They should be trained just before they start a QFD project, so that QFD is practised while the training is fresh.
  - The expectations of management should be structured so that they are not led to anticipate miraculous or instantaneous results from QFD. The process is heavily front loaded by the training, practice and tailoring necessary to match the technique to company, culture and the type of product.
  - It is advisable to start with a QFD project that is likely to result in a positive outcome in a short timescale. This will probably be a simple project with well bounded requirements.
  - To support this point, Raychem used the example of the successful application of QFD to the development of its application equipment which is used by the customer to install Raychem products. Such tools (which are sometimes quite complex) are usually developed without a complete knowledge of the customer's requirements and are thus often the subject of more than one redesign and/or on site modification. In the case quoted, QFD enabled a "50 per cent reduction in development and customer installation cycle" over previous similar tools developments – the product was "right first time".
  - Do not make extravagant claims for QFD until there is documentary evidence to back them up.
- QFD projects should be run by a project leader drawn from the QFD team. A facilitator should be available to help with the QFD process, but should not get actively involved in making QFD deliverables.
- An influential QFD champion and management commitment to provide the necessary resources and allocate the necessary staff time to training are vital components of any QFD programme.
- The implementation of QFD should be planned, resources and executed as a project.
- QFD relies heavily on team working. It is necessary to have a culture of teamworking before introducing QFD, or to develop such a skill as part of a QFD training package.
- When involving customers in a QFD project there is a risk that they will share the results with competitors in order to gain commercial (in particular price) advantage.

- QFD teams should be formed from those people who currently manufacture, design, sell and market a product.
- QFD can be used very effectively for deriving new solutions to existing problems.

Benefits
Raychem identify the following benefits:
- Building close relationships with customers.
- Meeting (and possibly exceeding) customers' expectations.
- Engineering customers' expectations.
- Building and encouraging team working and hence company effectiveness, through understanding of the problems of other functions.
- Products more likely to be right first time.
- Defining internal requirements.

Problems
- The introduction costs, particularly in training and practising the technique prior to its productive exploitation.
- Management expectations of a quick return.
- Where a customer has many potential suppliers of a product or service, there is a danger that a customer will share results with your competition in order to gain a cost advantage for themselves.

Recommendations for setting up in QFD
- Work with consultants to develop training material that is matched with your company's culture and of direct relevance to your products and organization structure.
- Ensure that management understands the size of the investment costs and the time that QFD takes to mature into a productive technique.
- Tailor the QFD methodology to your product development and manufacturing process. For example, when using continuous processes, like extrusion, link the process with part deployment, as the two are very much integrated. Follow the maxim: "right product – right process – achievable; right product – wrong process – not achievable".
- Ensure that your QFD team has appropriate teamworking and interviewing skills.
- Find a champion who will introduce QFD in the context of a simple product.
- Facilitation (in the form of expertise in the QFD process and techniques) should be available at the request of the QFD team leader.
- Only publicise QFD when claims can be supported by quantified evidence.

Figure 14.1 Two approaches: negative vs. positive quality

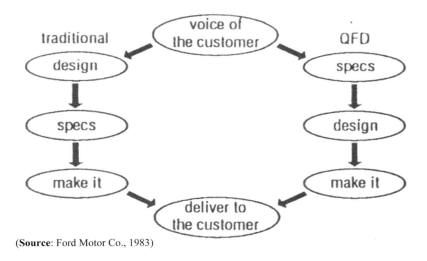

(**Source**: Ford Motor Co., 1983)

Figure 14.2 Ford CFE-QFD nine rooms QFD phase 1 matrix

Customer Axis

i   Customer Wants – as defined at a total vehicle level, for that attribute, through market research.

ii Customer Desirability Index – an Importance Rating identified by Market Research from the Customer.

iii Adjusted (Strategic) CDI – takes account of futuring, sales points, PALS, and Customer Satisfaction data.

iv Customer Competitive Assessment – customer image benchmarking exercise, to identify the position of the Ford product versus its key competitor, organised by Marketing Research.

Technical Axis

v   Roof Correlation – will identify attribute impact on each other.

vi Technical Systems Expectations – translation of the Customer Wants into engineering measurables.

vii Technical Importance Rating – the relative importance of the TSEs.

viii How Much – target value for each TSE.

ix Engineering Competitive Assessment – the technical benchmarking of current Ford and competitor vehicles against the TSEs. The results should correlate with the CCA.

Relationship Matrix

x   Relationships – identify the strength of the links between TSEs and Customer Wants.

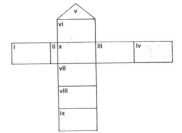

(**Source**: Ford Motor Co., 1994a)

221

Figure 14.3 Ford Quick-QFD nine rooms QFD phase 1 matrix

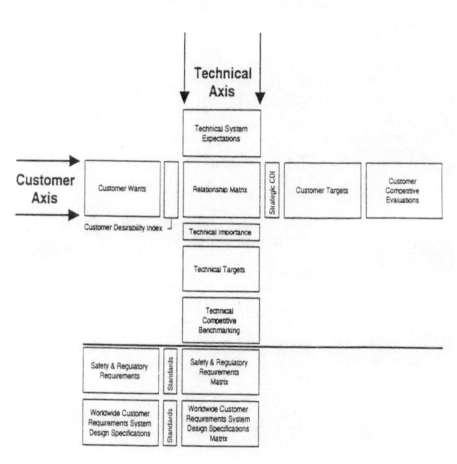

(**Source**: Ford Motor Co., 1994b)

Figure 14.4 Example QFD phase 1 house of quality

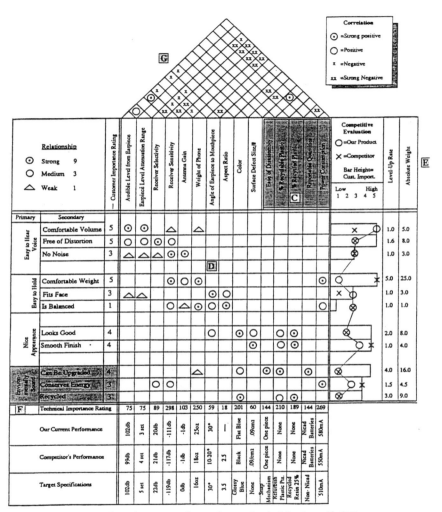

. Integrating customer environmental concerns into the design of a portable phone.

(**Source**: Hochman & O'Connell, 1993)

Figure 14.5 Example cyclical QFD process: phases for product development

(**Source**: Ford Motor Co., 1983

Figure 14.6 Ford CFE-QFD process clock

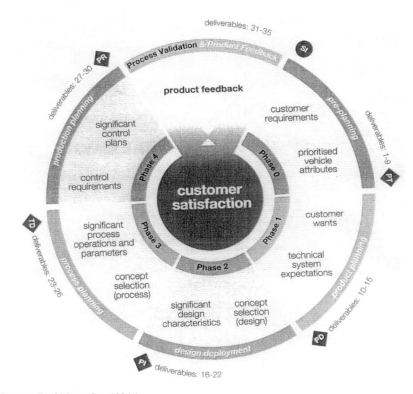

(**Source**: Ford Motor Co., 1994a)

Figure 14.7 Linked QFD houses convey the customer's voice to manufacturing

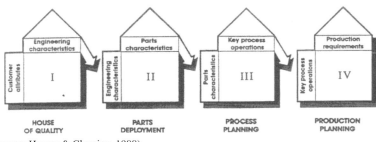

(**Source**: Hauser & Clausing, 1988)

Figure 14.8 Rear view mirror example, Ford phase 5 CFE-QFD process

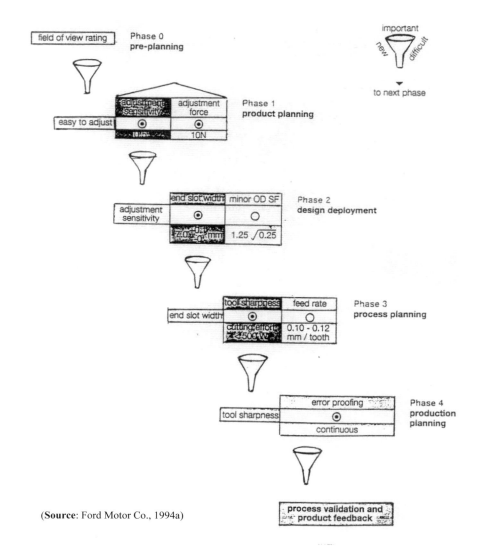

(**Source**: Ford Motor Co., 1994a)

Figure 14.9 Future scenarios of mutual overlap: customer/producer/supplier
satisfaction circle

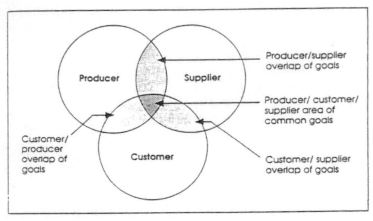

(**Source**: Chaston, 1993)

Figure 14.10 TQM as a promoter of common goals

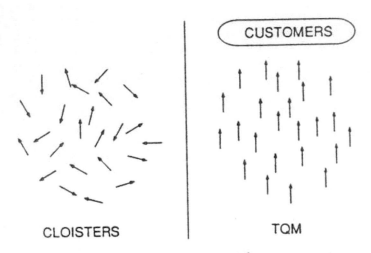

TQM as promoter of common goals.

(**Source**: Clausing, 1994)

Figure 14.11 Horizontal integration of QFD within TQM

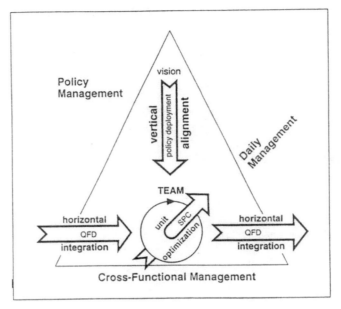

(**Source**: Zultner, 1993)

Figure 14.12 QFD positioning at Rover Group

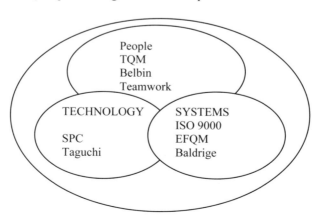

Chapter 15
Driving quality through policy deployment

There is an interrelation between quality planning and quality improvement. It is well described by the plight of the fabled manager who was up to his waist in alligators. Under the analogy each live alligator is a potential quality improvement project. Each completed improvement project is a dead alligator.

If our fabled manager succeeded in exterminating all alligators then quality improvement would be complete – for the moment. However, the manager would not be finished with alligators. The reason is that *the planning process has not changed.*

In effect, the quality planning process is a dual hatchery. A benign hatchery produces new, useful quality plans. A malignant hatchery produces new alligators. Quality improvement can take care of the existing alligators, one by one. However, to stop the production of new alligators requires shutting down that malignant hatchery (J.M. Juran).

The link between quality policy deployment and performance measurement
Quality policy deployment (QPD) is the necessary trigger for processes to perform well and for goals to be achieved. It is the mechanism by which the quality effort is cascaded down throughout the organization. QPD is a top-down approach and as such tends to be the responsibility of senior managers. Process improvement and measurement is a horizontal effort and quality deployment is a vertical (top-down) approach. As Figure 15.1 illustrates, quality improvement is a continuous effort and as such is not finite. However, quality effects have to be measured and quantified against set targets (Yoji, 1990).

Quality policy deployment is not merely a good communication process, it is a dynamic process where performance measurement is an integral part and where goals are translated into actions throughout the various activities. Quality function deployment is the horizontal process which ensures that performance will ensue from the goal communication effort.

The Deming cycle of plan-do-check-act (PDCA) can be applied in the context of QPD (i.e. strategical continuous improvement). As Figure 15.2 illustrates (American Supplier Institute, 1989) the PDCA can drive the strategy and ensure that goals are achieved, that adjustments are made as and when necessary and that learning takes place continuously.

The conventional methods of strategic planning and strategic implementation tend to be marred with problems. Many strategies fail to deliver for a variety of reasons including, among others:

- Poor communication of goals – people working in total darkness.
- Moving the goal post – too many disruptions and changes in direction.
- Pursuit of pet projects – short-term goals to the detriment of long-term competitiveness.
- Cost is the key driver for results at the expense of real improvement opportunities.
- Goals developed in remoteness from the process.
- Voice of customer not really captured.
- Achievements are not sustainable.

On the other hand, QPD is focusing on sustainability and building strengths for increased competitiveness. While this process focuses on results, it only does so by continuously improving the processes concerned so that repeatability of performance and consistency can be ensured.

QPD introduces discipline, conveys the same goal at all levels and ensures goal congruence or real alignment. Unlike management by objective (MBO), which focuses on individual performance and follows a rigid hierarchical route of line of authority and responsibility, QPD follows a process route and measures team performance. Unlike MBO, QPD is not concerned with the "one leap at a time" type of approach, the effect is to focus on continuous improvement to optimise process capability, to learn from mistakes, to capture winning practices and ideas and to manage quality proactively.

The relationship between QPD and performance management is illustrated in Figure 15.3. Perhaps the best description of quality policy deployment is the process by which congruence can be achieved and the "what to do" and "how to perform" questions can be answered. Performance measurement on the other hand measures motion, action and value added contributions. The business delivery process (BDP) reflects all the recommended effects which add value to the end customer, driven by a thorough understanding of customer requirements and process capability.

Figure 15.4 on the other hand describes the two activities of QPD and performance measurement in terms of:

1. *Process management*: this is a senior management responsibility, deciding on the right things to do, developing the right objectives and communicating them at all levels in the right way.
2. *Performance measurement*: quality improvements take place through team efforts and a multi-functional approach. Performance measurement therefore becomes the responsibility of process workers who have the ultimate task of carrying out the necessary improvements.

Figure 15.4 also highlights the fact that quality policy deployment and performance measurement have to focus not just on deficiency areas and negative gaps but also on pro-active quality and the protection of competitive advantages. Benchmarking therefore becomes very relevant at two levels:

1. *Strategic benchmarking*: to develop goals and critical success factors (CSFs) through a thorough understanding of customer requirements and process capability.

2. *Operational benchmarking*: to optimise process capability at all levels through the introduction of new practices, methods learned from leading organizations.

An example of a quality policy deployment process

This is a process described in Hronec (1993) who presents QPD as a model of seven key elements:

1. Strategy – its development and communication supported by having the right reward mechanisms in place, training and also reliance on benchmarking for doing the right things in the right way.
2. Goals.
3. Critical processes.
4. Output measures.
5. Key activities.
6. Process measures.
7. Implementation.

The "quantum performance measurement model", as it is referred to, is dynamically driven by continuous improvement (i.e. PDCA cycle). As Figure 15.5 illustrates, the corporate objectives could be to maintain customer loyalty through rapid product introduction.

The goals/CSFs could be to:

- increase speed to market by 50 per cent over the next two years;
- develop two new products each year; and
- get 25 per cent of company profits from new products in two years.

These goals are then cascaded down to all key activities and critical processes. Performance measurement and improvement start, therefore, once key performance measures have been developed (i.e. to capture core activity and high leverage in areas which impact most on customer satisfaction).

Soft measures, which are people related, could also be used to ensure that the right people with the required skills are used in the right way for all key processes.

Defining quality policy deployment

Policy management is the vehicle by which business plans are put together and communicated at all levels of the organization. Policy management is the translation of *hoshin kanri* as it is known in Japan: *hoshin* means direction; *kanri* means deployment/administration/ management. Rank Xerox defines policy deployment as follows:

> A key by which Rank Xerox can articulate and communicate the Vision, Mission, Goals and Vital Few Programmes to all employees. It provides the answers to the two questions: "What do we need to do?" and "How are we going to do it?"

At Rank Xerox, quality policy is used as a process by which company values and goals are translated into activities which, when carried out, can achieve the desired results.

Policy deployment is the propagation of a cycle where "whats" and "hows" are worked out at a very senior management team level (e.g. "What" = CSF = Be No. 1 supplier to major retailers by 1995; "How" = by focusing on on-time delivery, speed/quality of response, level of service). The "hows" can then become "whats" at the next management level, and so on. In this way performance measurement becomes an application which can be seen at major process level, sub-process level, activity and task levels.

Examples of quality policy deployment models
Procter and Gamble

The company, which was founded in 1837 by William Procter and James Gamble, is a global leader in areas such as health care, food, beverage, laundry, cleaning and beauty care products, amongst others. It employs over 100,000 people world-wide and has operations in 53 countries.

Procter and Gamble adheres to the TQ principles. It started implementing TQM in 1983 through a bottom-up approach. TQM is, however, endorsed by senior managers at the highest level, including the chairman and chief executive who argues that (Bemowski, 1992):

> Total quality, because of its focus on benchmarking customer and consumer satisfaction, is basically an insurance policy for sustaining competitive advantage over the long term, even when a company might not, at any given time, have a blockbuster advantage over the others. Total quality is the very essence of our long-term growth strategy.

P&G recognises that strategy development and implementation is a serious business. There is awareness of the various pitfalls of strategic implementation, reported by a 1989 Booz Allen study of strategy development and implementation (Huston, 1992). The study concluded that, of the respondents:

- 73 per cent of managers believed that implementation is more difficult than development;
- 72 per cent thought that it would take more time;
- 64 per cent believed that it impacted more on performance;
- 64 per cent of management lacked implementation skills;
- 75 per cent stated that employees misunderstood roles;
- 75 per cent maintained that groups did not co-ordinate;
- 48 per cent criticised inadequate measures for strategy achievement;
- 45 per cent said there was internal competition;
- 40 per cent stated there was insufficient employee involvement and commitment; and
- 85 per cent thought that implementation was the part of the strategy over which managers had least control.

As Figure 15.6 indicates, P&G is very serious about how they implement strategy. They use a four-stage approach. The process itself covers five key elements which include:
1. Strategic intent.
2. Year targets.
3. Annual deployment plans (based on each year's objectives, goals, strategies and measures (OGSM).
4. Management reviews.
5. Results feeding back to learning.

The whole process of strategic deployment is reinforced by a positive deployment of TQM. It is, however, recognised that TQM by itself does not lead to the production of winning strategies. There has to be a strong presence of management leadership. This was highlighted by P&G's chairman and CEO, who argues that (Bemowski, 1992):

Total quality does not guarantee that companies will produce winning strategies. Winning strategies have to come from the minds of the leaders.

An example of quality deployment at P&G
Figure 15.7 illustrates quality policy deployment (QPD) at the Soap Sector of P&G. The process consists of three stages:
1. the long-term vision;
2. strategic development; and
3. strategic deployment.

The third stage (strategic deployment) is perhaps a revolutionary addition from conventional methods of strategy implementation. In addition to clearly specifying how goals are to be measured, how competitive advantages are measured and how progress is tracked, a shadow set of questions are asked to ensure that organizational capability is strengthened through the deployment process and that lessons learned are used to ensure more effective strategic deployment. Organizational capability is achieved through management reviews and visits conducted for purposes such as ensuring the quality of results, to assess strengths and weaknesses of organization capability, to ensure that there is a goal congruence and total alignment within the organization and finally to use the learning captured for future strategic planning.

Komatsu Ltd

This company is one of the world's leading producers and suppliers of industrial machines. The product range includes over 300 different types and the market served represents a wide variety of customers including construction and industrial machinery. The Osaka plant which won the Deming prize back in 1964 employs 2,000 people and manufactures bulldozers, hydraulic excavators and underground machinery. Figure 15.8 illustrates quality policy deployment at Komatsu Ltd (Catherine and Daniel, 1991).

Excessive effort is placed on planning in a rigorous manner, this is the key to successful goal translation. Quality policy in this context is very similar to previous cases analysed in that the PDCA cycle tends to be used extensively:

- *Plan stage*: establishing policies and deployment of various objectives to all functions. This is done through a focus on external customers and the translation of their needs into tangible goods and services.
- *Do stage*: the translation of company goals at all levels in the organization, including individual employees.
- *Check stage*: regular monitoring of progress and performance checks to ensure that goals are still achievable.
- *Act stage*: feedback from performance and results achieved, including new learning that can be used for the development of the next batch of goals.

Hewlett-Packard

This company manufacturers and sells electronic products which are used in the computer industry and also for measurement purposes. The products manufactured are widely used and include hardware equipment, peripheral equipment, printing equipment and software systems including networking.

Quality at H-P started in 1978, an inspiration coming from Japan, at the Yokagawa H-P Plant, a joint venture with Japan. The Yokogawa H-P Plant won the Deming Prize in 1982 as a result of its excellence in quality. At the heart of the quality drive with H-P is measurement in all areas. Some of the customer related measures include (Carter and Edmonds, 1988):

234

- *Response time*: the time from the first customer call to the arrival of the customer engineer at the customer's site.
- *Repair time*: the time it takes the engineer to repair the customer unit.
- *System downtime*: the total elapsed time from the customer call to the unit being repaired.
- *Turn around time*: the elapsed time from the unit arriving at the service centre to it being repaired.

Managing quality at Hewlett-Packard takes place through *hoshin kanri* (a literal translation is "shiny metal pointing direction"). As illustrated in Figure 15.9 the process uses the PDCA cycle and goal translation takes place through various stages.

The benefits of QPD include:
- Relying on QPD gives senior management a disciplined approach to planning and highlights the importance of goals and measures.
- It encourages regular reporting and provides managers with the right documentation that enables them to set future plans, implement them and review their outcomes.
- *Hoshin kanri* ensures that TQM implementation succeeds and the various efforts deliver.
- It constantly reminds people of the importance of customers and relying on measurement and action.

The motto at Hewlett-Packard is "That which is measured gets better, but that which is measured and reported gets better faster".

Rank Xerox Ltd

Hoshin kanri is a key process at Rank Xerox Ltd. It is used for creating synergy among the various functional areas and, hence, optimise capability to deliver, but also to convert all customer needs (explicit and non-expressed) into value added contributions.

Rank Xerox deploys quality policy at all levels of the organization and integrates QPD with employee appraisal. Although the process is deployed in a top-down fashion, there is active participation at all levels, to ensure that goals are delivered. In order to gain company wide commitment, Rank Xerox relies on a process called "catchball", which essentially means that there is negotiation using facts and hard data to resolve differences and disagreements during the deployment of company goals. Like playing " catch", employees and managers can throw data and information at each other so that goals are accepted and people are committed to delivering them.

Figure 15.10 illustrates quality policy deployment at Rank Xerox Ltd. Similarly to previously discussed processes, Rank Xerox used the PDCA cycle for planning, implementing and taking necessary actions.

Florida Power & Light

The first non-Japanese company to have won the Deming Prize, in 1989, FP&L employs over 14,000 people and has over three million customers. FP&L uses Japanese techniques very extensively to deploy the quality effort.

FP&L used the techniques of Japanese quality gurus such as Dr Asaka who, in 1985, made the management realise the importance of quality policy deployment. The Japanese have always believed that quality has to be managed strategically and unless all the efforts are deployed for the same goals and in the same direction, there will be very little impact. Goal congruence is therefore a vital task for managers to achieve in their quest for directing people towards successful performance standards.

Table 15.1 illustrates the way QPD is deployed at FP&L. First, it was determined that the vital priorities needing improvement were:

- sales and service quality;
- delivery;
- safety; and
- price.

FP&L has developed a set of objectives, indicators and improvement targets for each measure. Similar to Rank Xerox, FP&L uses "catchball" to communicate and ensure commitment. The process is cascaded down to all levels, function-department-section-individual. The power of QPD at FPL is seen in its ability to instigate discipline in planning and in taking action to ensure that goals are achieved.

Figure 15.1 The quality deployment process

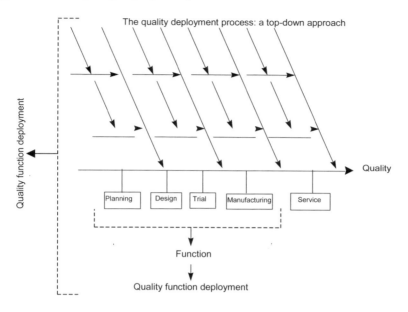

Figure 15.2 Strategic application of the PDCA cycle

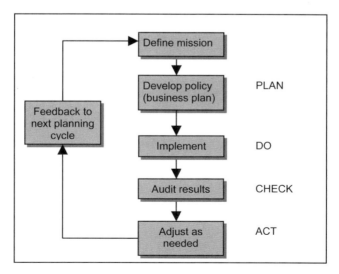

Figure 15.3 Integrating the voice of the customer with the voice of the process for goal congruence

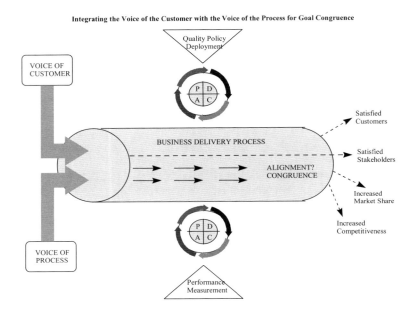

Figure 15.4 Integrating process management and performance measurement

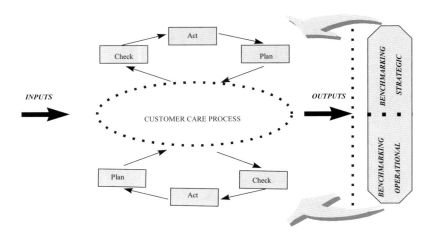

Figure 15.5 Example of quality policy deployment process

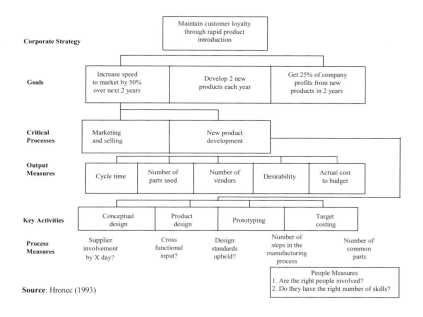

Figure 15.6 A four cycle approach to implementation of strategy

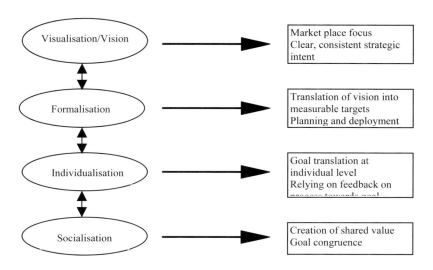

Figure 15.7 Quality policy deployment

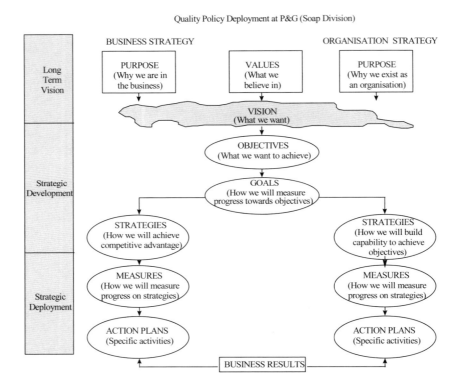

Quality Policy Deployment at P&G (Soap Division)

Figure 15.8 Quality deployment process at Komatsu Ltd

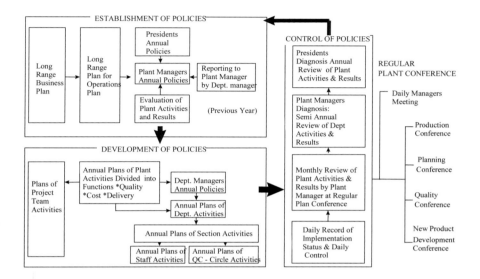

Figure 15.9 Quality policy deployment process at Hewlett-Packard

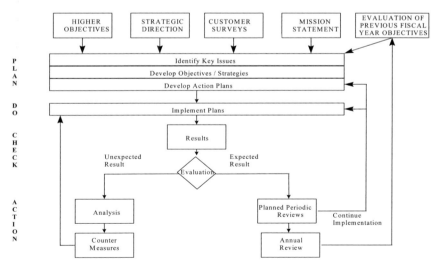

(**Source**: Catherine and Daniel, 1991)

Figure 15.10 Quality policy at Rank Xerox

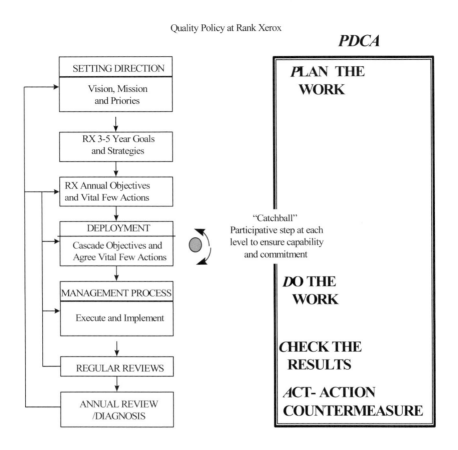

Quality Policy at Rank Xerox

PDCA

SETTING DIRECTION

Vision, Mission and Priories

RX 3-5 Year Goals and Strategies

RX Annual Objectives and Vital Few Actions

DEPLOYMENT

Cascade Objectives and Agree Vital Few Actions

MANAGEMENT PROCESS

Execute and Implement

REGULAR REVIEWS

ANNUAL REVIEW /DIAGNOSIS

"Catchball"
Participative step at each
level to ensure capability
and commitment

*P*LAN THE WORK

*D*O THE WORK

*C*HECK THE RESULTS

*A*CT- ACTION COUNTERMEASURE

Table 15.1 How QPD is deployed at Florida Power & Light

	Objectives	Indicators	% improvement targets	Quality categories			
				Sales and service quality	Delivery	Safety	Price
1.1	Improve the cost of electric service	Distribution service availability (customer minutes)	8		0		
		Transmission service unavailability (customer minutes)	13		0		
		Substation service unavailability (customer minutes)	9		0		
1.3	Improve customer satisfaction	Number of customer complaints to the FPSC/thousand customers (excluding current diversion)	12	0			
2.1	Improve the safety and competitiveness of nuclear power	Automatic trips (1991 St Lucie only)	100			0	
		Equivalent availability (1991 St Lucie only)	13		0		
		Turkey Point dual unit outage duration (days)	N/A		0		
		O&M cost variance to budget	0				0
		Capital expenditure variance to budget	0				0
3.4	Improve employee safety	Number of lost time injuries per 100 FPL employees	19			0	
		Number of doctor cases per 100 employees	13			0	
4.1	Improve O&M cost per PWH and achieve budget security and quality	O&M C/h WH	N/A				0
		O&M cost variance to budget	0				0
4.3	Establish fossil unit reliability, availability and maintenance targets and develop programmes to achieve those targets	Equivalent forced outage rate (%)	18		0		
4.4	Provide adequate energy supply capacity and maintain the energy of the delivery system during the Turkey Point emergency diesel generator (EDG) outage in an economical manner	MW required to ensure reserve margin 18>15%	N/A		0		

Chapter 16
A perspective on learning

People are different from one another. A manager of people must be aware of these differences, and use them for optimization of everybody's abilities and inclinations.

People learn in different ways, and at different speeds. Some learn a skill by reading, some by listening, some by watching pictures, still or moving, some by watching someone do it.

One is born with a natural inclination to learn. Learning is a source of innovation. One inherits a right to enjoy his work. Good management helps us to nurture and preserve these positive innate attributes of people (Deming, 1994, p. 108).

Where is the current focus of CEOs?
A report by the Royal Society for the Encouragement of Arts (RSA) (1995) refers to an enquiry made up of senior managers representing 25 top companies. It concluded that:

- there is an overall gap in performance at a world standard because companies suffer from complacency and ignorance of world standards;
- a national culture which is very adversarial; and
- an over-reliance on financial measures of performance and short-term focus.

The RSA report concludes that in order to create tomorrow's organization there has to be a radical shift through the creation of a more inclusive approach and taking a stakeholder perspective. In particular, the report stresses on the following:

- the need to define purpose, values and their effective communication at all levels;
- using the purpose, values etc. as a baseline for designing individually tailored formulas for success and a meaningful framework for performance measurement;
- organizations need to recognise the importance of reciprocal relationships, and learning from all those who have a stake in the business in order to compete effectively; and
- building close partnerships with customer and suppliers.

The imperative on business leaders, therefore, is to plan, define, discuss, measure and report on success in their organizations from an all encompassing way. There has to be a shift in the mind set for them to consider people as the key and only asset and therefore invest in the development of their potential, in engaging them in problem solving and continuous improvement activity and in harnessing their creative potential.

Learning and knowledge

Knowledge is power or should it be knowledge is powerful? Management gurus such as Peter Drucker advocate that productivity increases can only be measured beneficially through the harnessing of employee knowledge. A study conducted by Ikujiro Nonaka and Hirotaka Takeuchi of Hitotsubashi University (1995) has concluded that "it is the ability to create new knowledge, rather that manufacturing prowess, that puts firms ahead". According to the two authors concerned the difference between Western managers and their Japanese counterparts is that the former when referring to "knowledge" mean hard data, numbers and words (explicit). The Japanese on the other hand are more concerned with tacit knowledge which is embodied in employees' hunches, ideas and skills.

Tacit knowledge is thought to be deeply ingrained and very hard to share. However, once it is converted into explicit knowledge, then it automatically becomes part of innovation and,thus, becomes shareable. It is thought that there are three things which can help the sharing of tacit knowledge (Nonaka and Takeuchi, 1995):

1. Employees need to be encouraged to share each other's experiences as much as possible, perhaps through fluidity and team dynamics.
2. Making effective use of middle management. Although visions are created by top management and ideas originate from the bottom layers, middle managers are useful at bridging the two together.
3. Creating a "hypertext" organization made up of three structures:
   ◦ *Traditional structure*: useful for the running of day-to-day business and also for spreading the explicit knowledge referred to earlier.
   ◦ *Creative structure*: this is an arrangement where people can group and ungroup through team structures, in order to generate ideas.
   ◦ *Knowledge base:* this is a structure to bring together both explicit and tacit knowledge, including things such as databases, corporate culture and collected wisdom of all a firm's older citizens.

Both Deming and Juran have consistently argued that changing is not learning. Change is the net result of using SQC techniques and other problem-solving techniques to support teams in their quest to tackle variation, optimisation the performance of processes and activities and help achieve the desired standards of organizational performance. In so doing, teams must learn through their exposure to best practices and proven ideas through benchmarking for instance. True innovation and learning on the other hand, comes from big ideas, original thinking and unique creative suggestions that can tackle major parts of the system. The use of business process re-engineering is an approach which is used in this context (see Figure 16.1).

Juran's trilogy suggests that the control of chronic waste comes from using SQC techniques to stabilise the process and keep variation within the set limits. The new paradigm, where big leaps in improvement take place, can only come through injecting new learning and new ideas.

In order to avoid the practice of tampering and change for the sake of change, organizations will have to develop and progress through the following four key steps.

1. Having a process of learning

This is to ensure the inputs and the bank of knowledge which is available, the blend of skills and expertise that each individual can contribute. The corporate climate or heart of the process is a clear understanding of what the task really is and the innovation is reflected throughout the whole cycle of adding value to the end customer and that there is a positive climate of problem solving and continuous improvement. Of course this is all done in the context of multi-functional, horizontal involvement. The output from this is customer focus in terms of hard deliveries of products and services and soft deliveries in terms of value, professionalism, innovation etc. (see Figure 16.2).

2. Managing learning through a continuous process

TQM places the emphasis on the process and the use of PDC to optimise activities, reduce/eliminate waste and speed up the whole delivery cycle. Processes have to be managed through understanding and the application of knowledge, reflecting on outcomes and recycling again (see Figure 16.3).

3. Managing key ingredients for effective learning

Effective learning comes from having the right ingredients to start with a tireless approach (the engine) to constantly innovate and translate knowledge and know-how into customer benefits and competitive outcomes for the organizations concerned (Figure 16.4).

4. Strategic deployment process through learning

Business development and performance go hand in hand with organizational development. Business performance review processes are well understood and very often refer to the capability of "hardware" in terms of processes, sub-processes and activities which add value to the end customer. For effective learning, the goal transmission process has to be supported by a competence performance review process where the translation of corporate learning takes place to ensure effective implementation of corporate targets and the achievement of desired outcomes.

Very often the PDCA cycle is referred to at the operational level only. This is even the case when it comes to learning. The PDCA, however, can be applied at the strategic level and the process of learning is perhaps more enhanced and broader at the higher level, but there is a continuum of applying learning to achieve corporate goals.

Figure 16.5 illustrates the process discussed above. The deployment of various competencies will reflect roles and responsibilities. It is therefore expected that the organizational and business competencies will be exhibited more by senior managers, while at the lower levels, where people are expected to control the processes through SQC and other techniques, the skills are more technical/support in nature.

What and who are the learning organizations?

It is very hard to define the real meaning of corporate learning, learning organizations and the cycle of learning itself. Some view learning as a process closely linked to on-going training and education, others consider it as an outcome from the implementation of change and others will refer to the evolutionary process of corporate change and adaptation in the market place. It is however important, right from the outset, to put corporate learning in the right perspective. It is a continuous process, but the outcomes of which are not necessarily change for the sake of change but rather new knowledge which is capable of giving enhancements in overall corporate performance.

Types of learning organization

There are four distinctive types of learning organizations (McGill and Slocum, 1994):

1. *Knowing organizations*: this type refers to those organizations that are very current in their thinking and which are constantly seeking to pioneer or implement new thinking.

2. *Understanding organizations*: organizations that compete on the basis of clear understanding of their cultural norms and guiding principles which they the translate into strategy.

3. *Thinking/problem-solving organizations*: those that spend time identifying and solving problems which are impeding them from effective competitiveness.

4. *Learning organizations:* those that take time to learn, and take advantage of opportunities to develop and get smarter.

Table 16.1 compares the four types of organizations discussed above. The differences are highlighted in terms of management practices, employee behaviour, customer perspective and how change is applied.

Learning organizations are those that consider it to be an on-going cycle and a continuous process. It cannot and should not be measured in terms of single bursts of knowledge. Learning is not necessarily about blue printing and developing new thinking. Learning is what becomes imbedded and rooted in organizations and only can come through the application of knowledge. One quick lesson to be drawn from this is that learning is strongly associated with attitudes and behaviour.

How does learning happen?

Learning is about behaviour modification, the updating of the old with the new; it is about introducing better ways and not just about change for the sake of change; it is quantifiable and has a direct impact on corporate performance; it is transferable and the means necessary for corporate development providing new knowledge to be developed or exploited for enhancing overall standards of performance; learning organizations tolerate failure and encourage risk taking.

Bourgoyne (1992), for instance, suggests that learning organizations have the following features and implementation practices:

- a learning approach to strategy;
- participative decision making;
- informative, open information systems;
- formative accounting and control;
- mutual adjustment between departments;
- reward flexibility;
- adaptable structures;
- boundary workers as environmental scanners;
- inter-organizational learning;
- learning culture and climate; and
- self-development opportunities for all.

Learning-driven leadership

Jack Welsh, ex-CEO and chairman of General Electric introduced the philosophy of "change before you have to". Since he joined, this change master embarked on a programme which stretched GE to become a global competitor, lean and mean with annual turnovers well in excess of $60 billion. He believed that it is the role of leaders to create a climate which constantly reminds people that change is a continuous process. Some of Jack Welsh's famous words include: boundarylessness, speed and stretch. According to Welsh, "change should not be an event but rather a continuous process in the quest for success" (Salazar, 1995).

In order to create the learning organization visionary leaders have to focus on the following actions:

- the vision has to be very compelling and stretching;
- creating a value chain by breaking walls, taking a horizontal, customer-focused approach rather than relying on "prima donnas" and a functional approach to performance;
- excellence in business can only be measured in terms of degree of focus on key business priorities and the extent of capturing leverage from the core areas. A business that spreads itself too thinly by attempting to do

everything is highly unlikely to prosper and grow in a significant manner;

- managing the business as an extended chain and linking in customers and suppliers for total partnership; and
- managing complexity through a simplification process, defining everything in terms of customer benefits and developing means through processes, and measuring value in terms of quality, time, productivity etc. Anything which may not fit this scenario should not necessarily be included.

Above and below-the-line styles of leadership

Connors *et al.* (1995) suggest that there is a leadership style (below-the-line) which reflects a culture of blame, friction, confusion, demoralisation and an attitude of helplessness. Organizations which remain below-the-line will get into more trouble and will ultimately lose their abilities to respond effectively to pressures and threats from outside. On the other hand, the above-the-line style is characterised by openness, empowerment and the commitment to freeing people by encouraging them to be innovative, to question things and to make the right decisions.

In the above-the-line style, the emphasis is not on controlling people but rather on controlling events and activities and ensuring that the human potential is harnessed to the full. As Connors *et al.* (1995) argue:

No one can or should try to force another person to be more effective, more righteous, more knowledgeable, or in any way more politically "correct". Coach them, encourage them, teach them, give them feed back, admonish them, love them and lead them, but don't try to coerce them.

Figures 16.6 and 16.7 illustrate the difference between the two styles of leadership. In order to move from bottom to top, Connors *et al.* (1995) suggest five steps:

1. listening;
2. acknowledging;
3. asking;
4. coaching; and
5. committing.

It is therefore senior management's responsibility to ensure that there is constantly a stretch factor which demonstrates that corporate progress and advancement are very much in evidence and that new learning relevant to existing processes and practices is instigated. Strategies which do not seek to stretch organizations cannot be labelled as effective. Creating stretch factors means accepting the willingness to take risks, learn from past failures and build on achieved success. Building a stretch factor is almost about moving organizations to a new orbit. The fuel can only come through continuous experimentation.

Effective strategies for learning represent a clear shift in thinking from the conventional approach to competitiveness.

Leaders as role models for effective learning

Corporate learning starts with the leaders themselves. Very often the climate of learning reflects the style, type of leadership and the level of personal desire to learn and encourage others to learn. The role of leaders is described by McGill and Slocum (1994) in three areas:

1. Leaders as mentors of learning. This reflects a personal interest in seeing others develop and learn. The types of behaviours exhibited by leaders in mentoring can be reflected by:

    ○   the way they set agendas for learning, with a clear focus and targeting specific areas of learning;

    ○   creating a supporting environment for learning, where tasks/projects will stretch individuals, involve increased learning and where risk taking is allowed to take place;

    ○   channelling the process of learning positively by debriefing individuals on what they have learnt and how they have learnt it.

2. Leaders manage learning. In a sense this is expected behaviour from leaders and fits the slogan "walk the talk". In other words, leaders are expected to demonstrate that there is clear corporate development through learning by ensuring that the whole process is effectively managed and necessary actions can take place. A strategy for learning needs to be developed, with clear milestones and measures and implementation is regularly monitored. The mentoring behaviours are not sufficient to ensure that effective corporate development of learning is going to ensue.

3. Leaders monitor learning. This is a behaviour linked to the role of leaders in managing learning. Monitoring means that there are clear roles and responsibilities put in place for capturing and developing learning in all aspects of the organizations concerned. Although monitoring learning is not a process which is as straight forward as conventional systems of performance, which are product or service related, nevertheless, there have to be mechanisms in place to track progress in corporate learning development capability.

Leaders as designers, teachers and stewards

Some writers talk about a style of leadership through creative tension. This is basically establishing a current reality of being truthful and superimposing this on the vision of the organization. The gap between the two states then generates a natural tension. Peter Senge (1992) proposes a style of leadership based on three roles:

1. Leader as designer of:
   ◦ purpose, vision and core values;
   ◦ policies, strategies and structures; and
   ◦ effective learning organizations.
2. Leader as teacher:
   ◦ define reality; and
   ◦ bringing to the surface people's mental models of important issues
3. Leader as steward:
   ◦ wanting to serve, to serve first;
   ◦ stewardship for the people; and
   ◦ stewardship for the larger purpose or mission that underlies the organization.

Learning through focus on people

The emphasis has now shifted away from a clear emphasis on technology and more towards people. The jargon used in management nowadays is slowly shifting from the expected language of strategy, operational targets etc. to a "softer" type of language such as loyalty, self-respect, partnership, consensus, fairness, common values and co-peration (Fagerfjall, 1995). All the management gurus, including famous names such as Charles Handy, agree that there are several reasons why people are important nowadays:

- The emphasis nowadays is on creativity and innovation (i.e. people's brain power).
- The advantage of measuring not just in the hard areas but also the soft, non-financial areas is helping organizations significantly.
- Customers are becoming more and more demanding and performing on the "basics" of quality in terms of conformance is not necessarily adequate any longer. The delight factors are those which are going to help give a competitive advantage to an organization over its main rivals. The notions of "service" and striving for excellence have become very important.

A focus on people is, of course, a sound competitive strategy. There are various studies which have managed to establish a link between commitment to people and the impact on performance. For example, the Swedish consultant Lars Hessler, jointly with the Institute of Statistics at Stockholm University, has managed to establish a link between attitudes and business profitability levels in a large number of organizations. They have for instance, demonstrated that: business that have good standing in the market place and are known to be good performers, are those that have the best working climates; and people prefer to have respect and be involved in the everyday running of businesses rather than just being treated indifferently for giving assistance. This study (Fagerfjall, 1995) concluded by suggesting that there are ten rules to observe, if businesses are likely to compete effectively in the future, using "soft attributes":

1. Thou shalt treat thy people with respect.
2. Thou shalt encourage thy people to co-operate and resolve conflicts.
3. Thou shalt show thy people they can influence their work situations.
4. Thou shalt praise thy people for what they do.
5. Thou salt render unto thy people just rewards.
6. Thou shalt keep thy people informed.
7. Thou shalt explain to people their roles.
8. Thou shalt explain the objectives of thine organization and ensure all thy people work towards them.
9. Thou shalt help thy people to develop themselves.
10. Thou shalt create an organization in which it is easy to get things done.

Learning through teamwork

Teams make individuals shine and help put levels of energy together. Teams focus on work that needs to be done rather than just the fulfilment of trivial tasks. It is to provide a corporate performance through joining all various efforts together. The working environment which encourages teamwork is one where learning thrives and knowledge banks are greatly enhanced. Climates of effective learning through teamwork are characterised as follows:

- self-directed work teams;
- empowerment;
- flexible working hours;
- no hierarchical control; and
- wanting to unlearn in order to re-learn.

Rewarding contributions from learning means that changes will have to take place, moving away from task-related payments, to knowledge-based rewards. As such, employees are encouraged and rewarded for gaining expertise on ranges of products/technologies and processes. Employees in this context do not specialise but rather collect competence credits through team assignments and develop a wider variety of skills. The introduction of competence-based pay or knowledge-based compensation systems will preserve and encourage a learning-based work environment.

Creating a system of talent for effective learning

It has already been established that there is a close link between creativity and the development of effective learning. Bringing the two together means perhaps a radical shift in the way people, as individuals and in the context of working in teams, are selected, recruited, coached and managed.

First of all, one of the basic rules is to develop human resource practices which are in line with the vision of the organization concerned and its long-term ambitions. Second, if organizations are not going to be able to measure the contribution from creative potentials in enhancing competitive performance, it will always remain difficult to appraise the role of creativity as a core competence. Most prevalent HR systems are based on hiring for the task rather than hiring for creative contributions. Third, education and training are a continuous process, to ensure that changes in work processes and demands for new tasks are effectively met by the blend of skills and expertise levels available.

Effective creative contributions come from the deliberate corporate effort of stretching and making work a challenge at all levels. High performing organizations are those that create a climate of motivation and a desire to achieve superior performance levels.

Individual and team contributions go hand in hand. Each individual has to have high levels of expertise in their own specific domain. The expertise is, however, deployed flexibly in the context of a team, to address different needs and to tackle various specific projects. In this way, specialisation cannot be diluted and, through taking a process-based approach, high levels of synergy can be achieved by channelling all the individual efforts together.

Self-managing teams and the development of corporate learning
Self-managing teams (SMTs) use an extension of quality circles as an effective way of developing a culture of continuous learning. SMTs are totally autonomous. They get involved in the planning, execution and control of significant projects. They manage technological aspects, resources and approach to accomplishing the tasks which brought them together in the first place. Furthermore, SMTs deal with their own performance appraisal. This is often in the form of peer appraisal (giving individuals feed back on their contribution to the projects concerned) and also in terms of development by acknowledging whether individuals are certified or not in certain aspects of performance.

A model suggested by Haucks and Dingus (1990) suggests that the development of SMTs is a progressive process which requires a paradigm shift from being rigid, traditionally oriented through filtering information from a top-down approach and dividing work into specific functions and tasks to:

- breaking down walls between individuals and encouraging teamwork and process-based performance;
- moving away from rigid controls through the setting up of real empowerment, delegation of responsibility and power to make decisions and a bottom-up approach, to management and performance monitoring;
- slicing both vertically and horizontally and creating a climate of total flexibility, real alignment and core process orientation for effective business performance.

Teaming for innovation
The spirit of work through teams, a multi-functional approach and individual involvement in a wide variety of tasks will ensure a continuous flow of ideas, synergies and the effective development of innovation. Various pieces of research analysed the work of teams and the dynamics of groups of people. Four factors have been highlighted constantly as the key factors for team innovativeness:
1. *Vision*: sharing the same outcome from being together.
2. *Participative safety*: empowerment, encouragement in decision making and active participation. If people feel that the climate is non-threatening and supportive, they are likely to suggest ideas for improvement and change for positive ways forward.
3. *Climate for excellence*: total commitment to improving things and achieving superior standards without any compromises.
4. *Support for innovation*: by not just giving innovation activity "lip service", but demonstrating there is real commitment to innovation and creativity.

The learning organization: Xerox Corp.
Xerox Corp. articulates the importance of learning through its vision and has clearly defined and communication goals in relation to learning. Xerox uses an integrated model for driving learning through self-assessment and continuous improvement. The organizational model uses "hardware" aspects which represent structure processes, systems and such alike and "software" aspects which reflect leaderships, values, culture and the work climate. Figure 16.8 illustrates the model which drives organizational learning through individual learning. Figure 16.9 shows the management model which drives the hardware elements of Xerox's performance. The assessment is done at three different levels:
1. The individual – to assess their own commitment to learning, how they feel about learning and whether they are achieving their learning goals.
2. The manager – the individual can also assess his or her manager's commitment to them and to learning and how they assist them with their learning objectives.
3. The organization – the individual can assess his/her organization about its commitment to learning and how it facilitates learning activity and provides employees with opportunity for their individual development.

Figure 16.10 illustrates the scoring chart which is the basis for identifying the gaps and putting in place action plans for ensuring that learning takes place as a continuous process and in an integrated fashion. Figure 16.11 gives the assessment templates for the individual, manager and organizational levels.

Figure 16.1 Driving change through learning

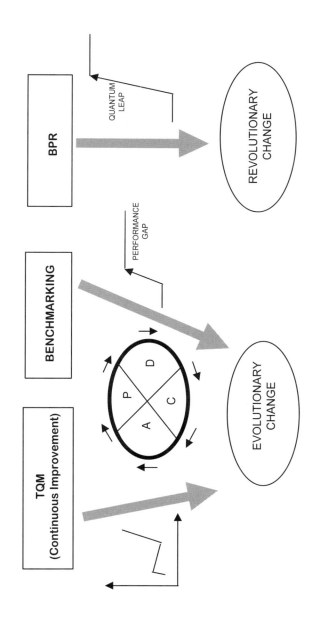

Figure 16.2 The process of learning and knowledge transfer

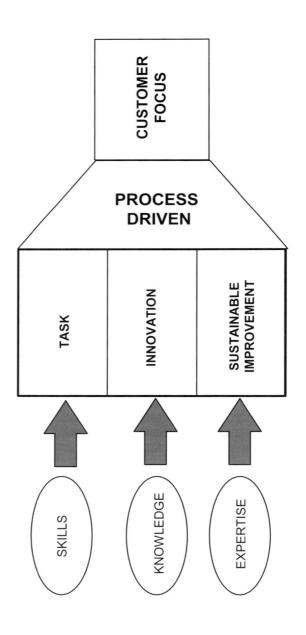

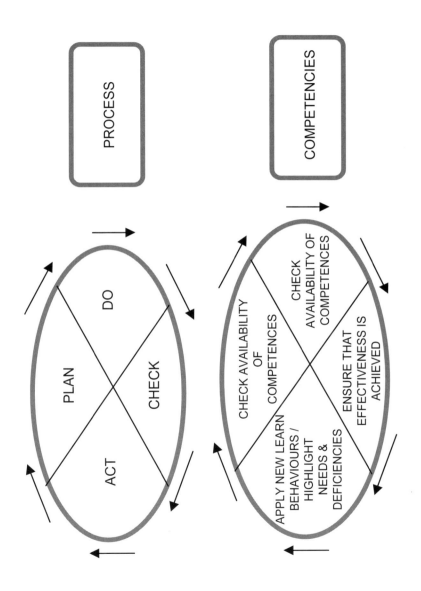

Figure 16.3 Management of learning through a continuous process

PROCESS

PLAN
DO
ACT
CHECK

COMPETENCIES

CHECK AVAILABILITY OF COMPETENCES

CHECK AVAILABILITY OF COMPETENCES

APPLY NEW LEARN BEHAVIOURS / HIGHLIGHT NEEDS & DEFICIENCIES

ENSURE THAT EFFECTIVENESS IS ACHIEVED

Figure 16.4 Management of key ingredients for effective learning

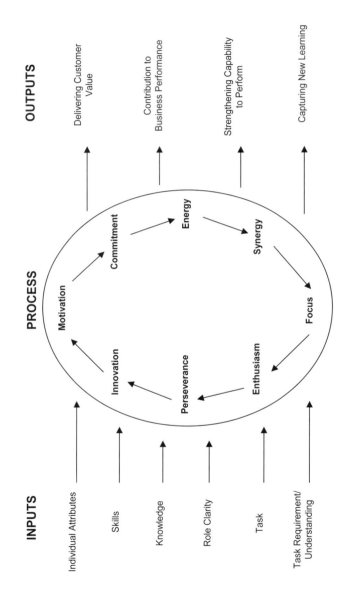

260

Figure 16.5 Strategic deployment process through knowledge deployment

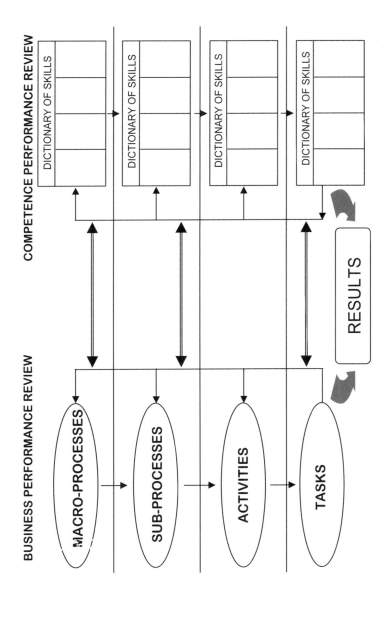

Figure 16.6 Above-the-line steps to accountability

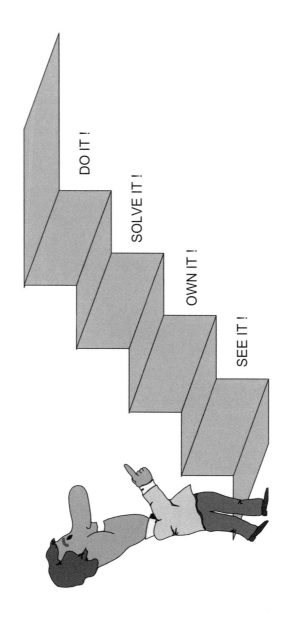

Figure 16.7 Below-the-line victim cycle

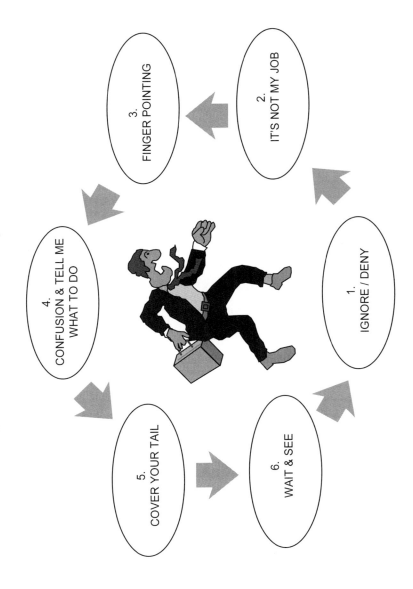

263

Table 16.1 Internal transfer of knowledge through best practice

	Knowing	Understanding	Thinking	Learning
PHILOSOPHY	Dedicated to finding the one "best way" that ensures a predictable, controlled, and efficient operation.	Strong cultural values guide strategy and action' belief in the "ruling myth."	Business is a series of problems; if it's broke, fix it fast.	Every business experience is an opportunity to improve.
MANAGEMENT PRACTICES	Control through rules and regulations; management by the book.	Clarify, communicate, and reinforce the company culture.	Identify problems, collect data, and implement solutions.	Model learning, encourage experimentation, and promote constructive dialogue.
EMPLOYEES	Follow the rules, and don't ask why.	Use corporate values as guides to behavior.	Embrace and enact programmed solutions.	Gather information, foster dissent, and promote network intimacy.
CUSTOMERS	Trust that the company knows best.	Believe company values will ensure positive experience.	Treat as a problem to-be-solved, as quickly as possible.	Participate in an open, continuous dialogue as part of a teaching / learning relationship.
CHANGE	Modification of the "best way" through incremental fine tuning.	Consideration of changes only within the ruling myth.	Implementation of problem-solving programs; each new "fix" is the answer.	Creation of new processes to re-define the competitive environment and provide a sustainable, competitive advantage.

Figure 16.8 Driving of organizational learning through individual learning at Xerox Corp.

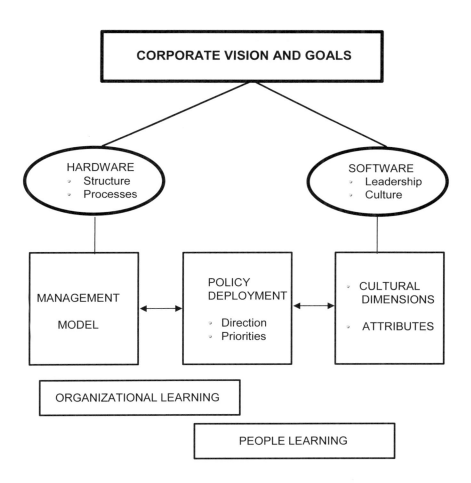

Figure 16.9 Management model driving hardware elements at Xerox Corp.

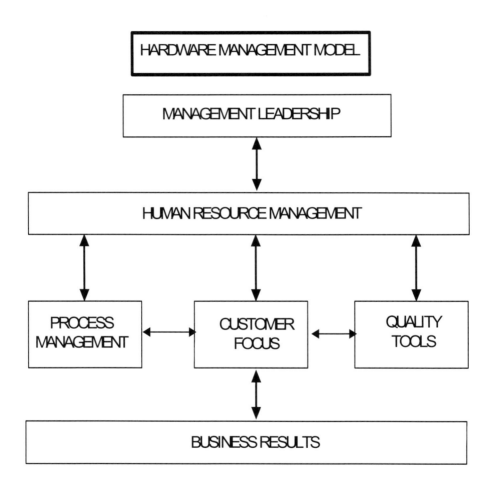

Figure 16.10 Knowledge transfer through best practice at Xerox Corp.

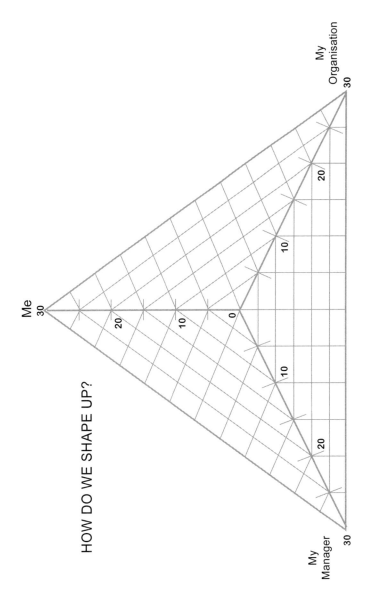

HOW DO WE SHAPE UP?

Figure 16.11 Assessment template for the individual level

Me as a learner			
	Scoring		
Dimension	**Disagree**	**Part agree/ disagree**	**Agree**
1. Learning is an active, enjoyable process for me, but it does not happen by accident			
2. I know my preferred learning style & take action to improve in any areas where I am not fully effective			
3. I am always open to feedback from others & actively seek the views of others (customers, colleagues, etc.) on my performance and behaviour			
4. In general at work I have a wide network of effective information sources, both people & systems			
5. I have a current, personal development action plan which I can remember & quote when required			
6. I have learning time set aside during my week, when I reflect on experiences to draw out lessons & required actions			
7. I am happy to take calculated risks at work, knowing that mistakes, within reason, will be seen as learning opportunities by others			
8. Learning and development are terms others say I use a lot at work			
9. I have a clear vision of where I am going in the future & I am taking actions today to pursue that path			
10. I believe others see me as an open, honest person prepared to share information to achieve better learning			
Sub-total (column score X no. of scores in column)			
TOTAL SCORE (max. 30)			

Figure 16.12 Assessment template for the manager level

My manager and learning			
		Scoring	
Dimension	Disagree	Part agree/ disagree	Agree
1. My manager is an effective learner & understands how to improve learning capabilities			
2. My manager sees developing people in his/her team as his/her responsibility			
3. My manager uses the words learning/development often & encourages others to learn from mistakes/successes			
4. My manager spends time coaching/developing members of his/her team			
5. My manager treats new ideas with respect & values diversity of views			
6. My manager communicates a clear vision, direction & targets			
7. My manager & I establish clear frameworks for short-term actions in line with long-term aims			
8. My manager provides challenging/stretch objectives			
9. My manager prefers me to draw my own conclusions/actions rather than tell me what to do			
10. My manager gives open, honest, constructive feedback			
Sub-total (column score X no. of scores in column)			
TOTAL SCORE (max. 30)			

Figure 16.13 Assessment template for the organization level

My organization as a learner			
		Scoring	
Dimension	Disagree	Part agree/ disagree	Agree
1. Commitment (values, resources, etc.) to learning as a strategic necessity exists at the top level			
2. Short & long-term organizational directions exist & are understood by everyone			
3. Clearly stated competencies, skills, knowledge etc. exist so employees know what is expected of them today & in the future			
4. Learning/development/training are integrated into work activities, rather than being one-off activities			
5. Personal performance reviews & feedback process exist for all employees			
6. Every employee takes personal responsibility for continuous learning			
7. Every manager sees their primary role as developing their team members			
8. Open, two-way communication is valued and effective			
9. My organization learns actively from other organizations and sets new standards as a result			
10. My organization regularly reviews its performance to identify/apply lesson learnt			
Sub-total (column score X no. of scores in column)			
TOTAL SCORE (max. 30)			

Chapter 17
A perspective on knowledge

The theory of knowledge helps us to understand that management in any form is prediction.

Rational prediction requires theory and builds knowledge through systematic revision and extension of theory based on comparison of prediction with observation.

A statement devoid of rational prediction does not convey knowledge.

Knowledge has temporal spread. Knowledge comes from theory. Without theory, there is no way to use the information that comes to us on the instant (W. Edwards Deming).

The new knowledge era

Knowledge management has moved a long way since the field first emerged; from being technology centric to a stage where it has started to serve wider purposes of real time feed reaction, right first time decision making and quality responsiveness. The days of relying on policies, procedures and technologies to drive the value chain are numbered. It is now vital to develop an ability to deal with emerging situations in the competitive world and tackle them with immediate effect. Furthermore, as the customer becomes integrated in the business, particularly with the use of e-commerce, the speed of reaction, the type of decision made, the quality of the outcome are going to decide on the competitiveness of organizations.

Is it, therefore, right and proper to understand the field of knowledge management properly and to implement its principles in the right way? The answer is simple, as Deming used to say: "survival is not compulsory". Managers have to solve problems all the time. They have the task of ensuring that the supply chain works consistently, reliably and with quality for the benefit of the end customer. Furthermore, they have the task of mobilising the collective know-how of all the employees and usingthe intellectual capital available for the end benefit of the customer. One more task is perhaps to encourage the creative potential of people to flourish and to have access to their tacit knowledge.

The intellectual capital of an organization is its real asset. It is the organization's future and with it the organization can predict the future and ensure its survivability. We are perhaps starting an era where for the first time, senior managers are going to be compelled to use facts, adopt scientific, logical reasoning, weigh up the evidence and exercise their judgement with the powerful support of reliable information. This may now signal the end of an era where decisions were made without having all the facts, where judgements were made based on bias rather than evidence, where there was huge reluctance to investigate and allow others to make the case and where the practices tended to be driven by obstinate behaviours concerned with short-term results.

The global knowledge growth phenomenon

We are witnessing a true revolution all over the world. Knowledge management has forced us to reconsider the way we practice management, the way we do research and everything we used to rely on in the past in terms of theories, concepts and principles. There are behavioural, social, economic, political and organizational factors related to the use of information technology and knowledge that are emerging and which are of great interest to researchers.

It is therefore right to acknowledge that knowledge management has affected our lives in an unprecedented way and it has also introduced a new paradigm of management where, for the first time, the power is in the hands of the individual employees rather than senior managers. It is feasible that in the future the following scenarios might dictate how the work climate might be shaped. Tacit knowledge is really the answer to all future problems, challenges and opportunities. Tacit knowledge is, however, triggered by events, by the need to think, interrogate, analyse and work out solutions and options. As Deming often said, the "power of the unknown and the unknowable". By working in a business environment which requires speedy responses, real time decision making and the ability to absorb a lot of information and react to it, the practices of controlling processes by using SQC techniques, to stabilise processes by controlling common and special causes of variation, is no longer sufficient. Real improvement will come through the innovative contributions, which are truly knowledge driven rather than the use of explicit, documented structured information which emphasises compliance and the adherence to systems and procedures. Knowledge workers will be making decisions which are dissimilar in nature, which are related to unique circumstances, with customer service more and more customised. This will create a challenge for evaluating the performance of the knowledge worker and recognising their contribution appropriately. We may have to accept a harsh reality that the terms and conditions of employment will change significantly. Knowledge workers will be those who have the needed asset and therefore able to negotiate with more than one employer at the same time, using their knowledge as leverage in a more lucrative fashion.

History of knowledge management

KM is a relatively new phenomenon in the field of management (Chan, 1999; Snyder and Wilson, 2000), and grew from organizational learning theories (Gable et al., 1998; Chan, 1999; Morse, 2000). Barclay and Murray (2000) and Sullivan (2000) trace the origins of KM to the early 1980s. Sullivan (2000) states that the

KM concept was utilised by Itami in the Japanese literature in 1980. This article, however, did not appear in English until 1987.

The development of systems for managing knowledge, relying on work done in artificial intelligence and expert systems during the 1980s, gave us such concepts as "knowledge acquisition", "knowledge engineering", "knowledge-based systems" and "computer-based ontology".

According to Barclay and Murray (2000), the International Knowledge Management Network (IKMN) began in Europe in 1989. By the mid-1990s, KM initiatives were prospering, thanks in part to the Internet. Further, the authors mention that by 1990, a number of management consulting companies had investigated an in-house KM programme, and several well-known US, European and Japanese firms had embraced a focused KM programme. KM was introduced in the popular press in 1991, when Tom Stewart published "Brainpower" in *Fortune* magazine (Barclay and Murray, 2000).

Finally, Balla *et al.* (1999) and Morten *et al.* (1999) support this view further, by arguing that KM as a concept has existed at least since the early 1990s when the large consulting firms, e.g. Andersen Consulting and Ernst & Young, began committing major resources to implement KM practices and technologies. Further, the KM trend began to gain some momentum in the mid-1990s, getting coverage in the trade press, at industry conferences and in business and academic fields.

Knowledge definition

The basic building block of knowledge is data, the processing of data resulting in information, and as a consequence of processing information knowledge is derived. Knowledge is the next natural progression after information; that is, a higher order than information (Grey, 1996; Lynn, 1998; Mullins, 1998; Zack, 1998; Newman, 1999; Bollinger and Smith, 2001).

Grey (1996) noted that knowledge is the full utilisation of information and data, coupled with the potential of people's skills, competencies, ideas, intuitions, commitments and motivations. Knowledge is people, money, leverage, learning, flexibility, power, and competitive advantage; it is stored in the individual brain or encoded in organizational processes, documents, products, services, facilities and systems. It is the result of learning which provides the sustainable competitive advantage.

Knowledge management (KM) definition

Many authors agree that KM requires a total organizational transformation, including organizational culture, structure and management style (Sveiby, 1997b; Buckman, 1998; Davenport and Prusak, 1998b). Many researchers have defined KM from different perspectives, and a large number of debates thus tend to centre around the difference in meaning between information and knowledge. For example, Snowden (2000, p. 63) defines KM as "the identification, optimisation, and active management of intellectual assets, either in the form of explicit knowledge held in artefacts or as tacit knowledge possessed by individuals or communities".

Poynder (1998) suggests that there are currently three major schools of thought on what KM is. One such school recommends that KM is mainly an IT issue, with networks of computers and groupware being the keys. If one constructs widespread computer networks and adds communication tools that allow group collaboration, people will be more disposed to share information and knowledge Grey (1996) defines KM as "an audit of 'intellectual assets' that highlights unique sources, critical functions and potential bottlenecks which hinder knowledge flows to the point of use. It protects intellectual assets from decay, seeks opportunities to enhance decisions, services and products through adding intelligence, increasing value and providing flexibility". Bertels (1996) defines KM as "the management of the organization towards the continuous renewal of the organizational knowledge base – this means, e.g. creation of supportive organizational structures, facilitation of organizational members, putting IT-instruments with emphasis on teamwork and diffusion of knowledge (as, e.g. groupware) into place". Finneran (1999) regards KM as a discipline that assists the spread of knowledge of individuals or groups across companies in ways that directly affect performance. KM envisions getting the right information within the right context to the right person at the right time for knowledge is seen as a capability, as something that can be said, as information plus something. It only makes sense that the knowledge created for solving problems will be re-used whenever the organization faces the same problems.

Knowledge management systems (KMS)
Pluskowski (2002) divided KM systems into three types: information knowledge systems (IKS), KM tools (KMT), and dynamic knowledge systems (DKS). Gupta and Iyer (2000) see KMS as capturing, transferring, storing, controlling, distributing and archiving knowledge within an organization. They state that effectual employed KMS could facilitate an organization's internal processes to operate easily and quickly, allow a company to take rapid action to customer feedback, supply the ability to react to its competitive situation in a timely manner, and empower workers with critical knowledge. A balanced KM system is shown in Figure 17.1.

Types of KM
People gain or create new knowledge from numerous activities. First, action-based learning that involves working on problems, and implementation of solutions. Second, systematic problem solving, which requires a mindset, disciplined in both reductionism and holistic thinking, attentive to details, and willing to push beyond the obvious to assess underlying causes. Third, learning from past experiences, which reviews a company's successes and failures, to take the way that will be of maximum benefit to the organization, as suggested by Morse (2000).

Hubert (1996), Lim *et al.* (2000), Nonaka and Konno (2000), Snowden (2000), Bollinger and Smith (2001), Mentzas *et al.* (2001) and Seubert *et al.*(2001) have classified KM into two primary types, namely tacit and explicit knowledge. These two types are discussed in the ensuing sections.

Tacit knowledge

Tacit knowledge resides in our mind and cannot be easily shared or it is difficult to communicate with others, as defined by Hubert (1996), Nonaka and Konno (2000), and Seubert *et al.* (2001). Nonaka and Konno (2000) add that tacit knowledge is deeply rooted in an individual's actions and experience, as well as in the ideals, values or emotions he or she embraces. It has two dimensions: the first is the technical dimension, which encompasses the kind of informal personal skills or crafts often referred to as "know-how". The second is the cognitive dimension. It consists of beliefs, ideals, values, schemata and mental models which are deeply ingrained in us and which we often take for granted. While difficult to articulate, this cognitive dimension of tacit knowledge shapes the way we perceive the world.

Explicit knowledge

Hubert (1996), Nonaka and Konno (2000) and Seubert *et al.* (2001) defined explicit knowledge as that which can be captured and expressed in words and numbers (i.e. quantitatively) and shared in the form of data by courses or books for self-reading, scientific formulae, specifications, manuals and the like. This kind of knowledge can be readily transmitted between individuals formally and systematically.

Nonaka *et al.* (1996) have suggested that knowledge is created through four different modes:

1. *Socialisation*: involves conversion from individual tacit knowledge to group tacit knowledge (watching somebody, then doing it).
2. *Externalisation*: involves conversion from tacit knowledge to explicit knowledge (doing it, then describing it).
3. *Combination*: involves conversion from separate explicit knowledge to systemic explicit knowledge (reading about it, then describing it).
4. *Internalisation*: involves conversion from explicit knowledge to tacit knowledge (reading about it, then doing it).

Whenever knowledge translates from one form to another it liberates energy, innovation and performance.

Knowledge as a strategy

Newman (1999) said that Probe Consulting presents how each of the separate departments of human resources (HR) and training and development (T&D), information systems, and the business unit sees its contribution to the organization. Each of these groups would merge and share the goal of developing strategic knowledge, which builds customer and shareholder value (see Figure 17.2).

According to Skyrme (2002a), there are two thrusts for strategy. The first is to make better use of the knowledge that already exists within the firm, for example by sharing best practices. The second major thrust of knowledge-focused strategies is that of innovation, creation of new knowledge, and turning ideas into valuable products and services. It is the most difficult, but it ultimately has the best potential for improved company performance. It is effective commercialisation of ideas that has taken companies like Netscape and Formula One to be multi-million dollar corporations in just a few years.

Zack (1998) suggests that there is a strategic gap between what a firm must do to compete and what it actually does in practice. Strategy, then, represents how the firm balances its competitive "cans" and "musts" to develop and protect its strategic position. In addition, knowledge gap is the gap between what a firm must do to compete and what it can do. Figure 17.3 illustrates the knowledge gap analysis.

How to manage knowledge
Knowledge itself cannot be managed, only its processes or systems (Platt, 1998; Newman, 1999). For example, Newman (1999) suggests managing knowledge means finding ways to create, identify, capture and distribute organizational knowledge to the people who need it. Platt (1998) is certain that only the processes of knowledge or its systems can be managed, such as through sharing knowledge.

Organizations are now starting to look at knowledge as a resource. This means they need ways of managing their knowledge. These organizations could use techniques and methods that were developed as part of KM to analyse their knowledge sources. While using these techniques, they can perform knowledge analysis, which is a necessary step in the ability to manage knowledge and knowledge planning (Sierhuis, 1996).

Radding (1998), Bassi (2000), Bednar, (2000) and Mertins et al. (2001) noted that there are some processes in KM which are useful to focus on in developing a KM strategy. These include creating, capturing, transferring and sharing knowledge, and Macintosh (1998) added some processes, e.g. developing knowledge, preserving knowledge and using knowledge. The success or failure of companies depends on how well they develop and use these processes. Therefore, Radding (1998) has added two more, which are storage and processing (storing, comparing, analysing, organizing, any of a variety of techniques).

KM focuses on understanding these processes as well as how they are to be acquired, stored and utilised within an organization. Technology has to support all activities involved in the knowledge life cycle and KM processes, as suggested by Duffy (2000). Also, Morse (2000) substantiates this view by warning organizations using technology to provide employees with an environment to learn and share knowledge, with the goal of enhancing their productivity. Figure 17.4 shows a generic KM model which is based on Morse (2000), but with technology added as an important element.

How to capture and transfer knowledge

Simply capturing and transferring data are only one part of KM. According to Bednar (2000) and Morse (2000), knowledge could be transferred or captured in many ways, by written communications, training, internal conference, internal publication, job rotation and job transfer, and mentoring. In addition, Bednar (2000) proposed and believed that interviewing (questions), writing (story), and video communication are effective methods of capturing and disseminating knowledge.

In order for an organization to capture all aspects for effective KM, it must direct attention and take account of four elements of the cost model (customer, organization, suppliers and technology) proposed by Pervaiz et al. (1999).

Bednar (2000) comments that the creation of knowledge occurs with the transfer of what is inside a person's mind (tacit or explicit) to other individuals or groups, in such a way that the transfer influences the beneficiary's future actions and decisions. The desired result in this interaction is an increase in the probability of a faster and more accurate decision.

Finally, Figure 17.5 illustrates the KM core process, as presented by Heisig (2001) and Figure 17.6 shows the building blocks for successful KM.

Some reported benefits from knowledge management

Dow Chemicals saved $4 million during the first year of its new programme, and expects to generate more than $100 million in licensing revenues that it might otherwise have forgone (Davenport et al., 1998). Also, Manasco (1997a) mentioned that it was increasing annual revenue from licensing by $100 million. Dow Chemicals has generated over $125 million in revenues from licensing and other means of exploiting intangible assets (Skyrme, 2002a, 2002c and 2003).

Glaxo Wellcome, by focusing on shareholder value and better understanding of the value of its R&D pipeline, has significantly increased its share price over the last few years (Skyrme, 2002c, 2003).

Texas Instruments went from last (1992) to first (1994) in on-time delivery satisfaction in customer ranking of suppliers (APQC, 1996), and it saved the $500 million cost of new plant by leveraging internal knowledge and best practices (O'Dell and Grayson, 2000a). Further, Skyrme (2002a) stated that TI has saved the equivalent of investing in a new plant by sharing best practice between its semiconductor fabrication plants.

Chevron realised $150 million annual saving in power and fuel expenses from knowledge sharing in energy use management (O'Dell and Grayson, 2000b).

Silicon Graphics reduced sales training costs from $3 million to $200,000 by managing its product information communications process (Manasco, 1997b).

Kaiser Permanent, in one of its branches (the Northwest Region), was able to implement an open access programme six to 12 months faster than it predicted by transferring internal best practice from another region (APQC, 1996).

Price Waterhouse's collaborative behaviour improved circulation of information by its implementation of Lotus Notes and the formation of a central group to capture and document best practices. Analysis and documentation time was reduced (APQC, 1996).

Regarding the final report of American Productivity & Quality Center (APQC) (1996), the benefits of KM are greater customer intimacy and satisfaction, improved cycle time and operational excellence, and better use of organizational knowledge to improve operations and deliver products and services.

Nonaka (1991) mentioned that some of the highly successful Japanese organizations like Honda, Canon, Mutsushita, NEC, Sharp and Kao have become famous because of their ability to respond quickly to customers, create new markets, rapidly develop new products, and dominate emergent technologies. The reason for their success is the way that they use management for the creation of new knowledge.

Figure 17.1 Balanced knowledge management system

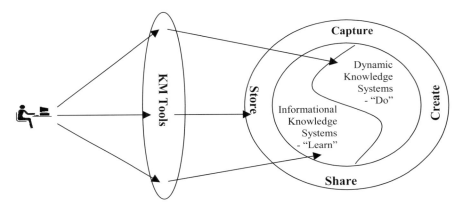

Source: Adapted from Pluskowski (2002)

Figure 17.2 Merging of separate departments to share knowledge

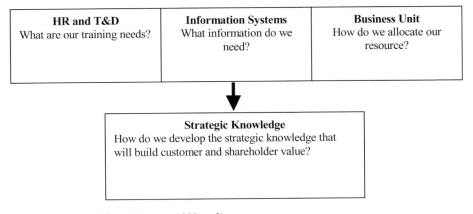

HR and T&D	Information Systems	Business Unit
What are our training needs?	What information do we need?	How do we allocate our resource?

Strategic Knowledge
How do we develop the strategic knowledge that will build customer and shareholder value?

(**Source**: adapted from Newman, 1999, p. 3)

Figure 17.3 Knowledge gap

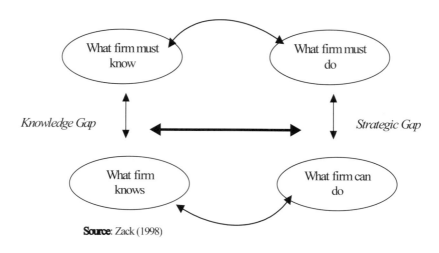

Source: Zack (1998)

Figure 17.4 Generic knowledge management model

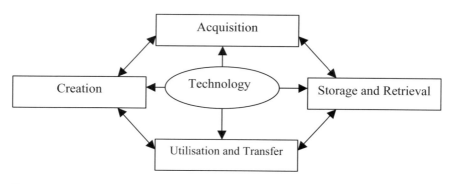

Source: Adapted from Morse (2000)

Figure 17.5 Core process of knowledge management

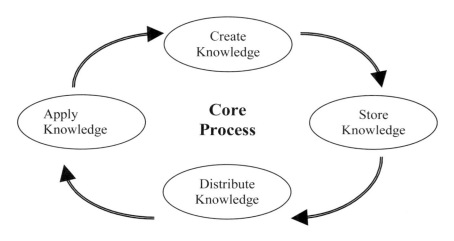

Source: Heisig (2001:28)

Figure 17.6 Building blocks of successful knowledge management

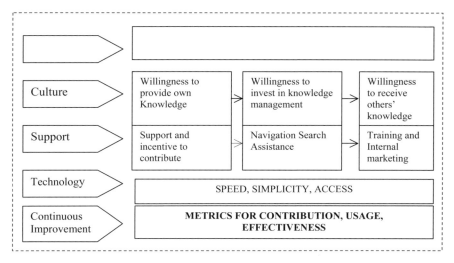

Chapter 18
A best practice model for TQM implementation

The practical framework

In constructing the TQM implementation framework, consideration was accorded to the objective of structuring it to be of as practical a value as possible. This was achieved by presenting the central component of the framework in the form of implementation guidelines, with the critical quality factors superposed as a useful checklist.

Information from TQM literature suggests that in developing guidelines for effective implementation, there is a need to:

- List the key quality levers that have to be manipulated to implement TQM. These are called key organizational requirements (KORs).
- Describe the organizational activities needed to deploy and implement the KORs.
- Present the guidelines in a recognisable structure.

As a framework is designed to be of as practical as possible, tools to assess the progress of TQM implementation and training needs during the early years are also included.

While the framework is constructed using inputs "closer to the phenomenon" to offer support for decision making during TQM implementation, it is not intended to be prescriptive. The quality management literature is clear that models and frameworks cannot take the responsibility from management as to how to go about implementing TQM.

Development of the framework

Before discussing the framework in detail, it is essential to introduce formally the elements of the central component of the framework and the form in which they will be presented.

Key organizational requirements (KORs)

Key organizational requirements (KORs) are the actual quality levers that the management need to deploy and manipulate to implement critical quality factors, the foundation factors and, hence, TQM. Critical factors form the basis for deriving KORs. A key organizational requirement is described in the form of a verb plus and an object(s).

The critical quality factors and foundation elements offer a practical step-wise framework of "most critical first" and "least critical last" in addressing the KORs. A three-stage approach is suggested and the three categories of KORs adopted:

1. Stage zero KORs: KORs needed during the pre-TQM introduction stage. Foundation factors and Tier I critical quality factors define stage zero (S0) KORs.
2. Stage one KORs: KORs needed during the early stages of TQM implementation. Tiers I and II critical quality factors define stage one (S1) KORs.
3. Stage two KORs: deployment of stage two (S2) KORs can be delayed after stage zero and stage one KORs. The KORs here are defined primarily by Tiers II and III critical quality factors.

Organizational activities (OAs)

Organizational activities (OAs) describe what it involves and/or what must be done to implement the key organizational requirements. OAs primarily aim to describe the tactics and techniques employed in deploying and implementing the key organizational requirements and, where appropriate, the structure of individual KOAs.

Structure

In presenting the critical quality factors and KORs, it was felt that a provision of a recognisable structure would assist in the moulding of a user friendly framework. The concept of finding a constellation of underlying constructs to represent variables offers the means of achieving such a structure.

Information from the TQM literature also suggests that there is a need to attempt to explain the constructs of TQM implementation. Writers of TQM find it all but impossible to discuss and explain TQM models without using words relating to constructs to define the important aspects of TQM. The constructs which come by different names – conditions, quality levers, tracks for change, general governing principles and pillars to name a few – are generally presented as areas that organizations planning to implement TQM should aim to excel at.

The concept of constructs was also used by researchers of TQM to group variables into a number of underlying factors. Given the nature of the task at hand, a judgmental process grounded in the literature was used to group variables into five underlying factors, and accord them recognisable labels. In finding the underlying constructs to group the critical quality factors and associated KORs, conscious effort was also made to: ensure that the constructs reflect the key findings to the three levels of investigations, maximise clustering of items of similar criticality, maximise clustering of items that can be actionable together, limit the number of groups, and enable recognisable labels that are simple to understand and use to be accorded to the groups. Such effort is intended to distil constructs that have empirical validity and practical values within the implementation framework.

Four separate but interrelated and mutually supportive categories can be identified. Each of the categories is accorded a recognisable label from a descriptive perspective. A descriptive perspective means that the label describes the inter-relationship between the items within the categories. As the categories are distilled from the critical quality factors and labelled appropriately, the categories will put in perspective the broad critical areas that an organization planning to implement TQM should aim to create. In tandem with other components of the TQM implementation framework, the categories will be identified as critical categories from hereon.

Critical categories
The four critical categories are:
- I: institute leadership.
- II: maximise internal stakeholders involvement.
- III: manage by customer-driven processes.
- IV: adopt continuous improvement.

As continuous customer satisfaction underlies the quality ethics that most of the sample of organizations strive for, the categories are also what must be in place in order for an organization to continually satisfy the customer.

Everything starts with committed leadership with a vision that to be successful in the marketplace means continually having to satisfy the customer by making fundamental changes. The cross-cutting theme in these changes is the shift from managing along the traditional organizational structure to focusing on business processes that add value to customer satisfaction. Customer satisfaction results from how effectively and efficiently an organization executes its business processes and organization-wide supports and involvement are the prerequisites here. Continuous improvement of the business processes is a basic philosophy that underlies continuous customer satisfaction.

Figure 18.1 conveys the inter-relatedness of the critical categories. The model is also portrayed to convey the soft-hard aspects of essentials of TQM implementation. Figure 18.2 shows the proposed structure of the TQM implementation framework and how the elements stack up.

Guidelines for TQM implementation
It should be noted that the guidelines, as presented here, are directed at top management.

Critical category I: institute leadership
Leadership and corporate quality strategy mean a united top management team committed to customer satisfaction, setting corporate sights on continually satisfying the customer and communicating the vision in such a way as to mobilise all employees towards its attainment.

Critical prerequisites to developing the necessary commitment are a clear belief in the tangible business and operating benefits of TQM and the recognition that the traditional management system is no longer an option in a competitive business environment. An effective TQM initiative cannot be mounted without this conviction and commitment.

An early responsibility of management is developing a corporate quality policy incorporating a statement of mission/vision, quality goals and guiding principles. Effective communication of the mission ensures all employees understand and are committed to the organization's direction. Effective deployment and implementation of goals at all levels ensure congruence of individual efforts and corporate expectations.

Given the considerable time and ability required during the early stages, a high-powered steering group for quality, chaired by the chief executive, is usually set-up to design and manage the implementation process. A TQM support manager may be appointed and co-opted into the steering group to assist in the early tasks.

As the quality process gets underway, the steering group continues to serve as the key custodian of the quality process by creating the enabling mechanisms and resources. Below the steering group, the management establishes additional steering groups to take ownership of the implementation of the quality process at divisional and site levels. Such sub-groups comprise the members of local management and staff. The TQM manager provides the vital links between the corporate steering group and the sub-groups, and takes on implementation support functions.

Implementation guidelines

- Senior executives assume active responsibility for evaluation and improvement of management system, and leading quality drive (T1).
- Visibility of senior executive commitment to quality and customer satisfaction (T1).
- Comprehensive policy development and effective deployment of goals (T1).
- Clear, consistent communication of mission statement and objectives defining quality values, expectations and focus (T1).
- Elements of quality management structure in place to manage the organization's quality journey (T3).

Build energy (S0)

Develop a clear belief in the tangible business and operating benefits of TQM in order to build the energy to start and sustain the transformation. It involves investing time and effort up front by becoming familiar with the content of TQM. This may require research into TQM literature and conducting benchmarking visits to quality leaders.

Develop consensus amongst the top team (S0)

Ensure that there is consensus among the senior executives on what should be done to implement and sustain TQM. It requires understanding the challenges and opportunities and involves finding out about the process of changing to TQM. This may require brainstorming, benchmarking visits to quality leaders and researching into TQM literature.

If the directive to implement TQM is an external one, ensure co-ownership of the decision. This may involve brainstorming on what TQM really means to the organization and developing an implementation plan accordingly.

Set-up quality council (S1)

Set up a quality steering committee/council to provide strategic direction on TQM and plan for its implementation. Ensure senior executives serve on the council, with the chief executive as the chairperson. Co-opt the TQM support manager into the council. Develop a TQM plan by active consensus.

Appoint a corporate TQM support manager (S1)

Appoint a TQM support officer to advise and assist the quality council in planning and implementation of TQM. The post may be on a full-time or part-time basis. Co-opt the manager into the quality council.

Develop an implement policy and strategy based on total quality (S1)

Develop a policy based on the concept of total quality that includes mission statement, corporate values, expectations and focus. Benchmark policy development and deployment process by researching and visiting quality leaders.

Take into account the needs of all organizational stakeholders, competitive position and process capability in developing the policy. Where appropriate, involve employees in the development process.

Incorporate conditions critical to the success of the organization achieving its policy, that is, identify critical success factors (CSFs). Define key performance indicators (KPIs) for each CSF. Set targets for KPIs for each CSF. Set targets for KPIs and measures to track gaps in target performance. Publish a timetable to review target performance.

Arrange for an effective policy deployment and implementation to ensure organizational goal alignment and congruence. Set goals and targets at process and individual levels. Provide the necessary resources and training for a successful implementation.

Communicate the statement of mission (S1)

Communicate the statement of mission and objectives defining quality values, expectations and focus organization-wide. Ensure senior executives accept responsibility for and commitment to the mission before communicating it to the rest of the employees.

Gather all employees together to communicate face-to-face and explain the mission. Where this is not possible, use a cascade approach. Use a wide variety of modes to communicate the statement of mission, with emphasise on face-to-face meetings rather than artefacts. Encourage discussion and feedback by allowing time for questions and answers.

Continue to accord high profile status to the mission statement using a wide variety of modes of communication.

Ensure visibility (S1)

Ensure visibility of senior executives' commitment to quality and customer satisfaction. This may require devoting a substantial portion of time to quality-related matters. For example, actively communicating the organization's vision, values and focus, attending quality courses first and teaching the courses to the next level managers, attending training courses with staff, regular meetings with staff, giving informal and formal recognition and celebrating successes, visiting customers, regularly reviewing quality issues during management meetings and using quality tools and techniques in their daily work.

Set-up local steering committees (S2)

Set-up steering committees at divisional and site levels to take up the responsibility of overseeing and managing the quality processes at the local level. Each committee is represented by local key personnel, and chaired by the manager. Effective liaison and links with the corporate quality council is vital. This may be done via the TQM secretariat, headed by the TQM support manager.

Critical category II: maximise internal stakeholder involvement

Internal stakeholders are middle management and non-management employees. Maximising internal stakeholders' support and involvement involves mobilising the entire workforce to attain the quality goals of the organization through buy-in, skills training and recognition.

Writers of TQM are unanimous that maximising employees' support and involvement in quality initiatives is the most basic requirement for making TQM work in an organization. It must be through the combined efforts of middle managers and employees, led by senior executives, that the offerings to customers can be continuously met and improved.

Once there is employee buy-in to adopting TQM and an understanding of the corporate mission and quality goals, employees need to develop the necessary skills and abilities to carry out the quality mandate. In addition to learning the fundamentals of TQM, early training should support values and expectations as defined by the quality policy, developing continuous improvement and problem-solving skills. Employees also need skills to work well together as a team. Aligning rewards and recognition is an important ingredient for maximising employees' involvement in the quality initiatives.

Implementation guidelines
A critical quality factors checklist is:

- The entire workforce understands and is committed to the vision, values and quality goals of the organization (T1).
- Supervisors, unit heads and divisional mangers assume active roles as facilitators of continuous improvement, coaches for new methods, and mentors and leaders of empowered employees (T1).
- Training for employees in problem identification and solving techniques, quality improvement skills and other technical skills (T1).
- System for recognition and appreciation of quality efforts and success of individuals and teams (T1).
- Training for employees to improve interactive skills (T2).

Soft sell TQM (S0)
Disseminate information about TQM in general, and its operating and business benefits in particular, before formally launching TQM. This may involve incorporating relevant TQM news and articles in the in-house bulletin, sending key personnel to TQM conferences and seminars.

Foster employee buy-in to TQM (S1)
Communicate the need to set-up a management system based on total quality. Gather all employees together to communicate the need face-to-face. Where this is not possible, use the cascade to approach. Provide training in the concepts and philosophies of TQM.

Orientate the perspective of everyone towards corporate objectives (S1)
Communicate the statement of mission and corporate objectives, defining quality values, expectations and focus organization-wide. Ensure the entire workforce understands and is committed to the mission. Gather all employees together to introduce and explain the mission. Where this is not possible, use the cascade approach.

Allay middle managers anxiety (S1)
Recognise and allay the anxiety and concern of middle managers as the organization develops a TQ ethic. Extend assurance by mentoring and guidance. Ensure greater direct interaction with middle managers during the early years. Organize visits to TQ organizations to allow middle managers to meet peer groups.

Nurture middle mangers to assume new roles (S1)
Recognise that middle managers' new roles under TQM demand new knowledge, skills and abilities. Provide training to assume roles as facilitators of continuous improvement, coaches of new methods and leaders of empowered employees. Align rewards and recognition to reinforce the behaviours needed for their new roles.

Provide the necessary training in scientific continuous improvement skills (S1)
Provide training in continuous improvement, problem identification and problem-solving techniques: for example, training in the seven basic QC tools and techniques.

Introduce teamwork and decision making based on facts and systematic analysis as one of the guiding values of continuous improvement.

Set up a reward system and recognition programmes (S1)
Align the reward system and recognition programmes as a tool in maximising employee support and involvement. Employees need to be consulted regarding what form of recognition is a motivator for them. An *ad hoc* committee may be set up to make recommendations. Visit best-in-class organizations to study best practice.

Have in place both monetary and non-monetary recognition. Also strive for balance between recognising individual and team performance based on the organization's quality goals.

Set up effective top-down and bottom up communication (S1)
Review the internal communication strategies in maximising employee support and involvement. This may involve using feedback from employee surveys and/or other measures. An *ad hoc* committee may be set up to review and make recommendations for improvements. Identify and act on areas for improvement. Identify opportunities for improvement by visiting best-in-class organizations.

Keep employees informed (S1)
Keep employees regularly informed of business performance and development and quality initiatives such as individual and team successes. Use a variety of modes of communication such as management presentations, and one-to-one meetings, in-house bulletins and posters and banners. Where possible, emphasis should be on face-to-face meetings rather than artefacts. Organizations with fragmented businesses may need to rely on effective use of the latter.

Institute training in interactive skills (S2)
Provide training in interactive skills such as leadership, training and effective communication.

Critical category III: manage by customer-driven processes
Manage by customer-driven processes for quality means the organization must conduct its business and implement its quality goals primarily by deploying its employees and other resources along processes, rather than the organization structure, which deliver values for the customers. Central to this approach is the concept of internal customer-supplier relationship.

Focus on processes and internal customer-supplier relationship and their management has been widely documented by authors in the area of TQM since

TQM revolves around effectively managing processes to continually satisfy customers.

For organizations that are managed on a functional basis, a critical early task is to promote internal customer-supplier attitude. The effort involves employees/functions seeing themselves as part of a customer-supplier chain by relating the things they are doing to delivering values for the customer and identifying the requirements of their immediate customers.

Implementation guidelines
A critical quality factor checklist is
- The entire organization understands that each individual and process has internal customer and supplier (T1).
- Comprehensive identification of customers and their needs (internal and external) and the alignment of processes to satisfy the needs (T2).
- Systematic review and analysis of key process measures that have a direct or indirect impact on value addition to customer satisfaction (T3).

Promote the concept of internal customer-supplier relationship (S1)
Promote the concept of customer-supplier relationship as a discipline to identify, control and improve activities that add value to customer satisfaction.

Ensure everyone, including senior executives, understands the concepts of process management and internal customer supply chain. Include the concepts as part of early quality awareness training.

Identify external and internal customer requirements (S2)
This may initially involve marketing and sales personnel providing inputs. The use of other formal techniques such as customer surveys and focus groups may be introduced at a later stage to collect data.

Request everyone within the organization to seek out his or her customer requirements. This may involve asking questions: who are my immediate customers? What are their requirements? Do I have the necessary capabilities to meet their requirements? Who are my immediate suppliers? What are my true requirements? And do I communicate my requirements?

Carry out process mapping (S2)
Conduct training in process mapping. This may involve just the senior managers and middle managers who will take on the responsibility of process champions of processes and sub-processes.

Carry out process mapping of major processes that together impact on the organization's ability to achieve customer requirements. Involve employees responsible for performing the processes in the exercise. Document the processes. Include information of process owners, internal customers and suppliers, their requirements, critical and non-critical activities and measures and targets.

Deploy resources around the major processes (S2)
Deploy resources, including manpower, for the effective and efficient execution of the major processes. Assign a process champion to be responsible for the execution of each business process. This may be a senior manager. Involve employees responsible for performing the processes. Identify new sets of process ownership. Set up process improvement teams wherever inter-process dependencies are identified. Recognise and reward individual's contribution to the process team. Improve communication across functional units involved in performing the critical processes, for example, by setting up new modes of communication, better management of meetings and the use of information technology.

Develop a performance measurement system (S3)
Develop a performance measurement system to track process performance and for continuous improvement of processes. Establish measures and targets to be used as evidence of the success of attaining customer values attached to business and sub-processes and benchmark standards. Ensure the measures and targets are mutually agreed by supplier and customers. These need to reflect the needs and wants of the customer, process capability and benchmark standards. Devise procedures for data collection. Measure performance against target performance. Develop plans for handling non-conformance, including establishing target time scales for resolving non-conformance. Incorporate mechanisms for continuously improving the business processes. Establish a standardised corrective action method to maximise the sharing experience.

Critical category IV: adopt continuous improvement
Adopting continuous improvement means every activity and process aligned to the customer must continuously undergo improvement. Continuous improvement of customer-driven activities and processes is a basic philosophy that underlies continuous customer satisfaction.

There are a number of early initiatives, some fundamental, that should be pursued to support continuous improvement. Among others, continuous improvement demands that every step taken is based on facts and teamwork to promote a bottom-up trust for quality improvement and deliver synergistic enhancement of quality efforts.

At a later stage, tools and techniques such as benchmarking, self-assessment and cost of quality should be introduced to initiate and guide continuous improvement efforts.

Implementation guidelines
A critical quality factors checklist is:
- Problem solving and continuous improvement processes based on facts and systematic analysis (T2).
- A team approach in problem solving and continuous improvement (T2).

- The use of customer surveys and feedback processes, and tracking of other key measures to assess customer satisfaction (T2).
- The use of self-assessment tools and other mechanisms to track and improve performance gaps in the implementation and effectiveness of systems, processes and practices (T3).
- Competitive benchmarking made against primary competitors (T3).
- Cost of quality process to track rework, waste, rejects and for continuous improvement (T3).
- Informal benchmarking and other forms of information sharing with organizations in different sectors and industries to identify best practice for improvements and opportunities (T3).

Instill discipline that continuous improvement and problem-solving decisions are based on facts and systematic analysis (S1)

Make decision-making based on facts and systematic analysis part of the organization's guiding values. Provide employees with training and assistance to help them use facts appropriate in their decision making. This may include training in the use of specific analysis tools such as the seven basic QC tools for employees and the seven management and planning tools for managers.

Make available a pool of assistance to individuals and teams to use the tools and make systematic analysis to arrive at decisions. This may be set up as part of the quality management structure. Encourage ideas for improvement that are substantiated with data.

Encourage team effort (S1)

Establish metrics to track customer satisfaction. This may include methods such as customer surveys to solicit information from customers and internal data, such as actively collecting delivery times. Use customer data to identify opportunities for continuous improvement.

Introduce tools and techniques (S2)

Introduce tools and techniques to identify opportunities for continuous improvement. This should include benchmarking, self-assessment and cost of quality process. Develop pools of personnel trained in the various tools and techniques.

Benchmark to identify best practices. Carry out both competitive and non-competitive benchmarking. Involve process owners in benchmarking exercises.

Carry out quality control exercises. Measure cost of prevention, appraisal and internal failure.

Summary
Construction of this TQM implementation framework is primarily based on findings representing the experiences of TQM organizations, the vast majority with

two to three years' implementation. Although it has been shown that three core elements – the critical quality factors – used to construct the framework are generalisable, the framework is presented more as a guide for organizations contemplating a TQM initiative. It is thought that the framework should be useful up to the critical two to three years into implementation. During that time, the framework is also useful as a practical and systematic tool for assessing, measuring and evaluating the progress made in the implementation of TQM.

The framework is applicable to organizations in a wide range of industries, since it provides for the development of a TQM implementation plan to suit, for example, their business situation and available resources, rather than as a prescriptive "to do" list.

Although the key concepts of the framework represent most, if not all, of the current philosophical understandings underpinning TQM, it is recommended that organization complement the guidelines by continually seeking out and studying best implementation practices to understand how others are achieving success in implementing and sustaining TQM. Even developers of well-established TQM frameworks such as the Baldrige award recognise the evolution of implementation approaches.

How the framework was developed
Measuring the criticality of TQM implementation
A critical quality factor has been defined as a quality factor that is critical and absolutely essential to the success of TQM implementation. This definition is qualified to mean that the implementation process stands a good chance of ending in failure if this critical quality factor is not part of TQM. It is also implied that the more critical a quality factor is, the higher the chances of failure if it is not part of TQM. A comparative quantitative measure of how critical a quality factor is, therefore, useful.

A comprehensive study conducted at the European Centre for TQM established that:

- A quality factor with critical as the modal category be defined as a critical quality factor.
- The extent of consensus in opinions among respondents in categorising a quality factor as critical can be equated to show how critical a quality factor is.
- Variation ratio as a measure of how descriptive the modal category is of the data can be equated to the extent of consensus in opinions.
- Variation ratio, thus, can be equated to show how critical a critical quality factor is.

By definition, variation ratio is corrected for the unequal valid responses (N). Thus, ratio values can be compared across response distributors with differing numbers of valid responses within a single survey sample. It also permits cross-cutting comparisons between survey samples of differing sizes with an identical number of categories. Variation ratio is, therefore, appropriate as a surrogate measure of comparative criticality.

A variation of zero for a critical quality factor is obtained when every single organization perceives a quality factor to be absolutely essential to the success of TQM implementation. Thus, a zero value represents the extreme end or pinnacle of criticality. Any value greater than zero means relatively fewer organizations returning the quality factor as critical. At the other extreme end of criticality, the maximal value is obtained when just a third of the organizations return the quality factor as critical.

The maximum value is never an integer and depends on the number of categories (K). This feature is awkward and does not allow easy interpretation when the measure is used as a stand-alone indicator of criticality. It would be more useful were the measure normed to go from 0 to 1. Introducing an index of comparative criticality for critical quality factors with end values of 0 for most critical and 1 for least critical is thus in order. Dividing the variation ratio by the maximal value norms the CC index so that the value of 1 always represents the least critical. The criticality index for each critical quality factor is, therefore, best calculated from a modified variation of the ratio equation:

CC index $= (1 - f\,critical/N)/(K - 1/K)$

Where critical is a maximal value.

The following list shows the critical index of the 22 critical quality factors distilled from this investigation. To enable ease of interpretation when used as a stand-alone indicator, the CC index is superimposed with tiers and the question numbers are given in parentheses so the factors can be identified on the criticality matrix shown in Figure 18.3:

- Tier I:
    - 0.000 Senior executives assume active responsibility for evaluation and improvement of management system and lead the quality drive (q1).
    - 0.132 Clear, consistent communication of mission statement and objectives defining quality values, expectations and focus (q3).
    - 0.166 The entire workforce understands and is committed to vision, values and quality goals of the organization (q9).
    - 0.171 Visibility of senior executive commitment to quality and customer satisfaction (q2).
    - 0.205 Training for employees in problem identification and solving skills, quality improvement skills and other technical skills (q16).
    - 0.240 The entire organization understands that each individual and each process has internal customers and suppliers (q8).
    - 0.304 Supervisors, unit heads and divisional managers assume active roles as facilitators of continuous improvement, coaches of new method, mentors and leaders of empowered employees (q12).

- ○ 0.370 Systems for recognition and appreciation of quality efforts and success of individuals and teams (q14).
  - ○ 0.388 Effective top-down, bottom-up and lateral communication (q6).
- • Tier II:
  - ○ 0.408 Problem solving and continuous improvement process based on facts and systematic analysis (q20).
  - ○ 0.493 Comprehensive policy development and effective deployment of goals (q4).
  - ○ 0.519 A team approach in problem solving and continuous improvement (q23).
  - ○ 0.519 Comprehensive identification of customers and customer needs and alignment of processes to satisfy the needs (q30).
  - ○ 0.519 The use of customer surveys and feedback processes and tracking of other key measures to assess customer satisfaction (q31).
  - ○ 0.544 Training for employees to improve interactive skills (q15).
- • Tier III:
  - ○ 0.759 Elements of quality deployment structure in place to manage the organization's quality journey (q7).
  - ○ 0.759 Employee suggestion scheme in place, with target time scales for management response (q11).
  - ○ 0.759 The use of self-assessment tools and other mechanisms to track and improve performance gaps in the implementation and effectiveness of systems, processes and practices (q22).
  - ○ 0.769 Competitive benchmarking made against primary competitors (q18).
  - ○ 0.769 Cost of quality process to track re-work, waste, rejects and for continuous improvement (q25).
  - ○ 0.787 Informal benchmarking and other forms of information acquisition and sharing with organizations in different sectors and industries to identify best practices for improvement and opportunities (q17).
  - ○ 0.826 Systematic review and analysis of key process measures that have a direct or indirect impact on value addition to customer satisfaction (q19).

Most if not all Tier I critical quality factors are acknowledged in TQM literature as prerequisites of fundamental elements that must be addressed early in the implementation. Namely, commitment and involvement from the top, communication of statement of mission, maximising employees' support and involvement, internal customer supplier attitude and effective communication. This validates the interpretation of Tier I critical quality factors as factors that impact on the success of the TQM implementation the most.

The development of a clear mission statement and the consistent communication of objectives defining values, expectations and focus (q3) is seen as one of the first steps for top management commitment. Quality and commitment to customer satisfaction is also seen to play an important part in the top management daily priorities (q2). Such commitment of top management, actively demonstrated, is the means for promoting organizational commitment, such as identification by the workforce with the vision, values and goals of the organization and middle management assuming their new roles (q12). Education and training is often reported as an important element in the development of a suitable continuous improvement culture. Many organizations view employee training in problem solving and continuous improvement (q16) as the main emphasis here. However, top management must sell the need to create such a culture to engage the commitment of the employees. Effective top-down and bottom-up communication (q6) is perceived as a critical enabler here. A system for recognition and appreciation of quality efforts and success of individuals and teams, as a core concept of TQM, needs to be set up by the top management to reinforce the message.

The critical quality factors list also shares most of the values covered by key principles espoused by the Baldrige award and EQA criteria, namely:

- Top management take responsibility for creating the enabling environment for quality to take root and to be sustained. Their role includes policy development and goal setting and planning process, promoting quality awareness, providing role models through demonstrated commitment and involvement, and setting up elements of a quality management structure.
- Aligning employee active involvement to corporate expectations by uniting them behind the vision, values and quality goals of the organization.
- Maximising employee involvement through teamwork, understanding and meeting their needs, setting up the means to tap improvement ideas, recognition for quality efforts and training and education.
- Creation of continuous improvement ethics and the use of quality improvement tools and techniques.
- Emphasis on management by fact.
- Importance of external customer focus; understanding of the concept of internal customer.
- Having a system for measuring key indicators that impact the way the organization adds value to customers.

A self-assessment tool using TQ quality factors

A self-assessment tool can be useful in two ways. First, to assess TQM implementation within an organization during the early years. The 22 critical quality factors provide a more realistic checklist for assessment of implementation progress during the early years of implementation than those suggested in national quality awards. It is generally recognised that self-assessment using the criteria of quality awards such as MBNQA and EQA are appropriate for organizations that are usually advanced in the use of TQM. Second, the self-assessment tool can be used to assess TQM understanding among the workforce. Such an assessment is of importance in an appraisal of training requirements especially during the early years.

In designing an instrument, consideration had to be given to subject matter for the assessment – the unit of analysis. For TQM implementation assessment, the organization is the unit of analysis. The instrument is designed to measure an individual's perception of the level of implementation of each quality factor, and therefore the development of the overall programme as a whole within the organization. To assess TQM understanding, an individual is the unit of analysis. The instrument is designed to measure an individual's perception of the relative importance of the quality factors.

The selection of measurement scales to solicit such responses must be taken into consideration for both respondents and those who administer the tools. Features like ease of completion and scoring are important to the former, while ease in interpretation are important to the latter.

The survey questionnaire used in this study could be used with minor modification as a tool for assessing the implementation of the critical quality factors. A significant modification to the questionnaire will be the exclusion of non-critical quality factors.

The use of a Likert-type scale with a rating of, say 1 to 5 or even 1 to 10 to express the extent of implantation can be limiting and pose difficulties in interpretation. The alternative of a continuous scale, where respondents rate the degree of implementation as a score out of the maximum points. The maximum score represents the organization performing to the full extent of the quality factors. It is convenient to work with a single maximum point for all quality factors; working with integers such as 10, 100 or 1,000 as maximum points are practical and convenient when it comes to interpretation and mathematical conversion; a maximum of 100 is ideal as it is neither limiting nor awkwardly large to score and sum.

Using the self-assessment tool for benchmarking

A useful analysis to perform is benchmarking using the comparative criticality index (CC index). The information gathered from the benchmarking analysis could be used as the basis to prioritise areas for improvement (implementation) action.

Benchmarking analysis involves the comparison of the degree of implementation of critical quality factors against the CC index as the standard. A gap analysis is performed on a matrix chart called a criticality matrix (see Figure 18.3). Critical quality factors in order of criticality are listed on the left y axis from top to bottom. Benchmark scores for each critical quality factor is incorporated on the matrix using horizontal lines with varying lengths representing values of the

CC index. Implementation scores of the respective critical quality factors, represented as lines, are plotted from right to left on the criticality lines. Implementation score plots that fall short of the benchmark line range are negative gaps (that is, the level of implementation falls short of standard). Positive gaps are ones where the implementation score plots fall short on the line range.

The information gathered from benchmarking analysis could be used as the basis to prioritise areas for improvement (implementation) action. Negative gaps indicate actions required. Prioritisation of actions is performed along the criticality scale from the top downwards. Positive gaps are of little concern, unless in instances where there are significantly large numbers of negative gaps. The management then needs to re-align quality strategies and tactics, resources and personnel to correct the imbalances.

Benchmarking analysis of past trends could also be done across departments using a similar approach.

Figure 18.1 Critical categories for reaching organizational excellence

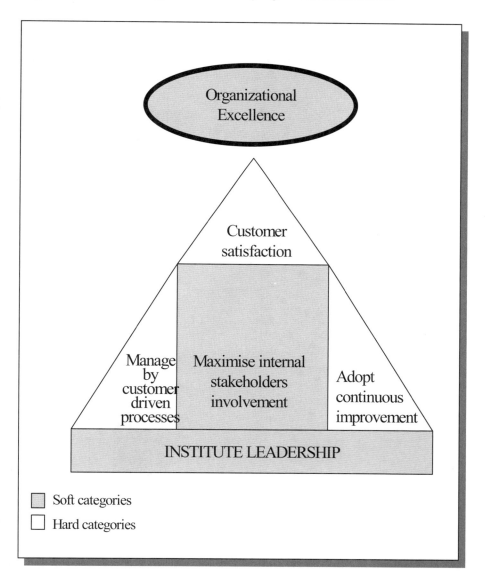

Figure 18.2 Elements of the TQM implementation framework

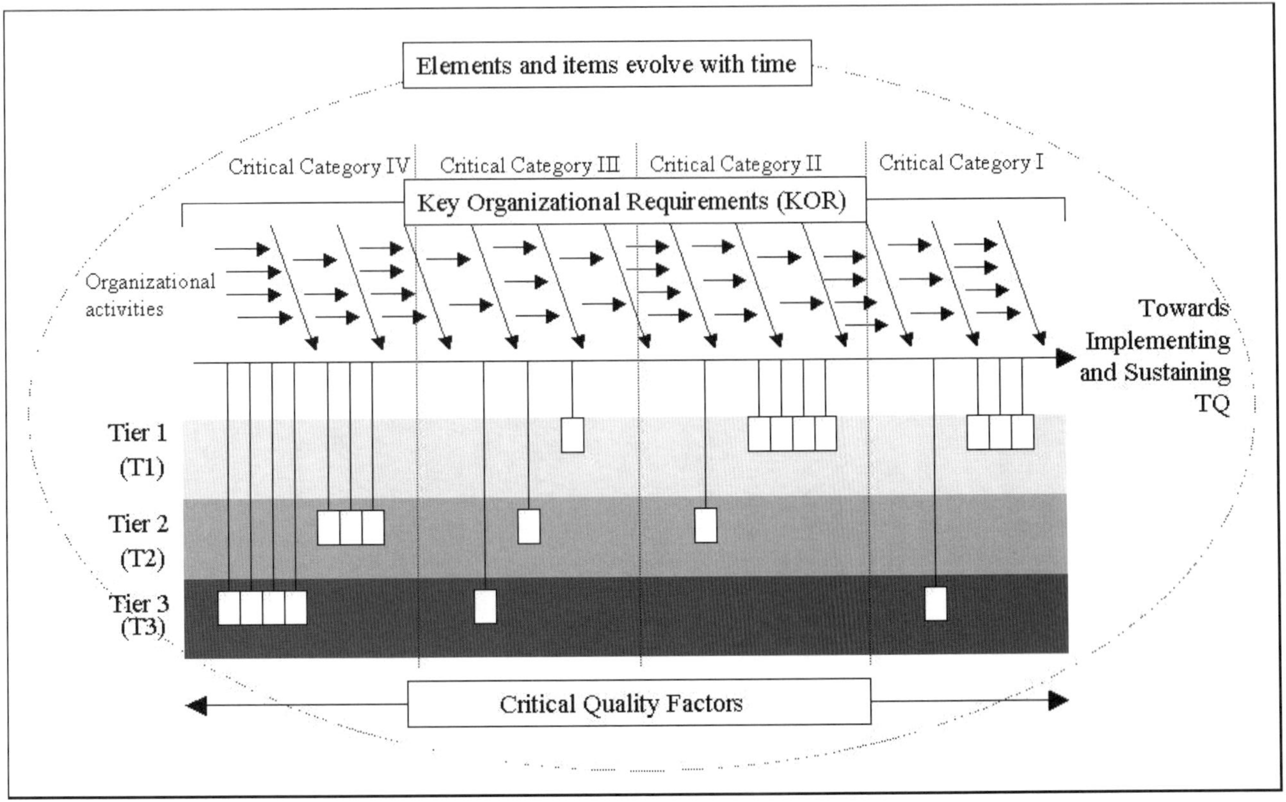

302

Figure 18.3 Criticality matrix

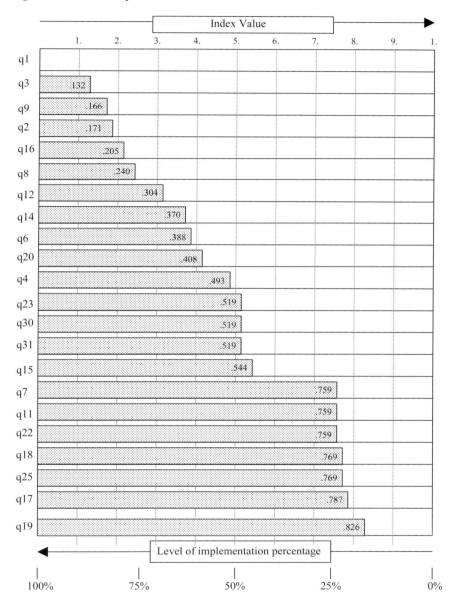

Chapter 19
Sustainability of TQM

Introduction
The organizational quest for quality has resulted in varied conceptualisations and paradigms (Hermel, 1997), with the following four principal trends becoming visible:

1. Quality, initially conceptualised as a quantitative aspect, gradually emphasising qualitative factors.
2. The reactive function of inspection became a preventive function, thus moving from a reactive to a proactive vision of quality.
3. The notion of quality gradually no longer focusing on the final product, but on quality of daily tasks and processes.
4. A global perspective of the organization emerged as a result of the increasing integration of different functional aspects of quality. Social and environmental aspects are now added to the commercial dimension of organizations.

Conceptualising total quality management (TQM)
As a concept, quality has emerged as a formal management function (Garvin, 1988), beginning from inspection to assurance to process management to best practice product development. This transformational path is shown in Figure 19.1. The process as outlined in Figure 19.1 is not only sequential, but also "walled" into separated product development functions. In essence, marketing threw the product goals over the wall to the product designers, who altered these goals and designed a product to meet the corrected market analysis, if they believed that the said goals were unrealistic and did not reflect a clear understanding of available technology. Product design then threw the design over the wall to both the process designers and purchasing. This has created haphazard interactions between functions within an organization. For example, in a traditional product development process, market analysis may have recorded the wants and needs of customers, whereas the customer is not really a part of the process. Little or no feedback occurred across the walls, no one was accountable for the results of the process, and the length of time from the market analysis to the point of sale was so lengthy that the market analysis was often no longer valid. This was because, at each stage, the entire product development process was restarted, creating expensive and time-consuming duplication. It is, therefore, obvious that this traditional product development process just did not work.

The shifting roles of quality and how quality management is managed occur in many facets of organizational processes beyond the product development function discussed above. A series of major events in the last four decades have brought quality management from functional focus to an integrated approach to managing an organization (Feigenbaum, 1961). Another major quality event of the 1980s was the establishment in 1987 of the Malcolm Baldrige National Quality Award (MBNQA). Suffice to add, that by the 1990s, a small number of US organizations had raised their quality to world-class levels and those successful Baldrige Award winners displayed characteristics that can be described as a TQM approach to quality.

Usability of self-assessment underpins continuous improvement by measuring the current performance of an organization against an "excellence". Two of the most frequently used self-assessment models are the MBNQA, and the European excellence model 2000.

Analysis of literature on MBNQA and EQA winners

The MBNQA and the European excellence model are now in widespread use in many organizations. Several approaches relative to the application of these models are documented in the literature and have emphasised some advantages in the area of TQM, which include improved approaches, measurement and benchmarking.

For the past decade or more, there seems to have been a proliferation of TQM frameworks in the literature, and Jamal (1998) provides a useful synthesis of this literature based on the work of several academics. His approach seeks to suggest that:

- TQM is strategically linked to business goals.
- Customer understanding and satisfaction are vital.
- Employee participation and understanding at all levels are required.
- Management commitment and consistency of purpose are compulsory.
- The organization is perceived as a series of processes that incorporate customer and supplier relationships.

McAdam and O'Neill (1999) cautioned that the EQA framework should not be viewed as being synonymous with TQM, although it has merit as a business audit approach. They argued that the EQA model is a technique within TQM, and not a model of the same and similar view applied to the MBNQA model.

This research has found that self-assessment techniques work well when employed with a long-term view. Other quality models still cannot be considered a panacea for all problems, neither will they guarantee immediate and everlasting success in improving quality.

Percentage weighting of MBNQA and EQA criteria

Despite their popularity, the MBNQA and the EQA models have been examined to see whether they achieve their aim. Both models have weighted scoring mechanisms (see Table 19.1) that are used to determine the performance of the organization within each of the model elements and identify an overall assessment.

306

It can be observed from Table 19.1 that differences exist in the point allocations placed on each criterion, as business results have the greatest weight for the MBNQA and customer satisfaction for the EQA. Results are the true indicator of success when it comes to assessing any improvement initiative. True TQM cannot, therefore, be successful without evaluating business results, which are extremely important for the implementation of any quality endeavour.

Comparative analysis of MBNQA and EQA models
Table 19.2 shows commonalities between the MBNQA and EQA models that claim to provide a holistic approach to assess effectiveness of TQM implementation. Each model places emphasis on customer-driven quality through streamlined processes, product design, leadership, human resource development, and customer-focused strategic plans. The literature on the MBNQA and EQA awards also reveals that both encourage continuous improvement of leadership techniques, strategic plans, company processes and stakeholder relationships, through the analysis and change of business results.

Growth of TQM transformational path
The literature suggests that in order to achieve "world-class" status, each MBNQA and EQA winner had closely to examine its entire operations, processes and its customers, so as to compare itself with the best-in-class. Self-assessment technique measures firms' standards and performance in their attempts to achieve world class rating. Both the MBNQA and EQA models provide the ideal framework against which this can be done.

The growth of the TQM framework was stimulated by economic and business pressures that drive an increased focus on the continuous benchmarking, global competitive benchmarking, adapting new best practice, and innovating to become world class. A world class organization is one that has the production and/or service capability that is competitive in the dynamic global economy.

A review of the literature about the 1988 and 1999 MBNQA winners, also the 1992 and 1999 winners of the EQA, with a view to examining the evolution of their TQM path, has reflected the four paradigm shifts as shown in Table 19.3. Managing this shift successfully is a key to TQM sustainability. From Table 19.3, the initial focus of management in 1988 was on increasing the efficiency of production. This involved an inward, product-orientated emphasis with the overriding objective to develop a standardised product at the lowest price possible. This production orientation philosophy represented an "inside-the-box" mentality, as this was an inward-looking approach to quality. It manifested itself in several ways, through "inspecting-in" quality, internal benchmarking, and being cost focused, then adopting a reactive approach to quality control with an emphasis on detection rather than prevention.

In later years, this old paradigm then changed to a transactional mode, and organizations became more responsive to customer needs. Customer satisfaction was given more credence, and this led to greater focus on internal organizational interactions and systems, as service orientation grew in importance across many Western industry sectors.

At the core of this service-oriented culture was an organization-wide understanding that the delivery of outstanding service quality meant examining the very nature of service. This required embracing a set of durable policies, practices and procedures like process mapping and improvement, along with employee training and rewards for creating and delivering "service excellence".

As competition increased, survival depended more on skills of organizations to become privy to different markets and improve sales techniques. This led to the philosophy which prompted organizations to start providing products they could sell, rather than trying to sell what they produced. Customer relations were now of paramount importance, and this customer orientation meant that organizations concentrated on providing products and services that fulfilled the needs of customers.

Organizations recognised that meeting customer needs and providing customer satisfaction were the most effective basis for planning and that an outward market-orientated emphasis was a key to being successful. The MBNQA and EQA criteria emphasise customer importance, and thus help organizations using these assessment models to understand better the customer roles which are a key to understanding customer orientation. Customer orientation therefore helped the organizations to deal with external and internal issues like market advantage and product/service design efficiencies and innovation (Reed *et al.*, 1996). Customer orientation is no doubt one dimension of market orientation (Kohli and Jaworski, 1990).

This final paradigm shift to market orientation that is found in the literature on the MBNQA and EQA winners shows that these models are not only applicable means of assessment, but can also form the basis for planning improvements. Market-oriented organizations should be adept at reacting to formal and informal feedback received from customers and competitors. The MBNQA and EQA thus offered tools for implementing a quality strategy, benchmarking best practices, performing self-assessments and, above all, achieving improvements.

Critical factors of success

The organizations using the Baldrige model are exposed to its criteria for a performance excellence framework, which has three basic elements:

1. *Strategy and action plans.* These guide overall resource decisions and drive the alignment of measures for all work units to ensure customer satisfaction and market success.
2. *System.* This comprises the six Baldrige categories that define the organization, its operations and its results.

3. *Information and analysis.* These serve as a foundation for performance management and are critical to ensuring the effectiveness of the organization, and support a system based on facts that are essential to improving performance and competitiveness.

The 1998 revised Baldrige criteria specify the needs of all stakeholders, with the aim of achieving a comprehensive coverage of strategy-driven performance. Greater emphasis is now placed on the alignment of company strategy, customer and market knowledge, a high performance workforce, key company processes, and business results. Additionally, there is an increased focus on all aspects of organizational and employee learning (NIST, 1998).

The European excellence model is also an inclusive framework for managing change and displays a nexus between cause and effect. The prevailing view is that an improvement of the enablers or the "how" of an organization's operations will lead to more excellent results for each of its key stakeholders.

This study of the MBNQA and EQA winners also found that each organization identified a mission and critical factors of success to drive and sustain continuous improvement. It is also worthy of note that the efforts employed by these winners were long term in nature, and even after their achievement, the business environment continues to change rapidly. To drive and sustain continuous improvement goes, therefore, beyond a mission, critical success factors, and the use of any of the self-assessment models. Emphasis must be placed on those factors which will keep the improvement momentum going between self-assessment checks, as the organization still has to cope with a dynamic business environment. This, therefore, requires an integrated effort to adapt strategy to comprehensive market needs. While both models have similar criteria, there is some variation in the approaches and definitions involved. An attempt is, therefore, made to demonstrate how the criteria for each award address seven quality areas - namely leadership, policy and strategy, customers, information and analysis, human resources, process management, and business results.

Further to an analysis of literature in relation to the award examination criteria of both the MBNQA and the EQA, the critical success factors covering the seven key areas are presented in Table 19.4.

Measures of success

The question of measuring the right dimensions of the models is necessary for the recipients of these quality awards to achieve business excellence in four key areas of enterprise. It is well documented and widely accepted that in order to remain a leader in this dynamic and unpredictable business environment, it is imperative to:

1. maximize stakeholder value;
2. achieve process excellence;
3. improve organizational learning; and
4. satisfy stakeholders (internal/external).

As implied in the models, it is essential to ensure that achievements in these key areas are mutually dependent, and thus form a cycle of continuous improvement, so that:

- customer satisfaction improves revenue generation and adequate returns on investment;
- increased revenue provides the necessary funding for investments in processes and learning; and
- more efficient and effective process and learning helps people to satisfy stakeholders and create business excellence.

Balanced scorecard approach

To achieve business excellence, many organizations have adopted the business scorecard approach for process improvement (Kaplan and Norton, 1992). The scorecard is designed to be comprehensive, includes a number of generic measures, and it is balanced because it has a balanced perspective which is both qualitative and quantitative (see Figure 19.2).

The business balanced scorecard is a powerful concept that helps to focus on different kinds of measures, which is the main ethos of performance measurement. It has increased in popularity since 1992, and has been further developed as an approach within TQM.

Traditionally, most organizations looked at their corporate performance by reviewing the financial aspects. However, financial measures alone do not give a balanced view of the critical success factors of any organization, for the simple reason that financial measurements provide historical data, since they tend to measure the past. While such measures inform the organization about what has happened, there are no explanations of why it has happened.

The Baldrige criteria create an avenue for looking across functional areas, and provide a more integrated and holistic view of the organization. In order to achieve business excellence, therefore, it is necessary to give equal weight to all four areas of enterprise rather than concentrating exclusively on the financial perspective. The balanced scorecard, being based on four key perspectives, allows organizations that use this approach to define a number of key corporate objectives, and assign an agreed set of measurement criteria to each factor. This allows everyone in the organization to capture at a glance how the big picture is shaping up, and how changes in one area are affecting achievement in another.

Assessment and improvement drive business results

Prior to the introduction of the Baldrige criteria, organizations had no effective way of performing company-wide self-assessments. There may have been ways of analysing processes or human resource programmes, but no way of looking more broadly at leadership systems, strategic planning, or the effective use of information and analysis. The Baldrige criteria thus create an avenue for looking across functional areas, and provide a more integrated and holistic view of the organization. They also act as a barometer to allow business leaders to predict business results and measure improvement trends.

There is mounting evidence that the Baldrige process produces result, as there is a direct correlation between "scores and business performance". Organizers of the MBNQA – the NIST – demonstrated that work on quality is an investment rather than a cost, and that the better the quality, the higher the return. This was done by NIST through a comparison of stock values. A hypothetical sum was invested in each of the 1988-1998 publicly-traded Baldrige Award recipients' common stock in the year they applied for the award. The investment was tracked from the first business day of the month following the announcement of the award recipients (or the date when they began public trading, if it was later) through December 1999. A sum of $1,000 was invested in each whole company, and for subsidiaries the sum invested was $1,000 multiplied by the percentage of the whole company's employee base that the sub-unit represents. The identical total dollar amount was invested in the Standard and Poor's (S&P) 500 on the same day. The stock performance analyses done by NIST show that Baldrige winners outperformed the S&P index by ratios up to 3.8 and 4.8 to 1 respectively. Using this index is one measure of the success of the companies that receive the Baldrige Award. Many improvements as a result of investing in quality management have been reported by award recipients. For example, cumulative manufacturing cost savings at Motorola, a 1988 winner, for the years 1987 through to the second quarter of 1994 were over $5.5 billion. For the 1992 winner, Ritz-Carlton Hotel Co., quality management helped the company to eliminate $75 million in waste through project improvements. The Ritz-Carlton, also a 1999 winner, is the only services company to receive a Baldrige Award twice, and reported sales in 1998 of more than $1 billion. Other studies have also found that organizations receiving quality awards show long-lasting improvements in their bottom-line results.

Rationale for a model
Increasingly, organizations in the USA and Europe accept that TQM is a way of managing activities to gain efficiency, effectiveness and competitive advantage, thereby ensuring longer-term success in meeting the needs of their customers, employees, financial and other stakeholders, and the community at large. The implementation of TQM programmes can deliver benefits such as increased efficiency, reduced costs and greater satisfaction, that all lead to better business results.

Regardless of business sector, size, structure or maturity, to be successful, organizations need to establish an appropriate management system. The MBNQA model and the EFQM excellence model are practical tools that can help organizations do this by measuring where they are on the path to excellence, helping them to understand the gaps and stimulate solutions.

It must be recognised that there are many approaches to achieving sustainable excellence, but within a non-prescriptive framework there are some fundamental concepts that underpin both models. Excellence, however, is dependent on balancing and satisfying the needs of all relevant stakeholders. Hence, to achieve business excellence, organizations must demonstrate that they excel across various performance areas, each of which is covered by agreed measurement criteria. This is expressed in Figure 19.3.

This business scorecard approach does not prescribe which performance areas should be used or how they should be measured. However, from the study of the literature, it is clear that organizations need to adopt a TQM process and the critical success factors if they are to achieve business excellence. While these two business excellence models are non-prescriptive frameworks, the issue of measurement is at the heart of everything that is done. It is a behavioural issue and not one of design or control.

Measurement gives strength, continuity and sustainable performance. As excellent organizations develop and improve, and regularly upgrade their strategic "scorecard", over time this will translate into effective leadership at all levels that practise management by fact, and inculcate a continuous improvement culture that enhances people performance that produces customer delight and good business results.

Proposed framework for sustainable TQM

The relevant literature suggests that organizations survive by constantly meeting the changing needs, wants and requirements of their customers, and withstanding the pressures of their competitors. Competition has forced organizations to think of delighting customers rather than simply satisfying them. This notion has been institutionalised by criteria under MBNQA or EFQA models.

It is also shown in the literature that the leadership system of the MBNQA/EQA winners demands models and assures continuous improvement in all business processes, and promotes an environment for innovation in products and services through the use of a strategic business plan, business environment, operating plan, and regular key indicator reports. An example of a leadership system is shown in Figure 19.4.

TQM maturity and sustainable performance model (proposed roadmap)

The literature also confirms that TQM is not a "quick-fix", "off-the-shelf" solution to competitiveness for any organization. It must be a totally integrated, continuous, professional system based on the commitment of employees and top management, working together with customers so that the needs of all are met. Against this backdrop, therefore, a proposed roadmap for creating a competitive advantage is developed from the literature, and is shown in Figure 19.5.

Model description

This TQM maturity and sustainable performance model (Figure 19.5) proposes the creation of an organizational system that fosters co-operating, learning, innovating, and facilitating process management. This in turn leads to continuous improvement of processes, products and services, and to employee fulfilment, both of which are critical to stakeholder satisfaction and ultimately to the survival of the organization.

Implicit in this proposition is the crucial role that organizational leadership plays in ensuring the success of quality management. It is the responsibility of leaders to create and communicate a vision that moves the organization towards continuous improvement. Management support also determines sustainability of an organizational system that is receptive to process management practices.

Need for TQM to drive sustainability

The "driver" can be interpreted as the TQM approach that exemplifies characteristics that an organization needs to display to compete successfully in the market place. As a business imperative, it must re-establish itself to be quicker to market, customer focused, innovative, flexible, and better able to cope with rapid change. A summary of the key drivers includes work process improvement, positive work experience, customer focus and satisfaction, supplier relationships and performance, support services, and competitive advantage.

Stages of evolution – (paradigm shift required: orientation)

As highlighted earlier, in support of the proposed TQM model (Figure 19.5), it bears repeating that several pundits have advanced different definitions and concepts of quality. However, the reality of present day globalisation is that markets have expanded in size, and the volume of activity in both manufacturing and service sectors has outgrown the capacity to manage by personal direction. With the emergence and growth of technology, products and processes have become increasingly complex, when one considers the totality of environmental forces.

The concept of orientation implied in this model, therefore, reflects the degree and nature of the organization's adaptation to a specific situation or environment in which it has to operate. It is thus suggested that the road to TQM requires a paradigm shift that takes into account the four significant transitional periods: "production, service, customer and market orientations".

Sustainable performance – (paradigm shift required: measures)

TQM looks at quality as a long-term business strategy, which strives to provide products and/or services to satisfy fully both the internal and external customers by meeting their explicit and implicit expectations. At the core is the issue of measurement, which is the source of strength, continuity and sustainable performance.

The "business balanced scorecard approach", which is an overall method of tracking performance, forms an integral part of the proposed model. This concept helps to focus on both the qualitative and quantitative measures, which are the main ethos of performance measurement. Such measures become indicators for two broad categories of consequences of the transformational path: learning culture and continuous improvement.

Key findings

TQM is an all-inclusive approach to improving competitiveness, effectiveness and flexibility of the entire organization through planning, organizing and comprehending each activity, with the involvement of each individual at every level.

The methods and techniques used in TQM are applicable throughout any organization, and are equally useful in every sector of industry, be it manufacturing or service. TQM ensures that management adopts a strategic overview of quality that eliminates the separation of planning from execution, and focuses on problem prevention instead of detection.

Managing for quality should not be delegated, and it is the responsibility of the senior executive leader to take charge of the commitment to a quality policy. An examination of all potential barriers to quality can help to achieve the correct mindset that maximises the use of time and resources by doing things right first time. The development of a culture for continuous improvement and communications is essential, as are training and development and use of the "Investors in People" standard. Customer and stakeholder focus is an imperative. The use of self-assessment techniques, performance measurement and feedback are vital.

Interpretation of findings

"Leadership" has to start with the organization's top managers, who must be the foremost buyers of the TQM programme, through leading and supporting the organization's vision with openness and objectiveness.

The introduction of TQM has sharpened the external focus of the organizations studied, which has led to an improvement in communication as well as greater involvement with stakeholders.

"Management" is the agent of integration among people, customers and competitors. Integration breaks down rigid structures, closed mind-sets, and entrenched cultures. It creates a strong force for change that provides a source of feedback, which adds value to the whole system.

Learning creates an environment where the organization's members perceive that they can increase their power as they expand their knowledge. Empowerment is the natural output of a well implemented TQM programme that promotes freedom among employees to use initiative in matters of customer care.

Innovation through implementation of new products or services can easily be copied by competitors. Improvements achieved by studying competitors are often difficult to perceive, and as a result they can be an important source of competitive advantage.

Implications for practice

The following implications were distilled:

- Ascertain that the product or service represents the output from an effective system to ensure capability and control.
- Optimise productivity by designing measures to relate to transformation processes.
- Set goals, measure and give feedback for all aspects of the business.
- Include quality principles into product and service design. A strategy for building customer needs into products and services that will create the opportunity for market orientation.

Recommendations

For practitioners, the following aspects need attention:

- The main driver as represented in the Baldrige criteria is that the leadership creates the values, goals and systems, and guides sustained activity of quality with the ultimate performance objective of delivering customer satisfaction and market success.
- The business excellence model criteria represent the role of leadership as one of the five "enablers" entailing what the organization does.
- The proposed model (Figure 19.5), however, sees the role of leadership as the fundamental driver, to guide the transitional stages of orientation in tandem with the business balanced scorecard approach, learning and innovation from a stakeholder perspective. Positioning these drivers will ensure the culture of continuous improvement is achieved and sustained.

In terms of theoretical challenges, the following aspects need attention:

- The model proposed provides an integrative and holistic approach for analysing the current status of continuous improvement within an organization.
- TQM is not a "quick fix", and thus has to be approached from a long-term perspective.
- To begin the journey using this quality process to create competitive advantage requires a well-defined strategy to allow the transition as depicted by the model.

Summary and conclusion

The MBNQA and EFQM models help organizations to establish the foundation and a culture for improvement and stretch goals. This research work has, however, found that the achievement of quality and continuous improvement is far from easy.

Although the literature promotes marked differences between the manufacturing and service sectors, this study wishes to deviate from that "split-mindset", and views the customer as integral to all transformation processes, irrespective of the industry.

This proposed model is thus advocated for all industry, and focuses on keeping the business aligned with stakeholder needs, measuring performance, and learning from results as the driving forces for improvement and creating a competitive advantage.

Figure 19.1 Traditional product development

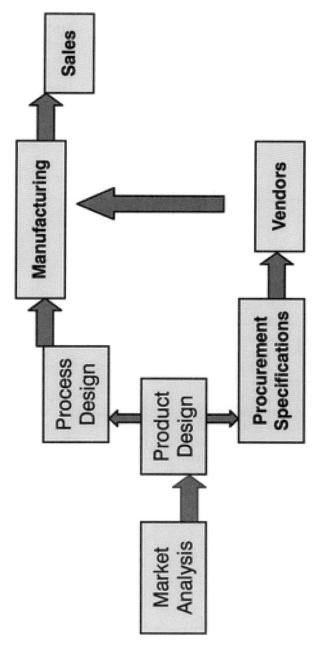

Source: Tompkins (1989)

Table 19.1 Percentage weighting of MBNQA and EQA criteria

EQA criteria	EQA % weighting	MBNQA % weighting	MBNQA criteria
Leadership	10	11	Leadership
People management	9	10	Human resources
Policy & strategy	8	8	Policy & strategy
Resources	9	8	Information & analysis
Processes	14	10	Process management
People satisfaction	9		
Customer satisfaction	20	8	Customer focus
Impact on society	6		
Business results	15	45	Business results
Total	100	100	

Table 19.2 Compatibility of models and criteria

	MBNQA	EQA
Leadership	Executive leadership	Inspirational leadership
	Corporate leadership	Supportive leadership
	Community leadership	Drive & reflect TQM
Planning	Strategic direction	Review of organization's
	Plan development	mission, values, vision, strategic
	Plan deployment	direction for policy & strategy
	Performance	
Customers	Market requirements	Measurement of external
	Customer satisfaction	customer satisfaction
	Customer relations	
Employees	Human resource development	Release of full potential through
	Participatory environment	people management
Processes	Process design	Process identification
	Process implementation	Process management
	Process management	Process review
	Process improvement	Process improvement
Suppliers	Improve partner process	Resource: management
	Evaluation of supplier performance	Utilisation & preservation
Results	Customer, financial	Objective achievement
	Human resource	Stakeholder satisfaction
	Supplier quality	Financial success
	Operational, competitive	Societal impact

Table 19.3 Evolution and history of the TQM path

1998 (world class)			▶ 1999 (world class)
Product orientation	**Service orientation**	**Customer orientation**	**Market orientation**
Six sigma	Customer service	Customer satisfaction	Quality management
Statistical variation measures	Service delivery	Customer loyalty	Customer loyalty
Cycle time reduction	Responsiveness	Customer complaints	Supplier management
Process efficiency	Quality audits	Customer retention	Customer service
Product reliability	Service business improvement	Customer service	Customer relationships
Zero defects	Customer satisfaction	Innovation	Innovation
Continuous improvement	Process mapping	Responsiveness	Responsiveness
Cost reduction	Service delivery	Customer partnership	Employee empowerment
Quality circles	Employee training/skills	Employee training/skills	Policy deployment
Technology	Quality culture	Quality culture	Benchmarking
Customer service	Service reliability	Continuous improvement	Process improvement
Employee incentive	Flexible job assignment	Quality leadership	Stakeholder management
Product design	Right first time	Flexible job assignment	Continuous improvement
Flexible job assignment	Continuous improvement	Right first time	Environmental impact
Employee training/skills	Quality leadership	Process improvement	Societal impact
Quality culture	Customer complaints	Communications	Quality culture
Quality leadership	Process improvement	Accountability	Process mapping
Benchmarking	Communications	Service reliability	Quality leadership

319

Table 19.4 Critical success factors

MBNQA/EQA criteria (condensed)	MBNQA (1986)/EQA (1992) success critical factors	MBNQA/EQA (1999) success critical factors
Leadership	Diagnosis of problems Maintaining status quo Management control Handling the task Directing quality improvement Results orientation Top level quality review programmes	Senior management commitment Senior management involvement Shared values Passion for excellence Inspire, guide, coach & support Corporate citizenship Public responsibility
Policy & strategy	Lowest cost/highest quality Excellence in product performance Divisional quality objectives Global market leader	Quality function deployment Strategic direction Performance tracking Planned development & implementation Strategic business/quality plans
Customer focus	Customer satisfaction Customer loyalty Customer visits Customer complaints	Customer quality measurement Customer relationships Customer satisfaction Market research
Information & analysis	Internal benchmarking Supplier information Competition comparison	Managing supplier resource Supplier performance evaluation Process partnership improvement Comparative benchmarking Organizational performance measures
Human resource focus	Employee skills Employee motivation Employee training	Human resource development Participatory environment Employee well-being/satisfaction
Process management	Product leadership Procedures Suppliers	Process design, implementation & management Process review & improvement Supplier/partnering processes
Business results	Market share Return on capital Product quality	Stakeholder satisfaction Societal impact Human resource & customer-focused results Organizational effectiveness, financial & market results

Figure 19.2 Four perspectives of the balanced scorecard

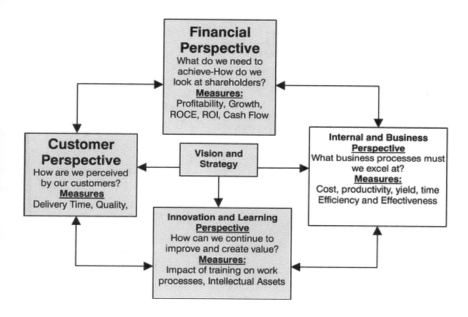

Figure 19.3 Business scorecard approach

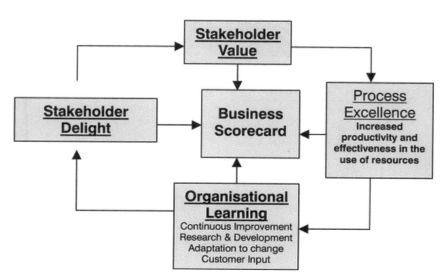

Figure 19.4 Leadership system

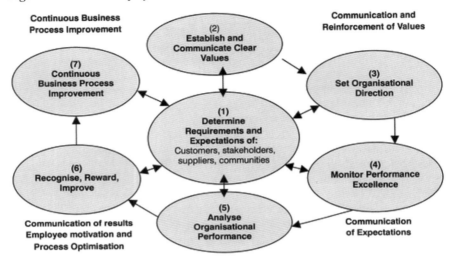

Source: Sunny Fresh Food

Figure 19.5 TQM maturity and sustainable performance model

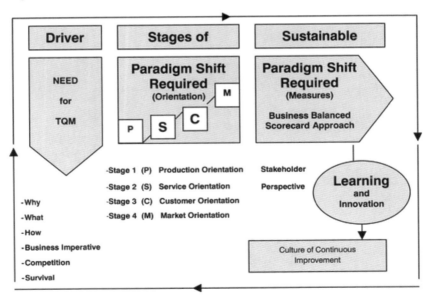

Chapter 20
Legacy of two great quality giants

Do you know that doing your best is not good enough? First you must know what to do (W. Edwards Deming).

A good rule in organizational analysis is that no meeting of the minds is really reached until we talk of specific actions or decisions. We can talk of specific actions or decisions. We can talk of who is responsible for budgets, or inventory, or quality, but little is settled. It is only when we get down to the action words – measure, compute prepare, check, endorse, recommend, approve – that we can make clear who is to do what (Joseph Juran).

Unique characters

There will probably never be another era where so many unique quality thinkers, philosophers, researchers, consultants and preachers will exist at the same time. Management thinkers in a contemporary age tend to impact more on organizations and individuals. In the case of Deming and Juran, their influence has served the purpose of building nations. They are truly renaissance men and their contributions are truly unique.

There are so many parallels between Deming and Juran's lives, philosophies and thoughts although they were two completely different characters. They both suffered hardship in their youth and started from very humble beginnings. They both had to endure poverty and hardship and were determined from an early age, to succeed and make their lives better. They both had the opportunity to work on quality problems in a similar work place (Western Electric) and have both known and worked with Water Shewhart (although in the case of Deming, a close friendship did develop between them). During the World War II, they were both summoned to work for the US Government in different departments. Deming worked in the application and teaching of statistical techniques and Juran helped re-design and optimise supply processes at the Lend-Lease Administration Department.

Their influence in Japan was through the Japanese Union of Scientists and Engineers (JUSE), the organization which had the responsibility for educating and training engineers and managers on SQC and quality management tools and techniques. They both consulted extensively in Japan by working with some of the very well known and established brands in the automobile, electronics and white goods sectors. Following on from Japan, they both continued to preach the quality message, to teach the concepts of quality and to consult widely all over the world.

As Landesberg (1999) argues:

Deming was a philosopher who desired to provide a new way to view the world. Juran was a practitioner who desired to teach people better management practices.

As a consequence, they had different appeals to different audiences. Deming was revered by theoretically minded individuals and particularly people interested in statistics, Juran on the other hand, appealed to practical-minded individuals, managers and consultants. They both, however, shared the same consensus about similar issues:

- For quality improvement to take place, top management must take full responsibility.
- They both rejected reliance on slogans and exhortations meant to motivate employees, since they both believed that very often faults lay in the system of work and not the employees.
- They were both highly critical of reward and recognition systems which were not based on quality-related contributions but rather on unfair and faulty methods.
- They both emphasised the importance of planning as a top-down process, for driving quality efforts.
- They both conveyed the message that variation is a fact of life and that senior management must understand the different types of variation and, therefore, design special remedies for each.

Deming – Juran: duel of the supremes

It has always been well-known that Deming and Juran hold different views and despite that fact their message to senior management has always been in accord, even though they have had major disagreements on many other things. Deming, for instance, has always acknowledged the work and contribution of Juran. In his book *Out of the Crisis* (Deming, 1986), he mentions that improvement of the process is not about putting control limits and managing SQC charts but real improvement starts once the control limits have been in place. Juran argues on the same point, that putting out fires is not improvement of the process, which concurs with Deming's view, that the process should go back to where it should have been in the first place.

Deming does also recognise the contribution that Juran has made in Japan. In relation to the courses and seminars that Juran undertook during his visits to Japan in 1954 and beyond, Deming says (1986, p. 488):

His masterful teaching, gave to Japanese management new insight into management's responsibility for improvement of quality and productivity.

Deming is also known to have said:

Anyone who wants to know how to implement quality must talk to Juran.

Juran, on the other hand, repays the compliments by saying the courses that Deming conducted in Japan in 1950 and beyond were extremely successful and useful. He says:

Prior to Deming's visits in the early 1950s, Japanese Quality Control had been butting its head against a wall created by adherence to difficult statistics theories. With Deming's help, this wall was torn down (Juran, 2004, p. 301).

Deep respect and admiration

Juran states that Deming and himself had known each other since World War II, although they never worked closely together. He said that he was pleased to have met Deming at the time and was impressed with his ideas and thoughts (he refers to a publication of Deming's without saying which one it was). He was interested to find that their careers had a lot in common. Deming moved from physics to statistics and Juran, from engineering to management. Juran recalls:

I took a liking to this dignified, even courtly scientist….those fields [statistics and management] managed to intersect, and we soon formed a warm friendship that endured until his passing in 1993 (Juran, 2004).

Juran (2004) goes on to say:

Deming and I agreed on most fundamentals. We were both crusaders for good quality. We agreed that the main quality problems had their origins in the system, not the workers. We deplored the efforts to solve problems by means of colourful banners and slogans. We were aware that the leadership in quality must come from top management (p. 303).

On Deming's death, Juran wrote the following note which he sent to the American Society for Quality (ASQ), The Japanese Union of Scientists and Engineers (JUSE) and the European Organization for Quality (EOQ). It read as follows:

We have been privileged to witness a dedicated professional, fully absorbed in his mission despite personal tragedies, despite old age, and despite serious illness, yet giving freely of his time even when he had little time left to give. For that privilege we should be grateful (Juran, 2004, p. 305).

Differences

There were several differences between Deming and Juran. Many of them are cited in Juran's memoirs (Juran, 2004). The biggest difference perhaps is that Deming had always believed that SQC was the solution to all the quality problems that industries encounter. He has always blamed senior managers for their lack of interest in understanding variation and for making rash decisions without doing root cause analysis and looking at facts on the limitations of their processes and which cause sub-optimisation. In a presentation to the French Deming Association in 1989 (Neave, 2000), discussing the importance of variation, Deming said:

...the harder they tried to achieve consistency and uniformity, the worse were the effects. The more they tried to shrink variation, the larger it got. They were naturally also interested in cutting costs. When any kind of error, mistake, or accident occurred, they were to work on it to try to correct it. It was a noble aim. There was only one little trouble – their worthy efforts did not work. Things got worse ...

He then went on to say:

... they were failing to understand the difference between common causes and special causes, and that mixing them up makes things worse ... Sure we don't like mistakes, complaints from customers, accidents – but if we weigh in at them without understanding, then we make things worse.

Deming always opposed the terminology of TQC and TQM and made his views felt very strongly. On the publication of Dr Val Feigenbaum's book on *Total Quality Control* in Japan in 1961, JUSE wanted to organize an international conference on QC (ICQC) in 1965. They wanted to include a track on total quality control (TQC). Dr Feigenbaum's work brought freshness to the subject of SQC since it was meant to show how the control of quality can be prevented from being "partially" controlled. Deming, however, had different views on this and at the time, he wrote to Mr Koyanagi from JUSE on 2 May, 1964, saying:

The word total quality control (TQC) is wrong for Japan and completely unnecessary anywhere. The statistical control of quality means total, and never meant anything else to Dr Shewhart, and this is what I taught my Japanese students and executives (Juran, 2004).

The Japanese were very hurt by Deming's comments and wrote to Dr Juran, seeking his guidance and advice on the matter. Dr Juran (2004) advised them to persevere with the planning of the conference and to ignore Dr Deming's comments. Reflecting on this incident, Juran (2004) wrote:

I was disappointed by Deming's reaction. He was contending that statistical tools could solve all quality problems – they were a panacea. I know from experience that this was simply not so; I concluded that his comment was narrow and self-serving...; I do not regard his opinions on the integrated approach as being based on experience. Moreover, while a number of mathematicians who had narrow approaches have broadened their views as they have been exposed to industry, Deming has not. He has remained a narrow specialist, one of the very best in his speciality, but his mind seems to have been closed to all else.

Deming's legacy

W. Edwards Deming's contribution in the twentieth century is immeasurable by all standards. He was often hailed as the man who has helped shape the style of Japanese management after the World War II. He was the recipient of the National Academy of Engineering Award in 1983. He also received the Second Order Medal of the Sacred Treasure, from the Emperor of Japan, in 1960. He got the Shewhart Medal from the American Society for Quality Control in 1955. He was enshrined in the Science and Technology Hall of Fame in Dayton, Ohio in 1986 and in 1987 he received the National Medal of Technology from President Reagan. He also received over 16 honorary degrees and became an honorary life member of several prestigious societies, including the Royal Statistical Society.

Despite his great success in Japan, Deming could not relate to managers and executives in the West. After returning from Japan, Deming spent his time teaching statistics. During the period 1946-1980 he managed to publish over 100 papers. The breakthrough for him came on 24 June 1980 when he appeared on a documentary broadcasted by NBC, entitled *If Japan Can, Why Can't We?*. Deming was very brutal with his remarks about US senior managers. This turnaround in the situation gave birth to quality in the USA and beyond. Deming even attacked business schools for teaching the wrong things to senior executives and not placing enough emphasis on variation and SQC. He was, however, sympathetic towards workers and was always a harsh critic of management practices that have stifled creativity and innovation by not developing employees and involving them in improvement activities.

His 14 points reflect his beliefs, together with the "deadly diseases" and later in his life, his "profound knowledge". His works were published and distributed all over the world, including his books *Quality, Productivity and Competitive Position, Out of The Crisis, The New Economics for Industry, Government, Education*.

Deming's contributions

Essentially Deming's theory of management rests on four key elements, which have formed the basis of his profound knowledge (Figure 20.1).

Understanding variation

Deming argues that variation is part of everything from suppliers' goods and services through manufacturing, delivery and customer handling. By getting to grips with the theory of variation, managers can improve processes and make rational decisions. They will be able to collect data, interpret the meaning of the data, evaluate performance accurately and deliver expected outcomes. He has always argued that this is the most powerful way to develop managers and ensure that they are doing the right things.

Deming's argument is that variation is a way of life and we need to understand its types and mange it better. To this end he has argued that all types of variations are caused. Variation due to common causes is due to a myriad of ever present factors (e.g. process inputs or conditions). This affects the overall system since this type of variation happens through random occurrences in small quantities but, overall, the impact it can create may be significant over time. Special causes variation, on the other hand, is on top and is due to identifiable sources. Common variation are, however, difficult to establish from the point of view of what leads to them happening in the first place. Deming refers to variation due to special causes as assignable causes.

There are two other types of variation often referred to in the literature: tempering caused by adjustments made to an unstable process and structural variation (regular, systematic changes in output). Unless managers can distinguish between the four different types of variation, improvement activity is not going to take place and a "hit and miss" phenomenon is going to ensue. The most important types that must be controlled and managed are however the ones related to common and special causes. Once we know that all the variation is due to common causes we can say that the process is in stable condition and is in statistical control. In other words, the performance of the process is predictable within some set bands or limits. On the other hand, special causes lead to the process being unstable because of the unpredictability of the special cause occurring again.

Deming has always argued that managers will only be able to make sound decisions if they can lead improvement activities from the top. This will only happen if they take an interest in control charts and looking at the performance of their operations and processes with a clear understanding of the whole system they are supposed to manage and control. They should stop being ignorant, halt the activity of tampering, and improve and control all the key processes through the management of variation.

Deming's 14 points
The premise behind Deming's 14 points is that managers must look at work as a whole system and that they must focus on optimising the organization as a whole by focusing on the needs of all stakeholders. He believes that all of these things need to be looked at in parallel and throughout, using a good understanding of variation.

1. Create constancy of purpose
Ensure that people are driven by common goals, tasks allocated are focused on delivering the ultimate goals that have to be defined in terms of stakeholders and customers. The implications of changing the goal post can have a negative impact on the organization concerned and may lead to its performance going down.

2. Adopt the new philosophy
Deming's argument here is that managers must learn to manage in accordance with the requirements of a modern economy. They have to learn first of all and acquire the deficient knowledge, they have to embrace the new management concepts and

they must do so in the context of managing a whole system. They must also stop the "hit and miss" approach caused by tampering.

3. Cease dependence on inspection
This is really an outmoded practice and organizations that still use it will be hugely disadvantaged in the competitive market. Inspection is really the "spike" to continuous improvement, particularly during this era of a digital economy, where predictability, reliability, agility are all key requirements for establishing a competitive advantage.

4. End purchasing on price tag
The modern practice is to work in partnership with carefully selected and managed suppliers, where costs are driven out through the control and management of variation and innovation is pushed in to give customers extra value.

5. Improve constantly
Using the PDSA (plan-do-study-act cycle), a culture of continuous improvement must be created to constantly eliminate problems and look for better alternatives. This must be based on employee total involvement and participation.

6. Institute training
Variation, according to Deming, is caused by the lack of commitment in organizations to equip employees with vital skills and knowledge that can enable them to improve their processes, take corrective action and deliver value to customers. In a knowledge-based economy, employees must be trained all the time since things change quickly and frequently. The dependability is going to be more and more on speed of action, competence and innovativeness.

7. Institute leadership
Deming argued that leaders cannot deliver constancy of purpose if they do not create and effectively manage a whole system. They first of all need to understand variation and what impedes their organization and employees from carrying out improvement activity and achieving the desired results. They then must develop goals and put in place the structure and key enabling factors so that the system is well managed. They must create total alignment by ensuring that everyone is working within the system and that there are shared goals and common objectives. They also have to spend time understanding each element of the work system, empathise with employees, mentor and coach them and enable people to perform and achieve. They must develop others and instigate succession leadership.

8. Drive out fear
Fear is a big impediment in many organizations. It gives senior management the lever to control and stifle. Fear manifests itself in so many different ways. It could be fear of reprimand, fear of failure, fear of the unknown. Companies which have

struggled with continuous improvement and are mainly "introverted" in their approach and performance, are ones that have created a big barrier between senior management teams and employees and they use knowledge, information, lines of authority, MBO amongst other things as tools to stifle and control.

Transformations that creates process orientation and a focus on customers, using quality and continuous improvement to drive value, are ones that have realised that there is no place for fear in an organization that needs to compete in the twenty-first century.

9. Break down barriers between departments
There is no place for silos in this modern age and no more opportunities for prima donnas. Process centric organizations (PCOs) are the ones which understand and appreciate the importance of leveraging, building synergy and optimising through common goals and shared resources.

10. Eliminate slogans, exhortations and targets for the work force
As the saying goes: "Insanity is hoping for different results while continuing to do the same thing".

People cannot be duped and suspicion, the "them and us" attitude, will persist for as long as there is no real change, no transparency, no respect for people and no leadership. Slogans only give a "veneer" and everything that shines is not gold in most cases.

11(a). Eliminate work standards (production quotas)
Quotas and standards are detrimental in this modern age. Standards make the assumption that if people have delivered a certain standard once, they can do it again and again and their performance can be judged on this "absolute" indicator. Deming argues that this is not the case, since in most cases senior managers have no knowledge of variation and employees may not be able to deliver set standards all the time because of variation that could be due to common or assignable causes.

Deming argues that performance improvement goals are more worthy of pursuing because these take variation as a challenge and the effort is to drive it out of the system as far as practically possible.

11(b). Eliminate management by objectives
Management by objectives (MBO) is a detrimental method, according to Deming. It creates sub-optimisation and kills innovation and improvement. It does not encourage people to look at new thinking, since on the whole it seeks to establish that set targets are achieved. In other words, people spend their time chasing their targets as opposed to spending time solving real problems. Furthermore, it creates a divided organization, sub-optimised because it rewards those who achieve their targets and forgets those who do not and in most cases for reasons due to circumstances outside of their control. MBO also creates unethical behaviours

since there are no shared goals, people will compete against each other as opposed to working together for the end benefit of the customer.

12(a). Remove barriers to pride of workmanship for hourly workers
This is often due to practices which tend to "robotize" workers and stop them from using their ideas and clever contributions. For instance, getting them to use defective materials in order to meet production quotas, applying inspection methods that have no logic, no understanding and no interpretation of what the numbers signify. It could also be caused by giving people the wrong tools, faulty equipment and poor or lack of supervision. The detrimental effect of this is poor productivity, increase in variation, frustration and demoralisation.

12(b). Remove barriers to pride of workmanship for management and engineering
Deming recommends that the annual merit schemes must be abolished and that the use of MBO encourages the practice of short-term goals as opposed to long-term quality improvement. He says that managers should not be glorified inspectors. They must improve the process, eliminate barriers and empower employees to deliver to the customer. They must be leaders instead. His point is that merit systems based on MBO appraisals tend to support behaviours that sub-optimise and encourage the increase in inherent variation. This is against the role of leaders who have the task of creating long-term sustainable performance by tackling variation head on and by not being distracted by short-term gains.

13. Institute a vigorous programme of education and self-improvement
In the twenty-first century, the power is really the intellectual capital and the knowledge residue that organizations possess. Employees have to be encouraged to take on life long learning as a goal, to be educated and supported with their quest for advancement and the betterment of their future. In this way, the other three pillars of Deming's profound knowledge can be practiced.

14. Put everybody to work to accomplish the transformation
Harnessing all the knowledge, expertise available through involvement, participation, positive engagement of all employees; ensuring that there is two-way communication and total alignment; using innovation and learning as powerful tools for achieving the desired transformation.

The most important thing for Deming was that his philosophy has to be implemented as a total knowledge system if benefits are to be expected from it. His ideas were packaged in this way and perhaps this is one of the reasons why managers have been intimidated, perhaps turned off and became cynical about the value of his ideas.

Appreciation for a system
In the days when quality used to be referred to as "conformance to requirements" the notion of a system was limited to product orientation and all aspects to do with

producing according to customer expectations and delivering to the customer. The system in the context of a modern business environment is, however, different. It requires a focus on the entire extended supply chain and has to include aspects which relate to servicing the customer, performance quality and, more recently, customer relationship management (CRM). Deming, therefore, argued that managers have to look at a holistic view of the system and must manage in an integrated way.

Deming has always warned about the negative effect of dividing organizations into various profit centres. His point is that even at the time when the customer is touching and using the product/service, this is still part of the system.

An extremely useful way of elaborating on what a holistic system might encompass is the example suggested by Myron Tribus (1990) (Figure 20.2).Tribus (1990) argues that organizations, generally speaking, tend to have a myopic view by focusing on the inner circle which deals with what he has termed, the technical system. This is mainly related to aspects affecting products and processes. He argues that the fabric of the organization in terms of its values, guiding principles, work climate, motivational schemes, communication on the importance of the customer and the cultural aspects are also part of the big system. He refers to this as the social system. Lastly, the outer ring that Tribus suggests is the managerial system. This is where the vision, strategy, goal development and deployment, aspects related to governance and performance measurement and control take place.

Tribus suggests that the optimisation of each of the three systems has to be related to the functional roles and responsibilities. It is therefore very likely that the technical system, which has an operational focus on it, will be dealt with in the lower ranks in the organization. Decisions for improvement of the system itself will involve senior management teams at all levels. Radical changes to the system itself is the sole responsibility of senior executives (Figure 20.3).

Tribus further suggests that according to the model he suggested (Figure 20.2), the logic is that senior managers should concern themselves more with enabling and empowering employees at the lower level to improve the technical system and optimise its operational aspects. They should, however, spend more time supporting the development and management of the social system and they certainly have to manage the managerial system, which cannot be delegated. Figure 20.4 depicts how the time should spent and who should take more responsibility and involvement in improving each of the three quality systems.

The diagram in Figure 20.5 appeared in Deming (1986) *Out of the Crisis* on page 4. Deming has always believed that this was the most important diagram that he drew during his entire life. In his final book *The New Economics for Industry, Government, Education* (Deming, 1993), Deming says:

> The flow diagram was the spark that in 1950 and onward turned Japan around. It displayed to top management and to engineers a system of production. The Japanese had knowledge, great knowledge, but it was in bits and pieces, uncoordinated. This flow diagram directed their

knowledge and efforts into a system of production, geared to the market – namely, prediction of needs of customers. The whole world knows about the results.

Deming used this diagram to convey his thoughts and ideas and it used to be referred to as the "blackboard for teaching engineers and managers".

Psychology

People are different and the way we communicate, interact with others, make decisions, contribute and make ourselves valuable is bound to differ from person to person. Deming argued that understanding human nature and what makes all of us tick will help build relationships and will assure the gaining of trust and commitment. Furthermore, management can play a key role in removing fear, building confidence, making people feel proud and valued. The intrinsic and extrinsic motivational factors are like levers that can be used to enthuse and motivate people.

Associated with this is the importance of learning. People learn in different ways and absorb knowledge at different speeds and with a preference for different styles. Learning has to be a joy for all employees and it is the responsibility of senior managers to ensure that learning takes place in the first instance and that it has an impact on the psychology and motivational aspects of employees and lastly that it leads to improvement and performance impact.

Theory of knowledge

Deming argued that management, at the end of the day, has to be equated with prediction. Knowledge does however require rigorous knowledge and understanding of the past, it has to be built on theory and it has to use reliable information. Deming argued that managers in the West have not been brought up with the knowledge of theory and this is reflected in the way they make irrational decisions. For instance, he questions the logic of deciding to lay people off when a business is not performing well instead of aggressively embarking on quality improvement schemes that can deal with the loss in the competitive market and can close the competitive gap. Deming said that the frenzy of cost reduction and efficiency drive that has characterised business practice in the West, based on data compiled internally or through consultants' reports, is wrong. He says that the true costs are those which are unknown and unknowable.

The "system of profound knowledge" comprises four major parts:
1. Appreciation of a system.
2. Theory of variation (right back to where it all started with Shewhart's breakthrough so long ago).
3. Theory of knowledge (how do we know things, how do we learn things, how do we improve that learning and knowledge?).
4. Psychology (the understanding of people and the way they interact with all that surrounds them).

This system is, as has been previously explained, a holistic, integrated management model. Deming's 14 points are reflected in the aforementioned four parts. Table 20.1 is an extremely useful attempt at linking in each of the 14 points to the four elements of Deming's management model.

How will Deming be remembered?

W. Edwards Deming died on 20 December 1993, at his home in Washington where he had lived since 1946, and just ten days after completing his final four-day seminar in California. It is estimated that at least a quarter of a million people attended his celebrated four-day seminars between 1980 and 1993.

His personality

As a person he was known to be impatient and brusque. A journalist who interviewed him just a few days before he passed away wrote:

> Unfortunately, Deming antagonized or intimidated many CEOs. Many were also put off by his obvious contempt for management. Yet he insisted on working only with them. Then he told them bluntly that they were the cause of the trouble, not lazy workers or outdated equipment.

Juran, in his memoirs (Juran, 2004), echoes these concerns about Deming's personality:

> What troubled me most was his random wondering over many matters he disliked – Crosby's offerings, the gullibility of managers who bought those offerings, the stupidity of chief executives who did not accept training in statistical methods, and so on. He wouldn't stop.... I was aware of his tendency to berate chief executives, even publicly, and had given thought to try and explain to him that the practice was detrimental to his goals (p. 305).

Deming was very sceptical about senior managers in the USA and the Western part of the world until the end. He was even more bitter because of years of rejection. He was reported to have said after his last seminar:

> The Japanese understand that quality is made in the boardroom. Not here. Here, too, it is made in the boardroom but the [people in the] boardroom don't understand their obligations.

To the question of whether one day US managers will be able to use his ideas effectively, Deming replied:

> I don't think so. They will have to limp along some other way.

Deming had no time to be patient. His frustration showed even with his own infirmity (he was confined to a wheelchair with an aide, he had a respirator, hearing aids, a pacemaker). His last words to an audience in Los Angeles, only ten days before he passed away, had double meaning:

Are we handicapped? Is your business the same? How long do we have?

The tributes

When Deming passed away, the *Washington Post* wrote:
> W. Edwards Deming dies; his lectures on quality control fueled Japan's rise.

From Japan, The President of Toyota Motor Corp. (Shoichiro Toyoda) wrote:
> There is not a day I don't think about what Dr Deming meant to us. Deming is the core of our management.

The Chairman Emeritus of NEC (Koji Kobayashi) said:
> Deming made a great contribution to the recovery of Japan's economy after the total war.

Yoji Akao (Engineering Professor at Temagawa University) wrote:
> He's the person who introduced quality control after the devastation of the war and was the starting point of the whole development of quality control in Japan. Japan owes a great deal to him.

His legacy

In a critique of Deming's management method and its failure, David Halberstam described Deming as a "prophet without honour". He said Deming fitted the description of a prophet but his message was not transferred. He tried to use revolutionary ideas which were contrary to current beliefs. He was advocating the return to some old values which do not reflect current business culture.

In a testimony to the life and works of Dr Deming, Myron Tribus concludes:
> Dr W. Edwards Deming's contributions to science, statistics and economics were important. But his development of a comprehensive theory of management overshadows all else. This theory has already changed the lives of millions of people. Applied to education it promises to change future generations. Dr Deming is gone. His legacy lives on.

While preparing for the 2001 Deming Lecture to Joint Statistical Meetings, Atlanta, GA, Gerry Hahn contacted various people for testimonies on Deming, from eminent statisticians to quality practitioners and experts. The following is a summary of what various people think of Deming, his contributions and his legacy.

Deming's greatest contribution(s)

> *Ed Baker*: Deming offered theories, ways of thinking, and methods to enable managers to lead people rather than to manage machines and numbers. In his later years he worked to integrate the various pieces of his general theory into one unified whole, which he called a "system of

profound knowledge", integrating statistical theory, epistemology, psychology and system thinking. This laid the foundation, not only of a general theory for management, but also a world view for living. He also generated in non-statisticians much interest in and appreciation of the discipline of statistics. He also showed some statisticians the broader and non-technical applications of statistical thinking and reasoning.

Tom Boardman: He got top management to understand its role in managing a "quality" organization.

George Box: I think I understand better why Dr Deming placed so much emphasis on continuous never ending improvement, profound knowledge and the distinction between what he called enumerative and analytic statistics...I am very happy about the Six Sigma initiative.

Cynthia Clark: In 1937 he invited Jerzy Neyman to Washington, C.C. to lecture on probability sampling...Since then the collection of federal statistics has never been the same (comment from Tommy Wright).

Peter Drucker: He made us realize that quality is not cost but yield.

Bill Golomski: His book on statistical methods in the census of human populations, and his editing of Shewhart's lectures in the 1939 book, re-energized statisticians and encouraged many executives, quality professionals and others on the importance of statistics and statistical thinking.

Lynne Hare: He paved the way for others to follow. He got the attention of top organizational brass by using methods most of us would avoid. (If most of us had tried what he did, we'd have been shot). He was effective.

Roger Hoerl: He gave statisticians a "window of opportunity" in that he made statisticians respectable and credible for a while (similar to Six Sigma today) – some statisticians took advantage of this; some didn't; reminded us that most real applications do not occur in the static populations of textbooks, but dynamic processes (enumerative versus analytic); forcefully made the point that statistical concepts can be applied generally, even to management, and do not have to be relegated to narrow, arcane work.

Don Holmes: Waking US management up to the need to gain high quality and continue to work on improving it.

Stu Hunter: His contributions to spreading the ideas of quality management and control; his method for fitting lines so that the distances from points to the lines were always least.

Alan Lasater: He got the big rock rolling.

Bill Latzko: Technical: distinction between enumerative and analytic statistics, replicated sample designs, editing Shewhart's second book, teach the Japanese SQC. Managerial: system of profound knowledge, 14 points, Ford Motor Company's success, Fiero's success.

Lloyd Nelson: He informed top management of what their job should be: in particular, how they should (and should not) deal with their employees.

Joyce Orsini: High up there would be his recognition of important thought. For example, his recognition of the importance of the four fields of knowledge (theory of knowledge, psychology, statistical variation, thinking of the organization as a system) not taught in most MBA programs; his earlier recognition of the work of Shewhart, Fisher and Neyman; and his development of practical methods to deal with statistics in the field (e.g. the half open interval – a major breakthrough for census-taking).

Bill Parr: Deming seriously prodded statisticians to think more broadly; he urged us to think about "variation" in ways other than that purely capturable via statistical formulae.

Gipsie Ranney: Although Deming contributed tremendously to statistical practice, his greatest contributions were his ideas about management of enterprise and people. His ideas in these areas have changed the worldview of countless managers all across the globe and have contributed to more humane and ethical practices. The contribution to improvement of the lives of employees, their families, and their communities is immeasurable.

Bill Scherkenbach: He was the bonfire that starts a prairie fire that consumes the whole world. He gave life to a movement that continued the relevance of Statistics to the improvement of the world.

Peter Scholtes: What I learned from Deming is to see things as part of a system, to see things in their larger context.

Ron Snee: His 14 Points for management, his red bead and funnel experiments, his focus on reduction of variation and systems thinking, and his system of profound knowledge. ("If I had to reduce my message for management to just a few words, I'd say it all had to do with reducing variation."). Six Sigma is an effective deployment process for Deming's teachings.

Bill Tucker: Deming's great impact was on the use of statistics – across the board – to promote continuous quality improvement.

Joe Voelkel: He made people think differently.

Areas in which Deming did not succeed

Ed Baker: He could see that he was not having the effect on management thinking he wanted. He felt a "bottom up" strategy also was needed. Hence he changed his strategy from transformation of organizations to transformation of individuals. He continued to be unhappy with the failure of educators (especially K-12) to understand the illogic of grading and the harm it does to the ability and motivation of children to learn. He was disappointed that he did not have much impact on the leadership of the U.S. Congress and executive branch. He was very disappointed that he did not have a profound impact on the teaching and application of statistics, especially the differentiation between "enumerative" and "analytic" problems.

Tom Boardman: Many organizations only gave his ideas "lip" service and went back to managing the numbers and doing it badly.

Peter Drucker: Japan reveres his memory, but doesn't use Deming.

Bill Golomski: He did not understand the complexity of new product development systems and reliability, and was not able to determine how one can organize broad scale change in efforts in companies.

Lynne Hare: He never established an organization of successors.

Roger Hoerl: He never showed managers how to change; he only convinced a small subgroup of statisticians; he exerted considerable fear on his audiences.

Don Holmes: He did not convince management to do away with slogans, exhortations, and targeting the work force asking for zero defects.

Stu Hunter: I fault the emphasis he placed on leaving the process alone. His funnel experiment delayed, nay continues to delay, the idea that processes can and should be adjusted given the immediate data. He placed excessive faith in stochastic independence.

Alan Lasater: He did not help management understand how to "do it".

Bill Latsko: Deming did not succeed in getting his cutting edge material accepted: statisticians still confuse analytical and enumerative statistics, Shewhart's books are little understood and often misused, the system of profound knowledge gets almost no play, the 14 points are used selectively, and there is over-reliance on testing.

Lloyd Nelson: He was not able to convince many managers that there are other measures than "How much money has your quality program saved you."...Also, many people did not react well to his "rough and ready" approach.

Joyce Orsini: I don't know of any areas where Deming did not succeed, at least in part...The newest texts for statistics include the distinction between enumerative and analytic studies and the hazards of using inappropriate tools. So, maybe it took some 50 years...but it's happening.

Bill Parr: His thoughts have survived and will survive, but he did not successfully create an organized "movement" which survived him. Also, he was disappointed with the extent to which statisticians have stayed within their boxes.

Gipsie Ranney: I don't believe Deming was successful in explaining to the statistical community the basis for the distinction between enumerative studies and analytic problems...Also, I don't believe Deming was successful in overcoming the intense and irrational belief in competition in the USA. He tried to convince people that they should cooperate when it was in their interest to do so, and his comments were often misinterpreted as some kind of advocacy of socialism. Also, I don't think people understood very well his concerns with the deterioration of education or have seen the hazards associated with the "teaching to the test".

Bill Scherkenbach: Because of his aversion to physical organizations, he failed to leave a lasting official organization, putting the movement into jeopardy.

Bill Tucker: His thinking on engineering process control was just wrong...just use of traditional SPC cannot solve all issues related to continuous improvement.

Joe Voelkel: He provided no real pudding, either instant or slow-cook. Like a Socratic-method philosopher, he would much prefer to ask questions than to provide (concrete) answers.

Bill Woodall: Deming's view was that the three-sigma Shewhart chart was unsurpassed as a method for detection of assignable causes...Why should control charting be exempt from Deming's exhortation to constantly and forever improve? (*Journal of Quality Technology*, October 2000).

Some famous quotes from Deming
We have learned to live in a world of mistakes and defective products as if they were necessary to life. It is time to adopt a new philosophy in America.

To the question of how long does it take to institute the philosophy of profound knowledge, Deming replied:
As long as you live, young man. No longer.

Juran's legacy

Juran is so different from Deming in so many respects and yet their philosophies are so inter-twined and compatible. Perhaps the main difference, as some authors put it, are in emphasis and scope rather than fundamentals. While Deming genuinely believed that managers must change the entire system (in his own description and definition, using the four tenets of profound knowledge), Juran was of the view that the system can be improved project by project with a long-term perspective of creating a world class status. Furthermore, Juran has always acknowledged that the use of statistics is not a panacea to all the organizational problems. On the other hand, Deming spent his life lamenting the fact that senior executives are not interested in statistics.

Juran has brought freshness with his approach by arguing that in order for TQM to replace Taylorism, it has to be implemented as an integrated system with senior managers assuming overall responsibility. He stresses that the effective implementation can only be done through proper planning and execution. He suggests that this could be done through: delegation of some of the planning to supervisors and non-supervisory staff; and re-designing jobs to enable workers to become more involved.

According to Juran (1991) the quality revolution in Japan has been successful because of the close involvement of CEOs, chairmen of companies and employees. In the USA, on the other hand, CEOs tended to concentrate their efforts on financial reports instead (Juran, 1993). Juran was always humble in acknowledging that the Japanese miracle was not due to his and Dr Deming's teachings as claimed, but rather to their commitment and dedication at all levels, to make quality work:

- The Japanese do not leave quality responsibility to individual functional managers.
- They concentrate on planning and execution (in Japan time spent on planning is approximately 67 per cent and 33 per cent on execution. In the USA about 40 per cent of time is spent on planning whilst 60 per cent on execution).
- Japanese senior managers take personal responsibility for quality, unlike their US counterparts.

During a recent speech Juran gave in Minneapolis he made a statement that leadership in quality can be attained. He said there are hundreds of organizations around the world that have demonstrated that TQM pays off and can lead to sustainable competitive advantage. He said that it takes on average ten years of firm commitment and perseverance for that position to be achieved. Most of the time spent is finding out how to avoid making mistakes, as Juran calls it not doing the wrong things.

Juran's own research indicates that the critical factors that have assisted world class organizations achieve their superior positions are leadership related:

- The chief executives personally led the quality initiative.
- They trained the entire managerial hierarchy in managing for quality.
- They enlarged the business plan to include strategic quality goals.
- The goals included improving quality at a revolutionary rate, year after year.
- They set up means to measure progress against the quality goals.
- The senior managers reviewed progress regularly.
- They provided for participation by the work force.
- They enlarged the system of recognition for superior performance in quality.

The Juran trilogy

Juran's trilogy is a universal methodology which is used to assist companies all over the world with the implementation of TQM. It has been developed over the years and tested with hundreds of Juran Institute clients who have managed to achieve world class status. Commenting on the similarities between organizations and the problems they face, Juran says:

> Many of my early consulting engagements involved improving quality by improving the yields of manufacturing processes. Each company confided to me at the outset that "Our business is different." From their perspective they were right; each did exhibit differences as to products, markets, technology, culture, and so on. Yet their quality problem exhibited commonality. To diagnose those problems I employed common diagnostic tools. To provide remedies I employed common remedial concepts and tools. To hold the gains I employed common control concepts and tools. As I moved from one "different" company to another, I was going through the same cycle of events, over and over. The concepts, methods, and tools I used turned out to be applicable to any company.

> I was intrigued by the existence of those commonalities, and I gradually identified the elements of that common cycle of events. In 1964 I devoted half of my book *Managerial Breakthrough* to the universal process for improving quality (or improving anything else). I

then continued to refine that process, which became an integral part of my training manuals on managing for quality.

By the year 1964 I had unbounded confidence in the validity of that universal approach. I had field-tested it in many client companies; it had repeatedly produced stunning results. I had witnessed the miracles and had thereby acquired the faith of the true believer.

The Juran trilogy is perhaps the best known, universal and well tried methodology that can guarantee results. It has been validated in different organizational contexts, used in different cultural settings and applied in different industry sectors. It could perhaps be proven as a scientific method for total quality implementation and management with more rigorous research and further scientific validation.

The Juran methodology is based on three processes (see Figure 20.6):
1.   Quality planning.
2.   Quality control.
3.   Quality improvement.

Figure 20.6 reflects an intersection of cost and time axis. The logic is that the planning function kicks off the process by identifying customer needs and translating them into proper functional requirements. These functional requirements result in the design and development of products and services, engineering processes which are expected to satisfy customer requirements. This will then mark the end of the planning process and will signal the start of the involvement of operations – who will have the task to run the existing process in order to produce the expected products with their design, engineering and aesthetic features and which hopefully will be able to fulfil the needs of the external customers.

As operations proceed, and as indicated in Figure 20.6, it soon emerges that the processes are unable to have 100 per cent quality output, (hence the chronic and sporadic spikes). The Juran trilogy demonstrates that over 20 per cent of the work is scrap and must, therefore, be re-done. Juran calls the waste chronic because it goes on and on and this happens because the operating processes were planned with limitations (variability). In the normal conventional way, chronic waste is tackled by using SQC, putting teams together so that they can use the PDCA cycle, identify root causes and stabilise the process. Juran refers to this as quality control, which is a reactive, fire fighting approach through corrective action.

To illustrate the difference between common causes of variation and special causes, Juran uses a sporadic spike to show that the process is way out of control and the cost of poor quality has all of a sudden shot up to 40 per cent. This could have been due to power failure, process breakdown or human error. Using SQC, this is easily restored and the chronic waste continues at the level which is satisfactory.

Figure 20.6 also shows the area of quality improvement, where the chronic waste has been reduced significantly. This is due to the fact that chronic waste was seen as a challenge and an opportunity for improvement rather than the previous approach, which looked at process control as the end goal. Similarly to the previous discussion on the improvement of the system (Titus, 1990), in the Juran trilogy senior managers can be expected to spend most of their time in planning and improvement activities while employees and process owners will have the task to control the quality of the output and the consistency of the performance of their processes.

The quality planning process
Figure 20.7 is a simplified input-output diagram showing the universal quality planning process as it progresses step-by-step. The quality planning process is a structured, systematic process which guides every organization through the various stages of establishing customer needs and requirements and translating them through the supply chain into tangible products and services that are capable of satisfying their expectation. Figure 20.7 illustrates the various stages of the quality planning process. Various tools and techniques can be used to bridge the gap between customer expectations and customer perceptions of quality of service and delivery.

Juran insists that planning has to be conducted with a long-term view rather than on a project-by-project basis, although the improvement of quality has to be done by taking projects one by one:

He (the manager) undertakes to slay alligators, one by one – a reptilian version of project by project improvement. But there will never be an end to it, because more and more alligators keep emerging from the swamp. The ultimate answer is to drain the swamp.

The quality control process
The quality control process exists to prevent adverse change. It is based on the universal feedback loop (Figure 20.8). The whole purpose of quality control is to provide stability and ensure consistency in processes and operations. This is done by identifying and reducing variation and preventing change from taking place. The evolution of quality control took place in the era of mass inspection (after the effect) to prevention-based QC.

Figure 20.8 depicts the feed back loop which is the approach used for controlling quality through the following stages:

1. A sensor is used to evaluate the actual quality of either the process or product or both. In the case of the process, its performance is identified by examining its features (directly) or through the product features (indirectly). The product "tells" on the process.
2. The sensor reports the performance to an umpire.

3. The umpire also receives information on the expected quality goal or standard.
4. The umpire compares the actual performance against the desired standard. If there is a big difference, the umpire energizes an actuator.
5. The actuator stimulates the process (human or technological) to rectify the performance so that there is conformance to the required quality level.
6. The process will now restore the performance to the desired standard.

The feedback loop is used as a universal methodology and forms the basis for an integrated quality control process (based on a PDCA principle). It uses the following distinctive steps:
1. Choose control subject.
2. Establish measurement.
3. Establish standards of performance.
4. Measure actual performance.
5. Compare standards.
6. Take action on the difference (use feedback loop for learning).

The quality improvement process
Improvement means creating a breakthrough situation where unprecedented gains can be expected through the attainment of new performance levels, higher than those achieved previously. Quality improvement can result from improvements to the products with a measurable impact on customer satisfaction or through process improvement so that deficiencies and disruptions are minimised and/or eliminated.
Quality improvement that impacts on profitability and competitiveness can result from innovations through product or process development or through radical changes to the organization and its operations using concepts such as business process re-engineering, for instance.

The quality improvement process requires a major departure from status quo and will need new sets of behaviours and attitudes from senior managers. The "don't rock the boat" mentality will impede any chance of achieving breakthrough gains. The concepts described in the following paragraphs must be observed in the context of quality improvement.

Improvement has to be distinguished from control. There has to be a clear standard achieved which reduces, for instance, chronic waste to an unprecedented level (see Figure 20.6).

All improvement takes place project by project. Improvement, as Juran argues, should not be used without clear definition. Improvement can only be gained by tackling quality challenges project by project.

Quality improvement is applicable universally. This has been demonstrated through the Juran Institute's experience in supporting thousands of businesses.

Quality improvement extends to all parameters. The benefits from improvement activity will affect several areas of the business, including for instance cycle time, productivity, human safety, the environment etc.

The backlog of improvement projects is huge. Juran argues that the backlog is due to the planning process (Juran and Godfrey, 1999):

> The backlog of improvement projects exists in part because the planning of new products and processes has long been deficient. In effect, the planning process has been a dual hatchery. It hatched out new plans. It also hatched out new chronic wastes, and these accumulated year after year. Each such chronic waste then became a potential improvement project.

Reduction in chronic waste is not capital intensive. Projects that tackle chronic waste reduction, very rarely require additional financial results. Teams who work on these projects will find ways within the existing resources and knowledge to improve and further optimise the processes. This is a good way of ensuring good return on investment, as opposed to new product development projects which require a lot of capital outlay to support all the operations involved in identifying and establishing customer needs, designing, developing, planning, producing, delivering. The ROI in this context can be expected to be lower.

The return on investment is among the highest. NIST has, since 1988, been publishing studies which demonstrate that companies that have attained quality leadership are performing among the very best of the 500 S&P list. Other studies in Japan and in Europe have come to similar conclusions.

The major gains come from the vital few projects. The most significant gains that can be expected from improvement activity, come from the"vial few", strategic projects which tend to be multi-functional. Small improvements in these will have drastic reductions in waste, cost and significant performance improvement. The "useful many" projects are those which are operational in nature and tend to address local and departmental issues. The improvements in these areas are ultimately not going to be as significant as the vital few projects. Juran does, however, argue that by sponsoring "useful many" projects, senior managers can ensure that the lower hierarchy people are involved, they feel valued and will commit further to their organizations.

In his address at Minneapolis, Juran added the following comments in relation to quality improvement:

- Annual quality improvement is one of the essential success factors; without it there can be no quality leadership.
- It is a big advantage for companies to have available a field-tested, proven managerial process as an aid to annual quality improvement.
- Training is needed to enable company personnel to attain mastery of the quality improvement process.
- The training should include participating in actual improvement projects.

Juran poses the question as to why is it that senior managers do not apply the concepts of quality improvement, since these are existing, sound methodologies which are well tried, credible and universal and where the benefits are demonstrated beyond any doubt and present at all levels. He suggests the following as some of the prevalent reasons:

- They are sceptical; many have tried and failed.
- They have learned not to trust the advocates, internal as well as external. They do not know who to trust; there are many advocates and agendas.
- They cling to the mistaken belief that "Our business is different".
- They believe that getting certified to ISO 9000 will solve their quality problems.
- They are aware that mediocre quality is still saleable.
- There is confusion in language – the belief that "higher quality costs more".
- The belief of the CEO that he can lead the company to quality leadership without personally becoming deeply involved.

He suggests that further research should be undertaken to identify the reasons why improvement activities are not evident in all organizations and to understand better the obstacles which stop senior managers from not committing to quality improvement initiatives.

Juran's contributions
Juran's contributions are far too many to recall in this section. Perhaps in a summarised fashion, the essential aspects of Juran's main thrust can be briefly described.

Quality definition
Juran argues that quality has two main perspectives to it. The first is the aim of satisfying customer needs and requirements and the second is the elimination of internal waste and key obstacles that interfere with quality. This has led Juran to describe quality as "fitness for use". Meaning that in order for organizations to provide "conformance to requirements" they have to focus on the improvement of the vital few areas which tend to have high leverage potential and impact on customer satisfaction more significantly. Juran suggests that there are five main aspects to his definition of quality as "fitness for use":

1. Quality of design, meaning design concept and specifications of the product should be flawless.
2. Quality of conformance, product engineering and design should match the intended use.
3. Availability, meaning the product should be reliable and easy to maintain.
4. Safety, assessed by risk of injury and hazards.

5.   Field use, when in the hands of the customer the product should work as intended.

For improving quality with fitness for use in mind, Juran suggests the following ten steps:
1.   Build awareness of the need and opportunity to improve.
2.   Set goals for that improvement.
3.   Create plans to reach the goals.
4.   Provide training.
5.   Conduct projects to solve problems.
6.   Report on progress.
7.   Give recognition for success.
8.   Communicate results.
9.   Keep score.
10.   Maintain momentum.

In a sense, this is his interpretation of the PDCA cycle and in his trilogy, Juran argues that chronic and sporadic variation can be tackled through quality control and quality improvement (two stages of Juran's trilogy).

Cost of quality
In his trilogy Juran shows the cost of poor quality as a function of time. Emphasis on quality control to tackle chronic variation will only stabilise the cost of non-quality. SQC techniques can also help dealing with sporadic variation by bringing back the cost of non-quality to its previous level. It is only with quality improvement by focusing on the entire value chain, upstream by examining raw materials, supplier issues through operations all the way to customer delivery and satisfaction.

By using statistical tools and techniques Juran suggests that there are three types of costs that can be tackled:
1.   Internal failure costs (the costs of making products that could not be sold).
2.   External failure costs (the costs of replacing defective products that were shipped), appraisal costs (the costs of evaluating products and processes for failure).
3.   Prevention costs (the amount of money it takes to product defect-free products).

This model became known as the PAF model (prevention, appraisal and failure costs). The model helps establish the percentage of costs which are not necessary and, therefore, provides a great impetus for improvement activity. Costs of non-quality are typically at the level of 20-30 per cent and in some industries the figures are even higher. Juran has always argued that there is an optimum level where costs of quality can be accepted. For instance when the costs associated with defects are equal to the costs of ensuring quality, perhaps this level will signal that quality management has achieved its desired effect and that further refinement may not be necessary because the cost of doing so may not be justifiable.

Juran, like Deming, does not believe in zero defect or "quality is free" concepts which were developed by Philip Crosby. Juran argues that the pursuit of quality can be done through project-by-project improvement using SQC techniques. He does however warn that SQC should not become the obsession or "the tool-oriented approach".

The Pareto principle

The Pareto principle represents a phenomenon whereby in any population which contributes to a common effect, a relative few of the contributors account for the bulk of the effect (Juran, 1992). The Pareto principle is a state of nature (the way things happen) as well as a process (a way of thinking about problems). The Pareto principle argues that there is a mal-distribution of quality losses. It suggests that most effects come from relatively few causes.

It is one of the most powerful tools of quality improvement since it helps people focus on areas with big impact. It can be used on a regular basis for identifying causes of problems and attempting to eliminate or greatly reduce those with the biggest impact. Concerned by comments that the Pareto principle is attributable to Vilfredo Pareto, Juran (1992) writes:

> Years ago I gave the name "Pareto" to this principle of the vital few and trivial many. On subsequent challenge, I was forced to confess that I had mistakenly applied the wrong name to the principle ... The Pareto principle as a universal was not original with Pareto. Where then did the universal originate? To my knowledge, the first expression was by myself. Had I been structured along different lines, assuredly I would have called it the Juran principle. However, I was not structured that way. Yet I did need a shorthand designation, and I had no qualm about Pareto's name. Hence the Pareto principle.

Internal customer

An important contribution from Juran is the argument that we should not just focus on the external customer. Alongside the value chain, he argues, are several internal customers who also become suppliers and the cycle propels itself forward. There are three role models which represent opportunities for improvement by looking at the full cycle of adding value to the end customer.

The spiral of progress that Juran suggests shows that the cycle of managing and improving quality in all aspects of the value chain goes through supplier-customer relationships, feedback on performance, learning and innovation, optimisation and integration and so on, until the ultimate impact on the customer is achieved.

Management-controllable and operator-controllable errors
Juran argues that defects to be "operator-controllable" if workers have working arrangements that enable them to meet quality standards. In other words, training has to come first and then proper empowerment and involvement in improvement activity. In the event that these errors continue to accumulate, it will demonstrate that management has not done its job properly, so the emphasis is shifted on to management controlling these errors (i.e. management-controllable errors). Using his famous Pareto approach, Juran argues that 80 per cent of the problems are management related and only 20 per cent are under employee control. The 80 per cent category means that the types of errors and problems need proper investigation of the entire system, processes, methods and policies, technology and materials. These are, of course, all under the jurisdiction of managers and not the employees.

Deming (1986, p. 315), similarly to Juran, says:

I should estimate that in my experience most troubles and most possibilities for improvement add up to proportions something like this: 94 per cent belong to the system (responsibility of management) 6 per cent special.

Subsequently he re-adjusted these figures to 98 per cent and 2 per cent.

In so far as those errors which fall under the remit of employees, Juran argues that "If the managers have met the criteria, then the means for doing good work are clearly within the hands of the operators".

Juran refers to three types of operator-controllable errors:

1. *Inadvertent errors.* These are due to poor attention, very often unexpected and unpredictable. They are certainly unwitting and unintentional. These errors exhibit randomness and the best way to tackle them is to fool proof the system.

2. *Technique errors.* These are due to lack of training and knowledge. They are not deliberate or intentional. They tend to be specific, of course consistent and ultimately unavoidable. Remedies require studying the system, process and methods and ensuring that employees are competent to operate the processes or change the system and processes so that employees can operate with fool proofing.

3. *Wilful errors.* These are witting, intentional and persistent errors. They are due to anti-social elements whose actions cannot be defended. Juran says that the fault very often lies with managers who foster a climate of fear, blame and suspicion by constantly moving the goal post, focusing on cost rather than quality and using scrap figures to apportion blame. Even for these types of errors, Juran argues that ultimately it is the responsibility of managers to work on fool proofing the system and creating a positive work climate where there is high concentration, high commitment and high competence to produce quality that can satisfy the customer and bring competitive benefits to the organization.

Juran's influence on ISO 9000

Juran has been very critical of the earlier version of ISO 9000 because according to him it encouraged mediocrity rather than real improvement. Furthermore, it did not emphasis the importance of leadership and senior management commitment. During an interview, Juran gave a lot of praise to the ISO 9000 movement for bringing quality to the fore and encouraging its uptake. His point of contention is that those who are responsible for certification need to certify excellence and not encourage mediocrity by insisting on compliance to poorly written procedures that are fundamentally wrong in the first place because they do not focus on doing the right things:

> I have a lot of quarrels with the criteria in the ISO 9000 series, the original criteria....They ask for a level of quality which I would label as mediocrity level. They did not publish criteria which would lead to quality leadership. I think the standards should b at an excellence level and if there's an assessment, the assessor will indicate the extent to which the criteria are met and which criteria are not met.

John Davies, Chairman of Subcommittee 2 of the International Organization for Standardization (ISO) Technical Committee 176 (TC 176), did admit that the 1994 version of the standard did not go far enough. In response to Juran's comments, he said: "I am sympathetic towards the opinion and we'll see what we can do about it". The result of course was the launch in 2000 of a much better, much improved version of the standard.

Some of the testimonies in recognition of Juran's role and contributions over the years include:

> Juran is the greatest authority on quality control in the entire world (Jungi Noguchi, Executive Director of JUSE).

> Whatever advances American manufacturing has made in the last thirty to forty years, we owe to Joe Juran and to his untiring, steady, patient, self effacing work (Peter Drucker).

> Joe is like a river. He just flows on and on. You don't know where it starts, you don't know where it ends. You just know it's rich and there's always water in it and it's always for good use (Lawrence Appley, Chairman Emeritus of the American Management Association).

Quality leadership

Famously, Juran calling for the need to have strong leadership has said: "What we need are leaders, not cheerleaders". Together with Deming, he was against exhortations and hype which might do managers' ego a lot of good, but would not solve the problem of identifying the key priorities for improvement, carefully selecting key projects and working on creating an effective organization that can deliver high value to its end customer. Juran's suggested recipe is for leaders to have clear goals to focus on, clear plans to help them deliver, proper involvement of people at all levels, effective performance measurement and monitoring systems and good reward and recognition schemes that are linked to quality improvement contributions only.

Quality leadership for Juran is to learn not to manage the sporadic spikes but to be aware and conscious of what chronic waste can do in impeding progress and the achievement of superior performance. Good practice is to work beyond stabilising the process by injecting real improvement activity that can reduce costs of non-quality very significantly. Doing so will require the project-by-project approach, following Juran's universal sequence for breakthrough. Juran describes breakthrough as: "The organized creation of beneficial change".

The steps of breakthrough include: proof of the need; project identification; organization to guide each project; organization for diagnosis/analysis of projects; diagnosis; breakthrough in knowledge; remedial action on the findings; breakthrough in cultural resistance to change; and control at the new level.

Juran emphasizes the importance of having senior executives lead the improvement activity. Very often the establishment of quality councils is to select the vital few projects, appoint improvement teams, authorise the activity to take place, allocate resource. Juran suggests the following steps and roles:

- Quality council: with the overall responsibility for:
  - establishing processes for nominating projects, assigning teams and making improvements;
  - providing resources;
  - establishing processes for review of progress, dissemination of results and recognition; and
  - revising the merit rating and business planning systems to include quality improvement.
- Role of upper management:
  - serve on the quality council;
  - approve strategic quality goals;
  - allocate the needed resources;
  - review progress;
  - give recognition to teams;
  - serve on some project teams; and
  - revise the merit rating and business planning systems.

Juran the person
Juran is described as being an astute observer, attentive listener, brilliant synthesizer and prescient prognosticator. He has been called the father of quality, a quality guru and the man who taught quality to the Japanese (he refutes this claim all the time). Juran has added the human dimension to quality thus broadening it from the SQC origins.

His philosophy which is based on two tenets: higher quality means a greater number of features that meet customer expectations and freedom from trouble, has been preached and practiced all over the world by thousands of organizations.

At the celebration of his 100th birthday, hundreds of testimonies have been made by great admirers, appreciative CEOs, influential thinkers, consultants, eminent academics among others. The following are some of the main testimonies:

Joseph Juran is and will continue to be a fundamental leadership force in the constantly growing economic, social and educational service of quality to America as well as to the world community. His combination of consistently innovative and intensely practical contributions has created much of what the quality field is today and is one of the foundations for its continued development. The breadth of his abilities—from highly sought after guidance to leaders of business and government to hands-on help for individual quality practitioners – has provided a unique legacy spanning a remarkably large number of generations. And, throughout it all, he has always marched to the drumbeat of his own convictions and provided a model of what a quality leader and engineer should be (Armand V. Feigenbaum, President and CEO, General Systems Co. Inc., ASQ past president and honorary member)

The links between Europe and Dr Juran are deeply rooted. He was a fundamental reference for the development of the quality culture in Europe. Many Europeans felt a deep cultural affinity with Dr Juran because of his rational, rigorous way of thinking. He was a symbol for those who did not appreciate over-statements, fads, distortions or oversimplifications in quality thinking. In 1993, as president of the European Organization for Quality (EOQ), I had the honour of expressing the gratitude of the European quality community to Dr Juran by granting him the EOQ Gold Honorary Medal. Now I wish to join the multitude of people around the world who greet Dr Juran as both a great "architect of quality" and an admirable man (Tito Conti, author, consultant and assistant editor of *A History of Managing for Quality*, past president, European Organization for Quality).

Joe Juran's contribution to society equals the most valuable contribution by anyone in the recent century. His inspiration and instruction, which in a practical way have been applied by countless institutions, improved the quality and efficiency of all institutions that serve others, be they commercial or even in the public sector. He did this in a most appealing personal way. My guess is many who took their lead from Joe did so as admiring friends. I consider myself one of those, and then all of us translated what he taught us into employable means for the betterment of those we served. Joe has ably served more people in our society than any other man I have known (Bob Galvin, chair, Motorola Executive Committee).

Joe Juran's stellar contribution: the Juran trilogy of the three quality processes. The processes show us how to manage quality during operations. The six steps of quality planning help us develop new products or processes; the six steps of quality control explain how to track performance; the nine steps of quality improvement guide us to make breakthroughs to superior levels of performance. This framework integrates the managerial, technological and statistical concepts of quality. As new concepts evolve, they will easily splice into the trilogy. A structured approach always wins the day over trial and error (Frank Gryna, Professor Emeritus, ASQ honorary member).

Since his first visit in 1954, Dr Juran has come to Japan many times during the last half-century. We learned a lot from him. Dr Juran summarized the following three features of quality control (QC) activities in Japan that created the revolution in quality: a massive quality-related education and training program; an annual program of quality improvement; and upper management leadership of the quality function. In 1954, he was invited by the Japanese Union of Scientists and Engineers and started the QC courses for top and middle managers. These courses had an immeasurably large impact on Japanese QC and positioned quality as the important management tool. *Hoshin kanri* (policy management) is the company-wide activity to rotate the plan-do-check-act cycle every year. An internal QC audit by top managers is included. Without the leadership of top managers of this kind, it is impossible to continue to promote total quality management of the company (Yoshio Kondo, Professor Emeritus, Kyoto University, Japan).

The world owes Dr Juran much for his unique contributions as a premier scholar and historian in the quality sciences. He has worked tirelessly and effectively to elevate quality's technical foundations and enable its beneficial applications in all sectors – in the United States and abroad. In his 100th year, he continues to lead, inspire and build, with the conviction the best days for quality lie ahead. Those of us in the Baldrige National Quality Program will always treasure Dr Juran. His support, guidance and friendship convinced us it was possible to create an award and continuously improve the resulting framework for cooperation and sharing to strengthen performance in businesses, healthcare, schools and non-profit organizations (Curt Reimann, past director, Harry Hertz, director, Baldrige National Quality Program).

Some famous quotes from Juran

At the age of 91, Juran was asked about retirement and he said that he did not agree with the word "retirement". He says (about dying):

When I go, please let me go at my word processor.

In 2004 (age 100), he wrote (Juran, 2004):

When I am gone, let no one weep for me. I have lived a wonderful life.

My job of contributing to the welfare of my fellow man is the great unfinished business

Honours received by W. Edwards Deming

- Taylor Key Award, American Management Association, 1983.
- The Deming Prize was instituted by the Union of Japanese Scientists and Engineers and is awarded each year in Japan to a statistician for contributions to statistical theory. The Deming Prize for application is awarded to a company for improved use of statistical theory in organization, consumer research, design of product and production.
- Recipient of the Second Order Medal of the Sacred Treasure, from the Emperor of Japan, 1960, for improvement of quality and of Japanese economy, through the statistical control of quality.
- Recipient of the Shewhart Medal for 1955, from the American Society for Quality Control.
- Elected in 1972 most distinguished graduate from the University of Wyoming.
- Elected in 1983 to the National Academy of Engineering.
- Inducted into the Science and Technology Hall of Fame, Dayton, 1986.
- In 1980, the Metropolitan section of the American Society for Quality Control established the annual Deming Medal for the improvement of quality and productivity.
- Recipient of the Samuel S. Wilks Award from the American Statistical Association in 1983.
- Recipient of the Distinguished Career in Science Award from the National Academy of Sciences in 1988.
- Recipient of the National Medal of Technology from President Reagan in 1987.

Deming's 1950 lecture to Japanese management

This is an "informal" translation of the Japanese transcript commissioned by John Dowd. It has been checked by several translators and is the only known English translation of Dr Deming's 1950 lecture. (Contents, images, and structure copyrighted by the Deming Electronic Network, © 1995-2000. All rights reserved.)

To management: Dr W.E. Deming, Presidential Adviser on Sampling Methods for the US Treasury.

Introduction

The opportunity to speak with all of you is my greatest honor. I will not give a sermon on statistical techniques. I leave that to the statisticians. Henceforth I shall speak of the truly important problems of manufacturing and sales, the statistical techniques which are helpful in the solution of these problems, and how all of you can use these techniques. Afterwards, I will answer your questions.

The problems and methods I will now discuss are extremely important to both Japanese and American manufacturers, as well as those of England, New Zealand and other countries around the world. As all modern-day manufacturers are striving to make their business prosperous in the long term, the following issues are necessary:

1. Better design of products to improve service.
2. Higher level of uniform product quality.
3. Improvement of product testing in the workplace and in research centers.
4. Greater sales through side [global] markets.

First of all, I am not a miracle worker. I am not an economist, or an expert in business sales or research. Neither am I a manufacturer. However, I firmly believe that statistical techniques and associated practices are useful to all of you. As a statistician, while being in close contact with the problems that all of you encounter, I have had the honor of doing research about those problems with statisticians, salesmen and other experts from diverse groups. Such groups include manufacturers, economists and technicians, as well as university professors and the world's largest, most successful trade associations. We all have our different perspectives, but I believe that we can solve the various problems facing modern Japanese manufacturers through co-operation.

Of course, you all have heard about statistical product quality administration before. However, if you do not understand it, or if you do not support your sales researchers, statistical product quality administration is not useful and your business will not be able to expand.

I must point out that I do not mean it would be good if you were simply to sell factory products. These days it is not enough only to sell goods. Next year, if you have that concept you all probably will want to sell a lot, or at least as much as you can. The English word "marketing" does not just mean sales; it is in fact a science, the science of knowing such things as: what the people who buy these products month after month think of them, whether they buy them again, and the reasons why. Afterwards, I will return to this, but now, I would like to continue my discussion of statistical product quality administration.

Statistical product quality administration

Statistical product quality administration is a splendid new tool. It is being applied in every industry, beginning in modern Japan and America as well as England, New Zealand, and various other countries. Whether it be on a large scale or a small scale, it is being researched and executed in an extremely large number of manufacturing plants. Some results of this are:

- Costs go down.
- Producers can economize on raw materials.
- Production levels increase, and waste decreases.
- Product quality becomes more uniform.
- Producers and consumers gain the ability to agree on product quality.
- Quality is improved, so inspections may be reduced.
- Appliances and techniques can be used to a higher degree.

It is already 25 years since statistical product quality administration was implemented in America, but it was not developed much until 1942, and the extent of its use was narrow. However, for the following two reasons, in about 1942, we developed statistical product quality administration. In that year, a pamphlet commenting on the principles of statistical product quality administration in simple language, easily understandable by general technicians, was published by the American Standard Association.

Secondly, beginning in 1942 an eight-day course on statistical product quality administration opened in the US, and several hundred technicians were trained. I ran this course in Tokyo for 220 Japanese technicians this July through the sponsorship of the League of Japanese Scientific Techniques; and its content was similar to that of one I ran again in August at Fukuoka's Kyushu University.

In modern Japan many technicians, mathematicians, and statisticians are researching statistical product quality administration. Furthermore, since coming to Japan I have learned that the splendid achievement these people have made in statistical product quality administration is already apparent. The results from all these countries are surprising. They have demonstrated superb ability in the statistical sphere.

The knowledge and brains applied to statistics by the Japanese are an essential national resource; it is important in the same way as water power, forests, and railroads. And that statistical knowledge, much like water power, is not useful at all unless it has an impact on work opportunity and work. With water power, if one were to get rid of turbines and generator machines, no power would emerge.

Similarly it may be recognized that without effective use, all of modern Japanese statistical knowledge would not be helpful to the advance of products, product quality, or product uniformity. You all must look for people who have both statistical knowledge and excellent experience with technical knowledge and employ them in factories. In addition, to aid your technicians you must seek mathematical statisticians as consultants.

However, no matter how excellent your technicians, you who are leaders, must strive for advances in the improvement of product quality and uniformity if your technicians are to be able to make improvements. The first step, therefore, belongs with management. First, your company technicians and your factories must know that you have a fervor for advancing product quality and uniformity and a sense of responsibility for product quality.

Nothing will come of this if you only speak about it. Action is important. If you demonstrate enthusiasm for the improvement of product quality, your product quality administration will certainly advance. Responsibility for product quality means guaranteeing one's own factory's products to the utmost degree possible. The greatest guarantee of product quality is not words, but executing product quality administration. When you effect product quality administration, show administrative charts or methods as an indicator, as there is no better way to guarantee product quality to the consumer. By showing enthusiasm toward product quality and uniformity and responsibility to product quality. You will gain the opportunity for your technicians to put product quality administration into effect.

However, product quality administration at the factory cannot be implemented in a single day. It requires along time. At first do it on a small scale, and once you think that has value, then expand. The process of product quality administration, consisting of the combination of statistical and manufacturing techniques is long and tiring.

Well, I think you must share an interest in how I define statistical product quality administration. Product quality administration is most useful, and moreover it illustrates the methods by which producers can economically produce the goods that buyers indicate they want.

All of the words in this definition have their respective meanings. "Economic production" means low price production: in other words, elimination of waste; faster production; fewer defects in products, raw materials or machines; the practical use of techniques; improved uniformity in product quality; and the opportunity for producers and purchasers to agree on product quality.

"Most useful" means the design and product quality must suit the purpose of the good; raw materials, mechanical manufacturing techniques, transport, and products must be the best as we consider them from the viewpoint of the marketplace. If you do not conduct market surveys about what quality or what design will be in demand, your products will not succeed in being "most useful".

The product must match the market. The product quality must be adapted to that market. If product quality is too high, or too low, it w ill not be right. If product quality is too good, the price is very high, and only a quite limited group of people can afford to purchase it. Even so, if product quality is too low, despite low prices, people will not repeat the purchase, and before long the business will slow down. Therefore, in order to make the most useful product, you must conduct market surveys about what kind or product quality and what kind of design are required. Additionally, through market surveys, you must make sure of the price buyers can pay for the product.

On this subject, there are other reasons why continuing market surveys are useful to economical production. Every month you must make roughly the right amount of product, or you cannot achieve economical production. If you are left with 10 percent, or 25 percemt, of your goods unsold, your profits will disappear. Further, if you cannot respond to a large number of orders, you will not maximize your profit. As a result, in order to achieve economical production, it is necessary to conduct market surveys. Based on market surveys, you will be able to stand on a stable foundation of monthly product sales. Then you can find out what kind of people (e.g. wage workers, farmers, businessmen) demand that product; or whether, having bought the product once, they will not but it again; or whether the people who bought it are satisfied with the product; or again if they are unsatisfied, why they are not satisfied. Thus by means of market surveys, you can effect administration of advertising, product design changes pricing, and production.

No matter what kind of manufacturer you are, if you have long-term plans, you must work to implement product quality administration in the wider meaning, as in the definition which I laid out a moment ago.

In the last ten years there has been no scientific method which has experienced such rapid expansion as has statistical theory. In the context of today's Japan, the most useful thing for manufacturers could be nothing but the appropriate application of statistical techniques.

At the end of my discussion of market surveys, I would like to explain my thoughts on the problem of statistical product quality administration with a diagram. This diagram not only makes clear my thoughts on product quality administration and market surveys, but I think it is extremely easy to understand. Below I have drawn a pie graph "wheel" divided into four sections [this refers to Figure 20.9 at the end of this chapter]. This wheel rolls along the line of "concepts regarding product quality" and "sense of responsibility for product quality." The fact that the four stages of the wheel are connected one to the other with no beginning and no end is very important. This is the reason why I drew a circle. You must not stop product design or testing. When your products emerge into the real market, after having inquired into how the product is useful to people, and what they think of it, you redesign it. There is no end to product quality administration. Using product quality administration, producing goods continually being improved, I want you to make more and more adapted items that buyers will want, designing, redesigning, and then finding cheap, better ways to make them. While this certainly benefits the purchasers, it benefits you as well.

Finally, I would like you to understand that the latest stage of statistical product quality administration for factories lies in pertinent market surveys.

Now I will add to this two or three explanations of market research.

Special advice concerning market surveys
This year is 1950. The current markets and manufacturing techniques are considerably different from those of 1935. In Japan the recent changes may possibly be greater than those in any other country. However, businessmen from

everywhere are facing the necessity for new methods. In the past, in 1935 and before, businessmen simply made things they wanted to sell, and sold those things they had made. They tried to sell these products both in domestic and international markets. There were those who succeeded, and those who failed. There was no way to determine how much their enterprise would improve if they made products of a different design, better adapted to the buyers' needs, with better methods. The stages of manufacture and sales of that time were as follows: product design (shoes, cotton materials, silk materials, magnetic products, electrical appliances); manufacture; sales. Today, in 1950, we all must design, manufacture, and sell in the same way, nut science has expanded. Rather than following the example of these three steps, four stages, including market surveys which I have just highlighted have become necessary.

These days we cannot compel people to buy. When, selling a product, whether it be on domestic or international markets, we must deliver the things people truly want. Moreover, we must manufacture at a price that invites purchase, furthermore, when markets are far away, at a price which is competitive. As I mentioned before, if the product quality is either too high or too low, it is no good.

In the past two or three years, market surveys have come to be extremely successful in America. However, I cannot say their evolution is complete. Market research by modern manufacturers themselves, or through market research specialist companies, is progressing swiftly. I think if it were not for that progress, many of those businesses would not be prosperous now.

I firmly believe that if product quality administration and market surveys, prudently and scientifically, were used in a correct manner you would be able to create a market for Japanese goods overseas, and the Japanese standard of living would greatly rise.

Market surveys give answers to the following kinds of questions: "What kind of goods would it be profitable to produce that people would demand and be able to buy?" I would probably say this about that subject: the techniques of statistical product quality administration count the methods of making cheap and uniform high-quality products for you. The manufacturing and market surveys that comprise the four stages of product quality administration consider not only the manufacturers, but also the consumers.

The process of sales is not something that finishes simply with transporting the products to the marketplace, and receiving money. In today's sales, after selling the product, the businessman must think about whether he has satisfied the customer, and how improvements can be made from then on. Market surveys accomplish better service for the consumer, and moreover they serve the purpose of increasing profit for management and workers.

As I have said before, I am visiting here as a statistician, but I strongly believe that, as in the four parts of that wheel diagram, we must not fail to use statistical techniques in today's industrial world. If it is the case that businessmen try to perform a great service to the public, I emphasize that they should find and put excellent statistical techniques into each of those four categories.

To conclude, I want to offer you one or two things I have realized about the statistical techniques that are currently being used. Number one: at the first stage, design, you must conduct market surveys and inspections, applying the statistical techniques for experimental and planning methods and inspection of samples. Furthermore, you must perfect the manufacturing process, using the technical skills of factory workers and machines, and utilizing these techniques to conduct inspections of raw materials.

Number two: in manufacturing in the second stage good product quality and uniformity of product quality are important. This means that by the time of shipping, you can transport quality products through the use of statistical techniques of inspection of samples, experimental planning methods and marketing surveys. Number three: at the third stage, sales, the statistical technique of the market survey is used. Number four: at the fourth stage of service research the techniques of sample inspections, experimental planning methods, and market surveys are used.

After you have reached the fourth stage, you return once again to the beginning stage in wheel. Here, then, putting together thoughts from your previous results, you may begin to implement product design changes.

I repeat myself, but the necessity of statistical techniques must not be ignored. Without them I deeply believe that businessmen cannot long sustain their prosperity. What I just spoke about now is true not only in Japan, but equally in Chicago, Manchester, or Amsterdam. Every businessman around the world is now facing these same problems.

By the way, I believe you all probably have many questions to ask. You probably want to know more about market survey techniques, or about how they are managed. Anticipating one of your questions, why don't I give an answer now. What they are doing to carry out market surveys in America may be answered as follows: it is fine to request the services of a trustworthy market research company on your own.

On this topic, I would like to ask for your care on one more issue. Even if you hear developments from professional buyers in New York, they are not necessarily all correct. Therefore, because you do not know what American shop for in a basic product, and you only respond to orders, you may be driven out of the market. This is due to lack of knowledge about what kind of design or product quality Americans are demanding, or what markets may prosper in the future. You, Japan's skillful technicians, can manufacturer items that businessmen of American and the rest of the world cannot. You don't know whether the things you want to sell are what Americans want to buy, but you know the way to find this out. That method is statistical research in the realms of manufacture and market surveying.

Brief biographical synopsis of Dr Joseph M. Juran and honours awarded to him

The following is a brief synopsis of the biography of Dr. Joseph M. Juran, highlighting important data and facts in his fruitful life of longevity and service to the quality profession.

Born:
- 24 December, 1904, Braila, Romania.
- Emigrated to USA, 1912.
- Naturalized US citizen, 1917.

Education:
- B.Sc., Electrical Engineering, University of Minnesota, 1924.
- J.D., Law, Loyola University, 1936.

Employment:
- 1924-1941 engineer, manager, Western Electric Company.
- 1941-1945 assistant administrator, Lend-Lease Administration, Foreign Economic Administration, US Government.
- 1945-1951 Professor and chairman, industrial engineering, New York University.
- 1951-1979 self-employed consultant.
- 1979 present founder, chairman, Juran Institute (Emeritus 1987).
- 1986 founder, chairman, Juran Foundation.

Honorary doctorates:
- Doctor of Engineering, Stevens Institute of Technology, 1988.
- Doctor of Science, University of Minnesota, 1992.
- Doctor of Science, Rochester Institute of Technology, 1992.
- Doctor of Laws, University of New Haven, 1992.

Honorary memberships, USA:
- American Society for Quality Control (ASQC), Honorary 1981.
- American Society of Mechanical Engineers (ASME), 1993.
- International Academy of Management.
- National Academy of Engineering, 1988.
- The Academy of the Association for Quality and Participation.
- Alpha Pi Mu.
- Sigma Xi, 1946.
- Tau Beta Pi.

Honorary memberships, international:
- Australian Organization for Quality Control, 1974.
- Argentine Organization for Quality Control , 1977.
- British Institute of Quality Assurance, 1976.

- European Organization for Quality Control.
- Philippine Society for Quality Control, 1974.
- Spanish Association for Quality Control.
- Romanian Academy, 1992.

Society affiliations, USA:
- American Association for the Advancement of Science, 1967.
- American Institute of Industrial Engineers, 1967.
- American Management Association, 1941.
- Malcolm Baldrige National Quality Award, Board of Overseers, 1988 to 1991.
- Member Illinois Bar, 1936.
- Professional Engineer, New York, New Jersey.

Medals, USA:
- Alumni Medal, University of Minnesota, 1954.
- American Management Association, Hall of Fame, 1983.
- Brumbaugh Award, ASQC, 1958.
- Chairman's Award, American Association of Engineering Societies, 1988.
- Edwards Medal, ASQC, 1961.
- Eugene L. Grant Medal, ASQC, 1967.
- Gilbreth Award, American Institute of Industrial Engineers, 1981.
- Managing Automation, Hall of Fame, 1995.
- National Medal of Technology, 1992.
- Soichiro Honda Medal, ASME, 1995.
- Stevens Medal, Stevens Institute of Technology, 1984.
- Wallace Clark Medal, ASME, AMA, 1967.
- Worcester Reed Warner Medal, ASME, 1945.
- Xerox Quality Award.

Medals, international:
- 250th Anniversary Medal, Czechoslovakian Higher Institute of Technology, 1965.
- Medal of Technikhaza, Esztergom, Hungary, 1968.
- Medal of Honor, Camera Official de la Industria, Madrid, 1970.
- Order of Sacred Treasure (Emperor of Japan), 1981.
- Medal of European Organization for Quality, 1993.

Placques, scrolls of appreciation, USA:
- American Management Association,Wall of Fame, 1983.
- Department of the Army.
- Department of Commerce.
- Department of Defense.

- Department of the Navy.
- Malcolm Baldrige National Quality Award.

Placques, scrolls of appreciation, international:
- Scroll of Appreciation, Japanese Union of Scientists and Engineers (JUSE), 1961.
- Taiwan Productivity Center, 1974.
- Plaque of Appreciation, Republic of Korea, 1978.

Nomination letter sent to The White House by ASQ

October 1, 2002

Hon. George Bush
Presidential Medal of Freedom
The White House
Washington, DC 20500

Mr. President:

It is my honor to place into nomination for the Presidential Medal of Freedom the names of three individuals whose lives and teachings have already had a giant impact on our economy, our society, and our way of life – and whose influence will only grow stronger in the decades to come.

I nominate the three individuals most responsible for the creation and development of the discipline of *quality* today:
William Edwards Deming
Joseph Moses Juran
Armand Vallin Feigenbaum

This nomination is unusual in two ways. First, the nomination is for *three* individuals, instead of one. Second, the nominations are of *statisticians* – not soldiers or statesmen or artists; statistics is not a profession people intuitively associate with the theme of freedom.

Honoring these men does more than acknowledge their unusual careers. It sends a signal to Americans everywhere that quality matters, that the United States of America stands behind businesses that try to do better, and that every action every individual takes to improve quality strengthens our country and our society for the competitive years that lie ahead.

In this letter and attached supporting statement, I hope to make clear that the award must be shared three ways, that each of the three is equally deserving of this highest recognition. I also hope to show that, while each man began his career as a statistician, each came over time to address issues of far greater breadth and significance to our society than abstract industrial statistics.

Sincerely,

Michael Finley
(American Society for Quality)

Figure 20.1 Deming's system of profound knowledge

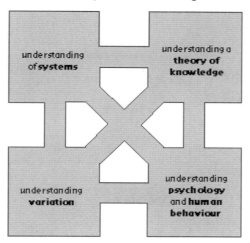

Figure 20.2 Three management systems

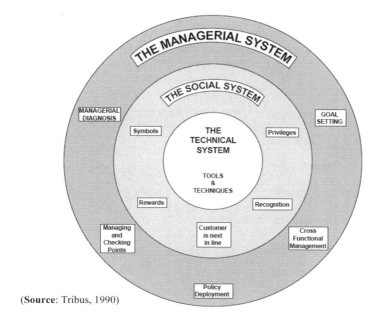

(**Source**: Tribus, 1990)

Figure 20.3 Distribution of time and responsibility for improvement, operations and the future of the enterprise at various levels

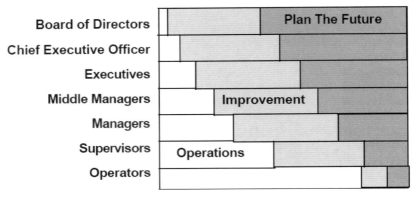

(**Source**: Tribus, 1990)

Figure 20.4 Division of responsibilities for the three systems as a function of level of responsibility in the enterprise

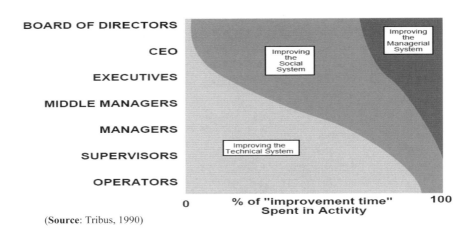

(**Source**: Tribus, 1990)

Table 20.1 Deming's theory of profound knowledge

Theory of profound knowledge	Relation to the 14 points	Relation to seven deadly diseases & obstacles
Appreciation for a system A leader must understand the system he/she is attempting to manage. Without this understanding the system cannot be managed or improved. A system cannot understand itself or manage itself. Optimisation of the parts does not optimise the whole. System optimisation requires co-ordination & co-operation of the parts, which requires leadership	Relates to points 1-13	Lack of constancy of purpose Emphasis on short-term profits/performance Evaluation by performance reviews, merit rating building fear, destroying teamwork Management mobility Running the company on visible figures alone distracts from the purpose All above prevent optimisation
Knowledge about variation Refers to Shewhart's concept of common or system causes of variation & outside assignable or special causes of variation. Relates to the red bead experiment & blaming people for variation caused by the system	Joiner & Gaudard (1990) compare each of the 14 points to the concept of variation, but points 5, 6, 7 & 11 appear to be the most relevant. A knowledge of variation helps one understand the system so that it can be managed & improved	Annual reviews & ranking employees show absence of knowledge of variation or understanding of the system – merely ranks effect of system on the people. This causes tampering which destroys motivation & teamwork
Theory of knowledge Knowledge depends on theory. Information is not knowledge. Experience teaches nothing without theory. Practice makes permanent, not perfect. Copying examples does not lead to knowledge	Relates to points 5, 6, 7, 10 & 11 since the emphasis is on teaching people how to think on a continuous basis and not to assume any two problems are the same	Relates to seeking examples to follow rather than developing solutions. Theory leads to questions which lead to knowledge & subsequent improvement – plan-do-check/study-act cycle
Knowledge of psychology Leader must understand human behaviour to motivate, co-ordinate and manage people to optimise the system	Relates to points 7, 8, 9, 10, 11 and 12	A lack of knowledge of psychology causes or supports evaluation with annual reviews, merit ratings & ranking people; running the company on visible results alone. People need a method to improve, not objectives, quotas & rankings

(**Source**: Martin, Management and Accounting Web)

Figure 20.5 The organization viewed as a system

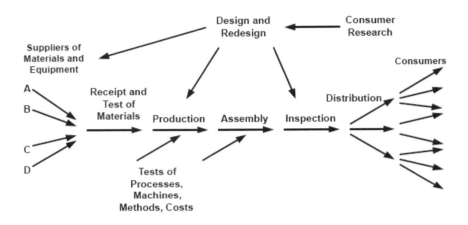

Figure 20.6 Juran's trilogy diagram

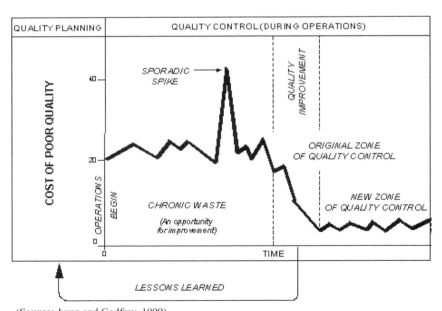

(**Source:** Juran and Godfrey, 1999)

Figure 20.7 The quality planning road map

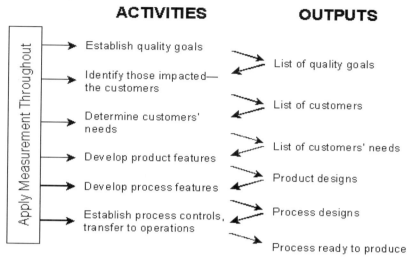

(**Source**: Juran and Godfrey, 1999)

Figure 20.8 The feedback loop

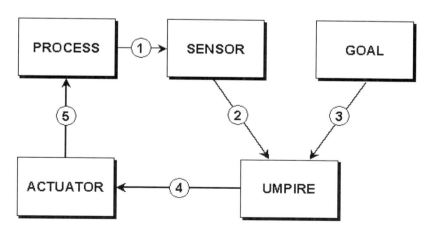

(**Source**: Juran and Godfrey, 1999)

369

Figure 20.9 Diagram from Deming's 1950 lecture to Japanese management

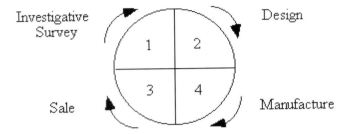

Bibliography

Ahire, S.L., Golhar, D.Y. and Waller, M.A. (1996), "Development and validation of TQM implementation constructs", *Decision Sciences*, Vol.27, pp. 23-56.

Akao, Y. (1990), *Quality Function Deployment: Integrating Customer Requirements into Product Design*, English translation, Productivity Press, (originally published as *Hinshitutenkai katsuyo no jissai*, Japan Standards Association, 1988).

Al Azmi, M. and Zairi, M. (2005), "Knowledge management: a proposed taxonomy", Working Paper, School of Management, University of Bradford, January.

Al Nofal, A., Al Omaim, N. and Zairi, M. (2005), "TQM: theoretical insights", Working Paper, School of Management, University of Bradford, January.

Al Omaim, N., Al Nofal, A. and Zairi, M. (2005), "Critical factors of TQM: an update on the literature" Working Paper, School of Management, University of Bradford, January.

Ali, A.N. and Zairi, M. (2005), "Service quality in higher education", Working Paper, School of Management, University of Bradford, January.

Alloway, J.A. (1994), "The card drop shop", *Quality Progress*, Vol. 27 No. 7, pp. 99-104.

American Suppliers Institute Incorporated (1989), *Policy Management – Executive Briefing Manual*, American Suppliers Institute, Michigan.

American Suppliers Institute Incorporated (1992), *Phase 1 – Product Planning, Analysing and Diagnosing the Product Planning Matrix*, ASI Quality Systems QFD, pp. 51-4.

American Productivity & Quality Center (APQC) (1996), *Knowledge Management*, Consortium Benchmarking Study, Final Report, APQC, Houston.

Anderson, M. and Sohal, A.S. (1999), "A study of the relationship between quality management practices and performance in small businesses", *International Journal of Quality and Reliability Management*, Vol. 16 No. 9, pp. 859-77.

Andersen, B. and Moen, R. (1999), "Integrating benchmarking and poor quality cost measurement for assisting the quality management work", *Benchmarking: An International Journal*, Vol. 6 No. 4, pp. 291-301.

Andersen, T. and Rasmussen, M. (1999), "Decision support in a condition based environment", *Journal of Quality in Maintenance Engineering*, Vol. 5 No. 2, pp. 89-102.

Anderson, D., Groves, D., Lengfelder, J. and Timothy, D. (2001), "A research approach to training: a case study of mystery guest methodology", *International Journal of Contemporary Hospitality Management*, Vol. 13 No. 2, pp. 93-102.

Angel, L. and Chandra, M. (2001), "Performance implications in continuous quality improvement", *International Journal of Operations & Production Management*, Vol. 21 No. 1/2, pp. 108-25.

Ansari, A. and Modarress, B. (1994), *Quality Function Deployment: The Role of Suppliers*, National Association of Purchasing Management, Inc., October, pp. 28-35.

Appelbaum, S., Gandell, J., Shapiro, B., Belisle, P. and Hoeven, E. (2000), "Anatomy of a merger: behavior of organisational factors and processes throughout the post-stages", *Management Decision*, Vol. 38 No. 10, pp. 674-84.

Asaka, T. and Ozeki, K. (1990), *Handbook of Quality Tools, The Japanese Approach*, English translation published by Productivity Press, Inc., (originally published as *Genbacho no tameno QC Hikkei*, by Japanese Standards Association, Tokyo, 1988).

Ashton, C. (1992), "Employing habitual success", *The TQM Magazine*, Vol. 4 No. 4, pp. 225-58.

Atkinson, G.S. (1993), "The 1993 state of US total quality management: a Baldrige examiner's perspective", *California Management Review*, Vol. 35 No. 3, pp. 32-54.

Atkinson, P.E. (1990), *Creating Culture Change: The Key To Successful Total Quality Management*, IFS Publications, Bedford.

Aune, A. (1991), "A recipe for success", *TQM Magazine*, February, pp. 33-7.

Badri, L., Badri, M. and Ferdenache, S. (1995), "Towards quality control metrics for object-oriented systems analysis", *Proceedings of TOOLS Europe '95*, Versailles, France, March, pp. 193-206.

Badri, M., Davis, D. and Davis, D. (1995), "A study measurement the critical factors of quality management", *International Journal of Quality and Reliability Management*, Vol. 12 No. 2, pp. 36-53.

Ball, A., Bowerman, M. and Hawksworth, S. (2000), "Benchmarking in local government under a central government agenda", *Benchmarking: An International Journal*, Vol. 7 No. 1, pp. 20-34.

Balla, J., Harty, J. and Andrew, L. (1999"), Knowledge management comes of age", *Inform Journal*, Vol. 13 No. 7, pp. 22-9.

Bank, J. (1992), *The Essence of Total Quality Management*, Prentice Hall, London.

Barcala, M., Martin, D. and Gutierrez, J. (2000), "Training in retailing: a guide for improving the supply of courses", *International Journal of Retail & Distribution Management,* Vol. 28 No. 6, pp. 243-60.

Barclay, O. and Murray, C (2000), "What is knowledge management?", http://www.media-access.com/whatis.html#whatis, accessed 10 March 2002.

Bardenstein, R.L. and Gibson, G.J. (1992), "A QFD approach to integrated test planning", *ASQC Quality Congress Transactions*, Nashville, pp. 552-9.

Barker, R.L. (1991), "Basic improvement tools and total quality management" in Oakland, J.S. (Ed.), *Proceeedings of the 4th International Conference on Total Quality Management*, Warwick.

Barlow, K. (1995), 'Policy deployment in action at Kawneer", ASI Quality Systems 6th European Symposium for Taguchi Methods & QFD, Kenilworth, England, 16-18 May.

Bass, B.M. and Avolio, B.J. (1993), "Transformational leadership and organisational culture", *Public Admistration Quarterly*, Vol. 17 No. 1, pp. 112-21.

Bassi, L.J. (2000), "Measuring knowledge management effectiveness", in Hermans, J. (Ed.), *The Knowledge Management Yearbook 1999-2000*, Butterworth-Heinemann, pp. 422-7.

Bate, P. (1994), *Strategies for Cultural Change*, Butterworth Heinemann, Oxford.

Batten, J. (1994), "A total quality culture", *Management Review*, Vol. 83 No. 5, p. 61.

Beadle, L. and Searstone, K. (1995), "An investigation into the use of benchmarking within quality programme", in Kanji, G.K. (Ed.), *Total Quality Management, Proceedings of the First World Congress*, Chapman-Hall, London.

Beckford, J. (1998), *Quality: A Critical Introduction*, Routledge, London.

Bednar, C. (2000), "Capturing and packaging knowledge", in Hermans, J. (Ed.), *The Knowledge Management Yearbook 1999-2000*, Butterworth-Heinemann, pp. 211-19.

Bemowski, K. (1992), "Carrying on the P&G tradition", *Quality Progress*, Vol. 28 No. 5, pp. 21-5.

Bemowski, K. (1994), "A pat on the back is worth a thousand words", *Quality Progress*, Vol. 27 No. 3, pp. 51-4.

Bemowski, K. (1995a), "1994 Baldrige Award recipients share their expertise", *Quality Progress*, Vol. 28 No. 2, pp. 35-40.

Bemowski, K. (1995b), "To boldly go where so many have gone before", *Quality Progress*, Vol. 28 No. 2, pp. 29-33.

Bendell, T., Boulter, L. and Kelly, J. (1994), *Benchmarking for Competitive Advantage*, Pitman Publishing, London.

Bergendahl, S. and Wachmeister, A. (1993), "Creating an index", *Managing Service Quality*.

Berling, C. (2000), "Continuous improvement as seen from groups and 'improvement agents'", *Total Quality Management,* Vol. 11 No. 4-6, pp. S484-9.

Berry, T.H. (1991), *Managing the Total Quality Transformation*, McGraw-Hill, NY.

Berry, L.L., Bennett, D. and Brown, C.W. (1989), *Service Quality: A Profit Strategy for Financial Institution*, Irwin, NY.

Berry, L.L., Davidson, P.H. and Thompson, T.W. (1988), *Banking Tomorrow – Managing Markets Through Planning*, Van Nostrand Reinhold, NY.

Bertram, D. (1991), "Getting started in total quality management", *Total Quality Management*, Vol. 2 No. 3 pp. 279-82.

Bertsch, B. and Williams, R. (1994), "How multinational CEOs make change programme stick", *Long Range Planning*, Vol. 27 No. 5, pp. 3-11.

Bertels, T. (1996), "What is knowledge management,"? http://www.km-forum.org/whats. htm, accessed 15 January 2003.

Bester, Y. (1999), "Qualimetrics and qualieconomics", *The TQM Magazine*, Vol. 11 No. 6, pp. 425-43.

Binney, G. (1992), *Making Quality Work: Lessons from Europe's Leading Companies*, The Economist Intelligence Unit, London.

Bird, S. (no date), "Object-oriented expert system architectures for manufacturing quality management", *Journal of Manufacturing Systems*, Vol. 11 No. 1, pp. 50-60.

Black, S. and Porter, L. (1996), "Identification of critical factors of TQM", *Decision Sciences*, Vol. 27, pp. 1-21.

Black, R. (1993b), *Evaluating Social Science Research: Introduction*, Sage, London.

Black, S.A. (1993a), "Measuring the critical factors of total quality management", University of Bradford, unpublished PhD thesis.

Boaden, R.J. and Dale, B.G. (1994), "A generic framework for managing quality improvement: theory and practice", *Quality Management Journal*, July, pp. 11-29.

Bollinger, A.S. and Smith, R.D. (2001), "Managing organizational knowledge as a strategic asset", *Journal of Knowledge Management*, Vol. 5 No. 1, pp. 8-18.

Booth, D. (1995), "Benchmarking the essential phase of preparation", in Kanji, G. K. (Ed.), *Total Quality Management: Proceedings First World Congress*, Chapman & Hall, London.

Bowen, D. (1993), "One piece at a time", *European Quality*, pp. 55-8.

Boyer, S.M. (no date) "Total quality management and new product development", *Total Quality Management*, Vol. 2 No. 3, pp. 283-90.

Brah, S., Ong, A. and Rao, B. (2000), "Understanding the benchmarking process in Singapore", *International Journal of Quality & Reliability Management*, Vol. 17 No. 3, pp. 259-75.

Brah, S., Wong, J. and Rao, B. (2000), "TQM and business performance in the service sector: a Singapore study". *International Journal of Operations & Production Management*, Vol. 20 No. 11, pp. 1293-312.

Bratton, J. (2001), "Why workers are reluctant learners: the case of the Canadian pulp and paper industry", *Journal of Workplace Learning*, Vol. 13 No. 7/8, pp. 333-44.

Brocka, B. and Brocka, B.S. (1992), *Quality Management: Implementing the Best Ideas of the Masters*, Business One Irwin, Homewood, IL.

Browning, S.A. and Shaw, W.N. (1990), "Employees' views of TQM at two Hewlett-Packard manufacturing plants" in Oakland, J.S. (Ed.), *Proceeedings of the 3rd International Conference on Total Quality Management*, Warwick.

Brown and Van der Wiele (1995), "Industry experience with ISO 9000", *Asia Pacific Journal of Quality and Reliability Management*, Vol. 4 No. 29, pp. 8-17.

Buckman, R. (1998), "Knowledge sharing at Buckman Labs", *Journal of Business Strategy*, January-February, Vol. 19 No. 1, pp. 11-15.

Burgoyne, J. (1992), "Creating a learning organization", *ESA Journal*, April, pp. 321-32.

Burton, D. (1995), "The ideal lunch, building the heart of quality, the complete 'how to' QFD", QFD Workshop Conference, Bradford Management Centre, University of Bradford, 27 June.

Buyukizkan, G. and Maire, J. (1998), "Benchmarking process formalization and a case study", *Benchmarking for Quality Management & Technology*, Vol. 5 No. 2, pp. 101-25.

Campanella, J. (Ed) (1999), *Principles of Quality Costs. Principles, Implementation and Use*, 3rd ed., American Society for Quality, ASQ Quality Costs Committee.

Canchick, M. (2001), "Comparing the Brazilian National Quality Award with some of the major prizes", *The TQM Magazine*, Vol. 13 No.4.

Capon, N., Kaye, M.M. and Wood, M. (1994), "Measuring the success of a TQM programme", *International Journal of Quality and Reliability Management*, Vol. 12 No. 8, pp. 8-22.

Carman, J. (1993), "Continuous quality improvement as a survival strategy: the southern pacific experience", *California Management Review*, Vol. 35 No. 3, pp. 118-32.

Carter, P. and Edmonds, T. (1988), "Service quality at the Hewlett-Packard company", in Spechler, J.W. (Ed.), *When America Does It Right*, Industrial Engineering and Management Press, Norcross, GA.

Cashbourne, B. (1991), "Organising for total quality management", in Oakland, J. S. (Ed.), *Proceedings. 4th International Conference On Total Quality Management*, Warwick.

Cassell, C., Nadin, S. and Gray, M. (2001), "The use and effectiveness of benchmarking in SMEs", *Benchmarking: An International Journal*, Vol. 8 No. 3, pp. 212-22.

Castka, P., Bamber, C.J., Sharp, J.M. and Belohoubek, P. (2001), "Factors affecting successful implementation of high performance teams", *Team Performance Management*, Vol. 7 No. 7-8, pp. 123-34.

Catharine, G.J. and Daniel, M.J. (1991), *Customer Satisfaction through Quality – An International Perspective*, The Conference Borad of Canada, Ottawa, Ontario, Canada.

Chan, K., Chan, S.F. and Chan, C. (2001), "Integrated management", in Ho, S.M. and Donnelly, M. (Eds), *Proceedings of the International Conference on ISO 9000 and TQM*.

Chan, S. (1999), "Architecture choice for ERB systems", *Proceedings of the Americans Conference on Information Systems (AMICS)*, Milwaukee, WI.

Chaston, J. (1993), *Marketing for Professionals: Customer Focused Marketing*, McGraw Hill, pp. 144-5.

Civi, E. (2000), "Knowledge management as a competitive asset: a review", *Marketing Intelligence & Planning*, Vol. 18 No. 4, pp. 166-74.

Clarke, S. (1998), "Trade union and the non-payment of wages in Russia", *International Journal of Manpower*, Vol. 19 No. 1/2, pp. 68-94.

Clausing, D. (1994), *Total Quality Development, A Step-by-Step Guide to World-Class Concurrent Engineering*, ASME Press.

Claver, E., Gasco, J., Llopis, J. and Gonzalez, R. (2001), "The strategic process of a cultural change to implement total quality management: a case study", *Total Quality Management*, Vol. 12 No. 4, pp. 469-82.

Clemmer, J. (1990), *Firing on All Cylinders*, Judy Piatkus (Publishers) Ltd, London.

Clemmer, J. (1993), "The coming team crisis: five stumbling blocks or stepping stones to success", *CMA Magazine*, Vol. 67 No. 4, p. 30.

Cole, R.E. (1989), *Strategies for Learning-Small-Group Activities in American, Japanese and Swedish Industry*, University of California Press, London.

Coleman, R. (1991), "People and training – the progressive evolution of a training strategy in support of the implementation of total quality management", in Oakland, J.S. (Ed.), *Proceedings of the 4th International Conference on Total Quality Management*, Warwick.

Collinson, M. and Edwards, P.K. (1998), *The Puzzles of Empowerment*, Mimeo Industrial Relations Research Unit, Coventry.

Conger, J.A. and Kanungo, R.N. (1988), "The empowerment process: integrating theory and practice", *Academy of Management Review*, Vol. 13 No. 3, pp. 471-82.

Connors, R., Smith and Hickman, C. (1995), "Breaking the victim cycle", *World Executive's Digest,* August, pp. 38-40.

Conti, T. (1999), "Vision 2000: positioning the new ISO 9000 standards with respect to total quality management models", *Total Quality Management,* Vol.10 Nos. 4 and 5, pp. 454-64.

Conti, T. (1991), "Company quality assessment", *The TQM Magazine*, June/July, pp. 14-27.

Conway, P. (1991), "How successful is world bank lending for structural adjustment?", *Policy Research and External Working Paper*, No. 582, World Bank, Washington, DC.

Conway, T. and Willcocks, S. (2000), "Relationship-based service marketing", *International Journal of Public Sector Management*, Vol. 13 No. 1, pp. 68-84.

Cornford, J. (2001), "Integrating local resource", *Library Management*, Vol. 22 No. 1/2, pp. 19-20.

Coulson-Thomas, C.J. (1992), "Quality: where do we go from here?", *International Journal of Quality & Reliability Management*, Vol. 9 No. 1, pp. 38-55.

Court, C.J. (1995), "Creating the learning organization", TQM8 Conference, Stratford-upon-Avon, 11-13 June.

Creech, B. (1994), *The Five Pillars of TQM*, Pengiun Group, NY.

Crosby, P. (1979), *Quality is Free: The Art of Making Quality Certain*, Penguin Books, NY.

Crosby, P. (1984), *Quality Without Tears: The Art of Hassle-Free Management*, McGraw-Hill, NY.

Crosby, P. (1989), *Let's Talk Quality: 96 Questions That You Always Wanted To ask Phil Crosby*, McGraw-Hill, NY.

Cullen, J. and Hollingum, J. (1987), *Implementing Total Quality*, IFS Ltd, Bedford.

Cunningham, I. and Hyman, J. (1999), "The poverty of empowerment? A critical case study", *Personnel Review*, Vol. 28 No. 3, pp. 192-207.

Cupello, J.M. (1994), "A new paradigm for measuring TQM progress", *Quality Progress*, May, pp. 79-82.

Curt W.R. (1991), "Winning strategies for quality improvement", *Business America*, pp. 8-11.

Dale, B.G. and Blunket, J. (1990), *Managing Quality*, Philip Allen.

Dale, B.G. and Duncalf, A.J. (1988), "Quality-related decision making: a study of six British companies", *International Journal of Operations and Production Management*, Vol. 5 No. 1, pp. 15-25.

Dale, B.G. and Plunkett, J.J. (1991), *Quality Costing*, Chapman and Hall, London.

Dale, B.G. (1999), *Managing Quality*, 3rd ed., Blackwell, Oxford.

Dale, B.G., Van der Wiele, A. and Williams, A.R.T. (2001), Quality – why do organisations still continue to get it wrong?", *Managing Service Quality*, Vol. 11 No. 4, pp. 241-8.

Dale, B.G., Y-Wu, P., Zairi, M., Williams, A.R.T. and Van der Weile, T. (2001), "Total quality management and theory: an exploratory study of contributions", *Total Quality Management*, Vol. 12 No. 4, pp. 439-49.

Davenport, T. and Prusak, L. (1998b), "Know what you know", reprinted with permission of Harvard Business School Press and special arrangement with CIO Magazine, www.brint.com/km/davenport/cio/know.htm, accessed December 2000.

Davenport, T., DeLong, W. and Beers, C. (1998a), "Successful knowledge management projects", *Sloan Management Review*, Winter, Vol. 39 No. 2, pp. 43-58.

Davidson, A., Chelson, L., Stern, L. and Janes, F.(2001), "A new tool for assessing the presence of total quality", *The TQM Magazine*, Vol. 13 No. 1, pp. 12-24.

Davies, A. and Kochhar, A. (1999), "Why British companies don't do effective benchmarking", *Integrated Manufacturing Systems,* Vol. 10 No. 1, pp. 26-32.

Davies, B. and Wilson, D. (1990), "TQM – organising for success", in Oakland, J.S. (Ed.), *Proceedings of the 3rd International Conference on Total Quality Management,* Warwick.

Davis, T. (1993), "Effective supply chain management", *Sloane Management Review*, Vol. 34 No. 4, pp. 35-46.

DDI (1994), *TQM: Forging Ahead of Falling Behind – A Study of Quality Practices*, Development Dimensions International Inc., Bridgeville, PA.

Deissinger, T. (2001), "Vocational training in small firms in Germany: the contribution of the craft sector", *Education + Training*, Vol. 43 No. 8/9, pp. 426-36.

Deming, W.E. (1982), *Quality, Productivity and Competitive Position*, MIT Centre for Advanced Engineering Study, Cambridge, MA.

Deming, W.E. (1993), *The New Economics for Industry, Government, Education*, MIT Centre for Advanced Engineering Study, Cambridge, MA.

Deming, W.E. (1986), *Out of the Crisis*, MIT Center for Advanced Engineering Study, Cambridge, MA.

Deming, W.E. (1993), "Leading quality transformations", *Executive Excellence*, Vol. 10 No. 5, p. 4.

Deming, W.E. (1994), "Leadership for quality", *Executive Excellence*, Vol. 11 No. 2, pp. 3-5.

Denison, D.R. (1996), "What is the difference between organisational culture and organisational climate? A native's point of view on a decade of paradigm wars", *Academy of Management Review*, Vol. 21 No. 3, pp. 619-54.

Department of Statistics (1990), *Singapore Standard Industrial Classification 1990*, Singapore.

DeRose, L.J. (1987), "Changing procurement practices", *Purchasing World*, Vol. 31 No. 3, pp. 32, 88.

Dobyns, L. and Crawford, M. (1991), *Quality or Else: The Revolution in World Business,* Houghton Miffin, Boston, MA.

Douglas, T.J. and Judge, W. Q. Jr (2001), "Total quality management implementation and competitive advantage: the role of structural control and exploration", *Academy of Management Journal*, Vol. 44 No. 1, pp. 158-69.

Dow, D., Swanson, D. and Ford, S. (1999), "Exploring the myth: do all quality management practices contribute to superior quality performance", *Production and Operations Management*, Vol. 8 No. 1, pp. 1-27.

Drew, E. (1998), "In pursuit of excellence: total quality approaches in Irish organisations", *The TQM Magazine*, Vol. 10 No. 6, pp. 452-7.

Duffy, J. (2000), "The KM technology infrastructure", *Information Management Journal*, Vol. 34 No. 2, pp. 62-6.

Dumas, R. (1989), "Organisational quality: how to avoid common pitfalls", *Quality Progress*, Vol. 22 No. 55, pp. 41-4.

Durrant, P.W. (1990), "TQM and the cultural changes required", in Oakland, J.S. (Ed.), *Proceeedings of the 3rd International Conference on Total Quality Management*, Warwick.

Dyer, J.H. and Ouchi, W.G. (1993), "Japanese-style partnerships – giving company a competitive edge", *Sloan Management Review*, Vol. 35 No. 1, pp. 51-63.

Ealey, L. (1987), "QFD – bad name for a great system", *Automotive Industries*, Vol. 167, July, p. 21.

Easton, G.S., (1993), "The 1993 State of US total quality management: a Baldrige examiner's perspective", *California Management Review*, Vol. 35 No. 3, pp. 32-54.

Edosomwan, J.A. (1992), "Six commandments to empower employees for quality improvement", *Industrial Engineering*, Vol. 24 No. 7, pp. 14-15.

Edson, J. and Shannahan, R. (1991), "Managing quality across barriers", *Quality Progress*, February, pp. 45-7.

Edvardsson, B. (1991), "Service design: a powerful tool in quality improvement", University of Karlstad.

EFQM (1999), *The EFQM Business Excellence Model*, The European Foundation for Quality Management, www.efqm.org

EFQM (1992), Total *Quality Management: The European Model for Self-Appraisal 1992*, ISBN 90-5236-035-9, European Foundation for Quality Management.

EFQM (2003), *European Foundation for Quality Management Excellence Model*, EFQM, Brussels.

Elbadri, A.N. (2001), "Training practices of Polish companies: an appraisal and agenda for improvement", *Journal of European Industrial Training*, Vol. 25 No. 2/3/4, pp. 69-79.

Elshennaway, A.K., Maytubby, V.J. and Aly, N.A. (1991), "Concepts and attributes of total quality management", *Total Quality Management,* Vol. 2 No. 1, pp. 75-98.

Evans, J.R. and Lindsay, W.M. (2001), *The Management and Control of Quality*, 5th ed., West Publishing, NY.

Fagerfjall (1995), "Gurus are putting faith in the people", *The European*, 12-18 May, p.21.

Fan, I., Russell, S. and Lunn, R. (2000), "Supplier knowledge exchange in aerospace product engineering", *Aircraft Engineering and Aerospace Technology*, Vol. 72 No. 1, pp. 14-17.

Fawcett, S., Calantone, R. and Roath, A. (2000), "Meeting quality and cost imperatives in a global market", *International Journal of Physical Distribution & Logistics Management*, Vol. 30 No. 6, pp. 472-99.

Feigenbaum, A.V. (1989), "Seven keys to constant quality", *Journal for Quality and Participation*, pp. 20-3.

Feigenbaum, A.V. (1993), *Total Quality Control*, 3rd ed., McGraw-Hill, NY.

Feigenbaum, A.V. (1999), "The new quality for the twenty-first century", *The TQM Magazine*, Vol. 11 No. 6.

Feigenbaum, A. (1961), *Total Quality Control*, McGraw-Hill, London.

Feigenbaum, A.V. (1983), *Total Quality Control*, 2nd ed., McGraw-Hill, NY.

Fernandez, P., McCarthy, I. and Rakotobe-Joel, T. (2001), "An evolutionary approach to benchmarking", *Benchmarking: An International Journal*, Vol. 8 No. 4, pp. 281-305.

Findlay, P., McKinlay, A., Marks, A. and Thompson, P. (2000), "Labouring to learn: organisational learning and mutual gains", *Employee Relations*, Vol. 22 No. 5, pp. 485-502.

Findlay, I., Wilshaw, G. and Dale, B.G. (1990), "Total quality management in sales and marketing organisation: introduction and development", in Oakland, J.S. (Ed.), *Proceedings of the 3rd International Conference on Total Quality Management*, Warwick.

Finn, M. and Porter, L. (1994), "TQM self-assessment in the UK", *The TQM Magazine*, Vol. 6 No. 4, pp. 56-61.

Finneran, T. (1999), "A component-based knowledge management system", Robert S. Seiner, http://www.tdan.com/i009hy04.htm, accessed February 2003.

Flood, R.L. (1993), *Beyond TQM*, Wiley, Chichester.

Floyd, D., Willis, R. and Adcroft, A. (1999), "Economic policy making in the UK: to what extent should this be endorsed by other EU member countries?", *European Business Review*, Vol. 99 No. 6, pp. 376-82.

Flynn, B.B., Schroeder, R. and Sakakibara, S. (1995), "Determination of quality performance in high and low quality plants", *Quality Management Journal*, Vol. 2 No. 2, pp. 8-25.

Fong, S., Cheng, E. and Ho, C. (1998), "Benchmarking: a general reading for management practitioners", *Management Decision*, Vol. 36 No. 6, pp. 407-18.

Ford Motor Company Limited (1983), *Module 7, Customer Focused Engineering, Level 2, QFD Manual*, EQUIP (Engineering Quality Improvement Programme), published by Education and Training, EQUIP Centre, GB-26/500, Boreham Airfield, Essex, England.

Ford Motor Company Limited (1994), *Quick QFD, The Marketing - Engineering Interface*, Automotive Safety & Engineering Standards Office, Ford Motor Company Limited, Fairlane Plaza, Dearborn (restricted access),Version 3.0.

Ford Motor Company Limited (1994), *Ford Customer Satisfaction Process*, European Automotive Operations Powertrain QFD Steering Team, issued by the Customer Focused Engineering Group, Ford Motor Company, Vehicle Centre 1, Dunton Research & Engineering Centre, Essex, SS15 6EE, UK, Version One (restricted access).

Fountain, M. (1998), "The target assessment model as an international standard for self-assessment", *Total Quality Management,* Vol. 9 Nos. 4 and 5.

Fowler, A., Wibberley, M. and Shears, M. (1992), "Two routes to quality" *Personnel Management*, November, Vol. 24, November, pp. 30-4.

Fowler, C.T. (1991), "QFD – easy as 1-2-3", *Proceedings of 1991 SAVE (Society of American Engineers)*, Kansas City, MO, SAVE National Business Office, Vol. 26, pp. 177-82.

Gable, G., Scott, J. and Davenport, T. (1998), "Cooperative ERP life-cycle knowledge management", *Proceeding of the 9th Australasian Conference on Information Systems*, Sydney, Australia.

Garvin, D.A. (1987), "Competing on the eight dimensions of quality", *Harvard Business Review*, Vol. 65 No. 6, pp. 101-9.

Garvin, D.A. (1988), *Managing Quality: The Strategic and Competitive Edge,* McGraw-Hill, NY.

Garvin, D.A. (1993), "Building a Learning Organisation", *Harvard Business Review*, Vol. 71 No. 44, pp. 78-91.

Garvin, D.A. (1983), "Quality on the line", *Harvard Business Review*, Vol. 61 No. 5, pp. 65-75.

Gehani, R. (1993), "Quality value-chain: a meta-synthesis of frontiers of quality movement", *Academy of Management Executive*, Vol. 7 No. 2, pp. 29-42.

George, P.L. (1998), "Implementing a quality management programme – three Cs of success: commitment, culture, cost", *The TQM Magazine,* Vol. 10 No. 4, pp. 281-7.

George, S. and Weimerskirch, A. (1998), *Total Quality Management: Strategies and Techniques Proven at Today's Most Successful Companies*, Wiley, Chichester.

George, D. (1990), "The routine involvement of senior managers in the quality improvement process", in Oakland, J.S. (Ed.), *Proceedings of the 3rd International Conference on Total Quality Management,* Warwick.

Ghobadian, A. and Woo, H. (1996), "Characteristic benefits and shortcomings of four major quality awards", *International Journal of Quality & Reliability Management*, Vol. 13 No. 2, pp. 10-44.

Gilbert, G.R. (1993), "Employee empowerment: flaws and practical approaches", *The Public Manager/The New Bureaucrat*, Vol. 22 No. 3, pp. 45-8.

Gilbert, J. (1992), "TQM flops – a chance to learn from the mistakes of others", *National Productivity Review*, Vol. 11 No. 4, pp. 491-9.

Gilroy, A.J., (1994), "Automotive purchasing management's comparative approaches to supplier interface and development", University of Bradford: unpublished MBA dissertation.

Ginn, D. and Zairi, M. (2005), "The role of QFD in capturing the voice of customers", Working Paper, School of Management, University of Bradford, January.

Glenn, T. (1992), "Getting people to do what they want to do", *The Public Manager/The New Bureaucrat*, Vol. 21 No. 3, pp. 14-16.

Glover, J. (1993), "Achieving the organisational change necessary for successful TQM", *International Journal of Quality & Reliability Management,* Vol. 10 No. 6, pp. 47-64.

Godfrey, J. and Godfrey, P. (1999), "Benchmarking quality management", *Benchmarking: An International Journal*, Vol. 6 No. 1, pp. 40-59.

Goodstadt, P. (1990), "Exceeding customer satisfaction", in Oakland, J.S. (Ed.), *Proceedings of the 3rd International Conference on Total Quality Management*, Warwick.

Gopalakrishan, K.N., McIntyre, B.E. and Sprague, J.C. (1992), "Implementing internal improvement with the house of quality", *Quality Progress*, September, pp. 57-60.

Gorman, R.F. (2001), "Historical dictionary of refugee and disaster relief organisations", *Reference Reviews*, Vol. 15 No. 2.

Goulden, C. and Rawlins, L. (1995), "A hybrid model for process quality costing", *International Journal of Quality & Reliability Management*, Vol. 12 No. 8, pp. 32-47.

Gouvea, M., Toledo, G. and Fiiho, L. (2001), "The prices of mailing services evaluated by companies", *Marketing Intelligence & Planning*, Vol. 19 No. 4, pp. 282-94.

Govers, C.P.M. (2001), "QFD not just a tool but a way of quality management", *International Production of Economies*, Vol. 69, pp. 151-9.

Grahn, D.P. (1995), "The five drivers of total quality", *Quality Progress*, Vol. 28 No. 1, pp. 65-70.

Grant, R.M., Shani, R. and Krishran, R. (1994), "TQM's challenge to management theory and practice", *Sloan Management Review*, Vol. 35 No. 2, pp. 25-35.

Greenall, R. (1995), "Policy deployment", ASI Quality Systems 6th European Symposium for Taguchi Methods & QFD, Kenilworth, England, 16-18 May.

Grey, D. (1996), "What is knowledge management?", http://www.km-forum.org/what is.htm, accessed February 2003.

Gronroos, C. (1985), "Internal marketing – theory and practice", in Bloch, T.M. et al. (Eds), *Services Marketing in a Changing Environment*, American Marketing Association, pp. 41-7.

Gronroos, C. (1990), *Service Management and Marketing: Managing the coments of cruth in Service Competition*, Lexington Books, Boston, MA.

Gronroos, C. (2000), *Service Management and Marketing: A Customer Relationship Management Approach*, 2nd ed., Wiley, London.

Groocock, J.M. (1986), *The Chain of Quality*, John Wiley, Chichester.

Groth J.C. and Dye R.J. (1999), "Service quality: guidelines for marketers", *Managing Service Quality*, Vol. 9 No. 5, pp. 337-51.

Gruenberg, G. (1998), "Papal pronouncements on labour union and workplace democracy", *International Journal of Social Economics*, Vol. 25 No. 11/12.

Gunasekaran, A. (1999), "A framework for the design and audit of an activity-based costing system", *Managerial Auditing Journal*, Vol. 14 No. 3, pp. 118-27.

Gunasekaran, A., Patel, C. and Tirtiroglu, E. (2001), "Performance measures and metrics in a supply chain environment", *International Journal of Operations & Production Management*, Vol. 21 No. 1/2, pp. 71-87.

Gupta, B. and Iyer, L. (2000), "Knowledge management systems: an imperative for supporting the e-commerce customer", *Proceeding of the 2000 IRMA International Conference*, Ancharge, Alaska.

Hahn, G. (2001), "The proactive statistician", gerryhahn@yahoo.com

Haksever, C. (1996), "Total quality management in the small business environment", *Business Horizons*, March-April, pp. 33-40.

Hardaker, M. and Ward, B.K. (1987), "How to make a team work", *Harvard Business Review*, Vol. 65 No. 6, pp. 112-20.

Harrington, H.J. (1999), "Performance improvement: a manager for the twenty-first century – Part II", *The TQM Magazine*, Vol. 11 No. 1, pp. 5-7.

Harris, C.R. (1995), "The evolution of quality management: an overview of the TQM literature", *Canadian Journal of Administration Science*, Vol. 12 No. 2, pp. 95-107.

Hart, C. and Schlesinger, L. (1991), "Total quality management and the human resource professional: applying the Baldrige framework to human resources", *Human Resource Management*, Vol. 30 No.3, pp. 433-54.

Hauck, W.C. and Dingus, V.R. (1990), *Achieving High Commitment Work Systems – A Practioner's Guide to Socio-technical System Implementation*, Industrial Engineering and Management Press, Norcross, GA.

Hauser, J.R. and Clausing, D. (1988), "The House of Quality", *Harvard Business Review*, May-June, pp. 63-73.

Heath, P.M. (1989), "The path to quality achievement through teamwork plus commitment", *International Journal of Quality and Reliability Management*, Vol. 1 No. 2, pp. 51-9.

Heisig, P., Vorbeck, J. and Nirbuhr, J. (2001), "Intellectual capital", in Mertins, K., Heising, P. and Vorbeck, J. (Eds), *Knowledge Management Best Practices in Europe*, Springer-Verlag, Berlin, p. 57.

Hellsten, U. and Klefsjo, B. (2000), "TQM as a management system consisting of values, techniques and tools", *The TQM Magazine*, Vol. 12 No. 4, pp. 238-44.

Hermel, P. (1997), "The new faces of total quality in Europe and the US", *Total Quality Management*, Vol. 8 No. 4, pp. 131-43.

Henderson, D. (1992), "Exotic produce: the changing market in the UK", *British Food Journal*, Vol. 94 No. 8, p. 10.

Heng, M. (2001), "Mapping intellectual capital in a small manufacturing enterprise", *Journal of Intellectual Capital*, Vol. 2 No. 1, pp. 53-60.

Hill, R.C. (1993), "When the going gets tough: a Bridrige Award winner on the line", *Academy of Management Executive*, Vol. 7, August, pp. 75-9.

Hill, S. and Wilkinson, A. (1995), "In search of TQM", *Employee Relations*, Vol. 17 No. 3, pp. 8-25.

Hillman, F.G. (1994), "Making self-assessment successful", *The TQM Magazine*, Vol. 6 No.3.

Hirschhorn, L. and Gilmore, T. (1992), "The new boundaries of the boundaryless company", *Harvard Business Review*, Vol. 70 No. 3, pp. 104-15.

Hochman, S.D and O'Connell, P.A. (1993), "Quality function deployment : using the customer to outperform the competition on environmental design", IEE International Symposium on Electronics and Environment, Arlington NA, pp. 165-72.

383

Hoevemeyer, V.A. (1993), "How effective is your team?", *Training & Development*, Vol. 47 No. 9, pp. 67-71.

Hoffman, J.M. and Mehra, S. (1997), "Management leadership and productivity improvement programs", *International Journal of Applied Quality Management*, Vol. 2 No. 2, pp. 221-32.

Hofstede, G. (1984), *Cultures Consequences*, Sage, London.

Hoopes, J. (2003), *False Prophets*, Perseus Publishing, Cambridge, MA.

Hrones, S.M. (1993), *Vital Signs Using Quality, Time and Cost Performance Measurrements to Chart Your Company's Future*, AMACOM, NY.

Hubert, S.O. (1996), "Tacit knowledge: the key to the strategic alignment of intellectual capital", *Strategy and Leadership*, Vol. 24 No. 2, pp. 10-14.

Hunt, D. (1993), *Managing for Quality: Integrating Quality and Business Strategy*, Irwin, Homewood, IL.

Hunt, W. and Hillman, G.P. (1990), "Achieving the real culture change necessary for TQM", in Oakland, J.S. (Ed.), *Proceeedings of the 3rd International Conference on Total Quality Management*, Warwick.

Huq, Z. and Martin, T.N. (2000), "Workforce cultural factors in TQM/CQI implementation in hospitals", *Health Care Management Review*, Vol. 25 No. 3, pp. 80-93.

Huston, L.A. (1992), "Implementing change – executing strategy at Proctor & Gamble", *Strategic Direction*, No. 84, October, pp. 28-30.

Hutchins, D. (1992), *Achieve Total Quality*, Director Books, Cambridge.

Hutt, G. (1990), Quality – The proper way to managing" in Oakland, J.S. (Ed.), *Proceedings of the 3rd International Conference on Total Quality Management*, Warwick.

Iaquinto, A. (1999), "Can winners be losers? The case of the Deming prize for quality and performance among large Japanese manufacturing firms", *Managerial Auditing Journal*, Vol. 14 No. 1/2, pp. 28-35.

Imai, M. (1986), *Kaizen: The Key to Japan's Competitive Success*, McGraw-Hill, NY.

Ingle, S., (1982), "How to avoid quality circle failure in your company", Training and Development Journal, Vol. 36 No. 6., pp 54-59.

Ishikawa, K. (1985), *What is Total QualityControl? The Japanese Way*, Prentice-Hall, Englewood Cliffs, NJ.

ISO (1990), *Quality Management and Quality Assurance Standards, Part III: Guidelines for the Application of ISO 9001 to the Development, Supply and Maintenance of Software*, ISO.

Israeli, A. and Fisher, B. (1991), "Cutting quality costs", *Quality Progress*, January, pp. 46-8.

Jackson, S. (1999), "Achieving a culture of continuous improvement by adopting the principles of self-assessment and business excellence", *International Journal of Health Care Quality Assurance*, Vol. 12 No. 2, pp. 59-64.

Jacqueline, A.M. and Shapiro, C. (1999), "Employee participation and assessment of an organisational change intervention three-wave study of total quality management", *Journal of Applied Behavioral Science*, Vol. 35 No. 4, pp. 439-56.

Jamal, T. (1998), "TQM drive for innovation: an Indian experience", *Proceedings of the Third International Conference on ISO and TQM*, Hong Kong, pp. 15-21.

James, P. (1996), *Total Quality Management: An Introductory Text*, Prentice Hall, London.

Japan Digest and Asia Pacific Economic Review (no date), "The legacy of W. Edwards Deming".

Jarrar, Y. and Zairi, M. (2000), "Best practice transfer for future competitiveness: a study of best practices", *Total Quality Management*, Vol.11 Nos 4/5 and 6, pp. 734-40.

Johnston, C.G. and Daniel, M.J. (1991), *Customer Satisfaction Through Quality, An International Perspective,* The Conference Board of Canada, Ottawa, Ontario, Canada.

Johnson, R.S. (1993), "TQM: leadership for the quality transformation", *Quality Progress*, Vol. 26 No. 1-5.

Joiner and Gaudard (1990), *Quality Progress,* December.

Juran, J.M. (1974), *Quality Control Handbook*, McGraw-Hill, London.

Juran, J.M. (1978), "Japanese and Western quality: a contrast in methods and results", *Management Review*, Vol. 67 No. 11, pp. 27-45.

Juran, J.M. (1979), "Japanese and Western quality", *Quality Assurance*, No. 1, March, pp. 12-17.

Juran, J.M. (1981), "Product quality: a prescription for the west (Part I)", *Management Review*, Vol. 70 No. 6, pp. 8-14.

Juran, J.M. (1986), "A universal approach to managing for quality", *Quality Progress*, August, pp. 19-24.

Juran, J.M. (1988a), *Juran on Planning for Quality*, Free Press, New York.

Juran. J.M. (1988b), *Juran's New Quality Roadmap*, Free Press, NY.

Juran, J.M. (1991), "The evolution of Japanese leadership in quality", *Journal of Quality and Participation*, Vol. 14 No. 4, pp. 72-7.

Juran, J.M. (1992), *Juran on Quality by Design*, Free Press, New York.

Juran, J.M. (1993a), "Made in USA: a renaissance in quality", *Harvard Business Review*, Vol. 71 No 4, pp. 42-50.

Juran, J.M. (1993b), "A Renaissance in quality", *Harvard Business Review*, Vol. 71 No. 4, pp. 42-50.

Juran, J.M. (1989), *Juran on Leadership for quality: An Executive Handbook*, Free Press, NY.

Juran, J.M. (1992), "Departmental quality planning", *National Productivity Review*, Vol. 11 No. 3, pp. 287-300.

Juran, J.M. (1993), "Why quality initiatives fail", *Journal of Business Strategy*, Vol. 14, pp. 35-8.

Juran, J.M. (1994), "The upcoming of quality", *Quality Progress*, Vol. 27 No. 1, pp. 29-37.

Juran, J.M. (Ed.) (1995), A History of Managing for Quality: The Evolution, Trends, and Future Directions of Managing for Quality, ASQC Quality Press, Milwaukee, WI.

Juran, J.M. (1997), "Early SQC Historical Supplement", Quality Progress, September, Vol. 30 No. 9, pp. 73-81.

Juran, J.M. (2002), *A Call to Action*, Minneapolis.

Juran, J.M. (2004), *Architect of Quality*, McGraw-Hill, NY.

Juran, J.M. and Godfrey, B.A. (1999), *Juran's Quality Handbook,* 5th ed., McGraw Hill, NY.

Juran, J.M. and Gryna, (1993), *Quality Planning and Analysis*, McGraw-Hill.

Kaplan, R.S. and Norton, D. (1992), "The balanced scorecard: measures that drive performance", *Harvard Business Review*, vol. 70 No. 1, pp. 71-9.

Kangis, P., Gordon, D. and Williams, S. (2000), "Organisational climate and corporate performance: an empirical investigation", *Management Decision*, Vol. 38 No. 8, pp. 531-40.

Kanji, G.K. (1990), "Total quality management: the second industrial revolution", *Total Quality Management*, Vol. 1 No. 1, pp. 3-11.

Kanji, G.K. and Yui, H. (1997), "Total quality culture", *Total Quality Management*, Vol. 8 No. 6, pp. 417-26

Kanji, G.K. and Asher, M. (1993), *Total Quality Management Process – A Systematic Approach*, Advances in Total Quality Management Series, Carfax Publishing Co., Abingdon.

Kanji, G.K. (1995), "Quality and statistical concepts", in Kanji, G.K. (Ed.), *Total Quality Management: Proceedings of the First World Congress*, Chapman & Hall, London.

Kanji, G.K. (1998), "An innovative approach to make ISO 9000 Standards more effective", *Total Quality Management*, Vol. 9 No. 1, pp. 67-78.

Kanji, G.K., Tambi, A.M. and Wallace, W. (1999), "A comparative study of quality practices in higher education institutions in the US and Malaysia", *Total Quality Management*, Vol. 10 No. 3, pp. 357-71.

Kano, N. (1993), "A perspective on quality activities in American firms", *California Management Review*, Vol. 35 No. 3, pp. 12-31.

Karabatsos, N. (1988), "Listening to the voice of the customer", editorial, *Quality Progress*, June, p. 5.

Kastetter, T. (1999), "Quality concepts and litigation: the role of record-keeping in products liability litigation in the USA", *Management Decision*, Vol. 37 No. 8, pp. 633-43.

Kathawala, Y.and Motwani, J. (1994), "Implementing quality function deployment, a systems approach", *The TQM Magazine*, Vol. 6 No. 6, pp. 31-7.

Keung, N. (2000), "Performance indicators and quality assurance", *Pang Sun Keung, Education Journal*, Hong Kong-Chinese University of Hong Kong, Vol. 28 No. 2, pp. 137-56.

Kim, S.H. and Ooi J.A. (1991), "Product performance as a unifying theme in concurrent design – II", *Software, Robotics & Computer-Integrated Manufacturing*, Vol. 8 No.2, pp. 127-34.

Kimmerling, G. (1993), "Gathering best practices", *Training & Development*, Vol. 47 No. 9, pp. 29-36.

Kite, P. (1990), "Quality purchasing", *Logistics Today*, May-June, pp. 19-25.

Kleiner, B.M. (1994), "Benchmarking for continuous performance improvement", *Total Quality Environmental Management*, Spring, pp. 283-95.

Kohli, A.K. and Jaworski, B.J. (1990), "Market orientaion: the construct, research propositions and managerial implications", *Journal of Marketing*, Vol. 54 No. 2, pp. 1-18.

Kolesar, P.J. (1993), "Vision, values, milestones: Paul O'Neill starts total quality at Alcoa", *California Management Review*, Vol. 35 No. 3, pp. 133-65.

Kordupleski, R.E., Rust, R.T. and Zahorik, A.J. (1993), "Why improving quality doesn't improve quality (or whatever happened to marketing?)", *California Management Review*, Vol. 35 No. 3, pp. 82-95.

Krantz, K.T. (1989), "How Velcro got hooked on quality", *Harvard Business Review*, Vol. 67 No. 5., pp. 34-40.

Krasachali, L. and Tannock, J.D.T. (1999), "A study of TQM implementation in Thailand", *International Journal of Quality and Reliability Management*, Vol. 6 No. 5, pp. 418-32.

Krasachol, L. and Tannock, J. (1998), "A study of TQM implementation in Thailand", *International Journal of Quality & Reliability Management*, Vol. 16 No. 5, pp. 418-32.

Kruger, V. (1999), "Towards a European definition of TQM: a historical review", *The TQM Magazine*, Vol. 11 No. 4, pp. 257-63.

Kyte, R. (1991), "Departmental purpose analysis/quality policy deployment", in Oakland, J.S. (Ed.), *Proceedings of the 4th International Conference on Total Quality Management*, Warwick.

Landesberg, P. (1999), "In the beginning, there were Deming and Juran", *Journal for Quality and Participation*, November/December, pp. 59-61.

Lashley, C. (1997), *Empowering Service Excellence: Beyond the Quick Fix*, Cassell, London.

Laszlo, G.P. (1999), "Implementing a quality management programme – three Cs of success: commitment, culture and cost", *The TQM Magazine*, Vol. 11 No. 4, pp. 231-7.

Lawler, E. (1994), "Total quality management and employee involvement, are they compatible?", *Academy of Management Executive*, Vol. 8 No. 1, pp. 68-76.

Lawler III, E.E. and Mohrman, S.E. (1985), "Quality Circle after the fad", *Harvard Business Review*, Vol. 63 No 1, pp. 65-71.

Lee, M. and Cunningham, L. (2001), "A cost/benefit approach to understanding service loyalty", *Journal of Services Marketing*, Vol. 15 No. 2, pp. 113-30.

Lee, H. and Howard, J.L. (1994), "Measuring the quality of services: the use of internal climate", *Benchmarking: An International Journal*, Vol. 1 No. 3, pp. 39-51.

Lee, R. and Dale, B. (1998), "Policy deployment: an examination of the theory", *International Journal of Quality & Reliability Management*, Vol. 15 No. 5, pp. 520-40.

Leitner, P. (1999), "Japan's post-war economic success: Deming, quality and contextual realities", *Journal of Management History*, Vol. 5 No. 8, pp. 489-505.

Lewis, R.G. and Smith, D.H. (1994), *Total Quality in Higher Education*, St. Lucie Press. FL.

Lidetka, J.M., Weber, C. and Weber, J. (1999), "Creating a significant and sustainable executive education experience", *Journal of Managerial Psychology*, Vol. 14 No. 5, pp. 404-20.

Liker, J., Kamath, R. and Wasti, S. (1998), "Supplier involvement in design: a comparative survey of automotive suppliers in the USA, UK and Japan", *International Journal of Quality Science*, Vol. 3 No. 3, pp. 214-38.

Lim, K., Pervaiz, A. and Zairi, M. (2000), "The role of sharing in knowledge management initiatives", Working Paper No. 0005, Bradford: Management Centre, University of Bradford.

Litwin, M.S. (1995), *How to Measure Survey Reliability and Validity*, Sage Publications, Thousand Oaks, CA.

Liu, J., Ding, F. and Lall, V. (2000), "Using data envelopment analysis to compare suppliers for supplier selection and performance improvement", *Supply Chain Management: An International Journal*, Vol. 5 No. 3, pp. 143-50.

Lloyds Register Quality Assurance Ltd (1994), *BS5750/ISO9000 – Setting Standards for Better Business*, Llyods Register Quality Assurance Services, Croyden.

London, C. and Higgot, K. (1997), "An employee reward and recognition process", *The TQM Magazine*, Vol 9 No 5, pp. 328-35.

Longenecker, C.O. and Scazzero, J.A. (1993), "Total quality management from theory to practice: a case study", *International Journal of Quality and Reliability Management*, Vol. 10 No. 5, pp. 24-31.

Longbottom, D. (2000), "Benchmarking in the UK: an empirical study of practitioners and academics", *Benchmarking: An International Journal*, Vol. 7 No. 2, pp. 98-117.

Lorentzen, P. (1992), "Public leadership 1986-1992: so what's different?, *The Public Manager/The New Bureaucrat*, Vol. 21 No. 3, pp. 31-4.

Lorenzen, J.A., Iqbal, A., Erz, K. and Rosenberger, L.M. (1993), "QFD, DOE and SPC in a process for total quality", *ASQC Quality Congress Transactions*, Boston, pp. 421-7.

Luzon, M.D.M (1988), "Quality circles and organisation culture", *The International Journal of Quality and Reliability Management*, Vol. 5 No. 4, pp. 46-56.

Lynn, B. (1998), "Intellectual capital", *Canadian Management Accountant (CMA)*, Vol. 72 No. 1, pp. 6-10.

Macdonald, J. (1998), "The quality revolution in retrospect", *The TQM Magazine*, Vol. 10 No. 5, pp. 321-33.

Macedo-Soares, T.D.L.V. and Lucas, D.C. (1996), "Key quality management practices of leading firms in Brazil: findings of a pilot study", *The TQM Magazine*, Vol. 8 No. 4, pp.55-70.

Macintosh, A. (1998), "Position paper on knowledge asset management", http://www.aiai.ed.ac.uk/~alm/kam.html, accessed 14 January 2002.

Mak, W. (2000), "The Tao of people-based management", *Total Quality Management*, Vol. 11 No. 4/6, pp. S537-43.

Makower, J. (1993), *The E-factor: The Bottom Line Approach to Environmentally Responsible Business*, Tilden Press Inc., NY.

Manasco, B. (1997a), "Dow Chemical capitalises on intellectual assets", *Knowledge Inc.*, Vol. 2 No.3, pp. 1-4.

Manasco, B. (1997b), "Silicon Graphics delivers powerful knowledge network", *Knowledge*, Vol. 2 No. 3, pp. 1-5.

Manasco, B. (1999), "The knowledge imperative: leverage it or lose it", http://webcom. com/quantera/empires5.html, accessed 14 January 2002.

Mangelsdorf, D. (1999), "Evolution from quality management to an integrative management system based on tqm and its impact on the profession of quality managers in industry", *The TQM Magazine*, Vol. 11 No. 6, p. 419.

Mann, R.S. (1992), "The development of a framework to assist in the implementation of TQM", University of Liverpool, unpublished PhD Thesis.

Mann, R.S. and Kehoe, D. (1995), "Factors affecting the implementation and success of TQM", *International Journal of Quality and Reliability Management*, Vol. 12 No. 1, pp. 11-23.

Manz, C.C. and Sims, H.P. (1993), *Business Without Bosses*, John Wiley, NY.

Marchington, M., Goodman, J., Wilkinson, A. and Ackers, P. (1992), *New Developments in Employee Involvement*, Department of Employment Research Series No. 2, HMSO, Sheffield.

Martin, J.R. (no date), Management and Accounting Web (MAAW).

Martinez-Lorente, A., Dewhurst, F. and Dale, B. (1998), "Total Quality Management: Origins and EVolution of the Term", The TQM Magazine, Vol. 10 No. 6, pp. 378-86.

Masella, C. and Rangone, A. (2000), "A contingent approach to the design of vendor selection systems for different types of co-operative customer/supplier relationships", *International Journal of Operations & Production Management*, Vol. 20 No. 1, pp. 70-84.

Master, W. (1992), "Introduction to forum: challenges for today's public manager", *The Public Manager/The New Bureaucrat*, Vol. 21 No. 3, pp. 11-13.

Mathews, B., Ueno, A., Kekale, T., Repka, M., Periera, A. and Silva, G. (2001a), "Quality training: needs and evaluation-findings from a European survey", *Total Quality Management*, Vol. 12 No. 4, pp. 483-90.

Mathews, B., Ueno, A., Kekale, T. and Repka, M. (2001b), "European quality management practices", *International Journal of Quality & Reliability Management*, Vol. 18 No. 7, pp. 692-707.

McAdam, R. and Bannister, A. (2001), "Business performance measurement and change management within TQM framework", *International Journal of Operation and Production Management*, Vol. 20 No. 63, pp. 634-55.

McAdam, R., Armstrong, G. and Kelly, B. (1998), "Investigation of the relationship between total quality and innovation: a research study involving small organisations", *European Journal of Innovation Management*, Vol. 1 No. 3, pp. 139-47.

McAdam, R. and O'Neill, E. (1999), "Taking a critical perspective to the European Business Excellence model using a balanced scorecard approach: a case study in the service sector", *Managing Service Quality*, Vol. 9, pp.191-7.

McAdam, R. and Reid, R. (2000), "A comparison of public and private sector perceptions and use of knowledge management", *Journal of European Industrial Training*, Vol. 24 No. 6, pp. 317-29.

McAdam, R. (1996), "An integrated business improvement methodology to refocus business improvement efforts", *Business Process Re-engineering & Management Journal*, Vol. 2 No. 1, pp. 63-71.

McAdam, R. and Welsh, W. (2000), "A critical review of the business excellence quality model applied to further education colleges", *Quality Assurance in Education*, Vol. 8 No.3, pp. 120-30.

McDermott, L. (1993), "Jump-starting managers on quality", *Training & Development*, Vol. 47 No. 9, pp. 37-40.

McGill, M.E. and Slocum, J.W. (1994), *The Smarter Organization – How to Build a Business that Learns and Adadpts to Marketplace Needs*, John Wiley, NY.

McElroy, J. (1989), "QFD, building the house of quality", *Automotive Industries*, January, pp. 30-2.

McNair, C.J. and Leibfried, L. (1992), *Benchmarking: A Tool for Continuous Improvement*, Harper Business, NY.

McTeer, M. and Dale, B. (1996), "The attitudes of small companies to the ISO 9000 series", *Journal of Engineering Manufacture*, Part B, Vol. 210, pp. 397-403.

Mentzas, G., Apostolou, D., Young, R. and Abecker, A. (2001), "Knowledge networking: a holistic solution for leveraging corporate knowledge", *Journal of Knowledge Management*, Vol. 5 No. 1, pp. 94-106.

Mercer, D.S. and Judkins, P.E. (1990), "Rank Xerox: a total quality process" in Dale, B.G. *et al.* (Eds), *Managing Quality*, Philip Allan, Hemel Hempstead.

Merron, K.A., (1994), "Creating TQM organisations", *Quality Progress*, Vol. 27 No. 1, pp. 51-4.

Mertins, K., Heisig, P. and Vorbeck, J. (2001), *Knowledge Management Best Practices in Europe*, Springer-Verlag, Berlin, Heidelberg, NY.

Millar, I. (1999), "Performance improvement. Part 1. Forget the acronyms", *Industrial Management & Data Systems*, Vol. 99 No. 4, pp. 172-80.

Mitchell, C.M. (1995), "Preparing for benchmarking: an effective benchmarking strategy", in Kanji, G.K. (Ed.), *Total Quality Management: Proceedings of the First World Congress*, Chapman-Hall, London.

Modaress, B. and Aussari, M. (1989), "Quality control techniques in US firms: a survey", *Production and Inventory Management Journal*, 2nd quarter.

Moen, R. (1998), "New quality cost model used as a top management tool", *The TQM Magazine*, Vol. 10 No. 5, pp. 334-41.

Mohanty, R.P. and Lakhe, R. (1998), "Factors affecting TQM implemention: an empirical study in Indian industry", *Production Planning and Control*, Vol. 9 No. 5, pp. 511-20.

Montes, J.L., Jover, A.V. and Fernandez, L.M (2003), "Factors affecting the relationship between total quality management and organisational performance", *International Journal of Quality & Reliability Management*, Vol. 20 No. 2, pp. 189-209.

Moran, J. (1998), "Patterns pointing to the future of HRMS", *IHRIM Journal*.

Morse, R. (2000). "Knowledge management systems: using technology to enhance organizational learning", Information Resources Management Association (IRMA), International Conference, Anchorage, Alaska, 21-24 May, pp. 426-9.

Motwani, J.G., Mohamoud, E. and Rice, G. (1994), "Quality practices of Indian organisations: an empirical analysis", *International Journal of Quality and Reliability Management,* Vol. 11 No. 1, pp. 38-52.

Mullins, C.S. (1998), "What is knowledge and can it be managed?" Robert S. Seine, www.tdan.com/i008fe03.htm, accessed 10 January 2002.

Nadkarni, R.A. (1995), "A not-so-secret recipe for successful TQM", *Quality Progress,* Vol. 28 No. 11, pp. 91-6.

Nanus, B. (1992), *Visionary Leadership: Creating a Compelling Sense of Direction for Your Organisation*, Joey-Bass, San Francisco.

Neave, H.R. (2000), "Inaugural address", Nottingham Trent University, 25 August.

Newman, R.G., (1988), "Primary source qualification", *Journal of Purchasing & Material Management*, Summer, pp. 10-17.

Newman, A. (1999), "Knowledge management", Info-line No.9903, March, pp.1-15.

Ngowi, A. (2000), "Impact of culture on the application of TQM in the construction industry in Botswana", *International Journal of Quality & Reliability Management,* Vol. 17 No. 4/5, pp. 442-52.

NIST (1999), *Malcolm Baldrige National Quality Award Criteria*, US Department of Commerce, National Institute of Standards and Technology.

NIST (1994), *Malcolm Baldrige National Quality Award: 1994 Award Criteria*, National Institute of Standards and Technology, US Department of Commerce, Gaithersburg, MD.

NIST (2003), *MBNQA Criteria 2003, Malcolm Baldridge Award 2003 Education Criteria for Performance Excellence*, National Institute of Standards and Technology, www.quality.nist.gov [accessed 1 November 2003].

Nonaka, I. and Konno, N. (2000). "The concept of "ba": building a foundation for knowledge creation", in Hermans, J. (Ed.), *The Knowledge Management Yearbook 1999 – 2000*, Butterworth-Heinemann, pp. 37-51.

Nonaka, I. (1991), "The knowledge-creating company", *Harvard Business Review*, Vol. 69 No. 6, pp. 96-104.

Nonaka, I., Umemoto, K. and Senoo, D. (1996), "From information processing to knowledge creation: the knowledge-creating company", *Technology in Society*, Vol. 18 No. 2, pp. 203-18.

Nonaka, I. and Takeuchi (1995), *The Knowledge-creating Company: How Japanese Companies Create the Dynamics of Innovation*, Oxford University Press, UK.

Nwabueze, U. (2001a), "An industry betrayed: the case of total quality management in manufacturing", *Total Quality Management*, Vol. 13 No. 6, pp. 400-9.

Nwabueze, U. (2001b), "Chief executives – hear thyselves: leadership requirements for 5-S/TQM implementation in healthcare", *Managerial Auditing Journal,* Vol. 16 No. 7, pp. 406-10.

O'Dell, C. and Grayson, J. (2000b), "Identifying and transferring internal best practices; the role of measurement", http://www.apqc.org/free/whitepapers/dispWhitePaper.cfm?ProductID=665, accessed 12 January 2002.

O'Dell, C. and Grayson, J. (2000a), "If we only knew what we know at TI: identification and transfer of internal best practices", http://www.apqc.org/free/whitepapers/dispWhitePaper.cfm?ProductID=665, accessed 12 September 2002.

O'Reilly, C.A. III, Chatman, J. and Caldwell, D.F. (1991), "People and organisational culture: a profile comparison approach to assessing person-organisation fit", *Academy of Management Journal*, Vol. 34 No. 3, pp. 487-516.

Oakland, J. (1989), *Total Quality Management*, 1st ed., Heinemann-Butterworth, London.

Oakland, J.S. (1993), *Total Quality Management*, 2nd ed., Butterworth-Heinemann, Oxford.

Oakland, J.S. (2000), *Total Quality Management – Text with Cases*, 2nd ed., Butterworth-Heinemann, Oxford.

Oakland, J.S. and Porter, L. (1994), *Cases in Total Quality Management*, Butterworth-Heinemann, Oxford.

Oakland, J.S. and Beardmore, D. (1995), "Best practice customer service", *Total Quality Management*, Vol. 6 No. 2, pp. 135-48.

Oakland, J.S. (1999), *Total Organizational Excellence: Achieving corld-class Performance*, Butterworth-Heinemann, Oxford.

Ohno, T. (1988), *Toyota Production System Beyond Large-Scale Production*, Productivity Press, Portland, OR.

Olian, J.D. and Rynes, S.L. (1991), "Making total quality work: aligning organisational processes, performance measures and stakeholders", *Human Resource Management*, Vol. 30 No. 3, pp. 303-33.

Ott, J.S. (1989), *The Organisational Culture Perspective*, Dorsey, Chicago.

Pannireselvam, G. and Ferguson, L. (2001), "A study of the relationships between the Baldrige categories", *International Journal of Quality & Reliability Management*, Vol. 18 No. 1, pp. 14-37.

Parasuraman, A., Zeithaml, V.A. and Berry, L.L. (1988), "SERVQUAL: a multiple-item scale for measuring customer perception of service quality", *Journal of Retailing*, Vol. 64 No. 1, pp. 14-40.

Patel, A. (1995), "The long view of total quality management pays off", *International Journal of Quality & Reliability Management*, Vol. 12 No.7, pp. 75-87.

Paton, R. (2001), "Developing businesses and people: an MBA solution?", *The Journal of Management Development*, Vol. 20 No. 3, pp. 235-44.

Pegels, C.C. (1993), "Total quality management defined in terms of reported practice", *International Journal of Quality & Reliability Management*, Vol. 11 No. 5, pp. 6-18.

Perlman, S.L. and Zacharias, M. (1991), "Can the quality movement succeed in healthcare?", *Journal for Quality and Participation*, January/February, pp. 54-8.

Pervaiz, A., Lim, K. and Zairi, M. (1999), *Measurement Practice for Knowledge Management*, University of Bradford.

Peters, T. (1989), *Thriving on Chaos*, Pan Book Ltd, London.

Peters, T. and Waterman, R. (1982), *In Search of Excellence*, Harper and Row, NY.

Pitt, D. (1999), "Improving performance through self-assessment", *International Journal of Health Care Quality Assurance*, Vol. 12 No. 2, pp. 45-54.

Platt, N. (1998), "Knowledge management: can it exist in a law office?", http://www.llrx.com/features/km.htm, accessed 13 January 2002.

Plunkett, J.J. and Dale, B.G. (1990), "Quality costing", in Dale, B.G. *et al.* (Eds), Managing Quality, Philip Allan, Hemel Hempstead.

Plunkett, J.J. and Dale, B.G., (1987), "A review of the literature on quality-related costs", *International Journal of Quality & Reliability Management*, Vol. 27 No. 1, pp. 69-81.

Pluskowski, B. (2002), "Dynamic knowledge systems", http://www.imaginatik.com/web.nsf/docs/idea_reports_imaginatik!open, accessed May 2003.

Porter, L.J. and Parker, A.J. (1993), "Total quality management: the critical success factors", *Total Quality Management*, Vol. 4 No. 1, pp. 13-22.

Porter, L.I. and Tanner, S.I. (1995), "Business improvement through self-assessment – a case study from financial services", in Kanji, G.K. (Ed.), *Total Quality Management, Proceedings of the First World Congress*, Chapman & Hall, London.

Porter, L.J. and Rayner, P. (1992), "Quality costing for total quality management", *International Journal for Production Economics*, Vol. 27 No. 1, pp. 69-81.

Potter, M. (1994), "QFD as a marketing tool", MBA thesis, Management Centre, University of Bradford.

Powell, T.C. and Dent-Micalef, A. (1997), "Information technology as competitive advantage: the role of human, business and technology resources", *Strategic Management Journal*, Vol. 18 No. 5, pp. 375-405.

Powell, T.C. (1995), "Organisational alignment as competitive advantage", *Strategic Management Journal*, Vol. 13 No. 2, pp. 15-37.

Powers, V. (1994), "The sweet smell of success", *Continuous Journey*, October/November, pp. 18-24.

Poynder, R. (1998), "Getting to the nuts and bolts of knowledge management", *Information World Review*, Vol. 135 No. 135, p. 20.

Prabhu, V.B. and Robson, A. (2000a), "Impact of leadership and senior management commitment on business excellence: An empirical study in the North East of England", *Total Quality Management*, Vol. 11 No. 4-6, pp. S399-S409.

Prabhu, V.B. and Robson, A. (2000b), "Achieving service excellence – measuring impact of leadership and senior management commitment", *Managing Service Quality*, Vol. 10 No. 5, pp. 307-17.

Price, M. and Chen, E. (1993), "Total quality management in a small, high-technology company", *California Management Review*, Vol. 35 No. 3, pp. 96-117.

Price, R.C. and Gaskill, G.P., (1990), "Total quality management in research – philosophy and practice", in Oakland, J.S. (Ed.), Proceedings of the 3rd International Conference on Total Quality Management, Warwick.

Prybutok, V.R. and Kappelman, L.A (1995), "Early empowerment creates productive outcomes during an organisational transformation", *Work Study*, Vol. 44 No. 7, pp. 15-18.

Pulat, B.M. (1994), "Total quality management: a framework for application in manufacturing", *The TQM Magazine*, Vol. 6. No. 4, pp. 44-9.

Quality Progress (1994), "Companies that link quality to reward program report success", *Quality Progress*, Vol. 27 No. 4, pp. 15, 18.

Quality Progress (1993), "Middle Managers can inhibit TQM", *Quality Progress*, Vol. 26 No. 7, pp. 97-100.

Quality Progress (1995), "Workforce study identifies most valued employee characteristics", *Quality Progress*, Vol. 28 No. 9, p. 14.

Quazi, H.A. and Padibjo, S.R. (1998), "A journey toward total quality management through ISO 9000 certification–a study on small and medium–sized enterprises in Singapore", *International Journal of Quality and Reliability Management*, Vol. 15, pp. 489-508.

Quiros, G.M. (1994), "Integrated performance measurement", University of Bradford, unpublished MBA dissertation.

Radding, A. (1998), *Knowledge Management; Succeeding in the Information-based Global Economy*, Computer Technology Research Corp., Charleston, SC.

Ramirez, C. and Loney, T. (1993), "Baldrige Award winners identify the essential activities of a successful quality process", *Quality Digest*, January, pp. 38-40.

Rao, A., Carr, L., Dambolena, I., Kopp, R., Martin, J., Rafii, F. and Schlesinger, P. (1996), *Total Quality Management: A Cross-Functional Perspective,* John Wiley and Sons.

Rao, S., Solis, L. and Raghunathan, T. (1999), "A framework for international quality management research: development and validation of a measurement instrument", *Total Quality Management*, Vol. 10 No. 7, pp. 1047-75.

Rao, S., Solis, L., Dambolena, I., Kopp, R., Martin, J., Rafii, F. and Schlesinger, P. H. (1996), *Total Quality Management: A Cross-Functional Perspective*, Wiley.

Rao, S.S., Raghunathan, J.S. and Solis, L.E. (1999), "The best commonly followed practices in the human resource dimension of quality management in new industrialising countries: the case of China, India and Mexico", *International Journal of Quality and Reliability Management*, Vol. 16 No. 3, pp. 215-26.

Rayan, J. (1993), "Employees speak on quality in ASQC/Gallup survey", *Quality Progress*, Vol. 26 No. 12, pp. 51-3.

Razmi, J., Zairi, M. and Jarrar, Y. (2000), "The application of graphical techniques in evaluating benchmarking partners", *Benchmarking: An International Journal*, Vol. 7 No. 4, pp. 303-14.

Reed, R.L., David, J. and Montgomery, J.C. (1996), "Beyond process: TQM content and firm performance", *Academy of Mangement Review*, Vol. 21 No. 1, pp. 173-203.

Reeves, C.A. and Bednar, D.A. (1993), "What prevents TQM implementation in health care organisations?", *Quality Progress*, April, pp. 41-4.

Rees, D. (1998), "Management structures of facilities management in the National Health Service in England: a review of trends 1995-1997", *Facilities*, Vol. 16 No. 9/10, pp. 254-61.

Reichers, A.E. and Schneider, B. (1990), "Climate and culture: an evolution of constructs", in Schneider, B. (Ed.), *Organisational Climate and Culture*, Jossey-Bass, San Francisco, pp. 5-39.

Remenyi, D., Williams, B., Money, A. and Swartiz, E. (1998), *Doing Research in Business and Management, An Introduction to Process and Method*, Sage, London.

Reynolds, M. (1992), "Quality assertive companies to benefit from recovery", *Elastometrics*, February, p. 19.

Richardson, T. (1996), *Total Quality Management*, Delmar Publisher.

Richbell, S. and Ratsiatou, J. (1999), "Establishing a shared vision under total quality management: theory and practice", *Total Quality Management*, Vol. 10 No. 4/5, pp. S684-9.

Robertson, M., Irensen, C. and Swan, J. (2001), "Survival of the leanest: intensive knowledge work and groupware adaptation", *Information Technology & People*, Vol. 14 No. 4, pp. 334-52.

Robin, M. and Dennis, K. (1995), "Factors affecting the implementation and success of TQM", *International Journal of Quality and Reliability Management*, Vol. 12 No. 1, pp. 11-23.

Robledo, M. (2001), "Measuring and managing service quality: integrating customer expectations", *Managing Service Quality*, Vol. 11 No. 1, pp. 22-31.

Roden, S. and Dale, B.G. (2000), "Understanding the language of quality costing", *The TQM Magazine*, Vol. 12 No. 3, pp. 179-85.

Rohm, C.E. (1993), "The principal insures a better future by reengineering its individual insurance department", *National Productivity Review*, Vol. 12 No. 1, pp. 55-64.

Rose, W. (Ed.) (1992), "Shifting sands? Trade unions and productivity at Rover cars", *Industrial Relations Journal*, Vol. 23 No. 4, pp. 257-67.

Ross, J.E. (1999), *Total Quality Management, Texts, Cases and Readings*, 3rd ed., St.Lucie Press, London.

RSA (1995), *Tomorrow's Company: The Role of Business in a Changing World*, Royal Society for the Encouragement of Arts, July, London.

Salazar, R. (1995), "Leading corporate transformation", *World Executive's Digest*, August, pp. 10-12.

Samuel, K.M. (1999), "TQM and organisational change", *International Journal of Organisational Analysis*, Vol.7, pp.169-81.

Samuel, M. (1992), "Catalysts for change", *The TQM Magazine*.

Sandberg, A. and Strimberg, U. (1999), "Gripen: with focus on availability performance and life support cost over the product life cycle", *Journal of Quality in Maintenance Engineering*, Vol. 5 No. 4, pp. 325-34.

Sanford, R.L. (1992), "Baxter Healthcare uses its own quality award to help achieve excellence", *National Productivity Review*, Winter, pp. 37-43.

Saraph, J.V., Benson, P.G. and Schroeder, R.G. (1989), "An instrument for measuring the critical factors of quality management", *Decision Sciences*, Vol. 20 No. 4, pp. 810-29.

Sarkis, J. (2001), "Benchmarking for agility", *Benchmarking: An International Journal*, Vol. 8 No. 2, pp. 88-107.

Sashkin, M. and Kiser, K. (1992), "What is TQM?", *Executive Excellence*, Vol. 9 No. 5, p. 11.

Sawchuck, P. (2001), "Trade union-based workplace learning: a case study in workplace reorganisation and worker knowledge production", *Journal of Workplace Learning*, Vol. 13 No. 7/8, pp. 344-51.

Saxton, J. and Locander, W.B. (1991), "A systems view of strategic planning at Proctor & Gamble", in Stahi, M.J. and Brunds, G.M. (Eds), *Competing Globally through Customer Value*, Quorum Books, NY.

Saylor, J.H. (1996), *TQM Simplified: A Practical Guide*, 2nd ed., McGraw-Hill, New York.

Schein, E.H. (1992), *Organisational Culture and Leadership*, Jossey-Bass, San Francisco.

Scheuing, E.E. (1999), "Achieving excellence – creating customer passion", *Hospital Material Management Quarterly*, Vol. 21 No. 1, pp. 76-87.

Scholtes, P. (1995), "Do reward and recognition systems work?", *Quality Magazine*, December, pp. 27-9.

Schroder, M. and McEachern, M. (2001), "ISO 9000 as an audit frame for integrated quality management in meat supply chains: the example of scottish beef", *Proceedings of the International Conference on ISO 9000 and TQM*, edited by Ho, S.M. and Donnelly, M.

Scott, G. (2001), "Customer satisfaction: Six strategies for continuous improvement", *Journal of Healthcare Management*, Vol. 46 No. 2, pp. 82-5.

Senge, P. (1992), *The Fifth Discipline – The Art and Practice of the Learning Organization*, Century Business, London.

Seubert, E., Balaji, Y. and Makhija, M. (2001), "The knowledge imperative", http://www.cio.com/sponsors/031501_km.html, accessed 13 January 2002.

Shewhart, W. (1931), *Economic Control of Quality of Manufactured Product.*

Shapiro, J.C. (1995), "The impact of a TQM intervention on teamwork: a longitudinal assessment", *Employee Relations*, Vol. 17 No. 3, pp. 63-74.

Shores, R.A. (1992), "Improving the quality of management systems", *Quality Progress*, June, pp. 53-7.

Sierhuis, M. (1996), "Definition of knowledge management and supporting concepts", http://www.km-forum.org/what_is.htm, accessed January 2002.

Simmons, D.E., Shadur, M.A. and Preston, A.P. (1995), "Integrating TQM and HRM", *Employee Relations*, Vol. 17 No. 3, pp. 75-86.

Simon, A. and Kumar, V. (2001), "Clients' views on strategic capabilities which lead to management consulting success", *Management Decision*, Vol. 39 No. 5, pp. 362-72.

Sinclair, D. and Zairi, M. (2001), "An empirical study of key elements of total quality-based performance measurement systems: a case study approach in service industry", *Total Quality Management*, Vol. 12 No. 4, pp. 535-50.

Sinclair, D.A.C. (1994), "Total quality-based performance management: an empirical study of best practice", University of Bradford, unpublished PhD thesis.

Singels, J., Ruel, G. and van de Water, H. (2001), "ISO 9000 series: certification and performance", *International Journal of Quality and Reliability Management*, Vol. 8 No. 1, pp. 62-75.

Sinha, G. and Ghoshal, T. (1999), "Quality customer service: strategic advantage for Indian steel industry", *Managing Service Quality*, Vol. 9 No. 1, pp. 32-9.

Skyrme, D. (2001), "Knowledge strategy development", http: //www.skyrme.com/ services/kmstrat.htm, accessed 13 January 2002.

Skyrme, D. (2002b), "Developing a knowledge strategy", http://www.skyrme. Com/pubs/knwstrat.htm, accessed 10 September 2002.

Skyrme, D. (2002c), "Measuring intellectual capital: a plethora of methods, http://www.skyrme.com/insights/24kmeas.htm#why, accessed January 2002.

Slinger, M. (1992), "To practice QFD with success requires a new approach to product design", Kontinuert Forbedring, Copenhagen, 20-21 February.

Small, M. and Yasin, M. (2000), "Human factors in the adoption and performance of advanced manufacturing technology in unionized firms", *Industrial Management & Data Systems*, Vol. 100 No. 8, pp. 309-402.

Smith, S. (1994), *The Quality Revolution*, Management Books 2000 Ltd, Didcot, UK.

Smith, P.K. and Tee, M.R. (1990), "Total quality – the issues and realities for a leading supplier of advanced surface treatment technology", in Oakland, J. S. (Ed.), *Proceedings of the 3rd International Conference on Total Quality Management*, Warwick.

Smock, D. (1982), "How to stem the tide of shoddy materials", *Purchasing*, Vol. May, pp. 51-7.

Snowden, D. (1991), "Business process management and TQM", in Oakland, J.S. (Ed.), *Proceedings of the 4th International Conference on Total Quality Management*, Warwick.

Snowden, D. (2000), "A framework for creating a sustainable knowledge management program", in Hermans, J. (Ed.), *The Knowledge Management Yearbook 1999 – 2000*, Butterworth-Heinemann, pp. 52-64.

Snyder, C. and Wilson, L. (2000), "Implementing knowledge management: issues for managers", 2000 IRMA International Conference, Anchrage, Alaska, USA.

Soin, S. (1992), *Total Quality Control Essentials: Key Elements, Methodologies and Managing for Success*, McGraw-Hill, NY.

Sommerville, J., Stocks, R.K. and Robertson, H.W. (1999), ICultural dynamics for quality: the polar plot model", *Total Quality Management*, Vol. 10 No. 4/5, pp. S725-32.

Southern, A. (2001), "How, where, why and when information technologies are seen as a regeneration policy", *The International Journal of Public Sector Management*, Vol. 14 No. 5, pp. 423-38.

Spechler, J.W. (1993), *Managing Quality in American's Most Admired Companies*, Berrett-Koehler Publishers, San Francisco.

Spring, M., McQuater, R., Swift, K., Dale, B. and Booker, J. (1998), "The use of quality tools and techniques in product introduction: an assessment methodology", *The TQM Magazine*, Vol. 10 No. 1, pp. 45-50.

Stamatis, D.H. (1997), *Total Quality Management in Healthcare: Implementation Strategies for Optimum Results*, St. Lucie Press, Daray Beach, FL.

Stark, J.A.L. (1990), "Experience of TQM at BP Chemicals" in Oakland, J.S. (Ed.), *Proceedings of the 3rd International Conference on Total Quality Management*, Warwick.

Stevens, T. (1994), "Dr Feigenbaum, Industry Week, Cleveland", *Total Quality Control*, Vol. 243 No. 13, p. 12.

Straker, D. (1995), "The tools of the trade", *Quality World*, Vol. 21 No. 1, January, pp. 28-9.

Sullivan, L.P. (1986), "Quality function deployment, a system to assure that customer needs drive the product design and production process", *Quality Progress*, June, pp. 39-50.

Sullivan, L.P. (1988), "Policy management through quality function deployment", *Quality Progress*, June, pp. 18-20.

Sullivan, P. (2000), "A brief history of the ICM movement", http://www.sveiby. com.au/articles/icmmovement.htm, accessed 10 January 2002.

Sun, H. (2000), "A comparison of quality management practices in Shanghai and Norwegian manufacturing companies", *International Journal of Quality and Reliability Management*, Vol. 17 No. 6, pp. 636-60.

Sunday, J.L. and Liberty, L. (1992), "Benchmarking the Baldrige Award", *Quality Progress*, Vol. 25 No. 9, pp. 75-7.

Superville, C. and Gupta, S. (2001), "Issues in modeling, monitoring and managing quality costs", *Total Quality Management*, Vol. 13 No. 6, pp. 419-24.

Sureshandar, G.S., Chandrasekharan Rajendran and Anantharaman (2001), "A conceptual model for total quality management in service organisations", *Total Quality Management*, Vol. 12 No. 3, pp. 343-63.

Sveiby, K.E. (1997a), *The New Organisational Managing Wealth: Measuring Knowledge Based Assets*, Berrett-Koehler Publishers, San Francisco, CA.

Sveiby, K.E. (1997b), "The intangible assets monitor", http://www.sveiby.com.au/ IntangAss/CompanyMonitor.html, accessed 12 December 2001.

Sweetman, J. (1996), "Reward your people and reap the returns", *Other Side Up – Business Ideas from a New Perspective*, May, pp. 1-2.

Szwejczewski, M., Goffin, K., Lemke, F., Pfeiffer, R. and Lohmuller, B. (2001), "Supplier management in German manufacturing companies – an empirical investigation", *International Journal of Physical Distribution & Logistics Management,* Vol. 31 No. 5, pp. 354-73.

Taguchi, G. and Clausing, D. (1983), "Robust quality", *Harvard Business Review*, Vol. 64 No. 4, pp. 65-75.

Takeuchi, H. and Quelch, J.A. (1983), "Quality is more than making a good product", *Harvard Business Review*, Vol. 61 No 4.

Tan, P.K. (1997), "An evaluation of TQM and the techniques for successful implementation", *Training for Quality*, Vol. 5 No. 4, pp. 150-9.

Taylor, C. (1997), "Baldrige winners learn that quality really does pay", *Managing Service Quality*, Vol. 7 No. 2, pp. 65-8.

Taylor, W.A. (1995), "Total quality management and the need for organisational self-assessment: Some empirical evidence", *Total Quality Management*, Vol. 6 No. 1, pp. 3-12.

Terziovski, M., Howel, A., Sohal, A. and Morrison, M. (2000), "Establishing mutual dependence between TQM and the learning organisation: a multiple case study analysis", *The Learning Organisation*, Vol. 7 No. 1, pp. 23-32.

The X Factor (1999), *Winning Performance Through Business Excellence,* European Centre for Business Excellence.

Thiagaragan, T. and Zairi, M. (1997a), "A review of total quality management in practice: understanding the fundamentals through examples of best practice applications, Part 1", *The TQM Magazine*, Vol. 9 No. 4, pp. 270-86.

Thiagaragan, T. and Zairi, M. (1997b), "A review of total quality management in practice: understanding the fundamentals through examples of best practice applications, Part 2", *The TQM Magazine*, Vol. 9 No. 5, pp. 344-56.

Thiagaragan, T. and Zairi, M. (1997c), "A review of total quality management in practice: understanding the fundamentals through examples of best practice applications, Part 3", *The TQM Magazine*, Vol. 9 No. 6, pp. 414-17.

Thiagaragan, T. and Zairi, M. (1998), "An empirical analysis of critical factors of tqm: a proposed tool for self-assessment and benchmarking purposes", *Benchmarking for Quality Management and Technology*, Vol. 5 No. 4, pp. 291-303.

Thiagaragan, T., Zairi, M. and Dale, B. (2001), "A proposed model of TQM implementation based on an empirical study of Malaysian industry", *International Journal of Quality & Reliability Management,* Vol. 18 No. 3, pp. 289-306.

Tith, A. (1998), "FDI and industrial relations in Central and Eastern Europe: the exceptional case of the Hungarian airline", *International Journal of Manpower*, Vol. 19 No. 1/2, pp. 115-33.

Titman, C.R. and Callum, W.S. (1991), "Recognition and Reward" in Oakland, J.S. (Ed.), *Total Quality Management: Proceedings of the 4th International Conference on Total Quality Management*, Warwick.

Tompkins, J.A. (1989), "The importance of product development to winning manufacturing", *Industrial Management*, Vol. 31 No. 4, pp. 10-14.

Townsend, P.L. and Gebhardt, J.E. (1992), *Quality in Action*, John Wiley & Sons Ltd, NY.

Townsend, P.L. and Gebhardt, J.E. (1986), *Commit to Quality*, John Wiley & Sons Inc., pp. 21-2.

Tracy, M. and Tan, C. (2001), "Empirical analysis of supplier selection and inVolvement customer satisfaction and firm performance", *Management Service Quality*, Vol. 6 No. 4, pp. 174-88.

Tribus, M. (1990), "The three systems of quality", paper presented at North Coast Business week, Community Quality Coalition, Jackson, MI, 10 October.

Tsai, W.-I., (1998), "Quality cost measurement under activity based costing", *International Journal of Quality and Reliability Management*, Vol. 15 No. 7, pp. 719-72.

Tsim, Y., Yeung, V. and Leung, E. (2001), "An adaptation to ISO 9001: 2000 for certified organisations, integrement", in Ho, S., Donnelly, M. and Leung, E. (Eds), *Proceedings 6th International Conference on ISO 9000 and TQM.*

Twomey, D. and Twomey, R. (1998), "UK business schools and business: activities and interactions", *Journal of Management Development,* Vol. 17 No. 3, pp. 160-76.

Vallely, I. (1993), "Why supervisors can with Nissan", *Works Management*, October, pp. 18-21.

Van Der Akker, G.J. (1989), "Managing quality across cultures", *The TQM Magazine*, IFS Publications, Bedford.

Van der Wiele, A. and company (1996), "Self-assessment: a study of progress in Europe's leading organisations in quality management practices", *International Journal of Quality & Reliability Management*, Vol.13 No. 1, pp. 84-104.

Van der Wiele, T., Dale, B. and William, R. (2000), "ISO 9000 series and excellence model: cad to fashion to fit", *Journal of General Management*, Vol. 25 No. 3, pp. 50-66.

Vandermerwe, S. (1993), "Jumping into the customer's activity cycle. A new role for customer services in the 1990s", *The Columbia Journal of World Business*, Vol. 28 No. 2, pp. 46-65.

Vaziri, H. (1992), "Using competitive benchmarking to set goals", *Quality Progress*, Vol. 24 No. 1, pp. 81-5.

Vermeulen, W. and Crous, M.S. (2000), "Training and education for TQM in the commercial banking industry of South Africa", *Managing Service Quality*, Vol. 10 No. 1, pp. 61-7.

Voehl, F. (1995), *Deming: The Way We Knew Him*, St Lucie Press, Delray Beach, FL.

Vokurka, R.J., Stading, G.L. and Brazeal, J. (2000), "A comparative analysis of national and regional quality award", *Quality Progress*, August, pp. 41-9.

Wacker, K.A. (1993), "Uncommon common sense", *Quality Progress*, Vol. 26 No. 7, pp. 97-100.

Watson, R. (1998), "Implementing self-managed process improvement teams in a continuous improvement environment", *The TQM Magazine,* Vol. 10 No. 4, pp. 246-57.

Watts , J. (1995), "The future for BPR", *Business Change and Re-engineering*, Vol. 2 No. 3, pp. 2-3.

Wemmenhove, R. and de Groot, W. (2001), "Principles for university curriculum greening – an empirical case study from Tanzania", *International Journal of Sustainability in Higher Education*, Vol. 2 No. 3, pp. 267-83.

Westbrook, R. and Barwise, P. (1995), "Total quality management in leading fast-moving consumer goods companies", *Total Quality Management*, Vol. 6 No. 4, pp. 365-82.

Whitford, B. and Bird, R. (1996), *The Pursuit of Quality*, Prentice Hall.

Widman, D. (1994), "Techniques that Momentum Graphics uses to balance the people and technical sides of quality", *National Productivity Review*, Vol. 13 No. 1, pp. 89-106.

Wiggenhorn, W. (1990), "Motorola U: when training becomes an education", *Harvard Business Review*, Vol. 68 No. 4, pp. 71-83.

Wilkinson, A. (1998), "Empowerment: theory and practice", *Personnel Review*, Vol. 27 No. 1, pp. 40-56.

Wilkinson, A., Redman, T. and Snape, E. (1994), "Quality management and the manager", *Employee Relations*, Vol. 16 No. 1, pp. 62-70.

Wilkinson, A. and Allen, Snape, P. (Eds) (1991), "TQM and the management of labour", *Employee Relations*, Vol. 13 No. 1, pp. 24-31.

Wilkinson, A. and Witcher, B. (1992), "Conference review: quality concerns for management", *International Journal of Quality & Reliability Management*, Vol.9 No. 2, pp. 64-8.

Williams, A., Dodson, P. and Walters M. (1993), *Changing Culture*, 2nd ed., Institute of Personnel Management, London.

Wilsy, H.D. (1995), "Leadership and human motivation in the workplace", *Quality Progress*, Vol. 28 No. 11, pp. 85-8.

Woon, K. (2000a), "Assessment of TQM implementation", *Business Process Management Journal*, Vol. 6 No. 4, pp. 314-30.

Woon, K.C. (2000b), "TQM implementation: comparing Singapore's service and manufacturing leaders", *Managing Service Quality*, Vol. 10 No. 5, pp. 318-31.

Wright, J. (1988), "Rank Xerox approach to implementation" in Oakland, J.S. (Ed.), *Proceedings of the 1st International Conference on Total Quality Management*, Warwick.

Yoji, A. (1990), "An introduction to quality function deployment", in Akao, Y. (Ed.), *Quality Function Deployment – Integrating Customer Requirements into Product Deisgn and Productivity*, Free Press, Cambridge, MA.

Yusof, S. and Aspinwall, E. (2000a), "TQM implementation issues: review and case study", *International Journal of Operation and Production Management*, Vol. 21 No. 6, pp. 634-55.

Yusof, S.M. and Aspinwall, E.M. (2000b), "Critical success factors in small and medium enterprises: survey results", *Total Quality Management*, Vol. 11 No. 4-6, pp. S448-62.

Zack, M.H. (1998), "Developing a knowledge strategy", *California Management Review*, Vol. 41 No. 3, pp. 125-45.

Zairi, M. (1991), *Total Quality Management for Engineers*, Woodhead Publishing, Cambridge.

Zairi, M. (1992a), "Managing user-supplier interactions: management of R&D activity", *Management Decision*, Vol. 30 No. 8, pp. 49-57.

Zairi, M. (1992b), *Total Quality Management for Engineers*, Aditya Books Pvt Ltd, New Delhi.

Zairi, M. (1992c), *TQM-based Performance Management: Practical Guidelines*, Technical Communications (Publishing).

Zairi, M. (1993), *Quality Function Deployment: A Modern Competitive Tool*, TQM Practitioner Series, European Foundation For Quality Management in association with Technical Communications (Publishing) Ltd.

Zairi, M. (1994a), *Measuring Performance for Business Results*, Chapman & Hall, London.

Zairi, M. (1994b), "TQM: What is wrong with the terminology?", *The TQM Magazine*, Vol. 6 No.4, pp. 6-8.

Zairi, M. (1995), "Strategic planning through quality policy deployment: a benchmarking approach in total quality management", in Kanji, G.K. (Ed.), *Proceedings of the First World Congress*, Chapman & Hall, London.

Zairi, M. (1996a), "Economic development and global competitiveness: why should arab managers take notice of total quality management", Arab Management Conference, Proceeding Book, Bradford University.

Zairi, M. (1996b), *Benchmarking for Best Practice*, Butterworth-Heinemann, Oxford.

Zairi, M. (1998), "Managing human resources in healthcare: learning from world class practices – Part1", *Health Manpower Management*, Vol. 24 No. 2, pp. 48-57.

Zairi, M. (1999a), "Managing excellence: leadership", *The TQM Magazine*, Vol. 11 No. 4, pp. 215-20.

Zairi, M. (1999b), "Managing excellence: policy and strategy", *The TQM Magazine*, Vol. 11 No. 2, pp. 74-9.

Zairi, M. (2002), "Beyond TQM implementation: the new paradigm of TQM sustainability", *Total Quality Management*, Vol. 13 No. 8, pp. 1161-72.

Zairi, M. and Youssef, M.A. (1995a), "Benchmarking critical factors for TQM: Part I: theory and foundation", *Benchmarking for Quality Management and Technology,* Vol. 2 No. 1, pp. 5-20.

Zairi, M. and Youssef, M.A. (1995b), 'Quality function deployment: a main pillar for successful total quality management and product development", *International Journal of Quality & Reliability Management*, Vol. 12 No. 6, pp. 9-23.

Zairi, M., Letza, S. and Oakland, J. (1994), *TQM: Its Impact on Bottom Line Results*, Technical Communications (Publishing), Letchworth.

Zairi, M. and Whymark, J. (2003), *Best Practice Organisational Excellence*, E-TQM College Publishing, Bradford.

Zeitz, G., Russel, J. and Ritchie, J.E. (1997), "An employee survey measuring total quality management practices and culture: development and validation", *Group and Organisational Management*, Vol. 22 No. 4.

Zhang, Z., Waszink, A. and Wijingaard, J. (2000), "An instrument for measuring TQM implementation for Chinese manufacturing companies", *International Journal of Quality and Reliability Management*, Vol. 17 No. 7, pp. 730-55.

Zhuang, L., Williamson, D. and Carter, M. (1999), "Innovate or liquidate – are all organisations convinced? A two-phased study into the innovation process", *Management Decision*, Vol. 37 No. 1, pp. 57-71.

Zink, K. and Schmidt, A. (1998), "Practice and implementation of self-assessment", *International Journal of Quality Science*. Vol. 3 No. 2, pp. 147-70.

Zink, K.J., (1995), "Total quality management and people management" in Kanji, G. K. (Ed.), *Total Quality Management: Proceedings of the First World Congress*, Chapman & Hill, London.

Zultner, R.E. (1993), "TQM for technical teams", *Communications of the ACM,* October, Vol. 36 No. 10, pp. 79-91.

Index

Market survey, 357, 358, 359, 360
Mass inspection, 10, 56, 343
Matrix, 189, 201, 202, 203, 204, 205, 298
MBNQA criteria, 92, 93, 100, 111, 129, 130, 147, 179, 180, 182, 184, 191, 192, 298, 306, 307, 308, 309, 311, 312, 316
Mentoring, 1, 251, 277, 289
Mercury Marine, 136, 146
Middle management, 144, 246, 288, 297
Milliken, 135, 138, 148, 180, 186
Mission, 30, 31, 61, 78, 83, 84, 90, 99, 132, 133, 141, 159, 160, 162, 173, 192, 210, 252, 286, 287, 288, 289, 295-7, 309, 325
Mission statement, 61, 78, 132, 173, 192, 286-8, 295, 297
Mitel Telecom Ltd, 135, 137, 145, 159
Mitsubishi, 53
Motorola, 132, 135, 179, 311, 353
Motwani *et al.* study, 118
Moving range chart, 24, 25
MR chart, 24
Multi-disciplinary teams, 206, 207, 217
National Westminster Bank plc, 135, 154, 188
NEC Japan, 135, 160, 161
Networking, 76, 234
Nissan, 135, 144, 147, 166, 169, 171
Non-conformity, 23, 183, 186
Norand Corp., 135, 144
Normal distribution, 19, 20, 25
Normal-predictable variance, 13
North Telecom Canada Ltd, 168
Notion of leadership, 128
np chart, 22, 28
On-the-job learning, 56
Operational results, 102
Operator-controllable errors, 348, 349
Organization capability, 234
Organizational activities, 283
Organizational change, 168, 196
Organizational effectiveness, 8
Organizational excellence, 94, 97
Organizational learning, 197, 249, 255, 272, 309
Organizational performance, 30, 94, 102, 116, 126, 141, 246
Organizational structure, 133, 171, 174, 177, 274, 285
Organizational system, 190, 313
Organizing for quality, 175
Ouchi, 54, 55, 69, 169

Out of control, 13, 14, 20, 21, 342
Ownership, 83, 132, 141, 142, 147, 149, 175, 177, 208, 215, 286, 287
p chart, 11, 22, 28
PAF model, 186, 347
Pareto analysis, 2, 16, 17, 18, 187, 204, 348, 349
Pareto chart, 16, 17
Pareto principle, 2, 17, 348
Participation, 50, 58, 62, 69, 75, 85, 93, 101, 112, 133, 134, 137, 138, 139, 141,
        152, 160, 171, 187, 195, 196, 235, 255, 306, 329, 331, 341
Partnership, 29, 94, 112, 156, 169, 250, 252, 329
Paul Revere Insurance Group, 132, 135, 149, 151
PDCA cycle, 12, 29, 173, 180, 229, 231, 234, 235, 247, 342, 344, 347
PDSA cycle, 15, 329
People management, 89, 144, 147, 150
Performance appraisal, 57, 122, 254
Performance gap, 89, 293, 296
Performance goal, 179
Performance management, 94, 230, 309
Performance objective, 315
Performance results, 52, 94, 96
Performance review, 247
Performance standards, 236
Philips Electronics, 132, 135, 166
Philips Signetics, 135, 166
Plan-do-check cycle, 55, 58, 85, 133, 180, 229, 353
Planning system, 351
Policy, 83, 85, 86, 95, 102, 119, 129, 143, 159, 160-3, 206, 207, 229, 232, 234,
        286, 287, 296, 297, 309, 353
Policy deployment, 83, 159, 160-3, 206, 207, 229, 232, 287
Policy deployment process, 160, 162
Policy management, 206, 353
Poor quality costs, 185
Post Office Counters, 135, 179
Post Office Counters Ltd, 135
PQC system, 185
Predictive models of performance, 9
Preferred supplier, 169
Prevention-appraisal-failure, 186
Price of non-conformance, 64
Principal Financial Group, 141
Prioritisation, 16, 163, 203-5
Private sector, 92, 101, 164
Probability plot, 16, 19, 20